Books in the series 'The Colonial Economy of NSW 1788-1835'

A Brief Economic History of NSW

The Colonial Economy of NSW 1788-1835 - A retrospective

The Government Store is Open for business - the commissariat operations in NSW 1788-1835

The Enterprising Colonial Economy of NSW 1800-1830 - Government Business Enterprises in operation

Guiding the Colonial Economy - Public Funding in NSW 1800-1835

Financing the Colonial Economy of NSW 1800-1835

Essays on the colonial Economy of NSW 1788-1835

Industries that Formed a Colonial Economy

FINANCING
the COLONIAL
ECONOMY
1800-1835

G ORDON B ECKETT

For book orders, email orders@traffordpublishing.com.sg

Most Trafford Singapore titles are also available at major online book retailers.

Printed in Singapore.

ISBN: 978-1-4669-2783-4 (sc)
ISBN: 978-1-4669-2784-1 (hc)
ISBN: 978-1-4669-2785-8 (e)

Trafford rev. 08/07/2012

 www.traffordpublishing.com.sg

Singapore
toll-free: 800 101 2656 (Singapore)
Fax: 800 101 2656 (Singapore)

CONTENTS

1. Background To The Colonial Accounting 1
2. Introduction To The Public Finance & The Reporting
   System In The Colony 92
3. Governance Of Public Finance.................................... 107
4. The Need For Manufacturing 207
5. The accounting & recording functions
   i.   Financial Statements For The First Period—1800-1810 ... 235
   ii. The Second Period 1811-1822 253
   iii. The Third Period 1823-1840.. 258
   iv. The Fourth Period 1841-1855.. 278
   v.   Special Economic Events 311

**The Financial Statements Of the Colony Of New South Wales
1800-1855**

1. Introduction To The Public Finance & The Reporting
   System In The Colony 349
2. Governance Of Public Finance.................................... 365
3. The First Post-Self Government Financial Statement—1855 406
4. Conclusions And Summary.. 417

THE PUBLIC FINANCE OF THE COLONY OF NSW

PREFACE

If Professor S. J. Butlin had been asked to write a preface to this work, he could have chosen the first paragraph of Chapter 1 in his splendid work 'Foundations of the Australian Monetary System 1788-1851' (1953 Edition), where he wrote "Australian Economic History is the major part of all Australian History; from the beginning, economic factors have dominated development in a way that should gladden the heart of any Marxist. What is true of any particular strand of economic growth—land settlement, labour relations and labour organisation, immigration, secondary industry—is also true of each major stage in the development of the community as a whole: each is characterised by economic changes which conditioned political, social and cultural change."

To explore the most important of the economic events in the Colony to 1856 is to inexorably (inevitably, as we have no choice but to) intertwine our history, both socially and economically, with the growth of wealth and the growth of the people.

These events don't fall naturally into importance by the tragedy of the circumstances like so many historical events can lay their focus to (such as like floods or wars, earthquakes or unnatural dramas such as social riots). These events were awakened by the wonderful aura of discovery. The exploration over the mountains to open up a new land, and unfold the story of the rivers; the discovery of gold, and the unfurling of the workers flag and untold riches; the amazing growth of the pastoral industry; the development of the great 'iron horse' and the opening of the vast inland to settlements; the unfolding of the education system to all young Australians 'free compulsory and secular' accompanied by the relief of seeing illiteracy drop from 75% to under 20% in the decade; and the development of communications. From bush telegraph to the electric telegraph, around the world, the natural advance of democracy and finally full self-government.

All these marvellous events had a major impact on the economy of the day. Revenue grew from 72,000 pound annually in 1826 to 13,000,000 40 years later, without demolishing (diminishing) the peoples will to work, and whilst they still respected the government's right to fairly tax its people and create a strong social infrastructure. Revenue per head rose only from 2.08 pound /head to 3.79 (during the 40 years from 1826 to 1866).

Export earnings kept pace with imports, so we did not buy overseas at the expense of the local ability to make new and worldly goods. By 1850 our exports, due to wool and gold, had out-run imports, but always the numbers grew. Exports grew from 3.08 per head in 1826 to 14.55 per head in 1860. Imports grew from 10.39 to 21.57 in the same period, often with imports less than exports during that time.

In 1850, in anticipation of full self-government, the Governors began playing with 'temporary' borrowing to meet monetary policy obligations and expectations; and to keep the budget ever in balance. Gold and wool exports came as immigration burgeoned and railways and other capital expenditure came into sight. The impeccable relationship between the Colony and the 'City' of London, allowed attractive and relatively easy borrowing of capital in Britain.

This work also includes studies of the early Colony and its financial establishment. The operations of the first Commissariats are considered, along with a consolidation and summary of the first Public Accounts in the colony (referencing the locally raised revenue), being the Gaol, Police and Orphan Funds. The first appropriation bill was brought down in 1832, after the 1823 reforms by the Governor and his advisory council. Full self-government in 1855 continued the slow reform of the treasury system and prompted further parliamentary reforms of financial statements prepared for the New South Wales Legislature. Finally, in 1856, the Parliament received full control of its financial destiny and was able to raise revenues and allocate funds for expenditure with only local franchised voters watching over their shoulders.

Each of the five distinct financial periods are analysed and examined, together with the economic and historical events, which so strongly shaped the life and future of the 'Mother' Colony—New South Wales.

FOREWORD

This research work embraces the whole picture of 'Public Finance in the Colony of New South Wales 1788-1856'. Its purpose is to follow the five main stages of public finance recording and reporting during this period and review the eight special events, which, during the 1800s shaped, promoted and guided the Colonial economy like no others. The economy, like most unplanned economies in the new world went through its two paces—boom and then bust. But the busts were essentially limited to two periods, the 1840s and the 1890s. The boom times came with the discovery of gold; exploration followed by the growth and expansion of the pastoral industry and the rise of the squattocracy. Free trade policies in the Colony of New South Wales set it aside from the protectionist and confining policies of Deakin in the Colony of Victoria. However with the discovery of gold came other side effects such as the termination of transportation, introducing self-government, further land reforms, a rise in wages, prices and rents due mainly to the shortage of a general labour supply.

The railway system underpinned the economic gains from the 1850s and set the pastoral industry onto a more comfortable plain. But mainly the railways allowed the policy of decentralisation to be formally adopted. The regions burgeoned especially Newcastle and the Riverina. Newcastle had been an ideal of Macquarie but it developed slowly until the rail system allowed coal extracts from the region to be moved quickly and cheaply to Sydney and then onto Victoria, which area became a major user of New South Wales coal.

The Treasurers of the Colony knew only the advantages of balancing the books each year—there was no deficit financing undertaken until after 1856 when overseas borrowing from the financial houses in the City of London, accepted the credit worthiness of the Colony and hastened to use this new outlet for surplus funds available for investment by Britain. The use of bank drafts for export commodities had commenced with the large wool exports to Britain and led to the creation of the Union Bank of Australia, the Bank of Australasia. This period also saw the rise of the great pastoral and financing houses—Brooks and Younghusband, Dalgety and Goldsbrough Mort. Shipping fleets grew rapidly for transporting convicts, and then free immigrants and returning with wool, and other commodities. The P & O operators, with its One million pound of paid up capital won the lucrative mail contracts from the British Government and commenced regular monthly trips from London to Australia.

The published public accounts reflect an annual cumulative surplus (of revenue over expenditures) each year from 1822 to 1900. What this meant was that the Colonial Treasurers and their advisers had the flexibility of running into temporary deficit, for instance in 1838 (-164102 pound) and 1839 (-121464) knowing that the cumulative surplus of 314517 pound would allow them to do so without having to borrow long-term. In this instance the cumulative surplus was reduced to only 28951 pound. The ways of recording in the various periods varied and opened the way for considerable mistake and misinterpretation, as we will see. The periods we speak of are:

There are five distinct periods:

* The goal and orphan fund period 1802-1810
* The Police and Orphan Fund period 1810-1821
* The 'Blue Book' period 1822-1855
* The self-government period 1856-1889
* The pre-Federation period 1889-1899

Governor Macquarie had appointed Darcy Wentworth and Reverend Samuel Marsden to be Treasurers of the Police and Orphan funds and we find their monthly reports published in the Sydney Gazette of the period 1810-1821.

The Blue Book period was recorded by clerical staff within the Colonial Secretary's office.

The Blue Book contains the comprehensive recording system of the times and the Consulting Accountant James Thomson introduced a new system after self-government, which was burdensome, intricate, and open to much abuse. After self-government, the ledgers were kept open until the funds appropriated to each line item in the budget were spent. This sometimes meant the ledgers could not be closed for upwards of three years, by which time the trail was cold in trying to keep track of annual revenues and expenditures. This problem was corrected in 1885, when a return was made to annual statements based on cash inflow and outflow.

Some interesting Observations

The Marsden and Wentworth transactions created major conflict of interest situations. It is interesting to muse how a Reverend gentleman who was paid from the Civil List at the rate of 180 pound per annum, could afford to operate 4,500 acres of pasture land and build up a flock of 3,500 sheep in a matter of less than twenty years. Even allowing that the land came about from grants, the sheep had to be purchased and although the convict labour assigned to him was unpaid, they had to be kept, with huts, food and clothing furnished. We might also ask why the monthly meat bill for the orphanage ran to over 60 pound even though the Orphanage owned and operated a farm, which regularly sold 'on the hoof' and then bought back dressed meat. For its annual sale of livestock in 1811-1812, Marsden received only 127 pound, but from the same source purchased over 700 pound of dressed meat. The means were easy to share the spoils between those that could help him gain wealth and reach his target of becoming a large landowner and successful grazier. Marsden housed only female orphans aged from under 5 to 14. On an average month, Marsden paid the butcher over 60 pound, being for an average of 2,500 lb of meat. By the 30th September 1818, Marsden held 3,033l (pound) in the Orphanage account, and on average disbursed 550 pound each month from that account. The only 'admonishment' that Macquarie made (if one can imply from a regulatory change, an act of admonition). Macquarie, at this time, chose to modify the basis of the Orphanage Fund revenue and deleted an item by redirecting that revenue to the Police Fund.

Macquarie made no objection to Marsden misdirecting funds from the orphan fund to repairing St. John's Church in July 1811 to the extent of 56 pound, nor to paying the Matron of the Orphanage a monthly stipend of 5 pound when the going rate would have been only 1 pound per month, nor of paying 4.5.0 for a bonnet for his wife from the fund.

Macquarie wrote approved on each monthly statement, when presented to him by Marsden, obviously without proper 'auditing' procedures being used.

Wentworth too had his dubious methods. He built up large surpluses of cash and bills receivable rather than spend funds on road and bridge or wharf construction; he expended large amounts through the military for 'repairs' to the streets of Sydney and other questionable contracts, never noted by Macquarie. Wentworth was also the town Magistrate, responsible for fines, which were an important source of revenue to the Police Fund. Two items of regular expenditure open to abuse, and which appear to be inordinately high were purchase of firewood and oil and payment for the capture of absconding convicts. The Military personnel were fleecing the Government stores, operating the barter system in the Colony and were obviously getting even more ample rewards in cash from Wentworth.

The Federation debates warrant a closer look at the figures furnished. As the official Colonial Statistician for New South Wales, Timothy Coghlan was trying to make a name for himself in the Commercial world and was in regular disagreement with the Premiers and Treasurers of the Colony. He had been publicly accused by Edward Pulsford, the leader of the Free Trade Movement of 'playing games' with his statistics, but the greatest self-serving abuse must have come with the request to furnish official statistics to the Federation debates in general and the Financial Sub-committee in particular.

He provided, in 1992, statistics for the year 1889 knowing that the figures were out of date, misleading and open to misinterpretation and misuse. But these figures became the guiding hand for the Finance Committee's recommendation on the structuring of the financial clauses for the Constitution. The 1889 figures remained in use until 1899 even though the scheduled collection of new statistics (which was scheduled for 1896) was delayed by Coghlan until 1902. Revised interim figures would have changed the course of Australian history, especially the fiscal nature of the Federation debates. A set of figures which should have formed the basis of the Federation debates and the Constitutional clauses is included in the Appendix to this work and the reader may judge for himself whether Coghlan's self serving submissions made sense. That New South Wales, being a free trade state, got great benefit from the incorrect figures being used is not questioned but the three smaller colonies—South Australia, Tasmania and Western Australia, were all significantly disadvantaged, although Western Australia was the only Colony to get preferred treatment under the Constitution. Coghlan's goal was to get appointed as Commonwealth Statistician and get recognition as a great Australian. Neither happened, but he did manoeuvre a knighthood in spite of a poor showing as Agent-general for NSW in London. His writings, especially the four-volume work of Labour and Industry Growth in New South Wales are illuminating, mischievous in their conclusions, self serving and misguided. His was a life spent on serving two masters. Himself and to a lesser extent the Government that paid him handsomely for many years.

CHAPTER 1

BACKGROUND TO THE COLONIAL ACCOUNTING

Colonial Origins of Public Accounts

The commencement of the Colony of New South Wales in 1788 was based on self-sufficiency for the colony even though it was a penal Colony. By 1823, the British Government had taken the approach it would be limiting its direct expenditure to the transportation of the convicts and their travelling food and supplies. The Colonial Administrators would be responsible for the convict's security, food, clothing and accommodation in the Colony. The proceeds from the sale of Crown land were to be the exclusive reserve of the British authorities, and not that of the colonists. The Governors commenced working the convicts for creating food, minerals (eg coal production), roads, housing and public buildings, and generally paying their own way. Other convicts had been assigned to land owners on a fully maintained basis, thus saving the British Treasury a great deal of money.

Such policy, of the Government maintenance of convicts, created the need for an accounting by a British Colony to the British Parliament and a Financial Controller come Colonial Accountant, prepared monthly and annual despatches to the British Colonial Secretary. Following self-government in 1856, the procedures changed as the Colony became fully responsible for their own economic planning and fiscal management.

1

Colonial Accounting in New South Wales

The Colony adopted the standards recommended in the 1823 'Blue Book', which replaced the 'gaol' and orphan funds. The 'gaol' fund was a record of funds raised by a surcharge on the citizens of Sydney town, as a means to complete the construction of the Sydney 'gaol'. Once customs duties were imposed on imports, and the gaol was completed with Government monies, the fund was renamed the police fund. The orphan Fund recorded the customs duties on spirits and tobacco and was later named the Orphan School Fund with the intention of creating a fund to erect a first school building in Sydney town.

Upon self-government in 1855, the government accounting procedures were again revised, since the Colony was now fully responsible for all its fiscal matters. After self-government was granted in 1851, the Colony was responsible for its own fiscal policy. At this time, gold was discovered and license fees, duties on exports of gold and duties on the domestic conversion of gold were applied and helped fill the Treasury coffers. Also came the first Appropriation Bills and 'Ways and Means' through the Legislative Assembly in 1832 under Governor Bourke. This was a major step forward in Government economic planning. As was the limited deficit budgeting that commenced at this time. Deficits were short term and recovered usually within 5 years, although the Colonial debt, mainly to overseas bondholders was kept very much in check after the surge of investment in railways and telegraph services.

The Federation debates were based around the role and adjustment to individual Colonial tariffs, their discussion in the Finance Committee of the Nation Debates, and their incorporation into the final Constitution of 1901. These trends from 1856 are discussed and analysed

Federation installed a new system within the structure of the new Commonwealth Treasury whilst the States revised their reduced revenue collection procedures and accounted for the grants of revenue from the Commonwealth.

Federation brought further changes to the raising of revenues, whilst the largest expenditure of the Commonwealth became the return of centrally collected funds to the States. The advent of the Commonwealth Treasury improved once again the quality of recording keeping and brought into being the first Commonwealth estimates and National budgets.

From the Exhibit, certain conclusions can be drawn, and these can be set out as follows:

a. There was a wide range of duties and taxes imposed on the early settlers, especially on alcoholic beverages. The general rate of duty on spirits was 10 shillings per gallon, and on wine it was 9 pence per gallon. On tobacco the rate was 6 pence per pound, while timber attracted a rate of one shilling per solid foot. General Cargo attracted duty at a flat 5% ad valorem rate.

b. There were also licenses and tolls. A Hawkers Licenses sold for 20 pound, and it cost a settler 2 pence (tuppence) to go from Sydney town to Parramatta town. A country settler (in the Hawkesbury) paid One penny to cross the Nepean River Bridge at Windsor.

c. References to crown land sales were recorded in the 1825 'Blue Book', and based on the decree by George 3rd in a Proclamation on 25th March of that year that there was to be imposed a new 'rent' on crown lands at the rate of One shilling for every 50 acres, to commence 5 years after the date of the original grant. To-date all crown lands had been disposed of by way of grants, and this rent was a form of back door compensation to the crown. In the official grant documents, the receiver of the land grant was given notice that further costs may attach at some future time to the land, and it was this opportunity that provided the Crown to raise this 'rent' charge on the land in 1828.

d. There was to be a Land-holders fee of Fifteen shillings per 100 acres of crown land reserved for each three years for free settlers, followed by a two shilling fee per 100 hundred acres redeemable after twenty years from purchase.

e. On the 18th May, 1825, the 'rent' was changed, by order of Governor Macquarie, to a flat rate of 5% of the estimated value of the grants, without purchase(as opposed to purchased land), to commence 7 years from the date of grant. 'Rents' on any 2nd and subsequent grants were payable immediately, without the benefit of the 7 years grace period.

f. Reference to Table 23 (Land Grants 1789-1850) shows the number of acres granted to settlers and the conclusion can be drawn that this revenue source of 'rents' on Corn Land grants could build into as considerable sum for the Crown.

g. By Proclamation, also dated 18th May, 1825, George III authorised the sale of crown lands at the rate of 10 shillings per acre, to a maximum of 4,000 acres per individual or a maximum of 5,000 acres per family. Payment was by way of a 10% deposit and four equal quarterly instalments.

h. The title pages to the 1822 'Blue Book' are entitled 'Abstract of the Net Revenue and Expenditure of the Colony of New South Wales for the Year 1822', which indicates (and as the detailed records also reflect) that all Colonial revenue and expenses were being accounted for in the 'Blue Book'. An interesting question to be answered, and a topic for further research is 'how does the British Colonial Office Accounting records (Table on Page 58) link with the 'Blue Book' figures. This area will be examined shortly. It is immediately recognisable that the Table is incomplete and misleading in that the outgoing expenditures do not reflect any offset revenues which would provide an 'offset' net expenditure. The official Table overstates the expenditure by the British Treasury on the Colony.

i. Table 14 (Civil List Salaries for 1792-1793) sets out the Governor's Salary at One Thousand Pounds. But in the 1822 statement of expenditures on the Civil Salaries, the Governor's Salary had increased to Two Thousand Pounds. By 1856 the Governor's salary had increased to 15,000 pounds.

j. In fact, the total of Civil List salaries in 1792 was only 4,726.0.0 pounds, but by 1822 the total had increased to 9,828.15.0 pounds, due to both individual salary increases as well as more people being placed on the Civil List.

k. The official 'Observations upon revenue for the Colony in 1828' (written by the Colonial Treasurer of New South Wales) makes an interesting point. It observes that the 'net colonial income' of the year 1828, as actually collected, is exclusive of sums in aid of revenue, which cannot be viewed in the character of income. This item is further defined as 'the proceeds of the labour of convicts, and establishments connected with them, being applied to the reduction of the amount of parliamentary grants for their maintenance'.

l.   The total quantity of alcohol imported and thus consumed in the Colony, even in 1828, and with only a population in 1820 of only 26, 000 people, of which adult numbers would be less than 15,000, was 162,167 gallons of spirits and 15,000 gallons of Colonial distilled spirits (distillation from sugar was prohibited in 1828, but the high price of grain and the higher taxing of local manufactured spirits became a natural deterrent). A final observation was made in 1829 that the only duties imposed on spirits in that year were upon spirits imported directly from H. M. Plantations in the West Indies. So the British authorities received double benefit in trading and duties.

m.   The quantity of dutiable tobacco in 1828 was 136,748 pounds (compared to 91,893 pounds in 1825). The Government experimented with locally grown tobacco at establishments in Emu Plains and Port Macquarie with the result being 51,306 pounds produced.

n.   Shipping companies also paid light house charges, along with wharfage.

o.   In 1828, the postage of letters attracted fees, for the first time, and the official Postmaster collected 598 pounds for general revenue.

p.   The commencement of sales of both crown lands and crown timbers increased general revenues to the extent that in 1828, the amounts realised were:

Sales of Crown Lands	5004.19.2
Sales of Cedar cut on crown lands	744.15.11
Sales of other Timber	9365.11.4

The Governor imposed a fee of One halfpenny per foot for all cedar cut on crown lands. The 'Blue Book' makes the further observation that this charge 'has checked bushrangers and other lawless depredators by depriving them of ready means of subsistence by the absence of all restraint from cutting Cedar upon unallocated lands'.

Colonial Accounting in Victoria

The new settlement of Port Phillip adopted the standards set out in the Governor George Gipps Report on Government Accounting and Reporting after 1836 Public Finance following separation from New South Wales to form the Colony of Victoria. The Blue Book was more accurately kept in the new settlement and full records are available concerning the commencement of the settlement and leading to the separation from New South Wales.

There was a major improvement in record keeping and reporting after self-government in 1855. The "Financial Statements of the Colonial Treasurers of New South Wales from Responsible Government in 1855 to 1881" provide a detailed accounting mechanism for recording classifications, and compilation of budgets and reporting to the Authorities. They contain 'explanatory memoranda of the financial system of New South Wales, and of the rise, progress and present condition of the public revenue'.

The interest in this period (from 1822 to 1881) is that these records, of the 'Blue Book' and the printed Financial Statements of 1881, provide the first identification of the items included in the revenue and expenditures for the Colony. This historical data is relevant to understanding the social conditions in the Colony, the application of duties, tariffs, tolls and fees which embraced the essential revenue of a Colony that was designed to be self-sufficient and which was being given minimal economic support by the British Government, even though the opportunity cost of housing 'prisoners' in the Colony was a fraction of the cost of housing them in England.

Table A
New South Wales Public Finance
Orphan, Gaol & Police Funds 1802-1821

Revenue

Year	Opng Balances	Customs	Total	Works Outlay
1802			900	
1803			5,200	
1804				
1805			3,100	
1806			1,900	
1807			1,200	
1808				
1809				
1810	0	1,384	3,272	2,194
1811	769	7,872	10,939	2,965
1812	5,016	5,579	13,494	3,259
1813	4,502	5,228	14,621	4,426
1814	6,016	4,529	13,325	4,993
1815	1,681	13,197	17,994	6,350
1816	3,327	11,200	17,782	5,582
1817	5453	16,125	24,706	7,048
1818	9363	17,739	31,008	6,219
1819	18900	22,579	42,968	17,131
1820	10725	27,891	44,507	14,700

Commentary on Table A

In 1876, the Colonial Financial Officer (the Treasury Consultant—James Thomson), acting for the Colonial Secretary of New South Wales, wrote in a report to the Imperial Government that "From the foundation of the Colony in 1788 to 1824, the records of local revenue and expenditure are too imperfect to render them of much value for statistical purpose, or for comparison with subsequent years."

However these figures (Table A) above, have been collated in the 'Historical Records of Australia—Statistics' from reports by the Colonial Governor to the British authorities and go someway to telling a story. The claim made by historian N. G. Butlin in his introduction to the Historical Records of Australia series—'The economy before 1850'—"that the British Colonial Office spent millions of pounds to start up the Colony"—does not seem to be verifiable. In fact, rather the opposite.

For instance we know that the British authorities had the choice of building new prisons in Britain and housing, feeding, guarding and clothing these prisoners, or relocate them to a 'penal colony'. The previous penal colony in America was no longer available because of the American Wars of Independence and the British were not welcome there. The recommendation of Sir Joseph Banks, after his voyage to the southern oceans with Captain James Cook, was to use the land and resources available in the newly charted east coast of 'Australia'. The opportunity cost of this arrangement was enormous. Britain was fighting wars in a number of areas and had numerous Colonies to administer, and one more Colony; supposedly rich in potential rewards and able to be converted to self-sufficiency was most attractive. So, the opportunity cost was one form of savings.

By 1824 the convicts were also paying their way (in opportunity cost terms) by removing coal from the ground in the Maitland area and used for heating purposes. No value was ever placed on this work, nor on the use of convicts as builders of roads, housing, barracks, storage sheds, port wharves, churches and government buildings. It would appear that the convicts earned their keep whilst the Colony paid its own way very quickly. Historians should recognise the value of the convict work as well as the opportunity cost of having transported the prisoners offshore, when an assessment is made of the 'investment' made by Britain in the new Colony of New South Wales.

The original estimate of direct gains by the British authorities from the original and continuing investment in the Colony of New South Wales was based on 5 (five) identifiable and quantifiable events

1. The opportunity cost of housing, feeding and guarding the convicts in the Colony compared with the cost of doing the same thing in Britain.

The original estimates, in this category, were based on an estimated differential of ten pound per head—an arbitrary assessment of the differential cost.

However recent and more reliable information has come to hand which gives further validity to a number of 20 pound per head per annum, compared with the original 10 pound per head per annum.

A letter to Under Secretary Nepean, dated 23rd August 1783, from James Maria Matra of Shropshire and London assists us in this regard.

It was Matra who first analysed the opportunity of using the new Colony as a Penal Colony; only his estimates were incorrect and ill founded. He had advised the Government that it would cost less than 3,000 pound to establish the Colony initially, plus transportation cost at 15 pound per head and annual maintenance of 20 pound per head.

In fact the transportation was contracted for the second fleet at 13 pound 5 shillings per head and Colonial revenues from 1802 offset annual maintenance.

However, Matra made a significant statement in his letter to Nepean, when he pointed out that the prisoners housed, fed and guarded on the rotting hulks on the Thames River were being contracted for in the annual amount of 26.15.10 per head per annum. He also writes that 'the charge to the public for these convicts has been increasing for the last 7 or 8 years' (Historical Records of NSW—Vol 1 Part 2 Page 7)

Adopting this cost as a base for comparison purposes, it means that the benefit to Britain of the Colony increased from 140,000,000 pound to 180,000,000 pound. This benefit assesses the Ground 1 benefit at 84,000,000 pound.

2. Benefit to Britain on Ground Two (2) is put at 70, 000,000 pound which places the value of a convicts labour at 35 pound per annum. Matra had assessed the value of labour of the Hulk prisoners at 35. 85 pound.

2. The valuation of convict labour in the new Colony should reflect the convicts not only used on building sites, but also on road, bridge and wharf construction. This would add (based on 35 pound per annum) a further 21,000,000-pound.

3. The Molesworth Committee (A House of Commons Committee investigating transportation) concluded that the surplus food production by the convicts would feed the Military people and this, over a period of 10 years, would save 7,000,000 pound for the British Treasury.

4. The benefits of fringe benefit grants of land to the Military etc can be estimated (based on One pound per acre) at over 5,000,000 before 1810.

5. We learn from Governor King's Report to Earl Camden (which due to a change of office holder, should have been addressed to Viscount Castlereagh as Colonial Secretary) dated 15th March 1806 that the Convicts engaged in widely diverse work. The Report itself (Enclosure #2) is entitled

"Public Labour of Convicts maintained by the Crown at Sydney, Parramatta, Hawkesbury, Toongabbie and Castle Hill, for the year 1805

Cultivation—Gathering, husking and shelling maize from 200 acres sowed last year—Breaking up ground and planting 1230 acres of wheat, 100 acre of Barley, 250 acres of Maize, 14 acres of Flax, and 3 acres of potatoes—Hoeing the above maize and threshing wheat.

Stock—Taking care of Government stock as herdsmen, watchmen etc

Buildings—
- At Sydney: Building and constructing of stone, a citadel, a stone house, a brick dwelling for the Judge Advocate, a commodious brick house for the main guard, a brick printing office
- At Parramatta: Alterations at the Brewery, a brick house as clergyman's residence
- At Hawkesbury: completing a public school
- A Gaol House with offices, at the expense of the Colony
- Boat and Ship Builders: refitting vessels and building row boats
- Wheel and Millwrights: making and repairing carts

Manufacturing: sawing, preparing and manufacturing hemp, flax and wool, bricks and tiles

Road Gangs: repairing roads, and building new roads

Other Gangs: loading and unloading boats"
(Historical Records of NSW—Vol 6 P43)

Thus the total benefits from these six (6) items of direct gain to the British comes to well over 174 million pound, and this is compared to Professor N. G. Butlin's proposal that the British 'invested' 5.6 million.

However, one item of direct cost born by the British was the transportation of the prisoners to the Colony, their food and general victualling. Although the British chartered the whole boat, some of the expense was offset by authorising private passengers, 'free settlers' to travel in the same fleet. A second saving was the authorities had approved 'back-loading' by these vessels of tea from China.

Only limited stores and provisions, tools and implements were sent with Captain Arthur Phillip, the appointed first Governor, and his efforts to delay the fleet until additional tools were ready was met with an order to 'commence the trip forthwith'. This turned out to be a mistake as the new Colony could only rely on minimal farming practices to grow a supply of vegetables and without the tools to scratch the land, remove the trees and vegetation, little progress was made. A potential big cost to the fledgling Colony.

i. The initial claim by the author that the cost to the British Treasury of establishing and operating the Colony was NOT the millions of pounds claimed by other economic historians is born out by examination. The accounting records as maintained by Governor Macquarie from 1822 leads to a statement of 'net revenue and expenses' which purports to offset all revenues against all expenses, and includes as revenue certain convict maintenance charges. Even in 1822 the Colony was showing a small operating surplus. This surplus grew through 1828 until, other than for transportation of convicts to the Colony, the charges on account of the British Treasury were less than One Hundred Thousand pounds for protecting, feeding and housing nearly 5,000 fully maintained convicts. Against this cost, the charge for housing, feeding and guarding this same number of prisoners in Britain would have been substantially higher, since in addition to the 5,000 gully maintained convicts there were a further 20,000 being paid for by free settlers and used as supervised labour. Britain surely had found a cheap source of penal servitude for at least 25,000 of its former prisoners, and found a very worthwhile alternative to the American Colonies as a destination for its prisoners.

j. Revenue from Crown Land sales and rents was used to offset Civil (Crown) salaries and expenses.

k. It is probably incorrect, at this stage, to say that it cost Britain nothing or at best, very little, to establish and maintain the Colony, but it can be said that from 1822 the costs were limited to maintaining fewer and fewer convicts. But from these convicts great value in terms of agricultural produce, coal and other minerals was derived. Just in terms of coal for lighting, heating and power, the cost to the government of purchasing these items would have been substantial. The 'Blue Book' reflects the use of the coal as a cost rather than a gain as would be the accounting standard today.

l. A final conclusion could be given that there are much more known records available for this period (the first One Hundred Years) than the author originally thought. The reproduction of the 'Blue Book' by the State Archives Office is a major step forward in understanding the economic challenges faced by settlers and convicts in the early Colony. The sourcing of material from the

Blue Book unveils the financial statements and conditions of these early years. It is still considered that finance records of the period 1788 to 1822 are not re-constructible, but the author feels that a deep search through the microfilms forming the Joint Copying Project will provide information on the two Colonial operating funds of the period—the 'Police Fund and the Orphan Fund'. This is a challenge for another time.

An interesting observation is found in_'The Constitutional History of Australia' by W. G. McMinn (1979), referring to the post 1855 financial arrangements. On P 33 he records "Subject to the need for a vice-regal message, accepting that any locally (Australian Colony) initiated legislation of a money bill nature requires The Sovereign's ratification, the New South Wales Legislative Council was to have a general right to appropriate revenue from taxation, except for an amount of 81,600 pounds, the expenditure of which was to be in accordance with 'three schedules' to the Act; 33,000 pound for the salaries of those on the civil list eg Governor et al, the superintendent of Port Phillip and its judges and for the expenses of administering justice; 18,600 pound for the chief civil officers and their departments, for pensions and expenses of the council; and 30,000 pound for the maintenance of public worship.

The Sale of Waste Land Act of 1828 raised the minimum reserve price of crown land to one pound per acre, except that large remote areas might be sold at a lower price, and established a formula for the use of the land revenue; fifty percent was to be spent on immigration, the rest was to be expended by the Governor in accordance with British Government directives from time to time. The Governor was to continue to have power to issue depasturing licences and to make regulations for the use and occupancy of unsold lands, but the existence of the Sale of Waste Lands Act placed an important restriction on the colony by implying a prohibition against the Legislative Council legislating on these matters. The first directive on how the Governor was to spend a portion of the fund, enjoined the Governor to spend a proportion on Aboriginal protection and another on the roads; he was left free to hand any surplus over to the Council for appropriation; but it was made clear that the whole of the fifty percent was to be considered as an emergency reserve if the Council proved difficult". McMinn sheds some further light on the Crown Lands mystery but there still remains the question of whether, year after year, these funds were fully used or just included as a contribution to general revenue. It would appear that somewhere there is a firm directive from the British Treasury that the revenues from Crown Lands sale was to be used to 'offset' British costs of maintaining the Colony. The 'Blue Book' is evidence that as general revenues, these funds were already being used to pay for the costs of feeding, clothing, housing convicts, and we know they were specifically used to pay for 'sponsored immigrants', aboriginal 'protection', and now roads. The costs of the military establishment were charged against general revenues so in the quite large 'pot', nearly all Colonial expenditures were subsidised or offset by revenues from the Sale of Crown Land. Britain put its hand in the till only, it seems, to pay for the shipping and supplies costs of getting their prisoners to the Colony. After 1828, we know that convict production—both agricultural and mineral—went a long way to paying their expenses, so perhaps the British Treasury did in fact get off very lightly indeed, especially fort the benefits it derived.

The vexing question of Crown Lands revenues still remains. It is apparent from the 'Blue Book' notations that this revenue was 'reserved' for specific allocation by the Crown and remained in the Colony as an offset against British Government fiscal obligations (eg Civil List salaries)until self-government in 1855. A relevant quotation from the 1887 Financial Statements of the Colonial Treasurer of New South Wales, follows:

"Prior to the passing of the Constitution Act, the Territorial Revenues of the Colony belonged to the Crown, but upon that coming into operation in 1855, they were placed at the disposal of the local Parliament, and together with the taxes, imposts, rates and duties were formed into one fund, under the title of the Consolidated Revenue Fund. In lieu of the Crown Revenues thus given up to the Colony, an annual Civil List of 64,300 pound was made payable to Her Majesty out of the Consolidated Revenues of the Colony." What this means is that the British Treasury allowed the offset of all direct British payments made on account of the Colony against revenues raised by the sale, rent or lease of Crown lands. A theory promoted by the writer but hithertobefore unable to be officially verified.

Governance of Public Finance

Included in the appendix to the 'Financial Statements of 1887' is the record (by the Colonial Treasury Consultant—James Thomson) that:

> "The Financial System of the Colony of New South Wales is regulated chiefly by the Constitution Act of 1855 and the Audit Act of 1870, and in matters relating to Trust Funds and Loans by special Appropriation Acts of the local legislature.
>
> The Imperial Act granting a constitution to the Colony of New South Wales was assented to on 16th July, 1855, and became effective on the 24th November 1855. This Act provides for a Legislative Council (Upper House) and a Legislative Assembly. The Upper House members were to be nominated by the Governor, while the Lower House members were to be elected by inhabitants of the Colony.

"Prior to the passing of the Constitution Act, the territorial revenues of the Colony belonged to the Crown, but on that Act coming into operation in 1855, these revenues were all placed at the disposal of the local Parliament, and together with the taxes, imposts, rates and duties, were formed into one fund, under the title of the Consolidated Revenue Fund. In lieu of the Crown Revenues thus given up to the Colony, an annual Civil List of 64,300 pounds was made payable to Her Majesty out of the consolidated revenues of the Colony.

The Constitution Act also provides that the legislature of the Colony shall have power to make laws for regulating the sale, letting, disposal, and occupation of the waste lands of the Crown within the Colony; and also for imposing taxes and levying customs duties. All Money Bills must, in the first place, be recommended to the Legislative Assembly by message from the Governor, and no part of the Public Revenue can be issued except on warrants bearing the Governor's signature, and directed to the Treasurer of the Colony.

The Audit Act of 1870 was passed to regulate the receipt, custody and issue of public monies, and to provide for the audit of the Public

Accounts. The Treasury is the Department entrusted with the collection
and disbursement of the revenues and other public monies of the Colony.
It is under the control and general management of the Treasurer and
Secretary for Finance and Trade. The permanent head of the Department
is responsible to the Minister for the efficient conduct of its business.

The revenue of the Colony is now to be classed under the following
general headings:

1. Taxation
2. Land Revenue
3. Receipts for services rendered
4. miscellaneous receipts

The main elements of the key items consist of

a. Taxation
    1. customs duties
    2. excise duties
    3. duty on gold exported
    4. trade licenses

b. Land Revenue
    1. Proceeds from land auctions
    2. sales of improved lands
    3. rents and assessments on pastoral runs
    4. quit rents
    5. leases of mining lands
    6. miner's rights

c. Services receipts, include:
    1. railway & telegraph revenue
    2. money orders
    3. mint charges
    4. gold escort fees
    5. pilotage & harbour fees
    6. registration of cattle brands
    7. other fees of office

d. Miscellaneous
   1. rents
   2. fines
   3. sale of government property,
   4. interest on bank deposits
   5. other general revenues

The revenue and expenditure of the Colony is increasing year by year in proportion to the prosperity of the people and the increase of population. This is naturally to be expected for as new lands are taken up and outlying districts occupied, demands upon the government for all those services which tend to promote the well-being of a community are constantly being made; and although these services when granted create an additional expenditure, there generally follows an augmentation of the revenue both from the sale and occupation of the waste lands of the Colony, and the larger consumption of dutiable articles"

When responsible government was established in 1855, the revenue amounted to 973,178 pounds and the population was then 277,000. In 1875, exactly twenty years after the introduction of responsible government, the population had increased to 606,000 and the revenue to 4,121,996."

From the Government Gazette of 2nd January, 1879, this condensed statement is taken:

REVENUE, 1878

Taxation	
Customs	1148,737
Duties	44,220
Duty on gold	6,898
Licenses	109,851
Land Revenue	
Sales	1915,466
Other	410,254
Services	1183,582
Miscellaneous	172,907
TOTAL REVENUES for 1878	4,991,919 pound

An interesting observation on latter day government finance and government involvement in entrepreneurial activities is made by Trevor Sykes in his book, 'The Bold Riders' 1994-Chapter 14, Page 438:

> "The Savings Bank of South Australia was formed in 1848 and the State Bank of South Australia was formed in 1896. By 1984 they had led stolidly blameless lives for 136 and 98 years respectively. In 1984 they merged to form a new, larger State Bank of South Australia.
>
> The chairman of Hooker Corporation, Sir Keith Campbell, headed the Campbell Committee, set up by Federal Treasurer, John Howard, in 1979. The Committee delivered its report in March 1981. The Report recommended deregulation of the financial system, a part of a world-wide trend, leading to deregulation in the federal sphere in 1984 by Paul Keating. The Campbell Report recommended that, once the banking system had been deregulated to make it more competitive, there would cease to be any justification, on efficiency grounds, for continued government ownership of banks, so that if government banks were to remain, should be no more fettered or subject to government interference than private sector institutions undertaking similar activities."

GOVERNANCE OF PUBLIC FINANCE IN THE COLONY

General observations on the origin and nature of the Colonial Revenue

"The Revenues collected within the Colony of New South Wales, from its establishment until the commencement of the administration of Governor Macquarie in 1810, were raised in support of the 'Gaol' and 'Orphan' Funds respectively. The Revenue thus levied for, and appropriated to the Gaol Fund consisted of a Duty of 1s. per gallon on Spirits, 6d per gallon on wine, 3d per gallon on beer, together with a wharfage duty of 6d on each cask or package landed. These duties appear to have been first established upon the authority of Governor John Hunter R.N. during his administration in 1795-1800 and were the earliest sources of local revenue in the Colony.

The Revenue raised for the Orphan Fund was derived from fees on the entry and clearance of Vessels, and for permits to land and remove spirits—both first levied in 1800; from licenses to retail liquor and from a duty of 1.5% on goods sold by auction (first collected in 1801); from a duty of 5% ad valorem on all articles imported, the produce of countries to the eastward of the Cape of Good Hope (first imposed in 1802) ; from fines levied by the Courts and Magistrates; from fees from grants of lands and leases, and quit rents on crown lands (Quit rents ceased in 1805). Other than quit rents and crown land fees, all revenues were levied upon Colonial authority.

The following is revenue raised in 1805 (James Thomson reports that the records from 1805 to 1810 are 'imperfect')

1805 Revenues in Gaol and Orphan Funds:

Duties on Spirits	1569.11.3
Fees on Vessels, licenses	595.13.7
Ad valorem duty	531.10.3
Fines by courts	86.5.8

Revenue raised in the Colony in 1805   2783.0.9

In 1810, Governor Macquarie changed the designation of these two funds to 'Police Fund' and Orphan School Fund. The designated revenues were split 3:1 into each fund. The Act 3 Geo IV c.96 of 1822 gave further powers of taxation to the Governor.

Concluding the background to Colonial Accounting

The analysis of Accounts extracted from the 'Blue Books' of 1822 through 1828 allows a number of conclusions to be drawn.

a. The initial claim by the author that the cost to the British Treasury of establishing and operating the Colony, was NOT the millions of pounds claimed by other historians, is born out by examination. The accounting records as maintained by Governor Macquarie from 1822 leads to a statement of 'net revenue and expenses' which purports to offset all revenues against all expenses, and includes as revenue certain convict maintenance charges. Even in 1822 the Colony was showing a small operating surplus. This surplus grew through 1828 until, other than for transportation of convicts to the Colony, the charges on account of the British Treasury were under One Hundred Thousand pounds for protecting, feeding and housing nearly 5,000 fully maintained convicts. Against this cost, the charge for housing, feeding and guarding this same number of prisoners in Britain would have been substantially higher, since in addition to the 5,000 gully maintained convicts there were a further 20,000 being paid for by free settlers and used as supervised labour. Britain surely had found a cheap source of penal servitude for at least 25,000 of its former prisoners, and found a very worthwhile alternative to the American Colonies as a destination for its prisoners.

b. Revenue from Crown Land sales and rents was used to offset Civil (Crown) salaries and expenses.

c. It is probably incorrect, at this stage, to say that it cost Britain nothing or at best, very little, to establish and maintain the Colony, but it can be said that from 1842 the costs were limited to maintaining fewer and fewer convicts. But from these convicts great value in terms of agricultural produce, coal and other minerals extraction was derived. Just in terms of coal for lighting, heating, the cost to the government of purchasing these items commercially would have been substantial. The 'Blue Book', however, reflects the use of the coal as a cost rather than a gain as would be the accounting standard today.

d. A final conclusion could be given that there are much more known records available for this period (the first One Hundred Years) than the author originally thought. The reproduction of the 'Blue Book' by the State Archives Office is a major step forward in understanding the economic challenges faced by settlers and convicts in the early Colony. The sourcing of material from the Blue Book unveils the financial statements and conditions of these early years. It is still considered that finance records of the period 1788 to 1822 are not re-constructible, but the author feels that a deep search through the microfilms forming the Joint Copying Project will provide information on the two Colonial operating funds of the period—the 'Police Fund and the Orphan Fund'. This is a challenge for another time.

e. An interesting observation is found in 'The Constitutional History of Australia' by W. G. McMinn (1979).

P 33 records "Subject to the need for a vice-regal message, accepting that any locally (Australian Colony) initiated legislation of a money bill nature requires The Sovereign's ratification, the New South Wales Legislative Council was to have a general right to appropriate revenue from taxation, except for an amount of 81,600 pounds, the expenditure of which was to be in accordance with 'three schedules' to the Act; 33,000 pound for the salaries of those on the civil list eg Governor et al, the superintendent of Port Phillip and its judges and for the expenses of administering justice; 18,600 pound for the chief civil officers and their departments, for pensions and expenses of the council; and 30,000 pound for the maintenance of public worship. Land and casual revenues were also reserved.

The Sale of Waste Land Act raised the minimum reserve price of crown land to one pound per acre, except that large remote areas might be sold at a lower price, and established a formula for the use of the land revenue; fifty percent was to be spent on immigration, the rest was to be expended by the Governor in accordance with British Government directives from time to time. The Governor was to continue to have power to issue depasturing licences and to make regulations for the use and occupancy of unsold lands, but the existence of the Sale of Waste Lands Act placed an important restriction on the colony by implying a prohibition against the Legislative Council legislating on these matters. The first directive on how the Governor was to spend a portion of the fund, enjoined the Governor to spend a proportion on Aboriginal protection and another on the roads; he was left free to hand any surplus over to the Council for appropriation; but it was made clear that the whole of the fifty percent was to be considered as an emergency reserve if the Council proved difficult". McMinn sheds some further light on the Crown Lands mystery by there still remains the question of how, year after year, were these funds fully used or were they just included as a contribution to general revenue. It would appear that somewhere there is a firm directive from the British Treasury that the revenues from Crown Lands sale was to be used to 'offset' British costs of maintaining the Colony. The 'Blue Book' is evidence that as general revenues, these funds were already being used to pay for the costs of feeding, clothing, housing convicts, and we know they were specifically used to pay for 'sponsored immigrants', aboriginal 'protection', and now roads. The costs of the military establishment were charged against general revenues so in the quite large 'pot', nearly all Colonial expenditures were subsidised or offset by revenues from the Sale of Crown Land. Britain put its hand in the till only, it seems, to pay for the shipping and supplies costs of getting their prisoners to the Colony. After 1828, we know that convict production—both agricultural and mineral—went a long way to paying their expenses, so perhaps the British Treasury did in fact get off very lightly indeed, especially fort the benefits it derived.

The vexing question of Crown Lands revenues still remains. It is apparent from the 'Blue Book' notations that this revenue was 'reserved' for specific allocation by the Crown and remained in the Colony as an offset against British Government fiscal obligations (eg Civil List salaries)until self-government in 1855. A relevant quotation from the 1887 Financial Statements of the Colonial Treasurer of New South Wales, follows:

> "Prior to the passing of the Constitution Act, the Territorial Revenues of the Colony belonged to the Crown, but upon that coming into operation in 1855, they were placed at the disposal of the local Parliament, and together with the taxes, imposts, rates and duties were formed into one fund, under the title of the Consolidated Revenue Fund. In lieu of the Crown Revenues thus given up to the Colony, an annual Civil List of 64,300 pound was made payable to Her Majesty out of the Consolidated Revenues of the Colony." What this means is that the British Treasury allowed the offset of all direct British payments made on account of the Colony against revenues raised by the sale, rent or lease of Crown lands.

Bigge in his first report to Lord Bathurst recommended that 'the number of convicts employed by the Government on public works should be reduced, both in the interests of economy and because it was argued that these men, especially if working in Sydney, were usually idle, and prone to misbehaviour in town. As far as possible, Bigge's recommended, convicts should be assigned to public service in the interior. He did, however, approve of sending convict offenders to penal settlements for further punishment, and he suggested that the settlements be expanded.

After the departure of Macquarie, administration of convicts became more efficient. The number of convict clerks in government service was gradually reduced, although the Marine and Survey Departments, the hospitals and domestic service for government officials became a reward for good conduct, although convicts were often placed in government service for breaches of discipline or failure to work effectively for private masters. In some areas, government service tended to be arduous.

The majority of convicts were 'assigned' to private employment and provided the bulk of the work force of the colony. Those 'assigned' were taken off commissary support and were entitled to be clothed and fed by their master in proscribed quantities of food and garb.

Quantity by year
How they worked—public or assignment by number
What they worked at
The cost to the British Government
What benefits they produced
Their talents and education
Their crimes and background

The Manonochie Report
Manonochie: 'Thoughts on Convict Management'
The Ovens Report
The Molesworth Committee Report 1837-38 'the present system of convict discipline in VDL
HRNSW
The Bigge Report—Vol I
Greenwood
Laidlaw
Report of the Select Committee on Transportation 1812

Bessant 'The Occupation of a Continent' P.85—defining an average convict

THE OPERATIONS OF THE COMMISSARY'S LUMBER YARD

We don't know a great deal about the operations of the Lumber Yard, other than where it was located, and the number of men it employed.

What we need to know, in addition, is

- Its size and building configuration
- How its harvesting operations were carried out
- Where were its main forests located
- Where and how did it cure the timber
- How was the timber transported from the forests to the Yard
- What type of timber did they produce; what were the most common dimensions
- How much finished timber did they keep in the Yard
- Who used the timber and how much did it cost to buy
- What security or fire prevention methods were in use
- Where did the nails and screws and specialty timbers come from?
- What was the most common method of connecting the timbers

There are only a few sources that can assist in answering these questions.

o Susanna de Vries-Evans in Historic Sydney
o Joseph Fowles in Sydney in 1848
o Peter Bridges in Foundations of Identity
o David Collins in An Account of the English Colony in New South Wales
o Geoffrey Scott in Sydney's Highways of History

Before we go delving into original sources such as Historic Records of NSW and Historic Records of Australia, we can see what we can learn from the above names secondary sources.

Historic Sydney tells us that the Lumber Yard was located on the corner of George Street and Bridge Street. Bridge Street earned its name from having the first wooden bridge constructed over the Tank Stream. The bridge, it tells us, 'was a rough affair of large logs, hastily rolled into place by convicts in 1788, but it soon collapsed and left the developing town once more divided into two by the stream. In June 1803, the Sydney Gazette reported that stonemasons and labourers were working on the foundations of a new bridge which would, upon completion, greatly add to the appearance of Sydney'. Governor King had made it compulsory for all residents of the town to work on the construction, either with goods or labour.

At the corner of George and Bridge Streets stood the Lumber Yard. De Vries writes in Historic Sydney 'these lumber or storage yards were a standard feature of British colonial penal settlements. They were in fact convict work camps and the Bridge Street Lumber Yard contained workshops for blacksmiths, carpenters, wheelwrights, tailors and shoemakers. There was also a tannery where the convicts made their own leather hats and shoes. Nails, bolts, bellows, barrels and simple items of furniture for the officer's quarters and the barracks were also made in the Lumber Yard. Convicts wore identification on their uniforms—P.B. for Prisoner's or Hyde Park Barracks or C.B. for Carter's Barracks. They worked from sunrise to sunset. If they failed to fulfil their allotted tasks they were flogged at the pillory, conveniently situated nearby, also on Bridge Street.

Sydney's Highways of History reminds us that Captain Dumaresq was the superintendent of the Lumber Yard and that bridge Street was possibly the second oldest street, and for some years, the most important, street in the country. It connected High Street (George Street) and Government House and residences of the senior administration officers (the commissary, Judge-Advocate, Chaplain and Surveyor-General). Between Bridge Street and the Tank Streams, Simeon Lord and other merchants built their homes and warehouses. Across the stream was the Lumber Yard, the great Government storehouse and factory where the convict mechanics laboured. The Lumber Yard adjoined the lease of Garnham Blaxcell, one of the builders of the Rum Hospital, and was opposite the elaborate garden of Lieutenant Kent, whose big brick house was taken over for the orphanage in 1800 by Governor King. The Lumber Yard continued in use as a convict workshop until 1834, at which time it was cut up and sold for up to 25 pound a front foot (for the best lots).

Foundations of Identity reveals that 'contracting for government work was a common path to independence for building craftsmen. Convicts or emancipists employed as supervisors of the government building gangs seldom wished to remain in service longer than they had to and there was always a shortage of reliable men to take their place. Macquarie, in his efforts to retain his supervisors in government employment, permitted them to combine their official duties with the business of private contracting. The supervisor would undertake the management of a building project to which the government contributed labour and materials from the Lumber Yard. The Superintendent of the Yard at that time, Major Druitt was unable to suppress the open practices of government men and tools being 'borrowed' and government materials from the Yard being diverted elsewhere.'

"Already by 1791 the government (Lumber) Yard had been established on the western side of the Stream to collect and prepare timber for building and was the recognised meeting place where the gangs picked up their tools and materials and were assigned to work. Here building materials were collected, prepared for use and distributed to the various work sites, tools were issued and gangs allocated and checked. It became the core of the government labour system after the devastating Hawkesbury floods in the winter of 1809. Lt-Gov Patterson had the Sydney working parties gather there for victualling before going to the relief of the settlers. Under Macquarie's expanding work program the Lumber Yard became the centre of the largest single industrial enterprise in the colony. Captain Gill, as Inspector of Public Works, exercised the general direction of the working gangs and controlled the issue of tools and materials, while William Hutchinson, Superintendent of Convicts distributed convicts to the work gangs.

With so much activity the Yard was an easy target for thieves and by September 1811, the loss of tools, timber, bricks, lime, coal, shingles and nails from the government stocks had become so great that a General Order was issued directing that offenders, including conniving supervisors, would be punished as felons. The same order directed that all tools had to be handed in and counted at the end of each day and banned men from borrowing tools or doing private jobs in the yard after normal working hours. (Sydney Gazette Sept 1811).

Gill's successor, Major Druitt, expanded the Yard to cope with Macquarie's work program. He took over the adjoining land in Bridge Street now abandoned by the debt-ridden merchant Garnham Blaxcell, who had fled the colony; and built new covered saw pits, furnaces for an iron and brass foundry and workshops for blacksmiths, nailers, painters and glaziers, and harness makers. He raised the walls surrounding the Yard and built a solid gate to discourage truancy and pilfering; he built moveable rain-sheds for jobs around the town and provided two drags drawn by draft animals to replace to replace the 90 to 100 men previously employed on the laborious task of rolling logs from the dock to the Yard. (HRA series I-vol 9 832; ADB I-324-5)

Men were selected off the convict transports based on their skills and background. They were told to find lodgings in the *Rocks* area. Each morning a bell "would call them to the Lumber Yard where they were set to work according to their trades or capabilities. Some went to the workshops, others to building sites or the Brickfields where they dug and puddled clay and pressed it into moulds for firing in the kilns. Unskilled labourers were allocated according to their physical condition; the fittest went to the gangs felling trees and cutting logs to length, others to barrowing heavy stones or dragging the brick carts to the building sites, with assignments often used as punishment for the recalcitrant. The unfit were not spared; weak and ailing men went to gangs tidying up the streets or weeding government land, a man without an arm could tend to the stock and a legless man could be useful as a watchman". (Bridges: Foundations of Identity). 'The days work started at 5 am, there was an hours break for breakfast at 9 am and at 1 pm for lunch and at 3 pm the men were free to go and earn the cost of their lodgings. When in 1819, Macquarie tightened the convict system, he housed them all in Hyde Park Barracks, and the working day was extended to sunset, and only married or trusted convicts were allowed to live in the town). The men from the Barracks were marched down to the Yards but 'control was lax and as they went through the streets, some would slip away to follow their own devices'. (Bridges)

'As a result of Macquarie's building activities, and partly as a means of employing more and more convicts, the range of activities expanded in the Lumber Yard'. (Bridges)

Every kind of tradesman was gathered: carpenters, joiners, cabinet makers, wood turners, sawyers, wheelwrights, cart-makers, barrow-makers, blacksmiths, whitesmiths, shoeing smiths, agricultural implement makers, tool makers, nailers, bell founders, iron and brass founders, brass finishers, turners and platers, brass wire drawers, tool sharpeners, steelers, tinmen, painters, glaziers, farriers, horse-shoers, saddle and harness makers, bellow makers, pump borers, tailors, coopers and many more.

The organisation was simple: the big work-sheds faced the central log yard where logs and sawn timbers from Pennant Hills and Newcastle were stacked. The Lumber Yard was the source of many of the colonial made goods and the centre of the Government's engineering and building activities. It was the first step in the creation of the Public Works Department. Although the Lumber Yard service most of Macquarie's building needs, he badly required the services of a skilled architect and he found those skills in a convict—Francis Greenway. Greenway had a solid background of practical experience as well as theoretical training and became influential in translating Macquarie's aims and ideas into reality.

Bridges records that 'Nathaniel Lucas was one of Sydney's earliest building contractors; Lucas was one of the few skilled craftsmen to come with the first fleet. Colonel Johnston appointed Lucas superintendent of carpenters at the Lumber Yard but in 1814, he returned to private contracting'.

THE ROLE OF THE COMMISSARY

(In The Operations of the Colonial Government)

Planning for a Commissary for the new Penal Colony was well under-way by the 1795, and such operation was to be operated and managed along the lines of the naval purser's office. The Commissary was to be responsible for all purchasing, storage, payment and distribution of goods.

However for a new colony, which had decided not to adopt a currency, the Commissaries role was made especially challenging. A currency was the traditional means of exchange. There would be no buildings initially available and only convict labour—'always unreliable and untrustworthy', said John Palmer the third Commissary.

The supply ships arrived with the rest of the first fleet on the 26th January, 1788 in Port Jackson. The unloading of bare essentials, such as tents and a few tools and minimal food was completed that day, but the balance of the supplies would be left aboard the Sirius and the Golden Grove until a storehouse was available.

Every carpenter available was busy with the building of barracks for the soldiers and military personnel, followed by a facility for the Governor and only then a storehouse. But first the land had to be cleared of trees and timber cut for the first makeshift buildings.

The first Commissary, Andrew Miller, had been hand picked by Governor Arthur Phillip, based on Phillip's past experience with Miller, rather than Miller's experience as a Commissary chief. Phillip had provided detailed instructions of how he wanted the operation performed. Phillip, in turn, had been given his instructions by the Lords of the Admiralty and the Colonial Secretary, and the most important of these were the overall goals:

- keep the cost per head per day for supplies as low as possible
- keep the number of fully victualled persons as low as possible
- establish the Colony to be self-supporting as quickly as possible
- put the convicts out to work to earn their keep (although this was a new and untried policy)
- assign convicts to non-government masters on a full support basis (again, this policy was untried and untested—but one strongly supported by Phillip)

Phillip had transported the first One thousand convicts and military without loss of life or loss of property. He had brought the first animals for breeding into the Colony, all healthy and was assigning duties by the

28th January 1788 for the general unloading of the animals, convicts and material supplies ready to commence his Colonial operations.

Convicts were set to clearing the ground for vegetable plantings and building sites.

Phillip decided that instead of relying on stores transported on an irregular basis from Britain, that he would commence a planting program to provide fresh vegetables and grain; fresh meat, fish and game and make it a happy colony in which to live and work. He did not plan, nor was prepared for the harsh climate and the periodic droughts and flooding rains, or the unhappy natives.

His goal of victualling the whole Colony for less than 14p per day was going to be difficult, but he could do it if some level of self—support could be accomplished. He had brought quantities of seed for planting, but his fears were that northern hemisphere soils and climate would be very different from local 'New Holland' conditions and his crops would fail or yields would be minimal. His first corn crop, however, returned his planting twenty times over (HRNSW), and he was pleased and hopeful of the future returns being plentiful. In fact, he wrote to the Lord Commissioners stating that 'this Colony will become the greatest investment ever made by the British'.

Phillip planned for other possible ways to reduce costs; such as reducing imports, commence an export trade, establish settlers on farming ground, establish remote settlements, establish jobs and trades and build the necessities and Phillip thus went about his work, putting these plans into practice. He assumed, incorrectly, that the convicts and the military shared his enthusiasm and commitment to hard work.

However, his experiment with tobacco planting, and grains, other than corn and wheat, and even sugar was encouragingly successful.

He planned for another new settlement at the head of the harbour, near fresh water, and with boat access at high tide. Rose Hill, soon to become Parramatta, was to be established with convict and military quarters, a church, and some emancipist settlers. To this end he released convicts for good conduct, who were willing to marry, and provided them grants of good land, usually 30 acres, and an admonition to become self contained and sell their surplus to the Commissariat store. He did allow the emancipists to retain access to the Government store for a period of two years. He would, in the future, exchange settler's grain for cows, to enable a breeding program to commence and further expand the likelihood of a successful colony.

His building and construction priorities changed. He saw the priority need for a hospital building, especially since he had a surgeon in his midst, and some of his convicts had been speared and even killed by the natives. So the barracks were completed and then the hospital and finally the storehouse was ready by early April. Phillip wrote in his journal that 'the timber has one very bad quality, which puts us to great inconvenience; I mean the large gum tree, which warps and splits in such a manner, when used green, to which necessity obliges us, that a storehouse boarded up in this wood is rendered useless'

David Collins, a military Lieutenant and Phillip's Private Secretary, wrote on the 5th April, 1788, 'As the winter of this hemisphere is approaching. It becomes absolutely necessary to expedite the buildings intended for the detachment, so, every carpenter that could be procured amongst the convicts was sent to assist, since as many as could be released from the transports were employed working on the hospital and storehouses.'

Collins recorded on the following day, the 6th April, 1788 'worship was moved indoors as divine service was performed in the new storehouse. One hundred feet by twenty-five feet were the dimensions of the building, constructed with great strength and covered in with thatching. But we were always mindful of fire since no other materials could be found and we became mindful of accidental fire.'

Obviously, the hospital was finished, the storehouse was complete, some female convict huts had been completed and the military barracks were well under way. Phillip's plan was now in full swing.

This first and temporary storehouse was built somewhere around the Sydney cove, where a landing wharf had been constructed and where the camp was getting into working order. Subsequently permanent storehouses were built nearer the hospital, using roof tiles instead of thatching, and connected from the landing area to the hospital past the storehouses via a convict constructed 'road'.

Andrew Miller grew sick and frail, in the service of Phillip and asked to be returned to England. He died on route but was replaced as Commissary by his former assistant, Zachariah Clark, who had come from England originally as agent to Mr Richards the contractor.

Collins reported on the 12th April,. 1788 that the 'issuing of provisions, was in future, under Mr Clark, to be once a week.'

Lieutenant John Hunter, soon to be Lieutenant Governor of Norfolk Island, recorded in his diary for 5th September 1788, that 'because of some failed crops, rotting food, and a plague of rats in the storehouse, that the colony would need more stores and provisions than any Pacific island could supply, and he would dispatch the Sirius to the Cape of Good Hope, in order to purchase such quantity of provisions as she might be capable of taking on board; and that she should be made as light as possible for that purpose. In consequence, eight guns and their carriages were removed and 24 rounds of shot for each gun, 20 barrels of powder, a spare anchor and various other articles were put on shore at Sydney Cove. I was also directed to leave the long boat behind for use by the Colony. The master of the Golden Grove store-ship was also ordered to get ready for sea to take supplies, convicts and some military personnel to Norfolk Island.'

Phillip was obviously panicking about the shortage of supplies and the empty storehouse. The proposed settlements at Rose Hill and Norfolk Island and a ship to the Cape had almost emptied the first settlement at Sydney Cove, of people as well as provisions.

A number of storehouses had been established. The first, a temporary one at the Cove, now the permanent one near the hospital on the first Sydney town street—High Street (now George Street), the lumber yard store, the military detachment store and the naval store. Clarke was nominally in charge of all stores but was also assigned other duties with the Governor, and with the hope of cutting rations even further by only opening the regular store once each week, was obviously in charge of only empty buildings.

In October, 1788, Warwick Tench observed, in his diary that 'we have now been here over half a year and are becoming acclimatised, even if we lack the shelters thought necessary. Since our disembarkation in January, the efforts every one has made was to put the public stores into a state of shelter and security and to erect habitations for the hospital convicts and ourselves. We are eager to escape from tents, where only a fold of canvas was between us and the hot beams of the summer sun and the chilling blasts of the winter wind from the south. Under wretched covers of thatch lay our provisions and stores, exposed to destruction from every flash of lightning and every spark of fire. A few of the female convicts had got into huts but almost all of the officers and all the men, were still in tents.'

In February, 1789, the only free immigrant, James Smith, who had procured a passage from England on the Lady Penrhyn was placed in charge of the new storehouse at Rose Hill and was also sworn in as a peace officer, or special constable. Claiming to be a 'practical farmer', Phillip gave him number of convicts to assist him in exercising his abilities. This was the first trial of the assigned convict system.

On the 18th March, 1789, Collins recorded the first major theft of stores and provisions from the secured commissary. There were seven of the military convicted of theft undertaken over a period of some weeks, robbing the store of liquor and large quantities of provisions. Phillip made an example of these men, but to little avail, as later that same year another six soldiers were convicted and hung for doing exactly the same thing.

The Economic Role of the Commissary

Over time Phillip increased and improved the operations of the Commissary and planned to offset the effect of having no currency in the Colony by creating a barter economy. To aid in this plan, Phillip arranged that all goods received into the Commissary would be recognised and accepted by 'store receipts'. Payment for goods arriving by ship or purchases made from other ports and brought to Sydney town was done via official 'bills' drawn for payment upon presentation on the British Treasury,.

By 1790 store receipts and the related official government bills formed the basis of the currency in the colony. The settlers would lodge their grain, wool, or meat with the store and receive an official receipt in exchange.

The receipt stated the recipients name, type and quantity of goods and the price paid. Because they were backed by the Government, the receipts became an increasingly popular instruments of exchange. They could be transferred between parties in payment for a debt, exchanged amongst settlers in the course of trade and for products from the Government stores, redeemed for the equivalent in coin and banknotes, and through the commissariat, exchanged for government bills drawn on the English Treasury. "Eventually when colonial banks became established, store receipts and government bills were accepted as deposits. In these early days, a store receipt was as good as cash and for many people, a lot more convenient." (Encyclopedia of Australia)

The Final Volume (# 7) of Historical Records of Victoria (Vol 7-Public Finance) sets out some background of what was happening in New South Wales whilst Victoria was still part of the Port Phillip colony.

"New South Wales was one of only three of the Empire's colonies established at the expense of British taxpayers. Most British colonies were begun by trading companies or settlement associations, and were expected to be self sufficient. The British Government was usually prepared to provide a civil administration and military protection, but wherever possible, these were to be funded from local sources. The commissariat was responsible for many of the early financial arrangements in New South Wales. From the beginning, practices had been highly unsatisfactory and allowed much corruption. The first fleet brought with it in 1788 only the most meagre of supplies of coin. This shortage of a circulating currency became increasingly acute. In the short term, the government used promissory notes, government store receipts, treasury bills, spirits and shipments of coins of various denominations and currencies to which varying values were assigned. All were part of a volatile and unstable money market."

Britain had, prior to the first fleet invoked its right to tax dependencies. The loss in the 1770s of its valuable American colonies, the previous dumping ground for convicts, was directly attributable to these taxes.

The Napoleonic Wars (1793-1815) almost beggared Britain, and ruthless experiments with new taxes and duties was tried in a desperate effort to meet national debts. Income tax was introduced in 1798, modified in 1805 and 1807 and discontinued in 1816. The unpopularity of direct taxation resulted in wider nets of indirect taxation, such as customs duties. The New South Wales experiment echoed some of these developments. But it became Governor Gipps' opinion that nowhere else was so large a revenue raised from so small a population." And this opinion is born out by the official Treasury reports of the time (refer attached Statistics).

Marjorie Barnard in her fine work—'A History of Australia' (P327) reflects on the early workings of the commissary and the financial dealings it accommodated.

"The commissariat had charge under the Governor of all stores and provisions. It acquired locally produced supplies, but the importation of food, clothing and other necessities from overseas was the responsibility of the home office, or in emergency, of the governor.

The commissariat was the colony's store and it also became the financial centre of the colony, where all transactions were by barter or note of hand. The only note in which there could be universal faith was that issued by the commissary as a receipt for goods received into the store. This department was the quasi-treasury, so that when a colonial treasury was set up, the commissary remained for provisioning of the convicts and only withered away at the end of transportation. Large sums could only be paid by the commissary's notes, for these alone had credit behind them, and they had to be eventually redeemed by bills on the treasury."

R. M. Younger in his work 'Australia & The Australians—'

writes (P78) "The only market for produce was the government store in the various farming districts, run by the commissariat under the ultimate control of the superintendent of public works. The governor fixed the price of grain, and it was left to the storekeepers to decide whose grain should be bought and whose refused. David Collins, former secretary to Governor Phillip wrote of this operation:

'The delivery of grain into the public storehouses when open for
that purpose was so completely monopolised that the settlers
had but few opportunities of getting full value for their crops.
The ordinary settler found himself thrust out from the granary
by the a man whose greater opulence created greater influence.
He was then driven by necessity to dispose of his grain at less
than half its value. He was forced to sell it to the very man who
had first driven him away and now whose influence was the
only available way to get the grain into the public store.'

Such incident evidenced a fundamental weakness in the economy. Farming
had to be expanded so that the community could become self supporting;
but since the demand was in fact small and inelastic, and since there was
no export, a glut or a shortage could easily occur. Because of strictly limited
demand the wheat acreage could not be expanded too greatly, yet when
two bad years occurred, there were dangerous shortages, and the colony
had to revert to imports.

The commissary store continued to be the centre of the colony's economy.
A great number of the population were still victualled from the store; these
included the military and civil list people and their families, together with
settlers receiving land grants, whether expirees or free, for the first two years
on the farm. And convicts unassigned or working for the government.
The requirement that the military officers clothe, feed and house assigned
convicts was not strictly enforced and so in 1800 Hunter's record must
show that 75% of the population was victualled by the government."

The anomaly was that by 1813 a few Sydney merchants were exporting,
even though the NSW Corps still dominated local business. Exporting had
begun in 1801 with Simon Lord, selling coal, whale oil and seal-skins to
the American boats visiting Sydney for the purpose of two-way trade; they
brought moderately priced cargo for general sale as well as provisions and
supplies for the commissary. Campbell, the biggest trader got around the
British support of the East India Company having a trade monopoly with
China by using French or American ships. Campbell had built a warehouse
in 1800 supplying wine, spirits, sugar, tea, coffee and tobacco and a wide
range of household articles However Campbell was additionally soon
selling livestock, grain and merchandise to the commissary and private

buyers, with the government spending several thousand pounds with his firm each year. He then entered the whaling and sealing trade and sent a trial shipment of each to England. This caused a dispute between the East India company on one side(pushing for exclusion), Sir Joseph Banks on the other (encouraging freedom of trade) and Simon Lord, whose cargo had now been seized in Britain as contraband."

One of the charges made to Justice Bigge when he was sent to Australia to investigate and report on the Macquarie governorship, was to review the cost of operating the colony in terms of its original charter. It was of great concern to Lord Bathurst that the British Treasury in 1820 was still paying so much of the colonial operations.

So Bigge reviewed and commented on the high number of persons still victualled from the government store as late as 1823. An extract from his third report (dated January 1823) into 'The Nature of the Expenditure in the Colony' sets out his observations.

He writes that in 1821 the Civil list salaries amounted to 8,474.17.6 but those paid from local revenues, from the 'Police Fund'_amounted to 9,824.05.0. So it is confirmed that within 22 years of the Colony being established, it was substantially on course to paying its own way. In fact Bigge writes, that "some of the salaries included in the parliamentary estimate (the Civil List) have not been drawn in this, or in some of the preceding years but have been defrayed by the police fund of NSW, including two government school masters, six superintendents and the clerk to the judge advocate, all amounting to 500 pound.

The clerks in the commissariat generally consist of persons who have been convicts and also of persons who are still in that condition (being ticket-of-leave individuals) They are paid variously from 18d to 60d per day, plus lodging money. They also receive the full ration. And a weekly allowance of spirits. Bigge recommended that to reduce the fraud on the commissary, along with the high cost to the public purse, that (a) all bread be baked by a variety of contractors in lieu of convicts, and (b) that contracts for the supply of hospitals with bread, meat and vegetables be also let. He likewise recommended that all meat to the King's stores be furnished by contract from the settlers at the 5d per lb. He reports that the number of provisioned convicts is constantly changing for instance, the total number of people provisioned from the Sydney store on 30ᵗʰ December,1820, was 9326, of which only 5135 were convicts unassigned."

As can be seen from the following table, the number of victualled convicts (and others) is surprisingly high, especially at the end of the last two periods (1810 & 1820). The Governor's were directed to assign convicts to settlers or military officers for assistance with farming operations; the intention was for the colony to supply its own provisions and stores. The settlers and officers were directed to house, clothe and feed all assigned convicts and take them off the public stores. However, by virtue of being in a special position in the colony, most civil list persons and military were still being supported by the public stores. Even emancipists or free settlers that carried out special duties (eg police constables) became entitled to support from the stores.

The number of people on Rations (number victualled from public store) between 1795 and 1820 were:

1795	1,775
1793	1,682
1799	1,832
1800	3,545
1804	2,647
1810	5,772
1820	9,326

(compiled from individual statistics in vols 1-7 HRNSW)

As Bigge's concluded "some rations were issued in higher allowance than decreed because of extra work or hard labour.

Government owned livestock is held at the Cow Pastures, Parramatta and Emu Plains. These facilities are operated by a Superintendent and 3 oversees, all paid by the police fund. In addition 75 convicts are employed as stockmen and general labourers. All these people in total draw 122 daily rations from the public stores. The cost of daily rations were estimated by Bigge at 4s 8d or 56 pound per annum, or nearly 4 (four) times the targeted cost.

There were also 451 head of wild cattle which had over the previous year run off from the holding areas, but were recovered in 1820 and used for public meat supply. In total, with slaughtered sheep and cattle from government herds, over 237,000 lb of fresh meat supplied at a savings of 5,000 pound to the government. This still left 6,000 animals in the government herd, but the settlers were increasing their pressure on the Governor to buy only meat from the settlers and not use government herds for slaughtering.

Of the total colony expenditure in 1820 of 189,008 pound, the cost of rations for troops, civil list and convicts amounted to 143,370 or 75%. Bigge did state that the general expense of erecting buildings in the Macquarie years in the colony of New South Wales is lessened by the use of convict labour and locally found timbers and locally made bricks, tiles and stone. He suggested that the cost of local funds used for buildings would be better spent on clothing, and feeding the convicts and taking them off the public stores.

Reviewing the Official Records on the Commissary

The HRNSW contains numerous references to original records reporting the instructions on how to operate, or the anecdotal reports on how the commissariat operated.

Phillip wrote that 'It is planned that a quantity of provisions equal to two years consumption should be provided (written 1786), which will be issued from time to time, according to the discretion of the Superintendent, guided by the proportion of food which the country and the labour of the new settlers may produce.'

'Clothing per convict was estimated to cost 2.19.6 including jackets, hats, shirts, trousers, shoes'. Phillip further wrote that 'the type of clothing was not always suitable for the climate, and should be ready made rather than relying on the convicts to sew their own.'

He noted that 'The Sirius brought seed wheat and barley and four months supply of flour for the settlement, together with a year's provisions for the ships company,'

And, 'Supplies of grain or flour from England will be necessary to maintain the colony until there is sufficient local crops in store rather than 'in the ground', because of grub, fire, drought and other accidents.'

And 'I have directed the commissary to make a purchase (9th January, 1793) and have thus augmented the quantity of provisions in the colony to 7 months at the established ration.'

On 6th January 1793, Phillip recorded his opinion that the expense for the settlement projected for 1794 was 25913 for 5,500 persons. With 3000 convicts this cost translated into a per head cost per annum of 13.14.0, (or approx. 9p per day) which he pointed out 'this sum cannot increase, but must gradually diminish.' This converted within the officially targeted allowance of 14p per head per day.

'Whitehall reported on 9th November 1794 that the stock of stores of provisions and ready-made clothing should now be sufficient for the settlement for one year.

With the quantity of clothing shipped in mid—1794, there would be a sufficient supply for 2,500 men and 700 women, according to the last official report of numbers.' Mr. Henry Dundas (British MP) insisted that the convicts should be made to wear the clothing for a full year.'

The Colonial Office insisted that 'Each ship was to carry supplies for the trip and for maintenance upon arrival, for both convicts soldiers and sailers.' (15th February 1794)

King, as Governor of Norfolk Island on the 20th July 1794, recorded that the island had produced a second crop in sufficient quantity for storage for the next year.—Being 11500 bushels + 4000 reserved for seed, stock, and the producing families.'

'Stores were ordered from the Cape of Good Hope for the settlement and the hospital on 22nd June 1788 to be selected by John Hunter, as captain of the Sirius

Governor Hunter submitted a plan on 10th June 1797 saying that "were Government to establish a public store for the retail sale of a variety of articles—such as clothing, or materials for clothing, hardware, tools, sugar, soap, tea, tobacco and every article that labouring people require—supported by a reputable shopkeeper who should produce regular accounts and charge a small premium to cover these other costs, then the people would get what they wanted with easer, and at far less expense than in any other way."

Governor Hunter repeated his request for a public store on 10th January 1798 "If my suggestion is adopted, a branch of the store should be placed on Norfolk Island. Such a store should lessen the expense of maintaining the convicts and into the store, I would also suggest the retailing of liquor and spirits, for the purpose of putting a stop to the importation of that article."

Again on the 25th May 1798 Hunter recommended "the public store as a means of controlling the high price of grain. Such a store would operate as an encouragement to industry. Without some form of price control on grain the settlers cannot live let alone provide for a family. The speculators and the monopolists all contrive to keep the settlers in a continual state of beggary and retard the progressive improvements of the colony." The success of Simon Lord's colonial merchandising in 1801 evidences that Hunter was on the right track with his 'public' store.

The Colonial Secretary wrote to Hunter in 3rd December, 1798 about the meat supply "when the livestock belonging to the crown, added to that of individuals, is in so flourishing a state as to supply the needs at 6d a pound or less, it is evident the Government will gain by supplying the settlement with fresh meat instead of sending salted provisions from England. This request was later modified to limit the store purchases for meat to those from farm settlers.

On 2nd February, 1800, William Broughton, a Churchman and Magistrate was also appointed to be the storekeeper at Parramatta to replace a man sacked by Hunter for fraud.

Governor King recorded his success in conserving the stores by writing that "since I took office, I have reduced the full rationed people relying on the public stores by 450. This has saved annually the amount of 10488 pound using the rate of 23 pound per head. I have also reduced the price of wheat to 8d per bushel, pork to 6p per lb, maize to 4s instead of 5s per bushel."

When Hunter was recalled to England, the Commissary was left with many debts owing by settlers. Hunter was concerned that these would be denied and he be held responsible. He wrote to Governor King, 'I trust it is clear that there has been no lavish waste, and no improvident use of the public stores during my authority. These debts are just, even though many of the individuals may doubt their being indebted to the Government for so much. "It appears there were doubtful debts of over 5,000 pound due to the store.

In response King made demand on the settlers and accepted grain at a higher price than usual in settlement of the debt. When the public demands became known it also produced an unusual response from John Macarthur, who suddenly recalled that much of what he had taken from the stores, and charged against the public account, over the previous twelve months was in fact his personal responsibility and he settled with the stores on this basis.

King appointed a new head of the store on 7th November 1800-A Mr Palmer. Other appointments included Broughton to Norfolk Island and Deputy Chapman from Norfolk to Sydney and William Sutter as Storekeeper at Parramatta.

In order to conserve grain, King reduced the ration to 13.5 lb of wheat per week.

Palmer, at the time of his appointment had been handed a set of instructions, which included the instruction that:

a. All troops and convicts in the territory were to be properly supplied and keep a stock of 12 months supply
b. Transmit annually a list of expected consumption

c. Purchases were to be made under the authority of the Governor and prices paid to be no greater than market prices

d. all bills of exchange must be accompanied with an affidavit of purchase countersigned by the Governor

e. you will make receipts for all payments in the presence of at least one witness—preferably a magistrate—and make three sets of all vouchers, one for the treasury, one with the accounts and one for the store use.

f. keep a separate account of all items transmitted from England.

g. make a survey of any stores lost or damaged—which goods are to be sold or destroyed at the Governors discretion.

h. Make up annually an account of all receipts and expenditures, accompanied by one set of vouchers.

i. You are responsible for the preservation of all stores and provisions and the employees who work for you, and to the public.

A set of notes on how the commissary should operate was prepared by the Duke of Portland and handed to Governor-in Chief Phillip Gidley King on 28th September 1800. These notes are attached for historical purposes.

OFFICIAL INSTRUCTIONS FOR THE COMMISSARY—28th September, 1800

Instructions to the Commissary by Captain Philip Gidley King, Governor-in-Chief, &c., in and over His Majesty's territory of New South Wales and its Dependencies, 28th September, 1800.

In consequence of my instructions, you are hereby required to conform to the following directions for your conduct:-

1st. You are to be present yourself as much as possible, and control the receipt and issue of all stores and provisions into and from His Majesty's stores; and as you are answerable for the conduct of those under you and about the different stores, if you should have any cause to be dissatisfied with their conduct in discharge of their duty you are to report the same to me, when a proper notice will be taken thereof.

2nd. You are not to receive or issue any articles whatever, either public or purchased, into or from the stores, but by a written order from me, delivering me an account thereof, on the receipt or issue having taken place, taking care to comply with all such general orders as I may judge necessary respecting your department.

3rd. When any grain or animal food raised by those at government work, or received from England or elsewhere, is delivered into your charge, you are to furnish me with a particular receipt for it, specifying the place and person you received it from, charging yourself with it as provisions received for the public use, and to observe the same with respect to all stores belonging to the Crown, and to deliver the quarterly accounts of the expenditure and the remains thereof, or oftener, if required.

4th. When there is not a sufficiency of grain and animal food raised by the convicts at public labour for the use of those necessarily maintained by the Crown, and that it becomes necessary to purchase the deficit required from the settlers, you are to give me an account of the quantity that may be absolutely necessary weekly, or at a stated period, but not to require more gain at a time than can be kept from the weevil. After my approval thereof, and the price at which such articles are to be purchased is fixed, you are to give public notice thereof, and open a list at the different settlements for the insertion of those persons' names who can spare any quantities of the articles required from the reserve necessary for seed and their own use; such persons being freemen, possessed of ground are known cultivators, are to be regularly entered on the list in preference to any other description of persons, as they offer themselves, and their required produce to be received in the stores without any preference or partiality. The grain thus purchased is to be measured at such times as I may direct in front of the storehouse, and from thence lodged in the store in the presence of a superintendent and another creditable person. When the receipt is ended for the day, a return thereof it to be made the next morning to me, specifying the person's name and quality from whom it is received, the superintendent and other witnesses attesting the same, one or both of whom are to sign their names to the witness column in the voucher when payment is made.

5th Being particularly directed to reform the irregularity that has existed in the mode hitherto followed in making payment for such articles as have been purchased from the inhabitants for the public use, the persons who take your printed receipts, audited by me, for their respective produce being lodged in the stores, may transfer them from one to another for their accommodation; all such receipts to be called in as often as I may judge proper, when payment will be made by me of all outstanding receipts by a bill on His Majesty's Treasury for the amount of such receipts as may be in the hands of individuals, such bills not to be drawn for less than (Pounds) 100, and the vouchers in support thereof to be verified by liquidating your receipts in rotation. And whenever such payments are made you are to take care that five complete sets of vouchers with their documents, agreeable to the annexed form, be prepared to be signed before me at the time of payment being made, which I am directed to control and superintend.

6th. When it is absolutely necessary for any stores, clothing or provisions being purchased from masters of ships, or other strangers, after the price is regulated by two proper persons on the part of Government, and the same on the part of the proprietors, the Commissary will be ordered to receive such articles into the stores in the presence of two respectable witnesses, who are to sign the vouchers, two of which are to be delivered to me, with the proprietor's receipt for the payment, witnessed by two other respectable persons.

7th. As I am directed to forward my account current, made up to the 10th of October annually, with the Right Honourable the Lords Commissioners of His Majesty's Treasury, to the Inspector General of Public Accounts, under cover to His Majesty's Principal Secretary of State for the Home Department, you are therefore not to fail in delivering to me, on or before the 10th day of October, for my inspection and auditing, the following books and papers in support of your account current with the Lords Commissioners of His Majesty's Treasury, together with the surgeon's account of the expenditure of stores and necessaries received from you, in order that those accounts may be sent with mine by the first opportunity after the above date, viz.:-

First—A census book, containing each man, woman, and child's name that has received any provisions from the stores during the year, distinguishing those in the different rations.

Second—A clothing and slop expense book, for those supported by the Crown, expressing as above.

Third—A book specifying the receipts of stores, provisions, and clothing from England or elsewhere, belonging to the Crown, also the quarterly expense thereof, and remains at the time of making up the public accounts, which is to be distinctly stated and carried over the next year's account, as a charge.

Fourth—A book of the particular expense, and the application of the above described provisions and clothing issued by you during the year, to those supported by the Corn, also another book stating the expense and application of the above described stores issued by you for the use of the public, and signed relatively by the superintendent, overseer, or other person to whom they have been delivered.

Fifth.—A store purchasing book, specifying the different quantities of grain and animal food bought from settlers, &c., noting the time of purchase, quantity and application thereof, with a reference to the proper vouchers in support of the receipt and payment, which documents are to be annexed to this book.

Sixth.—A similar book to the above, specifying the different quantities of stores, &c., purchased from masters of ships, or other strangers, verified by proper vouchers, &c., as last above, to which book you are to annex the general expenditure thereof and remains at the time of making up the public accounts, which is to be distinctly stated; and carried over to the next year's account as a charge. At the end of this book you are to insert whether such articles have been paid for in grain, meat, or money, and to debit yourself accordingly, either in your account current of cash, or store account, and to charge yourself in the same manner with any other payment made to you on behalf of the Crown.

Seventh.—A list of all births, deaths, and absentees during the year.

You are not to fail (on peril of being subject to an exchequer process) in delivering me for my examination all the above books and papers, with every other explanatory document, on the thirty-first day of October, annually, which accounts you are to attest before me previous to my transmitting them to England and you carefully to preserve correct copies thereof, in case of any accident happening to those sent to England. You are to keep an open list in your office, containing the names of each class of people in the colony, according to the form you are provided with, in which you are to make regular entries and discharges as they occur.

Eighth.—Exclusive of the above papers, when any ship is going from hence to England, you are to furnish me with a general return of the inhabitants, according to the annexed form, also a return of the expenditure and remains of Government stock.

Ninth.—The issue of provisions is to be attended by a superintendent, or principal overseer, and a non-commissioned officer, for the purpose of detecting and reporting any improper proceedings; but no report will be attended to that is not made on the day of the issue. A weekly victual and store-issue book are to be kept at each store by the person who has charge of it. No person whatever is to be put on or off the store but by a written note from me, or by a note from the person who has the superintendence of the district where the stores are. The master carpenter, and every other description of persons that has charge of the workmen supplied with materials from the different stores for the public use, as well as such individuals as are allowed to receive that indulgence, are to apply for the orders on Monday mornings, and to give receipts for the same to the Commissary, delivery an account of the expense thereof to me weekly. By this regulation, the necessity of persons frequenting the stores on the intermediate days between stores and victual issue will be prevented, and the stores properly appropriated. The different storekeepers are to deliver you a weekly return of their expenditure and remains, keeping the same ready for my inspection when required, and you are to furnish me with a quarterly return of Government stock, charging yourself with any that may be killed and issued as a ration, accounting for it under the head of provisions raised by those at public labour. And as it is necessary the Deputy-Commissaries and storekeepers at detached places should be supplied with regular directions how they are to conduct themselves, you

are to furnish them with such parts of these Regulations as relate to their duty, and you are to direct them to deliver their returns and receipts to me, if I should be on the spot, or to the officer who has the direction of the public concerns in the district where they are stationed.

Philip Gidley King then issued further directions:

> "In addition to the above instructions, the Commissary will give directions to the Deputy-Commissary and storekeeper to obey all such directions as they may from time to time receive from the Reverend Mr Marsden, at Parramatta, and Charles Grimes, Esq., at Hawkesbury, reporting to him all such orders on the day they send their weekly returns".

Major Ovens Reorganises the Clearing Gangs

On 27th January 1824, Sir Thomas Brisbane forwarded a *memorial* from timber merchants in the colony to Earl Bathurst. The *Memorial* quoted that in the previous year 1823-24 a large quantity of timber (15,994 tons) was imported from Britain and only 7,235 tons are being exported from the colony back to Britain, but those exports are attracting a duty on entry into Britain. They wanted the duty removed under the Act 3 Geo II, C 96 that allowed duty free timber into England, especially on Cedar.

Major Ovens had arrived in the Colony with Brisbane and was set the task of organising convict work gangs leading to more control and better productivity.

He reported to Brisbane in 1824. Ovens recommended that 'clearing' gangs (land clearing before settlement) be split into two divisions, each under a Superintendent, who in turn will be responsible to the Chief Inspector and Chief Engineer. The Southward gang would be headquartered in Liverpool, whilst the Northward gang would headquarter in Rooty Hill.

Ovens reported that the food rations, clothing, sugar, tea and tobacco made available to the 1,150 convicts working on the gangs amounted to approx 23,000 pound (HRA) whilst the value of the wheat being able to be grown on the 9,000 acres cleared would be 6 bu /acre x 9,000acres x

8/6 /bu = 23,000 pound. So Ovens was justifying the value of the clearing work, not as an addition to the selling price of the land per acre but to the yield of grain. Ovens recommended that 23 men be included in each gang under one supervisor, with 50 gangs in total (50 x 23 = 1,150 convicts). The amount of clearing by each gang was to be 15 acres monthly or 180 acres per annum, or 9,000 acres in total (50 x 180 = 9,000). The incentive payments to each supervisor was3/6 per acre, and to each convict was ½ lb tea, 6lb of sugar, 10 2/3 oz of tobacco

Ovens noted that certain of the timber being cleared was suitable for milling and would arrange for transportation to the Lumber Yard.

An Original Purpose of the Colony was to find Strategic Timber Reserves

It is worthy to note that the final paragraphs of the 'Heads of a Plan', prepared by James Matra included three non-convict motives for the colony of New South Wales

a. The obtaining of a supply of flax to make canvass, cables and cordage for British ships in Indian waters
b. The obtaining of a supply of masts and spars for these ships
c. The cultivation of 'Asiatic productions'

Of these three, the sourcing of masts and spars was by far the most important, as there was a crisis in Britain's supply of these naval materials.

At this time, Britain's ships were exclusively composed of timber and flax and hemp; their frames and hulls were of English or continental oak; their masts and spars were mostly made from Baltic and British flax and hemp. Blayney writes, "to a maritime nation such as Britain, timber, flax and hemp were then as important as steel and oil became in the 20th century" (G. Blayney *The Tyranny of Distance*).

The argument here is that without any knowledge that the Pacific area could supply these naval materials, and if their need was so great to Britain, why was a testing not undertaken, or why was no expertise sent out with the First Fleet? The recommendation to establish Norfolk Island, as a source was an afterthought and to be pursued only after Botany Bay was settled.

Frost conjectures in *Botany Bay Mirages* 'conventional wisdom is that it was only during the last decades of the 18th century that there was a crisis in Royal Naval timber supplies, however, Britain's naval failures after 1763 are directly attributable to a lack of materials'. Another view submitted was that 'there was no real shortage of large masts in the period 1775-83, but it was the lack of skilled artificers that the Royal Navy then lacked' (R.J.B. Knight *Forests & Sea Power*) He goes on to record that "When the North American supply was cut off in 1775, the Baltic filled the gap effortlessly'

Why then the inclusion of sourcing masts and spars as a role for the Botany Bay settlement?

Frost claims it is a matter of perception. In the '1770s influential people thought there was a problem. For instance, Sir John Jervis in explaining the peace settlement by the Shelburne Administration, refers to the *want of sticks of a proper size for masts, and the shameful neglect in working them up, particularly the cordage, which is the worst in Europe*'.

Frost concludes "Given the centrality of timber and fibre to Britain's national life in the late 18th century, it was inevitable that people then should think of exploiting the perceived resources of the Pacific area. When in August 1783 James Matra justified his colonial proposal on the grounds it would give rise to sources of timber and flax, he was only reiterating an idea that had be in the air for fifteen years."

King on Native Timbers (HRNSW—Vol 6 p397)

In a document dated December 1807, and addressed to the Board of Commissioners in London, ex-Governor King outlined the nature of some native Australian timbers.

"The iron & stringy barks are straight and from 40 to 80 feet high, and 18 to 20 inches in diameter, generally sound throughout, without much crooked or compass timber. It is heavy, but the latter not more so than oak. Both are well adapted to the different purposes of keels, beams, uprights and floor timbers of large scantling, and many other purposes where straight and durable timber is required. Of the stringybark several ships have had lower masts. The *Buffalo* now has a fore and mizzenmast and boltsprit of that wood, and two cheeks of the mainmast, all of which she had in 1799, and have had them ever since. Their excellence, as well as that of studding sails and other booms, was sufficiently tried in the blowing weather and high seas she experienced in two voyages round Cape Horn. Fifty-gun ships' foremasts and mizenmasts might be selected, and it may be presumed that spindles for larger ships' masts maybe made from those trees, which abound in all parts.

The box is a very fine timber and grows in great abundance about Parramatta from 60 to 100 feet high, and from 18 to 26 inches in diameter, tapering but little. The crooked wood, being the branches are of small size; but this timber answers every purpose of the foregoing species, except that growing so very straight it might not answer so well for floor timbers; but for every kind of straight work, gun-carriages etc is equal to any wood in the world. Much of it has been used at Portsmouth Yard for tillers of all rates.

The blue and black-butted blue gums are esteemed good woods and ideal in vessels.

Gov. Hunter built a 150 ton vessel frame to demonstrate the variety of timbers and after 7 years it was still perfectly sound"

Gov. King had in June 1803 issued a Government Order relating to the general consumption of timber in the colony.

"The great consumption of timber, and the requisition made by the Government for as much as possible being preserved for the use of the Navy, the following regulations are to be observed.

Timber in this colony includes she and swamp oaks, red, blue and black-butted gums, stringy and iron barks, mahogany, box, honeysuckle, cedar, lightwood, turpentine etc, the property of all which lies in the proprietor of the land, either by grant or lease, excepting timber for naval or other public purposes, which may be marked, cut and removed from any situation, public or private. None may cut timber suitable for ship-building, buildings, masts or mechanical purposes, without being answerable to the Governor".

A further letter from King to Earl Camden of 20th July 1805 intended to reserve all timbers for the use of the crown.

David Collins remarked early in his diary (1793) about the Norfolk Island pines "They have been found not to meet the purpose intended of them. Strikingly straight and tall, they are often hollow and unsuitable for large masts. *They are shaky or rotten at thirty or forty feet from the butt; the wood is so brittle that it would not make a good oar, and is so porous that the water soaked through the planks of a boat which had been built of it*" (Collins: An Account of the English Colony in New South Wales P63)).

Even Watkin Tench recorded in his diary of 1792 his observations about the future usefulness of Norfolk Island

> "*The New Zealand hemp, of which so many sanguine expectations were formed, is not a native of the soil of New Holland; and Norfolk Island, where we made sure to find this item, is also without it. So that the scheme of being able to assist the East Indies with naval stores, in case of a war, must fall to the ground*" (Tench P74)

As if expecting to be censured for not performing in his duty of finding suitable naval materials, Governor Phillip wrote to London "The pine trees, in the opinion of the carpenter of the *Supply*, who is a good judge, are superior to any he has ever seen; and the island (Norfolk Island) affords excellent timbers for ship-building, As well as for masts and yards, with which I make no doubt but his Majesty's ships in the East Indies may be supplied" (Phillip to Lord Sydney 28th September 1788 HRNSW)

Is the mistaken impression that the colony could supply naval materials, evidence that the British Government might also have erred in its other preconceptions of conditions at Botany Bay? Impressions such as the circumstances of Phillip having come ill prepared; his convicts were not an effective work force and Phillip had no one to direct them? The British Government had mistakenly assumed that convicts with few useful skills, used to manual labour and hostile to authority, could turn themselves into pioneers 'capable of taming a wilderness' (Bridges: *Foundations of Identity*)

Bridges suggests that the belief of the capacity of the prisoners had its roots in the class structures and barriers in Britain.—The upper-class belief that poverty was a product of indolence and that the indigent poor had only themselves to blame.

Early Building Methods

Early timber of useable quality was not to be found around Sydney Cove, and so Phillip required pine from Norfolk Island, until he found good stands of eucalypts, blue gum, Blackbutt, flooded gum and box around the upper reaches of Lane Cove River and Middle Harbour. These logs were so heavy (and unable to float) that they had to be cut to length for moving by boat. However, there was plenty of good stone and clay for bricks, but again shortage of skilled labour made these materials unusable in the early days of the colony. Bricks began to be more usable in 1789 when the early timber constructions were decaying and in need of replacement. Roofing tiles became necessary as well to replace grass or reed thatching previously used for storehouses but which needed other than highly inflammable materials to protect the valuable foodstuffs and other stores. Collins records that the living huts were constructed from pine frames with sides filled with lengths of cabbage palm plastered over with clay to form 'a very good hovel'.

In the colony of New South Wales, close confinement was neither necessary nor practical, and except for hospitalisation, most convicts before 1800 had to find their own shelter. Building huts for convicts had not been part of official building policy, although some huts were built especially for convicts. In Rose Hill for instance, Phillip designed and built huts as part of his town layout. Since the sawn timbers were used for officer or public buildings, convicts building their own huts would use saplings covered with a mesh of twigs and walls plastered with clay. Convicts were not given any special favours of the limited quantity of building supplies such as ironmongery and glass, which had been brought from England so that windows were covered by lattices of twigs. The best buildings in the town were those for Government use, such as the stores, the barracks and the hospital, housing for officials. Only when convicts became free or went on ticket-of-leave status was there any call or need for private building and a building industry began to emerge.

When Phillip returned home in 1792, Major Grose reallocated convicts to officers and small farmers and succeeded in depleting the government work gangs and could only complete public works by paying soldiers one shilling a day. 'With the depleted government gangs and with no firm direction', Bridges writes that roads and buildings were neglected and fell into disrepair. For lack of barracks, soldiers built their own homes along the road to the brickfield.

David Collins reflected on the difficulties of the time:

> "To provide bricks for the barracks, three gangs, each of 30 convicts with an overseer was constantly at work. To convey materials from the brickfields to the barracks site, a distance of about ¾ ths of a mile, three brick-carts were employed, each drawn by 12 men and an overseer. Each cart held 700 tiles or 350 bricks and each day, the cart made 5 loads with bricks or 4 loads with tiles. To bring the timber to the site, 4 timber carriages were used, each drawn by 24 men. So 228 men were constantly used in heavy labour in the building of a barracks or storehouse, in addition to the sawyers, carpenters, smiths, painters, glaziers and stonemasons".

Bricks were used mainly for government buildings or official houses, because of the cost, and private housing continued to use timber framing. Private buildings activities increased and slowly improved and in the year following Phillip's departure 160 houses were built in Sydney, with an allowance of 1,400 bricks for the chimney and floor. When Hunter finally arrived, public works had languished and his first action was to plaster soft brick buildings as some protection against wind and rain. Hunter ordered the collection of foreshore shells for lime making and plaster. In a map prepared by the Frenchman Leseur in 1802, some 260 houses are identified but in 1804 an official count listed 673 houses in Sydney, indicating a rapid building program between 1802 and 1804.

There was constant pressure on scarce funds within the colony, as the authorities had not planned on any urban development. Hunter promoted the common cause and encouraged private contributions of material and labour to build bridges and public gaols. In building the Sydney gaol, Hunter directed each settler to bring in ten straight logs of nine feet in length and seven inches in diameter, weekly. When this scheme did not succeed, Hunter 'loaned' the Gaol Fund One thousand pound. To repay this sum, he imposed a levy of sixpence on each bushel of wheat delivered to the Commissariat store. And when that did not produce sufficient, he imposed a 'landing fee on spirits, wines and other strong drinks'. This was the very first tax imposed on the colonists for local discretionary use by the Governor.

Tracing through the Early Maps

Sydney town produced quite a few early town maps.

a. The 1800 map by Charles Grimes shows the site on the corner of Bridge and High street as being leased by a Mr Turnbull

b. A 'Plan of the Town of Sydney' prepared for Governor Bligh by James Meehan, and dated 26th January 1808 shows the Lumber Yard in its location

c. The Macquarie Plan shows each corner occupied—the southeast corner occupied by the Male Orphan School (the property was purchased by Governor King from Lt Kent, at the time of Kent's return to England in 1802. The south—west corner was occupied b7y the Lumber Yard, including the area previously acquired from Blaxcell.

Major Ovens Reported on the Convict Work Operations in the Colony

In a report to Governor Brisbane, of June 1825, Major Ovens, who had arrived in the colony as part of the Governor's staff, recommended a 'government contract' system.

Oven's introduces his report by stating that "this colony was formed with a view prospectively of becoming in the course of years a useful appendage to Great Britain, and in the prospect of serving as a place for exercising that degree of discipline over the larger portion of its population who, forfeiting all claims to the more lenient laws of their own country, had rendered themselves fit subjects for a more coercive system of restraint. In the first case, therefore it was only reasonable that the Colony should be indebted to the Mother country for a large outlay of capital in its principal institutions; and in the second, that the labours of the convicts should be rendered available for that purpose. Hence the numerous works and Establishments, that became necessary in the march of the colony's progress, were furnished from the industry and labour of that class of its inhabitants".

Having tried to justify both the development of the colony and the use of convicts for that purpose, Ovens goes on to suggest that the assignment system should be temporary and 'used only when a benefit on the colony of encuating it natural productions, or enhancing the value of its material by the skill and industry of the convict labour". In other words, place the convicts into service, where they can do the most good, and reap the largest reward. He points out that to that time, priority has been given to town development, but the priorities should now change and concentration given to developing 'agricultural and pastoral industries'. Although the previous priorities 'was not the most consonant to the principles of political economy, it was the most natural at the then existing state of society; when the extent of the Agricultural resources of the country became better known, clearer and more enlightened views on the subject were entertained, and the labour of the prisoners could be applied to such pursuits as were eventually most likely to add to the wealth, comfort and independence of the community. A practical example of the happy result of such measures may be instanced in the system adopted in clearing the country by means of convict labour, and bringing into cultivation large tracts of land which otherwise would be dormant and useless to the colonist; this work has also improved the moral condition of the convicts as well as their habits assimilated to those of farming men".

Ovens then noted a new system (with incentives) for the land clearing gangs in the country areas. He suggests that convict labour should be used not only for land clearing, road making, and public works in the towns (government buildings etc) but for repair work as well (rather than free contractors imposing costs on the colony). Ovens noted 4 commonly held objections to the privatisation of contract work. To coordinate the government contract system, he recommended establishing an engineer's department, in order 'to give a systematic effect to the labour and exertions, as well as to the skill and mechanical arts of the prisoners'.

Ovens' reports on the state of the Lumber Yard: This report is extracted from HRA Volume XI Page 653.

Operating the Lumber Yard

As we have discovered to-date, littler is known about the operations of the Yard. We know it was part of the Commissary, and was originally one property off the corner off Bridge and George (High) Street.

When Blaxcell went bankrupt and was forced to leave the colony, his property was purchased by the Commissary for use as an enlarged Lumber Yard. There were well over 1,000 convicts on site prior to the Macquarie years.

Major Ovens in his report to Governor Brisbane unveils a littler about the operations of the yard.

"In the Lumber Yard are assembled all the indoor tradesmen who work in the shops such as Blacksmiths, carpenters, sawyers, shoemakers, tailors etc. The workmen, carrying on their occupations under the immediate eye of the Chief Engineer are probably kept in a better state of discipline than those, who working more remote, are dependent on the good behaviour of an overseer for any work they may perform".

'Whatever is produced from the labour of these persons, which is not applied to any public work or for the supply of authorised requisitions, is placed in a large store and kept to furnish the exigencies of future occasions; the nature of these employments, also renders it much easier to assign a task to each, for the due performance of which they are held responsible'.

In the Timber Yard adjoining the Lumber Yard is kept assorted all the timber, scaffoldings etc required for the execution of public buildings: and whatever materials are carried away from hence for these purposes to the different works, the same have to be returned, or the deficiency accounted for. The storekeeper of this Yard has charge of such timber as is brought from the out stations, or sawn and cut up in the Yard, such as flooring boards, scantlings, beams etc; and when these supplies exceed the demand for government purposes, the excess is sold by public auction, and the amount of the proceeds credited to government.

Ovens lists the workforce by category as well as their expected output (HRA Vol X1 P655-7)

- Carpenters' Gang   50 convicts + free apprentices
- Blacksmiths' Gang   45 convicts
- Bricklayers' Gang   10 convicts
- Sawyers' Gang   25 convicts
- Brick-makers' Gang   15 convicts + boy apprentices from Carters barracks
- Plasters' Gang   8 convicts (these men carry out lathing, plaistering and whitewashing)
- Quarrymen   15 convicts
- Loading, carrying, clearing the Quarries—3 bullock teams + 5 horse trucks—19 convicts
- Wheelwrights' Gang   23 convicts (wheel, body and spoke makers)
- Coopers Gang   6 convicts
- Shoemakers' Gang   8 convicts
- Tailors' Gang   8 convicts (the cloth is made at the Female factory in Parramatta)
- Dockyard   70 convicts working as mechanics and labourers
- Dockyard Town gang   22 convicts used for loading or discharging vessels
- Stone-cutters and setters   13 convicts
- Brass Founders' Gang   9 convicts (casting iron for all wheels and millwork)

Other occupations of convicts employed, includes: foundation diggers', rubbish clearers; Commissariat Store gangs, grass cutters, boats' crews; boat conveyance crews, gardeners

The attached plan shows the representation of the Yard operations. Convicts were marched, as arranged by Macquarie, from the Hyde Park Barracks along Macquarie, Bent and Bridge Street to the entrance to the Yard, which faced High Street. Inside the entrance, which was two large solid wood gates set into a high brick wall, we can picture a supervisor's office, with room for clerical staff. A tool shed would have been located near the front gate so that convicts could be issued with tools and have them collected at the end of the working day. We can assume that there was some form of 'inventory' control of tools; otherwise the Governor could not have been advised that tools were missing (assumed) stolen. In the centre of the half-acre site, there was a large open, but roofed building, under which the logs were stored, debarked and sawn.

Along one side of the site, probably the back fence, the five operating divisions would have been housed, probably also under an open sided roofed building. These 5 independent areas include, workshops for

- Blacksmiths
- Carpenters
- Wheelwrights
- Tailors
- Shoemakers.

Sawpits were located in the central area, (2 sawpits of about 70 feet in length + 1 in the Timber Yard + 1 in the Dockyard—Ovens) whilst furnaces, for safety reasons would have been located on a third boundary wall. The fourth boundary wall would have contained materials storage, since bricks, tiles; sawn lumber would have been stored in the Yard.

Quarries were located at *Cockle Bay, Domain, Gaol quarry, and the High Street quarry.*

Stored items included:

- Bricks
- Lime
- Coal
- Shingles
- Nails
- Tools
- Timber in process of drying
- Logs awaiting cutting

The products despatched through the front gate, included

- Sawn timber for framing, roofing battens, flooring supports (if used instead of bricks), window frames, doors and frames
- Nails
- Bolts
- Bellows
- Barrels
- Furniture for the various barracks

Employment was considerable, and was categorised into at least these groupings for control purposes:

- Construction gangs for building, houses, public buildings, wharves, bridges
- Gangs for moving logs from the wharf behind the commissary, further up High Street, to the Lumber Yard
- Gangs for dragging 'materials' carts from the Yard to building and construction sites
- Gangs for dragging the portable 'rain-sheds' to the various construction sites.
- Gangs for dragging brick-carts to and from the Brickfields
- Gangs for dragging the 'roofing tile' carts from the Brickfields
- Gangs working in the Stone-yard on the west side of High Street
- Gangs for dragging carts with large stones from the Stone-yard to building sites
- Gangs for land 'clearing'

- Gangs for felling trees in the selected timber harvesting areas (Pennant Hills and Castle Hill)
- Gangs for Road making

In all over 20,000 convicts were organised from the centre of manufacturing, with about 2,000 employed within the yard itself.

Commissioner John Thomas Bigge gives us a preliminary opinion of the convicts at work in his First Report on the Colony published in 1821. We also have the written report by Major Ovens to Secretary Goulburn in June 1824 to show how the clearing gangs and road gangs were re-organised under Governor Darling.

Bigge's report provides an interesting insight into convict operations as will see momentarily, but he makes a couple of observations about the Lumber Yard.

- 'The able bodied men who are lodged in the Hyde Park barracks and the Carter Barracks are divided into gangs, and are employed in the Lumber Yard'
- The principal place of convict labour, Bigge reported, 'is in the Lumber Yard, a large space of ground now walled in, and extending from George Street to the edge of the small stream that discharges itself into Sydney Cove'.
- The trades carried on in this place, writes Bigge, are those of

Other observations based on the Bigge assessment of the convict work in the colony can be made as follows:

- o In the seven years between January 1, 1814 and December 20, 1820, Bigge tells us that 11,767 convicts arrived in the colony.
- o Of the 11,767 we are also told that 4587 were placed into government service, whilst the remainder of 7,180 were assigned to the military officers and other land grant beneficiaries
- o The government assignees (of 4587) were placed into various enterprises as mechanics and labourers—they all (except for 594) were required to live in government barracks in Sydney (Hyde Park or Carters) Parramatta, Windsor, Bathurst

They were employed on
- Government farms, growing or looking after
    - Vegetables 150
    - Cattle 11
    - Hay/charcoal 110
    - Wheat/maize 269
    - Timber cutting 73
    - Lime preparation 27
    - Road making 362
    - Land clearing 386
    - Stone quarries 69
    - Cart operators 268
    - Brick/tile makers 124
    - Boat navigators 12
    - Official boat crews 120
    - Dockyard operations 47
    - Lumber Yard 1000
    - Construction work 1450

There were over 1,500 convicts employed as supervisors, foremen, leading hands and clerical assistants, as well as in the Governor's and official government offices.

The hierarchy was equally as simple in structure. The Governor was obviously the final arbiter, whilst the Chief Engineer, Major Druitt had overall responsibility for the works program—planning and completion. The principal superintendent of convicts was William Hutchinson, and the other two important figures were the chief architect for public buildings and quality control as well as convict productivity (Francis Greenway), and design chief for military and civil barracks and police posts, Lieutenant Watts of Macquarie's 46th regiment.

Worth of the Convict Labour

Henry Kitchen, a free settler architect and Francis Greenway, a convict architect offer us a brief sample of the value of work performed by the convicts.

Kitchen Estimates 922,857.13.11 as the cost of the Macquarie era building program

Since the actual material cost total for the estimated construction work completed in the Macquarie era is less than $500,000 (refer this author's valuation of each building in Appendix A), and it is most unlikely that the total could have reached $922,000, then it is safe to assume that Henry Kitchen, in producing this misleading estimate to Commissioner Bigge was provided with the intention of further blackening the names of both Greenway and Macquarie—both of whom disliked Kitchen and were, in turn, disliked by Kitchen. This estimate by Kitchen, offered to Commissioner Bigge in evidence, was a deliberately malicious and deceptive piece of disinformation by Kitchen.

There is another possible explanation that stretches credulity somewhat but could be justified as a possibility. It is always assumed that convict labour was essentially 'free', and should therefore not count or contribute to the total cost of the finished construction.

If we make a number of assumptions concerning day rates of equivalent pay, and about the productivity level of the convicts in a major construction job, keeping in mind they were supervised by other convicts, then we may be able to say that the 400,000 pound of cost assembled in the Table above is for materials and that the equivalent value of the convict labour makes the difference of the 522,000 to bring the total estimate up to Kitchen's estimates.

The relevant assumptions are (based on Greenways cost estimates on Page 59 above)

- The number of days of mechanics labour to complete the Government House Stables was 16,686.5
- The average cost per man day was 1 shilling
- Labour reflected a 33% content of the total finished cost.

So applying these assumptions to the construction work in the rest of the table, we find that all projects would have taken 2,683,108 days of mechanics labour or approx 8,450 man years. The convict population increased between 1812 and 1820 by 10,800 men and totalled 19,000 men by 1820, and to suppose that 44% of the male convicts were employed in construction work is not unreasonable. At the minimum rate of 1s per day, our labour cost total becomes 134155 pound; thus, at an average of 3 shillings (compared with Coghlan's cost for 'free' mechanics at 5s per day, we would achieve the difference of 480,000 pound. Coghlan estimates that a convict would only produce about 60% of a 'free' labourer.

Our conclusion, if we stretch the point, is that Kitchen's estimate of a construction cost for the period of 900,000 is valid if our materials are valued at 402,000 and our labour accounts (at the average rate of 3 shillings per day) to a further 470,000-pound.

1. APPENDIX A LIST OF GREENWAY BUILDING+

- General Hospital, Macquarie Street, Sydney
- Magazine, Fort Phillip
- Design of Government House, Sydney
- St. John's Parsonage, Parramatta
- Portico, Government House, Parramatta
- Macquarie Lighthouse, South Head
- Obelisk, Macquarie Place, Sydney
- Military Barracks, Sydney
- Government Wharf, Windsor
- Parramatta Gaol, Parramatta
- Hyde Park Convict Barracks
- St. Matthew's Church, Windsor
- Chief Justice's House, Sydney
- Colonial Secretary's House, Macquarie Place, Sydney
- Judge Advocate's House, Macquarie Place, Sydney
- Chaplain's House, Spring Street, Sydney
- Government Stables, Government Domain, Sydney
- Fort Macquarie, Bennelong Point, Sydney
- Public Fountain, Macquarie Place, Sydney
- St. Luke's Church, Liverpool
- St. Luke's Parsonage, Liverpool
- Female Factory and Barrack, Parramatta
- Female Orphan School, Parramatta

- Government House, Sydney
- Dawes Point Battery, Dawes Point, Sydney
- Turnpike Gate & Lodge, Parramatta Road, Sydney
- St. Andrew's Church (Foundations), King Street, Sydney
- Supreme court House, King Street, Sydney
- Lumber Yard, Bridge Street, Sydney
- Male Orphan School, George Street, Sydney
- Dockyard, George Street, Sydney
- Market House, George Street, Sydney
- Court House, Windsor
- Charity School, Elizabeth Street, Sydney
- Police Office, George Street, Sydney
- Granary & Store, George Street, Parramatta
- St. Mary's Catholic Chapel, Hyde Park, Sydney
- Princess Charlotte Memorial
- Liverpool Hospital, Liverpool.
- Pigeon House
- Governor Brisbane's Bath House, Government Domain, Sydney
- St. Matthews Rectory, Windsor
- Ultimo House, Ultimo Sydney
- House for Sarah Howe, Lower George Street, Sydney
- House for George Howe, Charlotte Place, Sydney
- Tomb for George Howe, Devonshire Street Cemetery, Sydney
- House for Sir John Jamieson, Charlotte Place, Sydney
- House for T.W. Middleton, Macquarie /Hunter Streets, Sydney
- Work for R.W. Loane
- Cottage, Parramatta
- Proposed House, George /Argyle Street, Sydney
- House for Sir John Wylde, Sydney
- Bank of New South Wales, George Street, Sydney
- Wharf House, Lower George Street, Sydney
- House for Jemima Jenkins
- Shop for John Macqueen, Lower George Street, Sydney
- Cleveland House, Bedford Street, Surrey Hills
- Cottage, Cockle Bay, Sydney
- Pair of Houses for Sir John Jamison, George Street, Sydney
- Shop for George Williams, George Street, Sydney
- House for Robert Campbell Sr, Bunkers Hill, Sydney

- Shop for Barnett Levy, George Street, Sydney
- Henrietta Villa, Point Piper
- House for Thomas Moor, Elizabeth Street, Liverpool
- Waterloo Warehouse, George /Market Streets, Sydney
- House for William Cox, O'Connell Street, Sydney
- Regentville near Penrith
- Glenlee, Menangle
- House for Robert Crawford, Lower Fort Street, Sydney
- House & Store for Robert Campbell Jr, Bligh Street, Sydney
- Bungarribee, Eastern Creek
- Hobartville, Richmond
- Warehouse for John Paul, George Street, Sydney
- Springfield, Potts Point, Sydney
- Jerusalem Warehouse, George Street, Sydney
- Grantham, Potts Point, Sydney—

RECONSTRUCTING THE MACQUARIE ERA CONSTRUCTION PROGRAM

The Bigge's Report provides a partial list of building work completed by Macquarie. The items, which to Bigge are the most useful buildings on the list, include:

(The numbers refer to references in Greenway's—1822 Map of Sydney)

Sydney Items

- The Commissariat (King's) Store at Sydney (8)
- St. Phillips Church at Sydney (12)
- Improvement of Government House at Sydney (1)
- Sydney Gaol (30)
- Clearing of grounds contiguous to the Government Houses (1)
- A Parsonage House at Sydney (30)
- Military Barracks at Sydney—Wynyard Square (13)
- Hospital in Sydney—"Rum" Hospital—Macquarie Street (21)
- Hyde Park Convict Barracks (20)
- Military Hospital in Sydney—Wynyard Square (27)
- Improvements to Lumber-Yard at Sydney (28)

- Improvements to Dockyard at Sydney (29)
- St. James Church (19)
- Colonial Secretary's House & Office (4)
- Sydney Cove-Governor's Wharf (26)
- Water Bailiff—House and landing (31)
- Houses for Judge-Advocate (Judge of Supreme Court)—(4)
- Court-house at Sydney (18)
- School-house at Hyde Park (16)
- Market house at George Street, Sydney (15)
- Government stables at Sydney (2)
- Fountain in Macquarie Place (6)
- Obelisk in Macquarie Place (7)
- The Turnpike Gate—Lower George Street (22)
- Fort (Macquarie) at Bennelong Point (3)
- Battery at Dawes Point (10)
- Greenway's House and office (9)
- Windmill—(built at Public Expense)—at Garrison barracks (23)
- Windmill—(built at Public Expense)—at the Domain. (24)
- Magazine at Fort Phillip (11)
- St.Andrew's Church foundation (15)
- Orphan House in Sydney (25)

Parramatta, Windsor, Liverpool & Outer Sydney Area Items

- Carters Barracks and gaol at Windsor
- Female Factory at Parramatta
- St. Matthews Church at Windsor
- Church at Liverpool
- Chapel at Castlereagh
- A Parsonage House at Parramatta
- A Parsonage House at Liverpool
- Hospital at Parramatta
- Hospital at Windsor (a converted brewery formerly owned by Andrew Thompson)
- Hospital at Liverpool
- Convict Barracks at Parramatta
- Improvement of Government House at Parramatta
- An asylum for the aged and infirm near Sydney

- Bridge at Rushcutter's Bay—South Head Road
- Macquarie Light-house at Sydney South Head
  (This list accounts for 46 items on Bigge's 63 reference)

Newcastle Items

- Hospital
- Gaol
- Commandant House
- Surgeons Quarter
- Workhouse
- Blacksmiths Forge
- Pier
- Windmill
- Parsonage House "(Bigge Report)
  (We now account for 55 out of the 63)

Greenway Items (drawn but under construction)

- Officer Quarters-Hyde Park
- Alterations to Judge Advocate's House
- Alterations to Lumber Yard building
- Alterations to Dawes Battery
- Alterations to Liverpool parsonage
- Portico, Gov House, Parramatta
- Alterations to Orphan School, Sydney
- Alterations to Government House, Sydney
- Judge Field's House—Sydney
- Plans for Mr. Marsden's House at Parramatta
- Survey for the new General (Rum) Hospital
- Plans for the Windsor Church
- Plans for the Liverpool Church
- Plans for Judge Field's house
- Plans for Parramatta Female Factory
- Survey of Parramatta Bridge
- Survey of Sydney Gaol
- Measuring work by contractors at Sydney Gaol
- Plans for Windsor Court-house

- Plans for new toll-gate
- Plans for Obelisk in Macquarie Place
- Plans for fountain in Macquarie Place.

(If we count 'alterations' to buildings, we can account for the whole 63 items stated by Commissioner Bigge to have been undertaken in the Macquarie Era)

The Commissariat (King's) Store at Sydney (8)		7500
St. Phillips Church at Sydney (12)		3250
Improvement of Government House at Sydney (1)	600	
Sydney Gaol (30)	6000	
Clearing of grounds contiguous to the Government Houses (1)		200
A Parsonage House at Sydney (30)		350
Military Barracks at Sydney—Wynyard Square (13)		11000
Hospital in Sydney—"Rum" Hospital—Macquarie Street (21)		0
Military Hospital in Sydney—Wynyard Square (27)		6750
Improvements to Lumber-Yard at Sydney (28)		2000
Improvements to Dockyard at Sydney (29)		1000
St. James Church (19)	6240	
Colonial Secretary's House & Office (4)		875
Sydney Cove-Governor's Wharf (26)		3500
Water Bailiff—House and landing (31)		1250
Houses for Judge-Advocate (Judge of Supreme Court (4)		4800
Court-house at Sydney (18)	6450	
School-house at Hyde Park (16)		3500
Market house at George Street, Sydney (15)	300	
Government stables at Sydney (2)	9000	
Fountain in Macquarie Place (6)		500
Obelisk in Macquarie Place (7)		375
The Turnpike Gate—Lower George Street (22)		2750
Fort (Macquarie) at Bennelong Point (3		21000
Battery at Dawes Point (10)		4675
Greenway's House and office (9)		1695
Windmill—(built at Public Expense)—at Garrison barracks (23)		2250

Windmill—(built at Public Expense)—at the Domain. (24)		2230
Magazine at Fort Phillip (11)	1240	
St.Andrew's Church foundation (15)	2500	
Orphan House in Sydney (25)	2180	
Parramatta, Windsor, Liverpool & Outer Sydney Area		
Carters Barracks and gaol at Windsor		9750
Female Factory at Parramatta		278500
St. Matthews Church at Windsor		5600
Church at Liverpool		5250
Chapel at Castlereagh		4750
A Parsonage House at Parramatta		1250
A Parsonage House at Liverpool	520	
Hospital at Parramatta		6500
Hospital at Windsor (a converted brewery formerly owned by Andrew Thompson)		3365
Hospital at Liverpool		5850
Convict Barracks at Parramatta		21500
Improvement of Government House at Parramatta	1120	
An asylum for the aged and infirm near Sydney		8625
Bridge at Rushcutter's Bay—South Head Road		2275
Macquarie Light-house at Sydney South Head	7050	
(This list accounts for 46 items on Bigge's 63 reference)		
Newcastle Items		
Hospital		6693
Gaol		8824
Commandant House		1356
Surgeons Quarter		1569
Workhouse		5228
Blacksmiths Forge		2135
Pier		3556
Windmill		2150
Parsonage House "(Bigge Report)		1189
(We now account for 55 out of the 63)		
Greenway Items (drawn but under construction)		
Officer Quarters-Hyde Park	10600	
Alterations to Judge Advocate's House	600	
Alterations to Lumber Yard building	2000	
Alterations to Dawes Battery	1200	

Alterations to Liverpool parsonage	520	
TOTALS	**55600**	**344865**

<u>Kitchen Estimates 922,857.13.11</u>

Since the actual total for the estimated construction work completed in the Macquarie era is less than $500,000, and it is most unlikely that the total could have reached $922,000, then it is safe to assume that Henry Kitchen, in producing this misleading estimate to Commissioner Bigge was provided with the intention of further blackening the names of both Greenway and Macquarie—both of whom disliked and were disliked by Kitchen. This was a deliberately malicious and deceptive piece of disinformation by Henry Kitchen.

There is another possible explanation that stretches credulity somewhat but could be justified as a possibility. It is always assumed that convict labour was essentially 'free', and should therefore not count or contribute to the total cost of the finished construction.

If we make a number of assumptions concerning day rates of equivalent pay, and about the productivity level of the convicts in a major construction job, keeping in mind they were supervised by other convicts, then we may be able to say that the 400,000 pound of cost assembled in the Table above is for materials and that the equivalent value of the convict labour makes the difference of the 522,000 to bring the total estimate up to Kitchen's estimates.

The relevant assumptions are (based on Greenways cost estimates on Page 59 above)

- The number of days of mechanics labour to complete the Government House Stables was 16,686.5
- The average cost per man day was 1 shilling
- Labour reflected a 33% content of the total finished cost.

So applying these assumptions to the construction work in the rest of the table, we find that all projects would have taken 2,683,108 days of mechanics labour or approx 8,450 man years. The convict population increased between 1812 and 1820 by 10,800 men and totalled 19,000 men by 1820, and to suppose that 44% of the male convicts were employed in construction work is not unreasonable. At the minimum rate of 1s per day, our labour cost total becomes 134155 pound; thus, at an average of 3 shillings (compared with Coghlan's cost for 'free' mechanics at 5s per day, we would achieve the difference of 480,000 pound. Coghlan estimates that a convict would only produce about 60% of a 'free' labourer.

Our conclusion, if we stretch the point, is that Kitchen's estimate of a construction cost for the period of 900,000 is valid if our materials are valued at 402,000 and our labour accounts (at the average rate of 3 shillings per day) to a further 470,000-pound.

The Benefits to Britain

The original estimate of direct gains by the British authorities from the original and continuing investment in the Colony of New South Wales was based on 5 (five) identifiable and quantifiable events

1. The opportunity cost of housing, feeding and guarding the convicts in the Colony compared with the cost of doing the same thing in Britain.

    The original estimates, in this category, were based on an estimated differential of ten pound per head—an arbitrary assessment of the differential cost.

    However recent and more reliable information has come to hand which gives further validity to a number of 20 pound per head per annum, compared with the original 10 pound per head per annum.

    A letter to Under Secretary Nepean, dated 23rd August 1783, from James Maria Matra of Shropshire and London assists us in this regard.

    It was Matra who first analysed the opportunity of using the new Colony as a Penal Colony; only his estimates were incorrect and ill founded. He had advised the Government that it would cost less than 3,000 pound to establish the Colony initially, plus transportation cost at 15 pound per head and annual maintenance of 20 pound per head.

In fact the transportation was contracted for the second fleet at 13 pound 5 shillings per head and Colonial revenues from 1802 offset annual maintenance.

However, Matra made a significant statement in his letter to Nepean, when he pointed out that the prisoners housed, fed and guarded on the rotting hulks on the Thames River were being contracted for in the annual amount of 26.15.10 per head per annum. He also writes that 'the charge to the publick fore these convicts has been increasing for the last 7 or 8 years' (Historical Records of NSW—Vol 1 Part 2 Page 7)

Adopting this cost as a base for comparison purposes, it means that the benefit to Britain of the Colony increased from 140,000,000 pound to 180,000,000 pound. This benefit assesses the Ground 1 benefit at 84,000,000 pound.

2. Benefit to Britain on Ground Two (2) is put at 70, 000,000 pound which places the value of a convicts labour at 35 pound per annum. Matra had assessed the value of labour of the Hulk prisoners at 35. 85 pound.

2. The valuation of convict labour in the new Colony should reflect the convicts not only used on building sites, but also on road, bridge and wharf construction. This would add (based on 35 pound per annum) a further 21,000,000-pound.

3. The Molesworth Committee (A House of Commons Committee investigating transportation) concluded that the surplus food production by the convicts would feed the Military people and this, over a period of 10 years, would save 7,000,000 pound for the British Treasury.

4. The benefits of fringe benefit grants of land to the Military etc can be estimated (based on One pound per acre) at over 5,000,000 before 1810.

5. We learn from Governor King's Report to Earl Camden (which due to a change of office holder, should have been addressed to Viscount Castlereagh as Colonial Secretary) dated 15th March 1806 that the Convicts engaged in widely diverse work. The Report itself (Enclosure #2) is entitled

"Public Labour of Convicts maintained by the Crown at Sydney, Parramatta, Hawkesbury, Toongabbie and Castle Hill, for the year 1805

Cultivation—Gathering, husking and shelling maize from 200 acres sowed last year—Breaking up ground and planting 1230 acres of wheat, 100 acre of Barley, 250 acres of Maize, 14 acres of Flax, and 3 acres of potatoes—Hoeing the above maize and threshing wheat.

Stock—Taking care of Government stock as herdsmen, watchmen etc

Buildings—
- At Sydney: Building and constructing of stone, a citadel, a stone house, a brick dwelling for the Judge Advocate, a commodious brick house for the main guard, a brick printing office
- At Parramatta: Alterations at the Brewery, a brick house as clergyman's residence
- At Hawkesbury: completing a public school
- A Gaol House with offices, at the expense of the Colony
- Boat and Ship Builders: refitting vessels and building row boats
- Wheel and Millwrights: making and repairing carts

Manufacturing: sawing, preparing and manufacturing hemp, flax and wool, bricks and tiles

Road Gangs: repairing roads, and building new roads

Other Gangs: loading and unloading boats"
(Historical Records of NSW—Vol 6 P43)

Thus the total benefits from these six (6) items of direct gain to the British comes to well over 174 million pound, and this is compared to Professor N. G. Butlin's proposal that the British 'invested' 5.6 million.

THE WORKING OF THE FUNDS

There were numerous 'funds' probably supported by accounts from 1818, when the surplus balance of the Orphan Fund was ordered to be placed on deposit with the Bank of New South Wales. This was followed by the Military Chest, the Land Fund, the Commissariat Fund and many others, all of which were probably raised to simplify accounting recording and reporting-a Bank account can be used to greatly simplify accounting records.

Governor Macquarie directed that:

a. The Police Fund is intended to cover the expense of all items relating to the goal and police, and replace the gaol fund but is entirely distinct from the female orphan fund. (31.03.1810 P323 Vol 7)—effective 1st April, 1810

b. ¾ ths of all the duties and customs collected in the port and Town of Sydney are to be paid into the Police Fund. The remaining 1/4th to be paid to the Orphan Fund, which will be necessary to defray the expenses of that institution.

c. Liquor Licenses are to be paid to the Police Fund. Darcy Wentworth is to be Treasurer of the Police Fund. Quarterly accounts for both funds to be completed, inspected and published.

d. The naval officer, previously responsible for collecting customs and duties to settle his accounts by the 31st May, 1810

e. John Palmer to close up and settle all accounts for the commissary and pass over control to his deputy William Broughton until Palmer's return from England

f. Samuel Marsden is to be treasurer of the orphan fund

On 30th April, 1810, Macquarie wrote to Castlereagh concerning the two funds.

"Previously all duties and customs collections have been allocated to the Gaol and Orphan Funds. I have revised this practice in favour of sharing the collections between the Police—¾ ths.—and Female Orphan 1/4ᵗʰ—Funds.

From the Police Fund is to be defrayed the expense of the jail and police establishments, the erection of wharves, quays, bridges and making/ repairing of roads. The second fund is to cover establishment of the orphanage and other charity schools.

Coghlan in 'Wealth & Progress' (P837) writes about the Land Fund

"When in 1831 it was decided to abolish the system of free land grants, and to dispose of the public estate by auction in lieu of private tender, it was also decided that the proceeds of land sales should be paid into what was called the Land Fund, from which were to be paid the charges incidental to the introduction of immigrants; and it was from the inability of the Land Fund to meet these charges that the public debt of NSW first had its rise. From 1831 to 1834 the Land Fund was sufficient, but in 1841 the engagements for immigration purposes were so heavy that it became necessary to supplement the fund in some way and it was decided to borrow against the security of the Land Revenue. On 28ᵗʰ December 1841 a debenture loan of 49,000 pound was offered in the colony through the Sydney Gazette, the first loan raised in any colony.

Sundry Funds 1864

From "The Epitome of History of NSW" P409, the Government Printer reports that:

"The deficiency for 1864 was 407,626.7.11 of which, the sum of 357,408 had been already paid with funds borrowed from accounts as follows:

- Treasury Bills 30,948.1.11
- 1865 revenue 98,714.10.8
- Bank of NSW 83,333.14.8
- Oriental Bank, Ldn 20,818.14.9
- Lodgements 92,238.16.4

- Church & School Fund 19,658.09.7
- Civil Service Super Fund 1,429.7.10
- Scab in Sheep Fund 10,267.2.10

It can be concluded from the above referenced statement by the NSW Treasurer of 1864, that these funds were established as 'collectives' or depositories of segregated receipts and a means of trying to simplify an accounting, recording and reporting system. It is probable that the Church & School Fund, was operated by The Church & School Lands Corporation (under the Act of 1834; 'to provide for the maintenance of the police and gaol establishments of the colony, the surplus of the land revenue (land fund) and of the other casual Crown revenues had been placed at the disposal of the Council.

TRACKING THE MANY COLONIAL FUNDS

From 1802, the first date that the Colony of New South Wales attempted to manage some of its fiscal destiny by recording certain transactions in the Colony, in the Orphan Fund or the Gaol Fund.

The Crown did not put its hand out for a share of colonial revenues until 1822, but as early as 1802, the colony applied duties and customs to imported items, as a means of raising necessary revenue to provide a small amount of independence to the Governor's operations. The first year's revenue of 900 pound did not amount to much but it was the start of something big. That revenue grew quickly to reach over 100,000 by 1829 and over 1 million pound by 1854.

The Goal & Orphan Funds were shortly replaced by the Female Orphan and Police Funds sponsored by Governor Macquarie in 1810.

Later, during the 'Blue Book' period, the number of funds grew. From 1802 and the Orphan & Gaols Funds, the colonial revenue was distributed eventually through the Female Orphan & Police Funds, the 'Military Chest' Fund, The Land Fund, the Colonial Fund, and the Commissary Fund. Each fund had a unique role and purpose.

From an accounting viewpoint, the matter of allocating certain revenues must have caused some confusion. Thus the 'parliamentary grant to reimburse the local expenditure on the convicts' was handled by placing the revenue in a new category—"Receipts in Aid of Revenue". This was soon changed to the heading of "Revenue of the Crown".

The Colony was initially operated through a series of 'funds' which were simply a bank account by another name. For the first 32 years of the colonial administration, there was no 'treasury'; and so that fact, along with the administration overwatching a mere penal colony, a treasury was neither demanded or necessary. But times changed. There became a demand for immigration of free people, of both families and single women; there were the demands of the traders for a means of purchasing their wares and paying for them via an acceptable means of exchange; and then the dereliction of duty by the Marine Corps led to officer's influencing, if not controlling much of the economy of the colony, especially the Commissariat. A Treasury became essential and the first token Treasury came with the local recording of colonial revenue from customs duties and tariffs, tolls and rents. There were a number of such funds going back to 1802. The Colonial Treasury commenced in 1822 under the auspices of the Colonial Secretary and until 1827 the Colonial Treasury was the sole source of deposits of revenue and the source of expenditures. In 1827 we find the first mention of the 'Military Chest'. It is safe to assume that the successor to the Military Chest was the Land Fund whose functions, not unlike the military chest was to pool the 'revenue of the crown' raised in the colony from the sale of its 'waste 'or crown lands. We will consider the role and function of the Military Chest momentarily, but first there were a number of funds between 1802 and 1855 including:

* The Goal Fund 1802-1809
* The British Treasury 1788-1835
* The Commissariat Fund 1822-1850
* The Orphan Fund 1802-1822
* The Police Fund 1810-1822
* The Blue Book Period 1822-1857-1875
* The Military Chest
* The Land Fund
* The Colonial Fund

* Scab on Sheep Fund
* Church & School Fund
* Civil Service Super Fund

Because these funds have never been discussed or identified in any texts, this section has been designed to uncover and discuss two of the many funds mentioned above and trace their use and activity.

It would appear from the use of these minor funds that a new accounting procedure was under-way. A simple and inexpensive recording and reporting mechanism could be maintained with a fair degree of accuracy, if separate bank accounts were used for each collection point, or each source of revenue was identified by a separate account, into which these funds could be deposited.

THE MILITARY CHEST

With a name as romantic as 'the military chest', this story may be expected to unfold as a historic novel, but the 'military chest' was the first fund identified following the initiation of the 'Blue Book' period being the first formal accounts transmitted to England from the birth of the colony in 1788.

Our story starts with Governor Macquarie in 1810 who, having decided that the accounting records for the colony were, in effect, in a shambles, and did not properly reflect the fiscal condition of the colony, re-allocated certain local revenues to firstly the gaol fund and other revenue to the Orphan fund, each of which was to have a Trustee and Treasurer. The treasurer for the Orphan Fund was the Reverend Samuel Marsden. Marsden was known and feared for his despotic ways, and we find from his records of the fund, as reproduced in the Sydney Gazette each quarter from 1811 to 1821 that certain unusual practices were undertaken with the accounts.

D'arcy Wentworth, the Treasurer for the Gaol Fund, by then renamed the 'Police' Fund, also took substantial liberties and bestowed fiscal favours upon many fellow officers of the Military Corps, and supported many of the non-trading military men with road repair work, which may or may not have ever been completed at least to any acceptable quality, since month after month the same men received rather large sums for road repairs, bridge and wharf repairs.

The successor to these early restricted funds was the British Government introduction of a standard recording and reporting format called the 'Blue Books' because they were, in fact, bound in blue covers.

A search of the "List of Colonial Office Records" preserved in the Public Records Office, published by HM Stationery Office, 1911, suggests that there was no Blue Book compiled prior to 1822 nor for the year 1824. The volumes continued to be compiled until 1855 in a set of four copies; two being sent to the Colonial Office, one went to the Governor and the other to the Colonial Secretary, and from 1855 to 1857 an additional copy was placed before the Legislative Assembly (after self-government). The volumes continued to be compiled after 1857 until 1870 but at that were being printed instead of being written out by hand and they contain much less information, usually only the returns of the Civil and Ecclesiastical Establishments. These latter years of 'Blue Books' were probably only prepared as a verification to the British Treasury that the Civil List was being maintained by the Colonial Government.

The Blue Books were compiled retrospectively from groups of returns sent out from the Colonial Secretary's Office, which were filled in by the various officials, and then sent back to the Office.

The first reference to the 'Military Chest' was in the 1828 'Blue Books' where we find, as one item of Revenue:

- 'The amount of Revenue & Receipts derived from local resources of the colony', together with a 'Loan from the Military Chest'

This first 'loan' from the military chest was in the amount of 5,000.00 pound. It was obviously a short-term loan, because there is a reference to the "Balance in the Colonial Treasury on the 31st December, 1828, applicable to the service of the year 1829 being 11722.09.5 ½ *."

A further footnote tries to clarify this item.

"*This Balance includes the sum of 5,000 pound, a loan which has been repaid into the Military Chest since the 31ˢᵗ December, 1828.'

The Blue Books for the year 1828 make for further interesting analysis.

a. In spite of the final accounts being audited by Wlm. Lithgow (Colonial Auditor) and certified by Alex. McLeay, as Colonial Secretary, there is a substantial arithmetic error in the statements. We can track this error by accepting the opening balance in the colonial treasury as of 1ˢᵗ January 1828; the closing balance on the 31ˢᵗ December 1828; and the total receipts and disbursements recorded and added. Viz

Opening balance	3962.16.8 ¾.
Total receipts	226,191.16.7 ¾.
Total expenditure	214,469.07.2 ¼.
Closing balance	11,722.09.5 ½.
Difference	2,962.16.8 ¾.

This is an error in addition in the items of expenditure, or else an error of transposition from one set of records to the next set.

b. We note that in the following year, 1829 that a notation on the 'Receipts in Aid of Revenue' is that these deposits have been paid into the Military Chest. These deposits include:

- Consignment of specie
- Proceeds of bills drawn by the Deputy Commissary
- Proceeds of sale of
- Stores sent from England
- Crown stock (livestock)
- Coals ex Newcastle
- Wheat from Bathurst
- Sugar & molasses grown at Port Macquarie
- Schooner 'Alligator'
- Sundry stores & articles
- Miscellaneous receipts

- The receipts in aid of revenue (i.e. revenue of the crown) are exclusive of the value of colonial produce delivered to the commissariat from the convict agricultural establishments

a. The Military Chest usually made payments in the following categories:

- Civil establishment
- Convict establishment
- Military establishment
- Retired army pay & pensions

b. The main revenue and expenditures were deposited into and paid out of the 'Colonial Treasury'. The first reference to the balance in the Military chest is found in 1828, but the first reference to a balance in the Colonial Treasury is not found until 1829. From those dates, the closing balance at the end of each year is identified until 1831 when there are headings such as "Paid into the Colonial Treasury" "Defrayed from the Colonial Treasury";"Paid into the Military Chest", "Defrayed from the Military Chest", providing the means of tracking balances in each account.

c. In 1829, the disbursements on account of miscellaneous civil services states

"Total disbursements out of the military chest, in aid of the civil establishment of the colony"

d. In 1834, the 'Receipts in aid of Revenue' used each year, was changed to 'Revenue of the Crown'.

The items included remain the same; viz. proceeds of land sales, quit rents, fees on delivery of deeds and leased land revenue.

e. Back in 1826, for the first and only time, there was an entry for the British "parliamentary grant for the charges of defraying the civil establishment of the colony for the year 1826". The amount involved is 8,283.15.0; however the financial statements show the full civil establishment as costing 62,554.18.2 ½. The British Government must have decided that the cost of supporting the full civil establishment was too expensive and that it would only contribute to the salary of selected personnel. The details as listed in the 1826 statement do not allow us to decipher how the 8,283-pound is made up; we can only assume that the Governor, the chief justice, and possibly the chief medical officer are covered. The reason we cannot identify the amount is that individual salaries were no longer being shown in the records, but rather the Governor and his establishment received a grant of 4933.06.5 ¾, whilst the judicial establishment receive a grant of 13,462.02.8 1/4.

f. The reference above to the 'notes' incorporated into each statement to the effect that 'the total is exclusive of the value of articles of colonial produce delivered to the commissariat from the convict agricultural establishment' stood until 1825 when the military chest received and deposited receipts from "the sale of articles of colonial produce delivered to the commissariat from the several convict agricultural establishments and coal mines". The first ever recognition that the production of convict labours should be shown as a 'crown receipt'.

g. The 1826 Financial Statements from the 'Blue Book' of that year record the consignment of specie as being 50,000.09.0 pound. Butlin "Foundations of the Australian Monetary System" refers to the copper coins sent to the colony at the instigation of Governor King in 1805, together with a second consignment in 1806 to Governor Hunter. Hunter recommended that the coins be circulated at "a greater value . . . . than their intrinsic worth."

h. Butlin suggests that the progress of government finance in the colony goes along these lines:

    •   the earliest coins arrive in the pockets of the first Fleeters
    •   Phillip's Bills & Dollars—bills on the English Treasury & Spanish dollars
    •   The 'Rum' Currency and Barter

- Promissory Notes—personally pledged
- Commissary's Store receipts and Bills of Exchange
- Paymaster's Bills & Notes—Copper coins of 1805
- Legal Tender & Colonial Currency
- 'Holey' dollars
- Macquarie's Bank & exchange rates

Butlin decided, rightly, that, between 1788 and 1803, the 'Colony had no treasury', but this omission was not to last long. The earliest funds were controlled out of England with even the colonial commissary operating purely on a barter system. The first colonial accounting was commenced in 1802 (through the Goal & Orphan Funds) with revenue amounting to 900 pound. The Colonial Fund commenced with the 'Blue Books'. The Land Fund according to the 'Australians: Historical Statistics' opened in 1833, although the 1833 financial statements do show the balance at the end of the year, in the Military Chest was 22,719 pound. It is logical, subject to further verification, that the Land Fund was the successor to the Military Chest; the main evidence being that, in 1834, the 'Receipts in Aid of Revenue' was changed to 'Revenue of the Crown' and included the proceeds from the sale of crown (waste) land, and other crown assets of the colony.

The names of the various funds changed at different times between 1802 and 1834, including:

- Police Fund
- Orphan Fund
- Gaol Fund
- Orphan School Fund
- 'Blue Books' & The Colonial Fund
- Military Chest
- Colonial Treasury
- The Colonial Fund
- Land Fund

This was the story of how the Military Chest which became, during the Blue Book era, the holder of large balances in the Colony; became the main lender to an malnourished colonial treasury; and the beneficiary of the 'profitable' commissariat trading and discounting of bills drawn on the English Treasury. Its successor was termed the Land Fund, but we have little official recognition of this fund, other than what we learn from some of the economic historians.

THE LAND FUND

The military chest, as an account style for the colonial treasury was identified in the financial statements contained in the 'Blue Books', and we can readily identify the revenues credited to that account as well as the expenditures charged against the military chest.

However the Land Fund is without mention in the 'Blue Books' at least through the end of 1838, and the origin of this nomenclature must be accepted as 'untraceable' without proper basic evidence. We know only of its existence in firstly, the Australians: Historical Statistics P112, and then its mention in the works of economic historian, S.J. Butlin.

We find the following table in Historical Statistics

New South Wales Public Finance
Land Fund 1833-1850

Revenue		'000		Expenditure	'000	
Year	Land	Other	Total	Immign	Other	Total
1833 **	26.1	0.1	26.2	9.0	17.2	26.2
1834	48.2	42.9	60.8	7.9	52.9	60.8
1835	88.9	121.3	131.9	10.7	121.2	131.9
1836	131.4	121.1	263.3	11.8	251.5	263.3
1837	123.6	202.6	254.9	44.4	210.5	254.9
1838	120.2	185.8	353.8	108.0	245.8	353.8
1839	160.8	148.8	321.8	158.3	163.5	321.8
1840	325.3	283.6	480.0	148.0	332.0	480.0
1841	105.8	21.4	386.5	331.6	54.9	386.5
1842	44.1	51.7	117.2	112.0	19.7	131.7
1843	29.3	49.3	56.5	11.6	44.9	56.5
1844	16.9	126.0	127.5	69.0	58.5	127.5

1845	38.0	131.0	127.9	20.0	107.9	127.9
1846	38.8	153.5	146.5	1.2	145.3	146.5
1847	51.7	109.7	212.3	1.0	232.6	233.6
1848	51.7	109.7	212.3	113.8	98.5	212.3
1849	109.0	237.4	296.0	138.5	157.5	296.0
1850	158.5	104.8	373.1	166.2	206.9	373.1

** Receipts in aid of Revenue (ie. paid into military chest—no record of land sales)

This table extracted from Historical Statistics can only be verified by reference back to the Blue Book Financial statements for those years, provided we make a generous assumption.

That assumption must be as follows:

a. If the military chest is accepted as a predecessor to the 'Land Fund' then its purpose must have been essentially the same. The military chest took its revenue from the proceeds of sale of crown lands, sale of stores sent from England, sale of produce from the Convict Establishments and sale of crown livestock. In other words, only material items possessed by the crown; and that is most probably why the notations on the Blue Books changed from 'Receipts in Aid of Revenue' to 'Revenue of the Crown'. This important change occurred in the 1834 financial statements.

b. Obviously the Land Fund was so designated either officially or by Australian Economic Historians to be the account into which official 'crown' revenue is deposited and from which crown reserved expenditures are drawn. The crown reserved its use of portion of the funds for conveying selected immigrants into the country, and for (15%) aboriginal welfare. We will return to the official sanctioning of these funds later.

c. S.J. Butlin in his masterwork "Foundations of the Australian Monetary System 1788-1851" makes several passing references to the 'Land Fund' without fully identifying its source or use.

Butlin writes that "in February 1838, William Rucker, a Melbourne storekeeper, announced the opening of a Derwent Bank agency, to 'receive deposits and discount bills and orders for account and under the responsibility of the Derwent Bank Company in Hobart. He fixed the discount rate at 20%, letting it be known that Hobart rates would apply when a court was established in which debts might be recovered. Attempts were made, with what success it is not clear, to secure the accounts of the Customs Officer and of the Land Fund for the agency. But the agency met with considerable difficulty."

In 1846 there was a squabble between Stuart Donaldson, NSW Treasurer, Murray MHR and Dr. Bland MLC as to where certain colonial debentures were to be funded. Donaldson wanted the subscription to come from the public; Murray thought the Trust and Loan Bank should do the funding, but "Dr Bland wanted the loans to come from the Land Fund"

"Because of its late settlement and mining boom, land purchase in South Australia was heavy in the late 'forties and the local accumulations in the Land Fund were more than the local commissariat required. The practice developed, with English blessing, that any surplus in the Fund was paid to the commissariat which shipped the specie to other colonial commissariats in need, especially that in New Zealand, the amount being credited to the colony's account with the Land and Emigration Commissioners in London"

Grey, in South Australia, decided to use, contrary to official directions from London, to use any bank he chose for Government business, and he used the Bank of South Australia. Being contrary to official direction, this action permitted a penalty. The Land Fund, which was a transient deposit remitted to England for immigration payments, was divided between the Australasia and the South Australia, but all other government business was given to the Australasia."

"In 1851, the SA Treasury decided to require banks to hold cash at least equal to the government deposit, and to insist on this for the Land Fund."

Some of these references through doubt on the strict governmental use of the Land Fund. Other quotes come from 'Historical Records of Victoria—Volume 7'

"It was Lord John Russell's opinion in 1840 that the general revenue ought to provide for the general expenditure, leaving the Land Fund, apart from 15 percent to be used for expenditure on Aborigines, free for immigration purposes as originally intended"

A. Coghlan in his extensive work "Labour & Industry in Australia "helps place some of these matters in relation to sale of crown land & immigration into perspective.

"It was upon emigration from England at the cost of the land revenue that the colonial authorities finally placed their confidence. They offered in 1822 to set aside 10,000 pound from the Land Fund for emigration purposes; of this sum they desired that about two-thirds should be devoted to promoting the emigration of unmarried women, as the proportion of men in the colony was excessive, and that about one-third should be used in loans for the emigration of mechanics. The colonial office objected vigorously but the British Treasury agreed to the proposal with the proviso that no further sum should be expended upon immigration until the money received from the sale of land had reached 10,000 pound."

"It had been Edward Gibbon Wakefield's philosophy that the idea of land disposition in the colonies was adopted . . . . If the land was sold, the proceeds of the sale might aptly be applied to transferring labour from Britain to the colony without which labour the land would be of very little value. In 1831 the English Government resolved to alter the land system of Australia with the view of throwing open the country more freely to settlement, and thereby increasing immigration."

In the first four months of 1832, 103 mechanics reached the colony but were disappointed to find pay rates considerably less than those promised in England. The female emigrants all found ready employment, chiefly as domestic servants.

"Considering its resources, the colony went into the immigration business in a big way. The estimated expenditure of 1838 was 120,000 pound of which 80,000 was spent in chartering 26 ships, and 40,000 expended on bounty immigrants."

"With the overall success of the program it was decided that the whole of the rapidly increasing land revenue of New South Wales should be devoted to immigration and in 1837. 3093 immigrants arrived of whom 2688 were sponsored and 405 arrived under the bounty regulation of the colonial government."

Introduction to Special Economic Events

A number of 'special' events that influenced the course of the early economy and impacted on the extent and rate of economic growth have been selected and outlined. The list of events is not extensive but indicative of sometimes obscure events which can impact on economic growth eg education.

Although it may be suggested that the Report by Commissioner Bigge did not largely influence the Colonial economy, it must be stated that his recommendations to continue with the new Bank of New South Wales, which had been chartered incorrectly by Governor Macquarie, moved the economy along, as did his support for the continuation of the transportation of convicts to the Colony. His lack of support for land grants and early release of convicts may have slowed the economic growth until the consequences of his recommendation that the sale of Crown land be made, is considered. The revenue from the Sale of Crown land was considerable and kept the economy afloat, even if it was being badly managed, until 1810 and the arrival of Macquarie, in terms of food production.

Other special events fed on each other. Exploration across the mountains and uncovering the mystery of the rivers opened up huge pastoral areas and fostered the growth of the sheep and wool industries. The continued growth of the pastoral industries all through the 1800s was eclipsed as the prime exporting commodity only upon the 'official' discovery of gold. The discovery of gold once again filled the Colonial coffers and set into motion the most remarkable of special events, the expansion of the rail system across the Colony and inter-Colony. Instead of relying on sea transport, the very reason that the major cities were located on harbours and bays, the cities were connected by rail. The senior colony of New South Wales, could now diversify its population, move livestock and produce from Tamworth to

Albury. The most powerful benefit of the advent of the rail system is the most simplistic one. The Colonial labour-force learned how to engineer bridges (the Hawkesbury); how to construct gradients (crossing the Blue Mountains); and engineer the iron horses themselves for local conditions. This new knowledge led directly to the coming engineering shops and the likes of business adventurers such as Thomas Mort, whose remarkable drive, ingenuity and entrepreneurial ability led to the Mort Dry Dock & Engineering complex in Balmain, NSW Fresh Food & Ice, refrigeration and abattoirs in remote locations rather than in Sydney town. We cannot overlook the value of education to a largely illiterate economy. Finally the growth of the free trade movement brought to the fore the likes of Parkes, Reid, Wise and Pulsford—politicians who stood for a sound policy and formed the first 'party' ticket in the country. Federation took centre stage in the second half of the century and changed the face of the country and our analysis of the fiscal considerations of Federation and the post-Federation relations between the Commonwealth and the States will set the stage for review as to whether the Federation movement was successful.

There may well be more 'special events 'than those discussed but it seems, at least to this writer, that these interlinking events boosted the Colonial economy in a remarkable way:

- the crown land policy and reform
- the growth of education
- the Report by Commissioner Bigge
- exploration
- pastoral expansion
- the expansion of the rail system
- the Fiscal impact of Federation
- Commonwealth-State Financial Relations

The Report of the Select Committee on Transportation-1812 pages 11-12-records that 'The convicts who were distributed amongst the settlers, were clothed, supported and lodged by them; they either work by the task or for the same number of hours as the Government convicts; and when their set labour is finished, they are allowed to work on their own account. The master has no power of corporal punishment over them as this can only be inflicted by the interference of a magistrate. The convict, if he feels abused by his master, can complain to a magistrate who, if justified, can deprive the master of his servant.

It is to be found in the evidence of Mr Commissary Palmer that the expense of each convict in the service of the Government was about 40 pound per annum, and that a free labourer at Sydney could be hired for about 70 per year, but would do twice as much work. Palmer reports the annual expense of a convict is 30 pound, compared with the cost of holding them in a prison hulk on the Thames at 24 pound, with the value of their work being about 8 pound or $1/3^{rd}$ of the cost of keeping them."

The system was fundamentally changed in 1836, and the 2nd Select Committee in 1837-38 P669 recorded that" All applications for convicts are now made to an officer—'Commissioner for assignment of Convict Servants' who is guided by Government Regulations. Settlers to whom convicts are assigned, are bound to send for them within a certain period and pay the sum of 1 pound per head for their clothing and bedding.

Each assigned convict is entitled to a fixed amount of food and clothing—in NSW of 12 lb of wheat, or equivalent in flour and maize meal, 7 lb of mutton or beef or 4 ½ lb of salt pork, 2 oz of salt and 2 oz of soap each week. 2 frocks or jackets, three shirts two pair trousers, 3 pair shoes and a hat or cap, annually. Plus one good blanket, a palliasse or wool mattress which remain the property of the master. Obviously they are well fed well clothed and receive wages of between 10 to 15 pound per annum."

The 2nd Select Committee also heard evidence on convicts who have been emancipated or their sentence has expired.

"These people find no difficulty in obtaining work at high wages; and having acquired experience in the Colony are generally preferred to new arrivals. They fill many positions of trust for instance as constables, overseers of pastoral; properties and road or building gangs, as superintendents of estates, clerks to bankers, lawyers and shopkeepers, and even as tutors in private families. Some have married free women and have become prosperous."

CHAPTER 2

INTRODUCTION TO THE PUBLIC FINANCE & THE REPORTING SYSTEM IN THE COLONY

BACKGROUND TO THE COLONIAL ACCOUNTING

Colonial Origins of Public Accounts

One goal of the Governor of the Colony of New South Wales in 1788 was to achieve self-sufficiency for the colony even though it was a penal Colony. By 1823, the British Government had taken the approach it would be limiting its direct expenditure to the transportation of the convicts and they're travelling food and supplies. The Colonial Administrators would be responsible for the convict's security, food, clothing and accommodation in the Colony. The proceeds from the sale of Crown land were to be the exclusive reserve of the British authorities, and not that of the colonists. The Governors commenced working the convicts for creating food, minerals (eg coal production), roads, housing and public buildings, and generally paying their own way. By 1796, other convicts had been assigned to landowners on a fully maintained basis, thus saving the British Treasury a great deal of money.

Such policy, of the Government maintenance of convicts, created the need for an accounting by the Colony to the British Parliament with the appointment of a Treasurer acting as a Financial Controller, who could prepare monthly and annual despatches to the British Colonial Secretary. Following self-government in 1856, the procedures changed, as the Colony became fully responsible for their own economic planning and fiscal management.

Colonial Accounting in New South Wales

The Colony went through two stages before adopting the standards recommended in the 1823 'Blue Book', which replaced the 'gaol' and orphan funds. These two phases were the Gaol and Orphan Funds pre-1810, and the Macquarie promoted Police and Orphan Funds of 1811-1821, which results were published quarterly in the Sydney Gazette. The 'gaol' fund was a record of funds raised by a surcharge on the citizens of Sydney town, as a means to complete the construction of the Sydney 'gaol'. The voluntary collections fell far short of the funds needed and a part-completed gaol required official support. Customs duties were imposed on imports, and the gaol was completed with Government monies, the fund was renamed the police fund. The orphan Fund started in 1802 accepted as its revenue the customs duties on spirits and tobacco and was later (1810) named the Orphan School Fund with the intention of creating a fund to erect the first school building in Sydney town. The advisory Legislative Council were appointed in 1823, and the first Appropriation Act was passed in 1832, even though, in the interim, the Governors were passing 'messages' of the financial condition of the Colony to the members of the Council.

Upon self-government in 1855, the government accounting procedures were again revised, since the Colony was now fully responsible for all its fiscal matters.

About this time, gold was discovered and license fees, duties on exports of gold and duties on the domestic conversion of gold were applied and helped fill the Treasury coffers.

This was a major step forward in Government economic planning. A limited deficit budgeting commenced at this time. Deficits were short term and recovered usually within 5 years, although the Colonial debt, mainly to overseas bondholders was kept very much in check after the surge of investment in railways and telegraph services.

The formal Federation debates commencing in 1888 were based around the role and adjustment to individual Colonial tariffs, their discussion in the Finance Committee of the National Debates, and their incorporation into the final Constitution of 1901. These trends from 1856 are to be discussed and analysed

Federation installed a new system within the structure of the new Commonwealth Treasury whilst the States revised their reduced revenue collection procedures and accounted for the grants (return of surplus) of revenue from the Commonwealth.

Federation brought further changes to the raising of revenues, whilst the largest expenditure of the Commonwealth became the return of centrally collected funds to the States. The advent of the Commonwealth Treasury improved once again the quality of recording keeping and brought into being the first Commonwealth estimates and National budgets. By 1901, the public finance mechanism had grown from a colonial exercise by appointed settlers to a fully charged Government instrumentality.

From the earliest records (HRNSW), certain conclusions can be drawn, and these can be set out as follows:

a. There was a wide range of duties and taxes imposed on the early settlers, especially on alcoholic beverages. The general rate of duty on spirits was 10 shillings per gallon, and on wine it was 9 pence per gallon. On tobacco the rate was 6 pence per pound, while timber attracted a rate of one shilling per solid foot. General Cargo attracted an ad valorem duty at a flat 5% rate.

b. There were also licenses and tolls. Hawker's Licenses sold for 20 pound, and it cost a settler 2 pence (tuppence) to go from Sydney town to the settlement of Parramatta. A country settler (in the Hawkesbury) paid One penny to cross the Nepean River Bridge at Windsor.

c. References to crown land sales were recorded in the 1825 'Blue Book', and based on the decree by George 3rd in a Proclamation on 25th March, 1825, that there was to be imposed a new charge on crown lands at the rate of One shilling for every 50 acres, to commence 5 years after the date of the original grant. To that date all crown lands had been disposed of by way of grants, and this rent was a form of back door compensation to the crown. In the official grant documents, the receiver of the land grant was given notice that further costs may attach at some future time to the land, and it was this opportunity that provided the Crown to raise this 'rent' charge on the land in 1825.

d. There was to be a Land-holders fee of Fifteen shillings per 100 acres of crown land reserved for each three years for free settlers, followed by a two shilling fee per 100 hundred acres redeemable after twenty years from purchase.

e. On the 18th May 1825, the 'rent' was changed, by order of Governor Sir Thomas Brisbane, to a flat rate of 5% of the estimated value of the grants, without purchase (as opposed to purchased land), to commence 7 years from the date of grant. 'Rents' on any 2nd and subsequent grants were payable immediately, without the benefit of the 7 years grace period.

f. The Table of Land Grants between 1789 and 1850 shows the substantial number of acres granted to settlers and we can conclude that the revenue sourced from 'rents' on Crown land grants could build into a considerable sum for the Crown in the future.

g. By Proclamation, also dated 18th May 1825, George III authorised the sale of crown lands at the rate of 10 shillings per acre, to a maximum of 4,000 acres per individual or a maximum of 5,000 acres per family. Payment was by way of a 10% deposit and four equal quarterly instalments.

h. The title pages to the 1822 'Blue Book' are entitled 'Abstract of the Net Revenue and Expenditure of the Colony of New South Wales for the Year 1822', which indicates (and as the detailed records also reflect) that all Colonial revenue and expenses were consolidated in the 'Blue Book'.

i. The Table of Civil List Salaries for 1792-1793 sets out the Governor's Salary at One Thousand Pounds. But in the 1822 statement of expenditures on the Civil Salaries, the Governor's Salary had increased to Two Thousand Pounds. By 1856 the Governor's establishment was costing 15,000 pounds per annum.

j. In fact, the total of Civil List salaries in 1792 was only 4,726.0.0 pounds, but by 1822 the total had increased to 9,828.15.0

pounds, due to both individual salary increases as well as more people being placed on the Civil List.

k. The official 'Observations upon revenue for the Colony in 1828' (written by the Colonial Treasurer of New South Wales) makes an interesting point. It observes that the 'net colonial income' of the year 1828, as actually collected, is exclusive of sums in aid of revenue, which cannot be viewed in the character of income. This item is further defined as 'the proceeds of the labour of convicts, and establishments connected with them, being applied to the reduction of the amount of parliamentary grants for their maintenance'. In subsequent reports, 'receipts in aid of revenue' included items such as—'sale of Crown livestock; sale of government farms produce; sale of clothing and cloth made at the Female Factory at Parramatta; sale of wheat, sugar, molasses and tobacco produced by the convicts at new settlements such as Port Macquarie.

l. The total quantity of alcohol imported into and thus consumed in the Colony, even in 1828, and with a population in 1828 of only 37,000 people, of which adult numbers would be less than 25,000, was 162,167 gallons of spirits and 15,000 gallons of Colonial distilled spirits (distillation from sugar was prohibited in 1828, however, the high price of grain and the higher taxing of locally manufactured spirits became a natural deterrent). A final observation was made in the 'Blue Book' compilation of 1829 that the only duties imposed on spirits in that year was upon spirits imported directly from H. M. Plantations in the West Indies. So the British authorities received a double benefit in trading and duties.

m. The quantity of dutiable tobacco in 1828 was 136,748 pounds (compared to 91,893 pounds in 1825). The Government experimented with locally grown tobacco at establishments in Emu Plains and Port Macquarie with the result being 51,306 pounds produced. So the total consumption of tobacco in 1828 was over 4 Lb. Per head of adult population.

n. Shipping companies also paid lighthouse charges, along with wharfage. The growth of shipping, into the Port of Sydney, was so great that it meant that by 1828, the revenue from lighthouse dues, harbour dues and wharfage was over 4,000 pound.

o. In 1828, the postage of letters attracted fees, for the first time, and the official Postmaster collected 598 pounds for general revenue. This revenue grew rapidly so that by 1832 the amount of postage collected was 2,00 pound. Each colony imposed its own postage and printed its own stamps until Federation.

The commencement of sales of both crown lands and crown timbers increased general revenues to the extent that in 1828, the amounts realised were:

Sales of Crown Lands	5004.19.2
Sales of Cedar cut on crown land	744.15.11
Sales of other Timber	9365.11.4

The Governor imposed a fee of One halfpenny per foot for all cedar cut on crown lands. The 'Blue Book' makes the further observation that this charge 'has checked bushrangers and other lawless depredators by depriving them of ready means of subsistence by the absence of all restraint from cutting Cedar upon unallocated lands'.

p. There was a major improvement in record keeping and reporting after self-government in 1855. The "Financial Statements of the Colonial Treasurers of New South Wales from Responsible Government in 1855 to 1881" provide a detailed accounting mechanism for recording classifications and compilation of budgets and reporting to the Authorities. They contain 'explanatory memoranda of the financial system of New South Wales, and of the rise, progress and present condition of the public revenue'.

The interest in this period (from 1822 to 1881) is that these records, of the 'Blue Book' and the printed Financial Statements of 1881, provide the first identification of the items included in the revenue and expenditures for the Colony. This historical data is relevant to understanding the social conditions in the Colony, the application of duties, tariffs, tolls and fees which embraced the essential revenue of a Colony that was designed to be self-sufficient and which was being given minimal economic support by the British Government, even though the opportunity cost of housing 'prisoners' in the Colony was a fraction of the cost of housing them in England.

Colonial Accounting in Victoria

The new settlement of Port Phillip adopted the standards set out in the Governor George Gipps Report on Government Accounting and Reporting after 1836 Public Finance following separation from New South Wales to form the Colony of Victoria. The Blue Book was more accurately kept in the new settlement (than in the colony of New South Wales) and full records are available concerning the commencement of the settlement and leading to the separation from New South Wales.

Table A
New South Wales Public Finance
Orphan, Gaol & Police Funds 1802-1821

Revenue

Year	Opng Balances	Customs	Total	Works Outlay
1802			490	
1803			5,200	
1804				
1805			3,100	
1806			1,900	
1807			1,200	
1808				
1809				
1810		1,384	3,272	2,194
1811	769	7,872	10,939	2,965
1812	5,016	5,579	13,494	3,259
1813	4,502	5,228	14,621	4,426
1814	6,016	4,529	13,325	4,993
1815	1,681	13,197	17,994	6,350
1816	3,327	11,200	17,782	5,582
1817	5453	16,125	24,706	7,048
1818	9363	17,739	31,008	6,219
1819	18900	22,579	42,968	17,131
1820	10725	27,891	44,507	14,700

Commentary on Table A

In 1876, the Colonial Financial Officer (the Treasurer—James Thomson), acting for the Colonial Secretary of New South Wales, wrote, in a report to the Imperial Government that "From the foundation of the Colony in 1788 to 1824, the records of local revenue and expenditure are too imperfect to render them of much value for statistical purpose, or for comparison with subsequent years."

However these figures, from Table A above, have been collated in the 'Historical Records of Australia—Statistics' from reports by the Colonial Governor to the British authorities and go someway to telling a story. The claim made by historian N. G. Butlin in his introduction to the Historical Records of Australia series—'The economy before 1850'—"that the British Colonial Office spent millions of pounds to start up the Colony"—does not seem to be verifiable. In fact exactly the opposite.

The British expected their colonies to pay their way

We know that the British authorities had the choice of building new prisons in Britain and housing, feeding, guarding and clothing these prisoners, or relocate them to a 'penal colony'. The previous penal colony in America was no longer available because of the American Wars of Independence and the British were no longer welcome there. The recommendation of Sir Joseph Banks, after his voyage to the southern oceans with Captain James Cook, was to use the land and resources available in the newly charted East Coast of 'Australia'. The favourable opportunity cost of this arrangement was enormous. Britain was fighting wars in a number of areas and had numerous Colonies to administer, and one more Colony, supposedly rich in potential rewards and able to be converted to self-sufficiency was most attractive. So, the opportunity cost was became one form of savings.

By 1824 the convicts were also paying their way (in opportunity cost terms) by removing coal from the ground in the Maitland area and using it for heating purposes. No value was ever placed on this work, nor on the use of convicts as builders of roads, housing, barracks, storage sheds, port wharves, churches and government buildings. It would appear that the convicts earned their keep whilst the Colony paid its own way very quickly. The 'Blue Book' of 1828 states that there was revenue from the sale of convict produce such as 'coal, wheat, sugar, molasses and tobacco' but the value of convict labour was to remain unreported. Historians should recognise the value of the convict work as well as the opportunity cost of having transported the prisoners off-shore, when an assessment is made of the 'investment' made, and the benefits gained by Britain in the new Colony of New South Wales.

The original estimate of direct gains by the British authorities from the original and continuing investment in the Colony of New South Wales was based on 5 (five) identifiable and quantifiable events, even though the convicts were assigned jobs on the basis of 'full keep'.

1. The opportunity cost of housing, feeding and guarding the convicts in the Colony compared with the cost of doing the same thing in Britain.

    The original estimates, in this category, were based on an estimated differential of ten pound per head—an arbitrary assessment of the differential cost.

    However recent and more reliable information has come to hand which gives further validity to a number of 20 pound per head per annum, compared with the original 10 pound per head per annum.

    A letter to Under Secretary Nepean, dated 23rd August 1783, from James Maria Matra of Shropshire and London assists us in this regard.

    It was Matra, who first analysed the opportunity of using the new Colony as a Penal Colony, only his estimates were incorrect and ill founded. He had advised the Government that it would cost less than 3,000 pound to establish the Colony initially, plus transportation cost at 15 pound per head and annual maintenance of 20 pound per head.

In fact the transportation was contracted for the second fleet at 13 pound 5 shillings per head and annual maintenance was offset by Colonial revenues from 1802.

However, Matra made a significant statement in his letter to Nepean, when he pointed out that the prisoners housed, fed and guarded on the rotting hulks on the Thames River were being contracted for in the annual amount of 26.15.10 per head per annum. He also writes that 'the charge to the public for these convicts has been increasing for the last 7 or 8 years' (Historical Records of NSW—Vol 1 Part 2 Page 7)

Adopting this alternative cost (of 26.75 pound) as a base for comparison purposes, it means that the benefit to Britain of the Colony over a twenty-year period increased from 140,000,000 pound to 180,000,000 pound. This calculation assesses the Ground 1 benefit at 84,000,000 pound.

2. Benefit to Britain on Ground Two is put at 70, 000,000 pound (again over a 20-year period) which places the value of a convict's labour at 35 pound per annum. Matra had assessed the value of labour of the Hulk prisoners at 35. 85 pound.

2. The valuation of convict labour in the new Colony should reflect the convicts not only used on building sites, but also on road, bridge and wharf construction. This would add (based on 35 pound per annum) a further 21,000,000 pound.

3. The Molesworth Committee (A House of Commons Committee investigating transportation) concluded that "the surplus food production by the convicts would feed the Military people and this, over a period of 10 years, would save 7,000,000 pound for the British Treasury.

4. The benefits of fringe benefit grants of land to the Military etc can be estimated (based on One pound per acre) at over 5,000,000 before 1810.

5. We learn from Governor King's Report to Earl Camden (which due to a change of office holder, should have been addressed to Viscount Castlereagh as Colonial Secretary) dated 15th March, 1806 that the Convicts engaged in widely diverse work. The Report itself is entitled

"Public Labour of Convicts maintained by the Crown at Sydney, Parramatta, Hawkesbury, Toongabbie and Castle Hill, for the year 1805

Cultivation—Gathering, husking and shelling maize from 200 acres sowed last year—Breaking up ground and planting 1230 acres of wheat, 100 acre of Barley, 250 acres of Maize, 14 acres of Flax, and 3 acres of potatoes—Hoeing the above maize and threshing wheat.

Stock—Taking care of Government stock as herdsmen, watchmen etc

Buildings—
- At Sydney: Building and constructing of stone, a citadel, a stone house, a brick dwelling for the Judge Advocate, a commodious brick house for the main guard, a brick printing office
- At Parramatta: Alterations at the Brewery, a brick house as clergyman's residence
- At Hawkesbury: completing a public school
- A Gaol House with offices, at the expense of the Colony
- Boat and Ship Builders: refitting vessels and building row boats
- Wheel and Millwrights: making and repairing carts

Manufacturing: sawing, preparing and manufacturing hemp, flax and wool, bricks and tiles

Road Gangs: repairing roads, and building new roads

Other Gangs: loading and unloading boats"
(Historical Records of NSW—Vol 6 P43)

Thus the total benefits from these six (6) items of direct gain to the British comes to well over 174 million pound, and this is compared to Professor N. G. Butlin's proposal that the British 'invested' 5.6 million.

However, one item of direct cash cost born by the British was the transportation of the prisoners to the Colony, their initial food and general well being. Although the British chartered the whole boat, some of the expense was offset by authorising private passengers, 'free settlers' to travel in the same fleet. A second saving was the authorities had approved 'back-loading' by these vessels of tea from China.

Only limited stores and provisions, tools and implements were sent with Captain Arthur Phillip, the appointed first Governor, and his efforts to delay the fleet until additional tools were ready was met with an order to 'commence the trip forthwith'. This turned out to be a mistake as the new Colony could only rely on minimal farming practices to grow a supply of vegetables and without the tools to scratch the land, remove the trees and vegetation, little progress was made. A potential big cost to the fledgling Colony.

i. The 'Blue Book' accounting records as maintained by Governor Macquarie from 1822 includes a reference to 'net revenue and expenses' which suggests an offset of all revenues against all expenses, and would include as revenue certain convict maintenance charges, to be reimbursed by the British Treasury. Such reimbursement was accounted for and reported only once—in 1825, when it is recorded as a 'receipt in aid of revenue' that an amount of 16,617 pound 'the amount of the parliamentary grant for the charge of defraying the civil establishment'. Prior to and since that date, there are only reports of payments and outgoings to the civil establishment, military and other personnel, without offset from reimbursement.

ii. Other notations in 1825 include revenues from rentals of government assets (Government outsourcing and privatisation obviously started back in 1825) such as;

Ferries	1584 pound
Toll gates	6554
Gardens	1835
mill	1749
canteen	910
church pews	1296

the hire of convict 'mechanics' raised 6853.27 pound

Slaughtering dues contributed 975.54 whilst duty on colonial distillation reaped 4901.30 pound.

The biggest revenue earners were duty on imported spirits (178,434 pound) and duty on imported Tobacco (21,817 pound)

i. Even in 1822 the Colony was showing a small operating surplus. This surplus grew through 1828 until, other than for transportation of convicts to the Colony, the charges on account of the British Treasury were less than One Hundred Thousand pounds for protecting, feeding and housing nearly 5,000 fully maintained convicts. Against this cost, the charge for housing, feeding and guarding this same number of prisoners in Britain would have been substantially higher, since in addition to the 5,000 gully maintained convicts there were a further 20,000 being paid for by free settlers and used as supervised labour. Britain surely had found a cheap source of penal servitude for at least 25,000 of its former prisoners, and found a very worthwhile alternative to the American Colonies as a destination for its prisoners.

j. Revenue from Crown Land sales and rents was used to offset Civil (Crown) salaries and expenses.

k. It is probably incorrect, at this stage; to say that it cost Britain nothing or at best, very little, to establish and maintain the Colony, but it can be said that from 1822 the costs were limited to maintaining fewer and fewer convicts. But from these convicts great value in terms of agricultural produce, coal and other minerals was derived. Just in terms of coal for lighting, heating and power, the cost to the government of purchasing these items would have been substantial. The 'Blue Book' reflects the use of the coal as a cost rather than a gain as would be the accounting standard today.

l. A final conclusion could be given that there are much more known records available for this period (the first One Hundred Years) than the author originally thought. The reproduction of the 'Blue Book' by the State Archives Office is a major step forward in understanding the economic challenges faced by settlers and convicts in the early Colony. The sourcing of material from the Blue Book unveils the financial statements and conditions of these early years. It is still considered that finance records of the period 1788 to 1822 are not re-constructible, but the author feels that a deep search through the microfilms forming the Joint Copying Project will provide information on the two Colonial operating funds of the period—the 'Police Fund and the Orphan Fund'. This is a challenge for another time.

An interesting observation is found in 'The Constitutional History of Australia' by W. G. McMinn (1979), referring to the post 1855 financial arrangements. On P 33 he records "Subject to the need for a vice-regal message, accepting that any locally (Australian Colony) initiated legislation of a money bill nature requires The Sovereign's ratification, the New South Wales Legislative Council was to have a general right to appropriate revenue from taxation, except for an amount of 81,600 pounds, the expenditure of which was to be in accordance with 'three schedules' to the Act; 33,000 pound for the salaries of those on the civil list eg Governor et al, the superintendent of Port Phillip and its judges and for the expenses of administering justice; 18,600 pound for the chief civil officers and their departments, for pensions and expenses of the council; and 30,000 pound for the maintenance of public worship.

The Sale of Waste Land Act of 1828 raised the minimum reserve price of crown land to one pound per acre, except that large remote areas might be sold at a lower price, and established a formula for the use of the land revenue; fifty percent was to be spent on immigration, the rest was to be expended by the Governor in accordance with British Government directives from time to time. The Governor was to continue to have power to issue depasturing licences and to make regulations for the use and occupancy of unsold lands, but the existence of the Sale of Waste Lands Act placed an important restriction on the colony by implying a prohibition against the Legislative Council legislating on these matters. The first directive on how the Governor was to spend a portion of the fund, enjoined the Governor to spend a proportion on Aboriginal protection and another on the roads; he was left free to hand any surplus over to the Council for appropriation; but it was made clear that the whole of the fifty percent was to be considered as an emergency reserve if the Council proved difficult". McMinn sheds some further light on the Crown Lands mystery but there still remains the question of whether, year after year, these funds were fully used or just included as a contribution to general revenue. It would appear that somewhere there is a firm directive from the British Treasury that the revenues from Crown Lands sale was to be used to 'offset' British costs of maintaining the Colony. The 'Blue Book' is evidence that as general revenues, these funds were already being used to pay for the costs of feeding, clothing, housing convicts, and we know they were specifically used to pay for 'sponsored immigrants', aboriginal 'protection', and now roads. The costs of the military establishment were charged against general revenues so in the quite large 'pot', nearly all Colonial expenditures were subsidised or offset by revenues from the Sale of Crown Land. Britain put its hand in the till only, it seems, to pay for the shipping and supplies costs of getting their prisoners to the Colony. After 1828, we know that convict production—both agricultural and mineral—went a long way to paying their expenses, so perhaps the British Treasury did in fact get off very lightly indeed, especially for the benefits it derived.

The vexing question of Crown Lands revenues still remains. It is apparent from the 'Blue Book' notations that this revenue was 'reserved' for specific allocation by the Crown and remained in the Colony as an offset against British Government fiscal obligations (eg Civil List salaries) until self-government in 1855. A relevant quotation from the 1887 Financial Statements of the Colonial Treasurer of New South Wales, follows:

> "Prior to the passing of the Constitution Act, the Territorial Revenues of the Colony belonged to the Crown, but upon that coming into operation in 1855, they were placed at the disposal of the local Parliament, and together with the taxes, imposts, rates and duties were formed into one fund, under the title of the Consolidated Revenue Fund. In lieu of the Crown Revenues thus given up to the Colony, an annual Civil List of 64,300 pound was made payable to Her Majesty out of the Consolidated Revenues of the Colony." What this means is that the British Treasury allowed the offset of all direct British payments made on account of the Colony against revenues raised by the sale, rent or lease of Crown lands

CHAPTER 3

GOVERNANCE OF PUBLIC FINANCE

Included in the appendix to the 'Financial Statements of 1887' is the record (by the Colonial Treasurer—James Thomson) that:

> "The Financial System of the Colony of New South Wales is regulated chiefly by the Constitution Act of 1855 and the Audit Act of 1870, and in matters relating to Trust Funds and Loans by special Appropriation Acts of the local legislature.

> The Imperial Act granting a constitution to the Colony of New South Wales was assented to on 16th July, 1855, and became effective on the 24th November 1855. This Act provides for a Legislative Council (Upper House) and a Legislative Assembly. The Upper House members were to be nominated by the Governor, while the Lower House members were to be elected by inhabitants of the Colony.

"Prior to the passing of the Constitution Act, the territorial revenues of the Colony belonged to the Crown, but on that Act coming into operation in 1855, these revenues were all placed at the disposal of the local Parliament, and together with the taxes, imposts, rates and duties, were formed into one fund, under the title of the Consolidated Revenue Fund. In lieu of the Crown Revenues thus given up to the Colony, an annual Civil List of

64,300 pounds was made payable to Her Majesty out of the consolidated revenues of the Colony.

The Constitution Act also provides that the legislature of the Colony shall have power to make laws for regulating the sale, letting, disposal, and occupation of the wastelands of the Crown within the Colony; and also for imposing taxes and levying customs duties. All Money Bills must, in the first place, be recommended to the Legislative Assembly by message from the Governor, and no part of the Public Revenue can be issued except on warrants bearing the Governor's signature, and directed to the Treasurer of the Colony.

The Audit Act of 1870 was passed to regulate the receipt, custody and issue of public monies, and to provide for the audit of the Public Accounts. The Treasury is the Department entrusted with the collection and disbursement of the revenues and other public monies of the Colony. It is under the control and general management of the Treasurer and Secretary for Finance and Trade. The permanent head of the Department is responsible to the Minister for the efficient conduct of its business.

The revenue of the Colony is now to be classed under the following general headings:

1. Taxation
2. Land Revenue
3. Receipts for services rendered
4. miscellaneous receipts

The main elements of the these four categories items consist of:

a. Taxation
    1. customs duties
    2. excise duties
    3. duty on gold exported
    4. trade licenses

b. Land Revenue
    1. Proceeds from land auctions

2. sales of improved lands
3. rents and assessments on pastoral runs
4. quit rents
5. leases of mining lands
6. miner's rights

c. Services receipts, include:
   1. railway & telegraph revenue
   2. money orders
   3. mint charges
   4. gold escort fees
   5. pilotage & harbour fees
   6. registration of cattle brands
   7. other fees of office

d. Miscellaneous
   1. rents
   2. fines
   3. sale of government property,
   4. interest on bank deposits
   5. other general revenues

The revenue and expenditure of the Colony is increasing year by year in proportion to the prosperity of the people and the increase of population. This is naturally to be expected for as new lands are taken up and outlying districts occupied, demands upon the government for all those services which tend to promote the well-being of a community are constantly being made; and although these services when granted create an additional expenditure, there generally follows an augmentation of the revenue both from the sale and occupation of the waste lands of the Colony, and the larger consumption of dutiable articles"

When responsible government was established in 1855, the revenue amounted to 973,178 pounds (or 3.51 pound per head) and the population was then 277,000. In 1875, exactly twenty years after the introduction of responsible government, the population had increased to 606,000 and the revenue to 4,121,996 (or 6.80 pound per head)."

From the Government Gazette of 2nd January 1879, this condensed statement is taken:

REVENUE, 1878

Taxation

Customs Duties	44,220
Duty on gold	6,898
Licenses	109,851
Land Revenue	
Sales	1,915,466
Other	410,254
Services	1183,582
Miscellaneous	172,907
TOTAL REVENUES for 1878	4,991,919 pound

An interesting observation on latter day government finance and government involvement in entrepreneurial activities is made by Trevor Sykes in his book, 'The Bold Riders' 1994-Chapter 14, Page 438:

"The Savings Bank of South Australia was formed in 1848 and the State Bank of South Australia was formed in 1896. By 1984 they had led stolidly blameless lives for 136 and 988 years respectively. In 1984 they merged to form a new, larger State Bank of South Australia.

The chairman of Hooker Corporation, Sir Keith Campbell, headed the Campbell Committee, set up by Federal Treasurer, John Howard, in 1979. The Committee delivered its report in March 1981. The Report recommended deregulation of the financial system, a part of a worldwide trend, leading to deregulation in the federal sphere in 1984 by Paul Keating. The Campbell Report recommended that, once the banking system had been deregulated to make it more competitive, there would cease to be any justification, on efficiency grounds, for continued government ownership of banks, so that if government banks were to remain, should be no more fettered or subject to government interference than private sector institutions undertaking similar activities."

The State Savings Bank of South Australia foundered and failed in 1989, only 5 years after deregulation and 140 years after its opening.

GOVERNANCE OF PUBLIC FINANCE IN THE COLONY

GENERAL OBSERVATIONS

On the origin and nature of the New South Wales Colonial Revenue:—

"The Revenues collected within the Colony of New South Wales, from its establishment until the commencement of the administration of Governor Macquarie in 1810, were raised in support of the 'Gaol' and 'Orphan' Funds respectively. The Revenue thus levied for, and appropriated to the Gaol Fund consisted of a Duty of 1s. per gallon on Spirits, 6d per gallon on wine, 3d per gallon on beer, together with a wharfage duty of 6d on each cask or package landed. These duties appear to have been first established upon the authority of Governor John Hunter R.N. during his administration in 1795-1800 and were the earliest sources of local revenue in the Colony.

The Revenue raised for the Orphan Fund was derived from fees on the entry and clearance of Vessels, and for permits to land and remove spirits—both first levied in 1800; from licenses to retail liquor and from a duty of 1.5% on goods sold by auction (first collected in 1801); from a duty of 5% ad valorem on all articles imported, the produce of countries to the eastward of the Cape of Good Hope (first imposed in 1802); from fines levied by the Courts and Magistrates; from fees from grants of lands and leases, and quit rents on crown lands (Quit rents ceased in 1805). Other than quit rents and crown land fees, all revenues were levied upon Colonial authority.

The following is revenue raised in 1805 (James Thomson reports that the records from 1805 to 1810 are 'imperfect')

1805 Revenues in Gaol and Orphan Funds:

Duties on Spirits	1569.11.3
Fees on Vessels, licenses	595.13.7
Ad valorem duty	531.10.3

| Fines by courts | 86.5.8 |
| Revenue raised in | 1805 2783.0.9 |

In 1810, Governor Macquarie changed the designation of these two funds to 'Police Fund' and Orphan School Fund. The designated revenues were split 3:1 into each fund. The Act 3 Geo IV c.96 of 1822 gave further powers of taxation to the Governor.

Understanding the Public Accounts of 1810-1822

In preparation for understanding the Public Accounts of the Colony as printed by the Sydney Gazette between 28th August, 1810 and the 28th November 1818, and published under the authority of the Governor (Lachlan Macquarie), we must understand firstly the nature of the two Treasurers.

The Orphan Fund, whose official nomenclature is 'The Female Orphan Institution Fund' (a successor by name—change to the Orphan & School Fund) was administered by the Reverend Samuel Marsden, an Anglican churchman, who, as an official (principal) chaplain was on the Civil List for receiving an annual stipend or salary, as well as being the principal trustee and administrator of the Orphanage, the rector of St. John's Church, Parramatta, livestock trader, a marriage celebrant, a large land and livestock owner and a pastoralist, as well as self-appointed moral censor of the Colony. Marsden was also a magistrate at Parramatta—'the hanging preacher'.

That a conflict of interest is perceived is acceptable but the nature of the accounting process allowed the distinct possibility of misappropriation of funds. For instance the orphan fund was designated as being used for the operation of the Female Orphanage within an existing building in Sydney town, with a larger building to be constructed at Parramatta. However, we find that the orphanage farm sold produce in the amount of less than 1,000 pound during seven years. Marsden also 'sold' the labour or services of orphans for 310 pound during that period, and deposited that cash as revenue to the fund, instead of either dropping fees from people having to place children in the orphanage (usually 3 pound per head) or giving the money (or its equivalent in goods) to the Orphans themselves.

The governor shared the import duties between the two funds so that the Orphan Fund received 17,649 pound and the Police Fund received 77,600 in funds or bills receivable during this period.

But Marsden acted with impunity in expending over 1,000 pound on expenses, repairs and improvements to St. John's church. At least this amount was recorded.

The frightening thought is that some of the higher, unexplained expenditures could well have been going into the Marsden personal fund and assisting with the expenses of operating his 4,000 head herd of sheep and cattle or of paying farm expenses for his 4,500 acres. The small 30-acre farm attached to the Orphanage cost 1,268 pound to run for seven years so it is reasonable to expect that Marsden's broad acres were costing a goodly amount to operate. His stipend of 150 pound per annum would not have stretched to paying farm expenses, especially with a wife and 5 children, 5 servants and 10 'assigned' convicts. He eventually became the largest sheep owner before 1819.

Without proper authorisation, the new orphanage building had cost 4,000 pound to construct. The original estimate to Macquarie (HRNSW) was 500 pound. This is just another example of Macquarie's extravagance, which could not be reined in, not even by Lord Bathurst. It demonstrates the deviousness that Marsden could show when he craved something badly enough.

It is questionable, as well, that the 45 orphans housed in the original buildings could consume a monthly average food bill, for meat (of 70 pound) or of flour (of over 50 pound). With meat selling at about or below 6d per lb, the supposed quantity of meat was unmanageable, in infants. It is possible that during the period, the butcher was being paid for extra sheep on the hoof going to the Marsden farm. The amount of firewood purchased was 278 pound, regardless of the available wood on the orphanage farm and the surplus labour available to the farm. Shoes and clothing, in the amount of 600 pound during the period from 1825, for the orphans suggests frequent new clothing items, whilst the monthly 'donation' to the orphanage matron of 5 pound made her the highest paid female in the Colony.

There were five 'charity' schools operating until Macquarie decided to bring them under the umbrella of the governor, leave the administration to Marsden but now using paid and supervised teachers and other staff. These schools paid over 2,000 pound in salaries to its staff plus a further 187-pound in school supplies, books during the period.

Darcy Wentworth's fiduciary responsibilities, as Treasurer of the Police Fund were marginally better but this is mainly due to his handling over 120,000 pound during his eight years as Treasurer. His areas of revenue raising were hotel and spirit licences, road tolls (mainly Sydney to Parramatta), auction and marketing licences, and the bulk of import duties.

Wentworth also had ample opportunity to salt some revenues away to his own use, although in the main his financial statements did not contain too many arithmetic errors. His main areas of expenditure were repair work and new work on the many streets and roads within the Sydney and Parramatta areas.

Wentworth was the Treasurer of the Police Fund as well as a Police Magistrate for the town, and the 'Commissioner' of Police, it was not surprising to find that all of his repair work was carried out by soldiers and police officers. The recapturing of escaped convicts was paid for handsomely and Wentworth again made most of these payments to police officers and soldiers. It may be questioned whether they were being paid more to guard to convicts or to re-catch them, after they escaped. So, if 'trading' was not the military people's forte, Wentworth remunerated them well with extra pay for services and assistance from within his bailiwick. Road repairs and minor new construction came to over 15,000 pound whilst new wharves came to 2,000 pound. His largest single item was for salaries to those many people not on the civil list. This amounted to over 53,000 pound during the period

For full details of revenue and expenditure of these two funds between 1810 and 1821, refer to the appropriate table of statistics, in the appendix.

The Funds available to Wentworth and the Governor from the Police Fund, at the end of 1818 was nearly 17,000 pound. This amount was directed (by Macquarie in 1818) to be placed on deposit in the new Bank of New South Wales.

Macquarie's policy's of improving the Colonial operations did work, as can be seen from the 'investment', from Wentworth's account, in new buildings and other contract work of over 25,000 pound.

In terms of revenue, the Colony increased its costs of living by over 173,000 pound in just 7 years. In terms of pounds per head per year, it is estimated that amount is equivalent to at an impost of nearly two pound per head per year of additional duty, tolls, fees etc.

That Macquarie's successor, Sir Thomas Brisbane, as well as Commissioner Bigge, demanded full, proper and regularised accounting of all revenue and expenditures is reflected in the transfer to the 'Blue Book' system in 1822 and the appointment of a full-time salaried financial officer, for the Colony, in the same year.

THE ROLE OF THE COMMISSARY

(In The Operations of the Colonial Government)

Planning for a Commissary for the new Penal Colony was well under-way by the 1795, and was to be operated and managed along the lines of a naval purser's office. The Commissary was to be responsible for all purchasing, storage, payment and distribution of goods. Its purpose was to provision the convicts, civil employees, the military personnel, and their families.

However for a new colony which had decided not to adopt a currency, the Commissaries role was made especially challenging. A currency is the traditional means of exchange. There would be no buildings initially available and only convict labour to work the stores in Sydney, Parramatta and the Hawkesbury area—'always unreliable and untrustworthy', said John Palmer the third Commissary.

The first supply ships arrived with the rest of the first fleet on the 26th January, 1788 in Port Jackson. The unloading of bare essentials, such as tents and a few tools and minimal food was completed that day, but the balance of the supplies would be left aboard the Sirius and the Golden Grove until a storehouse was available.

Every carpenter available was busy with the building of barracks for the soldiers and military personnel, followed by a facility for the Governor and only then a storehouse. But first the land had to be cleared of trees and timber cut for the first makeshift buildings.

The first Commissary, Andrew Miller, had been hand picked by Governor Arthur Phillip, based on Phillip's past experience with Miller(as a seaman), rather than Miller's experience as a Commissary chief. Phillip had provided detailed instructions of how he wanted the operation performed. Phillip, in turn, had been given his instructions by the Lords of the Admiralty and the Colonial Secretary, and the most important of these were the overall goals:

- keep the cost per head per day for supplies as low as possible
- keep the number of fully victualled persons as low as possible
- establish the Colony to be self-supporting as quickly as possible
- put the convicts out to work to earn their keep (although this was a new and untried policy)
- assign convicts to non-government masters on a full support basis (again, this policy was untried and untested—but one strongly supported by Phillip)

Phillip had transported the first One thousand convicts and military without loss of life or loss of property. He had brought the first animals for breeding into the Colony, all healthy and was assigning duties by the 28th January 1788 (2 days after arrival in Port Jackson or Sydney Harbour) for the general unloading of the animals, convicts and material supplies ready to commence his Colonial operations.

Convicts were set to clearing the ground for vegetable plantings and building sites.

Phillip decided that instead of relying on stores transported on an irregular basis from Britain, that he would commence a planting program to provide fresh vegetables and grain; fresh meat, fish and game and make it a happy colony in which to live and work. He did not plan, nor was prepared for the harsh climate and the periodic droughts and flooding rains, or the unhappy natives.

His goal of victualling the whole Colony for less than 14p per day was going to be difficult, but he could do it if some level of self—support could be accomplished. He had brought quantities of seed for planting, but his fears were that northern hemisphere soils and climate would be very different from local 'New Holland' conditions and his crops would fail or yields would be minimal. His first corn crop, however, returned his planting twenty times over (HRNSW), and he was pleased and hopeful of the future returns being plentiful. In fact, he wrote to the Lord Commissioners stating that 'this Colony will become the greatest investment ever made by the British'.

Phillip planned for other possible ways to reduce costs; such as reducing imports, commence an export trade, establish settlers on farming ground, establish remote settlements, establish jobs and trades and build the necessities and Phillip thus went about his work, putting these plans into practice. He assumed, incorrectly, that the convicts and the military shared his enthusiasm and commitment to hard work.

However, his experiment with tobacco planting, and grains, other than corn and wheat, and even sugar was encouragingly successful.

He planned for another new settlement at the head of the harbour, near fresh water, and with boat access at high tide. Rose Hill, soon to become Parramatta, was to be established with convict and military quarters, a church, and some emancipist settlers. To this end he released convicts for good conduct, who were willing to marry, and provided them grants of good land, usually 30 acres, and an admonition to become self contained and sell their surplus to the Commissariat store. He did allow the emancipists to retain access to the Government store for a period of two years. He would, in the future, exchange settler's grain for Government—owned cows, to enable a breeding program to commence and further expand the likelihood of a successful colony.

His building and construction priorities changed. He saw the priority need for a hospital building, especially since he had a surgeon in his midst, and some of his convicts had been speared and even killed by the natives. So the barracks were completed and then the hospital and finally the storehouse was ready by early April 1789. Phillip wrote in his journal that 'the timber has one very bad quality, which puts us to great inconvenience; I mean the large gum tree, which warps and splits in such a manner, when used green, to which necessity obliges us, that a storehouse boarded up in this wood is rendered useless' (HRNSW)

David Collins, a military Lieutenant and Phillip's Private Secretary, wrote on the 5th April, 1788, 'As the winter of this hemisphere is approaching, it becomes absolutely necessary to expedite the buildings intended for the detachment, so, every carpenter that could be procured amongst the convicts was sent to assist, since as many as could be released from the transports were employed working on the hospital and storehouses.'

Collins recorded on the following day, the 6th April, 1788 'worship was moved indoors as divine service was performed in the new storehouse. One hundred feet by twenty-five feet were the dimensions of the building, constructed with great strength and covered in with thatching. But we were always mindful of fire since no other materials could be found and we became mindful of accidental fire.'

Obviously, the hospital was finished, the storehouse was complete, some female convict huts had been completed and the military barracks were well under way. Phillip's plan was now in full swing.

This first and temporary storehouse was built somewhere around the Sydney cove (at the top end of High Street, now George Street), where a landing wharf had been constructed and where the camp was getting into working order. Subsequently permanent storehouses were built nearer the hospital, using roof tiles instead of thatching, and connected from the landing area to the hospital past the storehouses via a convict constructed 'road'.

Andrew Miller, the first Commissary, grew sick and frail (during 1788), in the service of Phillip and asked to be returned to England. He died on route but was replaced as Commissary by his former assistant, Zachariah Clark, who had come from England originally as agent to Mr Richards the shipping contractor.

Collins reported on the 12th April,. 1788 that the 'issuing of provisions, was in future, under Mr Clark, to be once a week.'

Lieutenant John Hunter, soon to be Lieutenant Governor of Norfolk Island, recorded in his diary for 5th September 1788, that 'because of some failed crops, rotting food, and a plague of rats in the storehouse, that the colony would need more stores and provisions than any Pacific island could supply, and he would dispatch the Sirius to the Cape of Good Hope, in order to purchase such quantity of provisions as she might be capable of taking on board; and that she should be made as light as possible for that purpose. In consequence, eight guns and their carriages were removed together with 24 rounds of shot for each gun, 20 barrels of powder, a spare anchor and various other articles. These were all put on shore at Sydney Cove. I was also directed to leave the long boat behind for use by the Colony. The master of the Golden Grove store-ship was also ordered to get ready for sea to take supplies, convicts and some military personnel to Norfolk Island.'

Phillip was obviously panicking about the shortage of supplies and the empty storehouse. The proposed settlements at Rose Hill and Norfolk Island and a ship to the Cape had almost emptied the first settlement at Sydney Cove, of people as well as provisions.

A number of storehouses had been established. The first, a temporary one at the Cove, now the permanent one near the hospital on the first Sydney town street—High Street (now George Street), the lumber yard store, the military detachment store and the naval store. Clarke was nominally in charge of all stores but was also assigned other duties with the Governor, and with the hope of cutting rations even further by only opening the regular store once each week, was obviously in charge of only empty buildings.

In October, 1788, Warwick Tench observed, in his diary that 'we have now been here over half a year and are becoming acclimatised, even if we lack the shelters thought necessary. Since our disembarkation in January, the efforts every one has made was to put the public stores into a state of shelter and security and to erect habitations for the hospital, convicts and ourselves. We are eager to escape from tents, where only a fold of canvas was between us and the hot beams of the summer sun and the chilling blasts of the winter wind from the south. Under wretched covers of thatch lay our provisions and stores, exposed to destruction from every flash of lightning and every spark of fire. A few of the female convicts had got into huts but almost all of the officers and all the men, were still in tents.'

In February, 1789, the only free immigrant, James Smith, who had procured a passage from England on the Lady Penrhyn was placed in charge of the new storehouse at Rose Hill and was also sworn in as a peace officer, or special constable. Claiming to be a 'practical farmer', Phillip gave him a number of convicts to assist him in exercising his abilities. This was the first trial of the assigned convict system.

On the 18th March, 1789, Collins recorded the first major theft of stores and provisions from the secured commissary. There were seven of the military convicted of theft undertaken over a period of some weeks, robbing the store of liquor and large quantities of provisions. Phillip made an example of these men, but to little avail, as later that same year another six soldiers were convicted and hung for doing exactly the same thing.

The Economic Role of the Commissary

Over time Phillip increased and improved the operations of the Commissary and planned to offset the effect of having no currency in the Colony by creating a barter economy. To aid in this plan, Phillip arranged that all goods received into the Commissary would be recognised and accepted by 'store receipts'. Payment for goods arriving by ship or purchases made from other ports and brought to Sydney town was done via official 'bills' drawn for payment upon presentation on the British Treasury,.

By 1790 store receipts and the related official government bills formed the basis of the currency in the colony. The settlers would lodge their grain, wool, or meat with the store and receive an official receipt in exchange.

The receipt stated the recipients name, type and quantity of goods and the price paid. Because they were backed by the Government, the receipts became an increasingly popular instrument of exchange. They could be transferred between parties in payment for a debt, exchanged amongst settlers in the course of trade and for products from the Government stores, redeemed for the equivalent in coin and banknotes, and through the commissariat, exchanged for government bills drawn on the English Treasury". Eventually when colonial banks became established, store receipts and government bills were accepted as deposits. In these early days, a store receipt was as good as cash and for many people, a lot more convenient." (Encyclopaedia of Australia)

The Final Volume (# 7) of Historical Records of Victoria (Vol 7-Public Finance) sets out some background of what was happening in New South Wales whilst Victoria was still part of the Port Phillip colony.

"New South Wales was one of only three of the Empire's colonies established at the expense of British taxpayers. Most British colonies were begun by trading companies or settlement associations, and were expected to be self-sufficient. The British Government was usually prepared to provide a civil administration and military protection, but wherever possible, these were to be funded from local sources. The commissariat was responsible for many of the early financial arrangements in New South Wales. From the beginning, practices had been highly unsatisfactory and allowed much corruption. The first fleet brought with it in 1788 only the most meagre of supplies of coin. This shortage of a circulating currency became increasingly acute. In the short term, the government used promissory notes, government store receipts, treasury bills, spirits and shipments of coins of various denominations and currencies to which varying values were assigned. All were part of a volatile and unstable money market."

Britain had, prior to the first fleet invoked its right to tax its dependencies. The loss in the 1770s of its valuable American colonies, the previous dumping ground for convicts, was directly attributable to these taxes. The Napoleonic Wars (1793-1815) almost beggared Britain, and ruthless experiments with new taxes and duties was tried in a desperate effort to meet national debts. Income tax was introduced in 1798, modified in 1805 and 1807 but discontinued in 1816. The unpopularity of direct taxation resulted in wider nets of indirect taxation, such as customs duties. The New South Wales experiment echoed some of these developments. But it became Governor Gipps' opinion (1838-46) that nowhere else was so large a revenue raised from so small a population." And this opinion is born out by the official Treasury reports of the time (refer attached Statistics).

Marjorie Barnard in her fine work—'A History of Australia' (P327) reflects on the early workings of the commissary and the financial dealings it accommodated.

"The commissariat had charge under the Governor of all stores and provisions. It acquired locally produced supplies, but the importation of food, clothing and other necessities from overseas was the responsibility of the home office, or in emergency, of the governor.

The commissariat was the colony's store and it also became the financial centre of the colony, where all transactions were by barter or note of hand. The only note in which there could be universal faith was that issued by the commissary as a receipt for goods received into the store. This department was the quasi-treasury, so that when a colonial treasury was set up, the commissary remained for provisioning of the convicts and only withered away at the end of transportation. Large sums could only be paid by the commissary's notes, for these alone had credit behind them, and they had to be eventually redeemed by bills on the treasury."

R. M. Younger in his work 'Australia & The Australians—'

writes (P78) "The only market for produce was the government store in the various farming districts, run by the commissariat under the ultimate control of the superintendent of public works. The governor fixed the price of grain, and it was left to the storekeepers to decide whose grain should be bought and whose refused. David Collins, former secretary to Governor Phillip wrote of this operation:

> 'The delivery of grain into the public storehouses when open for that purpose was so completely monopolised that the settlers had but few opportunities of getting full value for their crops.

> The ordinary settler found himself thrust out from the granary
> by the a man whose greater opulence created greater influence.
> He was then driven by necessity to dispose of his grain at less
> than half its value. He was forced to sell it to the very man who
> had first driven him away and now whose influence was the
> only available way to get the grain into the public store.'

Such incident evidenced a fundamental weakness in the economy. Farming had to be expanded so that the community could become self supporting; but since the demand was in fact small and inelastic, and since there was no export, a glut or a shortage could easily occur. Because of strictly limited demand the wheat acreage could not be expanded too greatly, yet when two bad years occurred, there were dangerous shortages, and the colony had to revert to imports.

The commissary store continued to be the centre of the colony's economy. A great number of the population were still victualled from the store; these included the military and civil list people and their families, together with settlers receiving land grants, whether expirees or free, for the first two years on the farm. And convicts unassigned or working for the government. The requirement that the military officers clothe, feed and house assigned convicts was not strictly enforced and so in 1800 Hunter's record must show that 75% of the population was victualled by the government."

The anomaly was that by 1813 a few Sydney merchants were exporting, even though the NSW Corps still dominated local business. Exporting had begun in 1801 with Simon Lord, selling coal, whale oil and seal-skins to the American boats visiting Sydney for the purpose of two-way trade; they brought moderately priced cargo for general sale as well as provisions and supplies for the commissary. Campbell, the biggest trader got around the British support of the East India Company having a trade monopoly with China by using French or American ships. Campbell had built a warehouse in 1800 supplying wine, spirits, sugar, tea, coffee and tobacco and a wide range of household articles However Campbell was additionally soon selling livestock, grain and merchandise to the commissary and private buyers, with the government spending several thousand pounds with his firm each year. He then entered the whaling and sealing trade and sent a trial shipment of each to England. This caused a dispute between the East

India company on one side(pushing for exclusion), Sir Joseph Banks on the other (encouraging freedom of trade)and Simon Lord, whose cargo had now been seized in Britain as contraband."

One of the charges made to Justice Bigge when he was sent to Australia to investigate and report on the Macquarie governorship, was to review the cost of operating the colony in terms of its original charter. It was of great concern to Lord Bathurst that the British Treasury in 1820 was still paying so much of the colonial operations.

So Bigge reviewed and commented on the high number of persons still victualled from the government store as late as 1823. An extract from his third report (dated January 1823) into 'The Nature of the Expenditure in the Colony' sets out his observations.

He writes that in 1821 the Civil list salaries amounted to 8,474.17.6 but those paid from local revenues, being the 'Police Fund'_amounted to 9,824.05.0. So it is confirmed that within 22 years of the Colony being established, it was substantially on course to paying its own way. In fact Bigge writes, that "some of the salaries included in the parliamentary estimate (the Civil List) have not been drawn in this, or in some of the preceding years but have been defrayed by the police fund of NSW, including two government school masters, six superintendents and the clerk to the judge advocate, all amounting to 500 pound.

The clerks in the commissariat generally consist of persons who have been convicts and also of persons who are still in that condition (being ticket-of-leave individuals) They are paid variously from 18d to 60 d per day, plus lodging money. They also receive the full ration. And a weekly allowance of spirits. Bigge recommended that to reduce the fraud on the commissary, along with the high cost to the public purse, that (a) all bread be baked by a variety of contractors in lieu of convicts, and (b) that contracts for the supply of hospitals with bread, meat and vegetables be also let. He likewise recommended that all meat to the King's stores be furnished by contract from the settlers at the price of 5d per lb. He reports that the number of provisioned convicts is constantly changing. For instance, the total number of people provisioned from the Sydney store on 30ᵗʰ December,1820, was 9326, of which only 5135 were convicts unassigned."

Author's Note: As can be seen from the following table, the number of victualled convicts (and others) is surprisingly high, especially at the end of the last two periods (1810 & 1820). The Governor's were directed to assign convicts to settlers or military officers for assistance with farming operations; the intention was for the colony to supply its own provisions and stores. The settlers and officers were directed to house, clothe and feed all assigned convicts and take them off the public stores. However, by virtue of being in a special position in the colony, most civil list persons and military were still being supported by the public stores. Even emancipists or free settlers that carried out special duties (eg police constables) became entitled to support from the stores.

Number of people on Rations (number victualled from public store) between 1795 and 1820 were:

1795	1,775
1793	1,682
1799	1,832
1800	3,545
1804	2,647
1810	5,772
1820	9,326

(compiled from individual records in vols 1-7 HRNSW)

As Bigge's concluded "some rations were issued in higher allowance than decreed because of extra work or hard labour.

Government owned livestock is held at the Cow Pastures, Parramatta and Emu Plains. These facilities are operated by a Superintendent and 3 oversees, all paid by the police fund. In addition 75 convicts are employed as stockmen and general labourers. All these people in total draw 122 daily rations from the public stores. The cost of daily rations were estimated by Bigge at 4s 8d or 56 pound per annum, or nearly 4 (four) times the targeted cost.

There were also 451 head of wild cattle which had over the previous year run off from the holding areas, but were recovered in 1820 and used for public meat supply. In total, with slaughtered sheep and cattle from government herds, over 237,000 lb of fresh meat was supplied at a savings of 5,000 pound to the government. This still left 6,000 animals in the government herd, but the settlers were increasing their pressure on the Governor to buy only meat from the settlers and not use government herds for slaughtering.

Of the total colonial expenditure in 1820 of 189,008 pound, the cost of rations for troops, civil list and convicts amounted to 143,370 or 75%. Bigge did report that the general expense of erecting buildings in the Macquarie years in the colony of New South Wales is lessened by the use of convict labour and locally found timbers and locally made bricks, tiles and stone. He suggested that the cost of local funds used for buildings would be better spent on clothing, and feeding the convicts and taking them off the public stores.

Reviewing the Official Records on the Commissary

The HRNSW contains numerous references to original records reporting the instructions on how to operate, or the anecdotal reports on how the commissariat operated.

Phillip wrote that 'It is planned that a quantity of provisions equal to two years consumption should be provided (written 1786), which will be issued from time to time, according to the discretion of the Superintendent, guided by the proportion of food which the country and the labour of the new settlers may produce.'

'Clothing per convict was estimated to cost 2.19.6 including jackets, hats, shirts, trousers, shoes'. Phillip further wrote that 'the type of clothing was not always suitable for the climate, and should be ready made rather than relying on the convicts to sew their own.'

He noted that 'The Sirius brought seed wheat and barley and four months supply of flour for the settlement, together with a year's provisions for the ships company,'

and, 'Supplies of grain or flour from England will be necessary to maintain the colony until there is sufficient local crops in store rather than 'in the ground', because of grub, fire, drought and other accidents.'

and 'I have directed the commissary to make a purchase (9th January, 1793) and have thus augmented the quantity of provisions in the colony to 7 months at the established ration.'

On 6th January 1793, Phillip recorded his opinion that the expense for the settlement projected for 1794 was 25913 for 5,500 person. With 3000 convicts this cost translated into a per head cost per annum of 13.14.0,(or approx. 9p per day) which he pointed out 'this sum cannot increase, but must gradually diminish.' This converted within the officially targeted allowance of 14p per head per day.

'Whitehall reported on 9th November 1794 that the stock of stores of provisions and ready-made clothing should now be sufficient for the settlement for one year.

With the quantity of clothing shipped in mid—1794, there would be a sufficient supply for 2,500 men and 700 women, according to the last official report of numbers.' Mr. Henry Dundas (British MP) insisted that the convicts should be made to wear the clothing for a full year.'

The Colonial Office insisted that 'Each ship was to carry supplies for the trip and for maintenance upon arrival, for both convicts soldiers and sailers.' (15th February, 1794)

King, as Governor of Norfolk Island on the 20th July 1794, recorded that the island had produced a second crop in sufficient quantity for storage for the next year.—being 11500 bushels + 4000 reserved for seed, stock, and the producing families.'

'Stores were ordered from the Cape of Good Hope for the settlement and the hospital on 22nd June, 1788 to be selected by John Hunter, as captain of the Sirius.

Governor Hunter submitted a plan on 10th June, 1797 saying that "were Government to establish a public store for the retail sale of a variety of articles—such as clothing, or materials for clothing, hardware, tools, sugar, soap, tea, tobacco and every article that labouring people require—supported by a reputable shopkeeper who should produce regular accounts and charge a small premium to cover these other costs, then the people would get what they wanted with easer, and at far less expense than in any other way."

Governor Hunter repeated his request for a public store on 10th January, 1798 "If my suggestion is adopted, a branch of the store should be placed on Norfolk Island. Such a store should lessen the expense of maintaining the convicts and into the store, I would also suggest the retailing of liquor and spirits, for the purpose of putting a stop to the importation of that article."

Again on the 25th May, 1798 Hunter recommended "the public store as a means of controlling the high price of grain. Such a store would operate as an encouragement to industry. Without some form of price control on grain the settlers cannot live let alone provide for a family The speculators and the monopolists all contrive to keep the settlers in a continual state of beggary and retard the progressive improvements of the colony." The success of Simon Lord's colonial merchandising in 1801 evidences that Hunter was on the right track with his 'public' store.

The Colonial Secretary wrote to Hunter in 3rd December, 1798 about the meat supply "when the livestock belonging to the crown, added to that of individuals, is in so flourishing a state as to supply the needs at 6d a pound or less, it is evident the Government will gain by supplying the settlement with fresh meat instead of sending salted provisions from England. This request was later modified to limit the store purchases for meat to those from farm settlers.

On 2nd February, 1800, William Broughton, a Churchman and Magistrate was also appointed to be the storekeeper at Parramatta to replace a man sacked by Hunter for fraud.

Governor King recorded his success in conserving the stores by writing that "since I took office, I have reduced the full rationed people relying on the public stores by 450. This has saved annually the amount of 10488 pound using the rate of 23 pound per head. I have also reduced the price of wheat to 8d per bushel, pork to 6p per lb, maize to 4s instead of 5s per bushel."

When Hunter was recalled to England, the Commissary was left with many debts owing by settlers. Hunter was concerned that these would be denied and he be held responsible. He wrote to the new Governor, King, 'I trust it is clear that there has been no lavish waste, and no improvident use of the public stores during my authority. These debts are just, even though many of the individuals may doubt their being indebted to the Government for so much. "It appears there were doubtful debts of over 5,000 pound due to the store.

In response King made demand on the settlers and accepted grain at a higher price than usual in settlement of the debt. When the public demands became known it also produced an unusual response from John Macarthur, who suddenly recalled that much of what he had taken from the stores, and charged against the public account, over the previous twelve months was in fact his personal responsibility and he settled with the stores on this basis.

King appointed a new head of the store on 7th November, 1800-A Mr Palmer. Other appointments included Broughton to Norfolk Island and Deputy Chapman from Norfolk to Sydney and William Sutter as Storekeeper at Parramatta.

In order to conserve grain, King reduced the ration to 13.5 lb of wheat per week per person.

Palmer, at the time of his appointment had been handed a set of instructions, which included the instruction that:

    a.   all troops and convicts in the territory were to be properly supplied and a stock of 12 months supply to be kept at the store.
    b.   transmit annually a list of expected consumption.

c. purchases were to be made under the authority of the Governor and prices paid to be no greater than market prices

d. all bills of exchange must be accompanied with an affidavit of purchase countersigned by the Governor

e. you will make receipts for all payments in the presence of at least one witness—preferably a magistrate—and make three sets of all vouchers, one for the treasury, one with the accounts and one for the store use.

f. keep a separate account of all items transmitted from England.

g. make a survey of any stores lost or damaged—which goods are to be sold or destroyed at the Governors discretion.

h. Make up annually an account of all receipts and expenditures, accompanied by one set of vouchers.

i. You are responsible for the preservation of all stores and provisions and the employees who work for you, and to the public.

A set of notes on how the commissary should operate was prepared by the Duke of Portland and handed to Governor-in Chief Phillip Gidley King on 28th September 1800. These notes are attached for historical purposes.

OFFICIAL INSTRUCTIONS FOR THE COMMISSARY—28th September, 1800

Instructions to the Commissary by Captain Philip Gidley King, Governor-in-Chief, &c., in and over His Majesty's territory of New South Wales and its Dependencies, 28th September, 1800.

In consequence of my instructions, you are hereby required to conform to the following directions for your conduct:-

1st. You are to be present yourself as much as possible, and control the receipt and issue of all stores and provisions into and from His Majesty's stores; and as you are answerable for the conduct of those under you and about the different stores, if you should have any cause to be dissatisfied with their conduct in discharge of their duty you are to report the same to me, when a proper notice will be taken thereof.

2nd. You are not to receive or issue any articles whatever, either public or purchased, into or from the stores, but by a written order from me, delivering me an account thereof, on the receipt or issue having taken place, taking care to comply with all such general orders as I may judge necessary respecting your department.

3rd. When any grain or animal food raised by those at government work, or received from England or elsewhere, is delivered into your charge, you are to furnish me with a particular receipt for it, specifying the place and person you received it from, charging yourself with it as provisions received for the public use, and to observe the same with respect to all stores belonging to the Crown, and to deliver the quarterly accounts of the expenditure and the remains thereof, or oftener, if required.

4th. When there is not a sufficiency of grain and animal food raised by the convicts at public labour for the use of those necessarily maintained by the Crown, and that it becomes necessary to purchase the deficit required from the settlers, you are to give me an account of the quantity that may be absolutely necessary weekly, or at a stated period, but not to require more gain at a time than can be kept from the weevil. After my approval thereof, and the price at which such articles are to be purchased is fixed, you are to give public notice thereof, and open a list at the different settlements for the insertion of those persons' names who can spare any quantities of the articles required from the reserve necessary for seed and their own use; such persons being freemen, possessed of ground are known cultivators, are to be regularly entered on the list in preference to any other description of persons, as they offer themselves, and their required produce to be received in the stores without any preference or partiality. The grain thus purchased is to be measured at such times as I may direct in front of the storehouse, and from thence lodged in the store in the presence of a superintendent and another creditable person. When the receipt is ended for the day, a return thereof it to be made the next morning to me, specifying the person's name and quality from whom it is received, the superintendent and other witnesses attesting the same, one or both of whom are to sign their names to the witness column in the voucher when payment is made.

5th Being particularly directed to reform the irregularity that has existed in the mode hitherto followed in making payment for such articles as have been purchased from the inhabitants for the public use, the persons who take your printed receipts, audited by me, for their respective produce being lodged in the stores, may transfer them from one to another for their accommodation; all such receipts to be called in as often as I may judge proper, when payment will be made by me of all outstanding receipts by a bill on His Majesty's Treasury for the amount of such receipts as may be in the hands of individuals, such bills not to be drawn for less than (Pounds) 100, and the vouchers in support thereof to be verified by liquidating your receipts in rotation. And whenever such payments are made you are to take care that five complete sets of vouchers with their documents, agreeable to the annexed form, be prepared to be signed before me at the time of payment being made, which I am directed to control and superintend.

6th. When it is absolutely necessary for any stores, clothing or provisions being purchased from masters of ships, or other strangers, after the price is regulated by two proper persons on the part of Government, and the same on the part of the proprietors, the Commissary will be ordered to receive such articles into the stores in the presence of two respectable witnesses, who are to sign the vouchers, two of which are to be delivered to me, with the proprietor's receipt for the payment, witnessed by two other respectable persons.

7th. As I am directed to forward my account current, made up to the 10th of October annually, with the Right Honourable the Lords Commissioners of His Majesty's Treasury, to the Inspector General of Public Accounts, under cover to His Majesty's Principal Secretary of State for the Home Department, you are therefore not to fail in delivering to me, on or before the 10th day of October, for my inspection and auditing, the following books and papers in support of your account current with the Lords Commissioners of His Majesty's Treasury, together with the surgeon's account of the expenditure of stores and necessaries received from you, in order that those accounts may be sent with mine by the first opportunity after the above date, viz.:-

First—A census book, containing each man, woman, and child's name that has received any provisions from the stores during the year, distinguishing those in the different rations.

Second—A clothing and slop expense book, for those supported by the Crown, expressing as above.

Third—A book specifying the receipts of stores, provisions, and clothing from England or elsewhere, belonging to the Crown, also the quarterly expense thereof, and remains at the time of making up the public accounts, which is to be distinctly stated and carried over the next year's account, as a charge.

Fourth—A book of the particular expense, and the application of the above described provisions and clothing issued by you during the year, to those supported by the Corn, also another book stating the expense and application of the above described stores issued by you for the use of the public, and signed relatively by the superintendent, overseer, or other person to whom they have been delivered.

Fifth.—A store purchasing book, specifying the different quantities of grain and animal food bought from settlers, &c., noting the time of purchase, quantity and application thereof, with a reference to the proper vouchers in support of the receipt and payment, which documents are to be annexed to this book.

Sixth._ A similar book to the above, specifying the different quantities of stores, &c., purchased from masters of ships, or other strangers, verified by proper vouchers, &c., as last above, to which book you are to annex the general expenditure thereof and remains at the time of making up the public accounts, which is to be distinctly stated; and carried over to the next year's account as a charge. At the end of this book you are to insert whether such articles have been paid for in grain, meat, or money, and to debit yourself accordingly, either in your account current of cash, or store account, and to charge yourself in the same manner with any other payment made to you on behalf of the Crown.

Seventh.—A list of all births, deaths, and absentees during the year.

You are not to fail (on peril of being subject to an exchequer process) in delivering me for my examination all the above books and papers, with every other explanatory document, on the thirty-first day of October, annually, which accounts you are to attest before me previous to my transmitting them to England and you carefully to preserve correct copies thereof, in case of any accident happening to those sent to England. You are to keep an open list in your office, containing the names of each class of people in the colony, according to the form you are provided with, in which you are to make regular entries and discharges as they occur.

Eighth.—Exclusive of the above papers, when any ship is going from hence to England, you are to furnish me with a general return of the inhabitants, according to the annexed form, also a return of the expenditure and remains of Government stock.

Ninth.—The issue of provisions is to be attended by a superintendent, or principal overseer, and a non-commissioned officer, for the purpose of detecting and reporting any improper proceedings; but no report will be attended to that is not made on the day of the issue. A weekly victual and store-issue book are to be kept at each store by the person who has charge of it. No person whatever is to be put on or off the store but by a written note from me, or by a note from the person who has the superintendence of the district where the stores are. The master carpenter, and every other description of persons that has charge of the workmen supplied with materials from the different stores for the public use, as well as such individuals as are allowed to receive that indulgence, are to apply for the orders on Monday mornings, and to give receipts for the same to the Commissary, delivery an account of the expense thereof to me weekly. By this regulation, the necessity of persons frequenting the stores on the intermediate days between stores and victual issue will be prevented, and the stores properly appropriated. The different storekeepers are to deliver you a weekly return of their expenditure and remains, keeping the same ready for my inspection when required, and you are to furnish me with a quarterly return of Government stock, charging yourself with any that may be killed and issued as a ration, accounting for it under the head of provisions raised by those at public labour. And as it is necessary the Deputy-Commissaries and storekeepers at detached places should be supplied with regular directions how they are to conduct themselves, you

are to furnish them with such parts of these Regulations as relate to their duty, and you are to direct them to deliver their returns and receipts to me, if I should be on the spot, or to the officer who has the direction of the public concerns in the district where they are stationed.

Philip Gidley King

In addition to the above instructions, the Commissary will give directions to the Deputy-Commissary and storekeeper to obey all such directions as they may from time to time receive from the Reverend Mr Marsden, at Parramatta, and Charles Grimes, Esq., at Hawkesbury, reporting to him all such orders on the day they send their weekly returns.

THE WORKING OF THE FUNDS 1800-1810

There were numerous 'funds' probably supported by accounts with the Bank of New South Wales from 1818, when the surplus balance of the Orphan Fund was ordered to be placed on deposit with the Bank of New South Wales. This was followed by the Military Chest, the Land Fund, the Commissariat Fund and many others, all of which were probably raised to simplify accounting recording and reporting—a Bank account can be used to greatly simplify accounting records.

a. The Police Fund is intended to cover the expense of all items relating to the goal and police, and replace the gaol fund but is entirely distinct from the female orphan fund. (from a dispatch by Governor Macquarie 31.03.1810 and effective 1st April, 1810

b. ¾ ths of all the duties and customs collected in the port and Town of Sydney are to be paid into the Police Fund. The remaining 1/4th to be paid to the Orphan Fund, which will be necessary to defray the expenses of that institution.

c. Liquor Licenses to be paid to the Police Fund. D'Arcy Wentworth to be Treasurer of Police Fund. Quarterly accounts for both funds to be completed, inspected and published.

d. The naval officer, previously responsible for collecting customs and duties to settle his accounts by the 31st May, 1810

e. John Palmer to close up and settle all accounts for the commissary and pass over control to his deputy William Broughton until Palmer's return from England

f. Samuel Marsden to be treasurer of the orphan fund

On 30th April, 1810, Macquarie wrote to Castlereagh concerning the two funds

Previously all duties and customs collections have been allocated to the Gaol and Orphan Funds. I have revised this practice in favour of sharing the collections between the Police—¾ ths.—and Female Orphan 1/4 th—Funds.

From the Police Fund is to be defrayed the expense of the jail and police establishments, the erection of wharves, quays, bridges and making/repairing of roads. The second fund is to cover establishment of the orphanage and other charity schools.

The Second Period 1810-20

Timothy Coghlan in 'Wealth & Progress 1900-01' (P837) writes about the Land Fund

"When in 1831 it was decided to abolish the system of free land grants, and to dispose of the public estate by auction in lieu of private tender, it was also decided that the proceeds of land sales should be paid into what was called the Land Fund, from which were to be paid the charges incidental to the introduction of immigrants; and it was from the inability of the Land Fund to meet these charges that the public debt of NSW first had its rise. From 1831 to 1834 the Land Fund was sufficient, but in 1841 the engagements for immigration purposes were so heavy that it became necessary to supplement the fund in some way and it was decided to borrow against the security of the Land Revenue. On 28th December 1841 a debenture loan of 49,000 pound was offered in the colony through the Sydney Gazette, the first loan raised in any colony.

Sundry Funds 1864

From "The Epitome of History of NSW" P409, the Government Printer reports that:

"The deficiency for 1864 was 407,626.7.11 of which, the sum of 357,408 had been already paid with funds borrowed from accounts as follows:

- Treasury Bills 30,948.1.11
- 1865 revenue 98,714.10.8
- Bank of NSW 83,333.14.8
- Oriental Bank, Ldn 20,818.14.9
- Lodgements 92,238.16.4
- Church & School Fund 19,658.09.7
- Civil Service Super Fund 1,429.7.10
- Scab in Sheep Fund 10,267.2.10

It can be concluded from the above statement by the NSW Treasurer of 1864, that these funds were established as 'collectives' or depositories of segregated receipts and a means of trying to simplify an accounting, recording and reporting system. It is probable that the Church & School Fund, was operated by The Church & School Lands Corporation (under the Act of 1834; 'to provide for the maintenance of the police and gaol establishments of the colony, the surplus of the land revenue (land fund) and of the other casual Crown revenues had been placed at the disposal of the Council.

ON THE TRACK OF THE MANY COLONIAL FUNDS

From 1802, the first date that the Colony of New South Wales attempted to manage some of its fiscal destiny by recording certain transactions in the Colony, in the Orphan Fund or the Gaol Fund.

The Crown did not put its hand out for a share of colonial revenues until 1822, but as early as 1802, the colony applied duties and customs to imported items, as a means of raising necessary revenue to provide a small amount of independence to the Governor's operations. The first year's revenue of 900 pound did not amount to much but it was the start of something big. That revenue grew quickly to reach over 100,000 by 1829 and over 1 million pound by 1854.

The Goal & orphan Funds were shortly replaced by the Female Orphan and Police Funds sponsored by Governor Macquarie in 1810.

Later, during the 'Blue Book' period, the number of funds grew. From 1802 and the Orphan & Gaols Funds, the colonial revenue was distributed eventually through the Female Orphan & Police Funds, the 'Military Chest' Fund, The Land Fund, the Colonial Fund, and the Commissary Fund. Each with a unique role and purpose.

From an accounting viewpoint, the matter of allocating certain revenues must have caused some confusion. Thus the 'parliamentary grant to reimburse the local expenditure on the convicts' was handled by placing the revenue in a new category—"Receipts in Aid of Revenue". This was soon changed to the heading of "Revenue of the Crown".

A BANK ACCOUNT BY ANY OTHER NAME ?

The Colony was initially operated through a series of 'funds' which were simply a bank account by another name. For the first 32 years of the colonial administration, there was no 'treasury'; and so that fact, along with the administration of watching over a mere penal colony, a treasury was neither demanded or necessary. But times changed. There became a demand for immigration of free people, of both families and single women; there were the demands of the traders for a means of purchasing their wares and paying for them via an acceptable means of exchange; and then the dereliction of duty by the Marine Corps led to officer's influencing, if not controlling much of the economy of the colony, especially the Commissariat. A Treasury became essential and the first token Treasury came with the local recording of colonial revenue from customs duties and tariffs, tolls and rents. There were a number of such funds going back to 1802. The Colonial Treasury commenced in 1822 under the auspices of the Colonial Secretary and until 1827 the Colonial Treasury was the sole source of deposits of revenue and the source of expenditures. In 1827 we find the first mention of the 'Military Chest'. It is safe to assume that the successor to the Military Chest was the Land Fund whose functions, not unlike the military chest was to pool the 'revenue of the crown' raised in the colony from the sale of its 'waste 'or crown lands. We will consider the role and function of the Military Chest momentarily, but first there were a number of funds between 1802 and 1855 including:

* The Goal Fund 1802-1809
* The British Treasury 1788-1835
* The Commissariat Fund 1822-1850
* The Orphan Fund 1802-1822
* The Police Fund 1810-1822
* The Blue Book Period 1822-1857
* The Military Chest
* The Land Fund
* The Colonial Fund
* Scab on Sheep Fund
* Church & School Fund
* Civil Service Super Fund

Because these funds have never been discussed or identified in any texts, this work has been designed to uncover and discuss two of the many funds mentioned above and trace their use and activity.

It would appear from the use of these minor funds that a new accounting procedure was under-way. A simple and inexpensive recording and reporting mechanism could be maintained with a fair degree of accuracy, if separate bank accounts were used for each collection point, or each source of revenue was identified by a separate account, into which these funds could be deposited.

UNDERSTANDING THE FUNDS

a. THE MILITARY CHEST

With a name as romantic as 'the military chest', this story may be expected to unfold as a historic novel, but the 'military chest' was the first fund identified following the initiation of the 'Blue Book' period being the first formal accounts transmitted to England from the birth of the colony in 1788.

The First Period 1800-1810

Historical Records of New South Wales records that Lieutenant-Governor King wrote to The Rev'd Richard Johnson 'and others' (these others included William Balmain, John Harris, Samuel Marsden and Mrs Paterson, the wife of Major George Paterson—all being the preferred committee to oversee the proposed orphanage in Sydney) on 7th August, 1800, and reported that he had (without proper authorisation) 'made a conditional purchase of Captain Kent's dwelling house. Offices and ground, in this town for the reception and education of orphans, the number of whom, are 398 out of the 958 children accounted for at the general muster.

There was already funds available to commence the project. As King writes 'I am informed by Mr Johnson that a sum of money and some property arising from former subscriptions for the use of the orphans, and fines, remains in his hands which he will deliver to Mr Marsden, who I have requested to act as Treasurer, to the establishment I am forming.

In relation to the operation of the orphanage, King recorded that 'as this house will not hold more than 100 children, it is my intention to make an addition to the back of it which will allow for greater numbers. Planks for bedsteads is now sawing, to be paid for out of the money in hand. Another building will be commenced in Parramatta to house 200 orphans and will be paid for out of the funds for this establishment.

The accounts produced by Mr Johnson in early September 1800 showed a balance due to the Orphanage of 114.16.0 pound, plus some articles of cloth and spirits (304 gallons of brandy) taken in settlement of fines; plus repayment of a loan to the Orphans fund by Mr Balmain of 200.10.9d.

In late September 1800, Marsden informed the Committee that 196 pounds has been subscribed since the beginning of that month of which he has received 60.18.6, plus repayment of the loan to the public jail of 200.10.9.

The first licence fee of 5 guineas was received, in all totalling 517.1.9 plus the cloth and brandy on hand.

On 11th October, 1800 Marsden informed his Committee that the sum of 55.9.11 had been subscribed since the last meeting of which 17.6.0 had been paid. The amount of subscriptions paid to date was 572.11.8. Marsden also advised that the cost of building the new building in Parramatta may be as high as 2,000 pounds.

King 'ordered' in the Sydney Gazette of 10th October, 1800 the fees on entries of ships, bonds, permits, certificates and assessments to be levied by the naval officer and clerk/assessor and which revenue was to be accepted by the Orphan Fund. Further revenue for the Fund was announced by King in late October, being port fees on visiting vessels.

The Commissary fund, being in operation at this time was due monies from departing settlers, and King decided to delay the sailing of the 'Buffalo' until debts due to the commissary of 2166 pound were collected.

King also announced that by removing 450 full rationed persons from the commissary list, he would save the Government over 10,488 pound per year at 23 pound per head per annum.

After a series of bad storms on 4th,5th, and 6th June 1799 had layed flat the old wooden jail, Governor Hunter met with the settlers and proposed a new jail to be built at the expense of the colonists by voluntary subscription. He wrote to the Duke of Portland on July 10, 1799 that 'The prison I have proposed is large and substantial, built of stone and which we have abundance of fit use for it' The gaol fund was set into operation in July 1799 with 'the expense of the building being defrayed by the inhabitants of the colony. When in January 1800, Hunter was still dissatisfied with the progress being made in the construction, in no small part the responsibility of the lower than anticipated subscriptions, he directed that a levy or toll of sixpence per bushel of wheat be collected at the public store on deliveries King reported in August 1801 that the gaol was completed and the cost was 3,954 pound—it included separate sections for debtors and six strong and secure cells for condemned felons. To complete construction, the public stores or commissary provided the iron as required

The Second Period 1810-1821

Our story starts with Governor Macquarie in 1810 who, having decided that the accounting records for the colony (contained in the early gaol and Orphan Funds from 1800-1810) were, in effect, in a shambles, and did not properly reflect the fiscal condition of the colony, allocated certain local revenues to firstly the gaol fund and other revenue to the Orphan fund, each of which was to have a non-government or public citizen Trustee and Treasurer. The treasurer for the Orphan Fund was the Reverend Samuel Marsden. Marsden was known and feared for his despotic ways, and we find from his records of the fund, as reproduced in the Sydney Gazette each quarter from 1811 to 1821 that certain unusual practices were undertaken with the accounts.

D'Arcy Wentworth, the Treasurer for the Gaol Fund from 1810, which was then renamed the 'Police' Fund, also took substantial liberties and bestowed fiscal favours upon many fellow officers of the Military Corps, and supported many of the non-trading military men with road repair work, which may or may not have ever been completed at least to any acceptable quality, since month after month the same men received rather large sums for road repairs, bridge and wharf repairs.

The Third Period 1822-1838

The successor to these early privately run funds was the British Government introduction of a standard recording and reporting format called the 'Blue Books' because they were, in fact, bound in blue covers.

A search of the "List of Colonial Office Records" preserved in the Public Records Office, published by HM Stationery Office, 1911, suggests that there was no Blue Book compiled prior to 1822 nor for the year 1824. The volumes continued to be compiled until 1855 in a set of four copies; two being sent to the Colonial Office, one went to the Governor and the other to the Colonial Secretary, and from 1855 to 1857 an additional copy was placed before the Legislative Assembly (after self-government). The volumes continued to be compiled after 1857 until 1870 but were then printed instead of being written out by hand and contain much less information, usually only the returns of the Civil and Ecclesiastical Establishments.

The Blue Books were compiled retrospectively from groups of returns sent out from the Colonial Secretary's Office, which were filled in by the various officials, and then sent back to the Office.

The first reference to the 'Military Chest' was in the 1828 'Blue Books' where we find, as one item of Revenue:

- 'The amount of Revenue & Receipts derived from local resources of the colony', together with a 'Loan from the Military Chest'
- This first 'loan' from the military chest was in the amount of 5,000.00 pound. It was obviously a short-term loan, because there is a reference to the "Balance in the Colonial Treasury on the 31st December, 1828, applicable to the service of the year 1829 being 11722.09.5 ½ *."

A further footnote attempts to clarify this item.

"*This Balance includes the sum of 5,000 pound, a loan which has been repaid into the Military Chest since the 31st December, 1828.'

The Blue Books for the year 1828 make for interesting analysis.

a. In spite of the final accounts being certified by Alex. McLeay, as Colonial Secretary, there is an substantial arithmetic error in the statements. We can track this error by accepting the opening balance in the colonial treasury as of 1st January, 1828; the closing balance on the 31st December 1828; both balances were represented by cash deposits in the Bank of New South Wales and the total receipts and disbursements recorded and added.

opening balance	3,862.16.8 ¾.
total receipts	226,191.16.7 ¾.
Total expenditure	214,469.07.2 ¼.
Closing balance	11,722.09.5 ½.
Difference	2,962.16.8 ¾.

This is an error in addition in the items of expenditure, or else, an error of transposition from one set of records to the next set.

THE REVENUE OF THE CROWN OR the first LAND FUND

b. We note that in the following year, 1829, that a notation on the 'Receipts in Aid of Revenue' is that these deposits have been paid into the Military Chest. These deposits include:

- Consignment of specie (transfer of coinage from Britain to the Colony)
- proceeds of bills drawn by the Deputy Commissary
- proceeds of sale of stores sent from England

Sale of :

- crown stock (livestock)
- coals ex Newcastle
- wheat from Bathurst
- sugar & molasses grown at Port Macquarie
- the Schooner 'Alligator'
- sundry stores & articles
- miscellaneous receipts

A special notation on the accounts is made for 'receipts in aid of revenue (ie revenue of the crown) which are exclusive of the value of colonial produce delivered to the commissariat from the convict agricultural establishments'

In subsequent years, this statement is modified because sale of produce from the Government farms is listed, but the notation is modified to say that the value of convict labour (other than labour for hire) is excluded

Military Fund—Items of Revenue & Outgoings

proceeds of bills	civil establishment
proceeds of sale of stores	convict establishment
Sale of crown livestock	military establishment

:coal	retired army pay
:wheat	retired military pensions
:sugar & molasses	
:sundry stores	

a. The Military Chest usually made payments in the following categories:

- civil establishment
- convict establishment
- military establishment
- retired army pay & pensions

b. The main revenue and expenditures were deposited into and paid out of the 'Colonial Treasury'. The first reference to the balance in the Military chest is found in 1828, but the first reference to a balance in the Colonial Treasury is not found until 1829. From those dates, the closing balance at the end of each year is identified until 1831 when there are headings such as "Paid into the Colonial Treasury" "Defrayed from the Colonial Treasury" ;"Paid into the Military Chest", "Defrayed from the Military Chest", providing the means of tracking balances in each account.

c. In 1829, the disbursements on account of miscellaneous civil services states "total disbursements out of the military chest, in aid of the civil establishment of the colony"

d. In 1834, the 'Receipts in aid of Revenue' used each year, was changed to 'Revenue of the Crown'.

The items included remained the same, viz. proceeds of land sales, quit rents, fees on delivery of deeds and leased land revenue. These revenues were claimed by the British Treasury for dedication to their exclusive use to offset treasury expenditure on items such as the civil list, the military and interim commissary expenditure on public stores for improvements, until the Commissary Fund was properly established in 1833.

e. Back in 1826, for the first and only time, there was an entry for the British "parliamentary grant for the charges of defraying the civil establishment of the colony for the year 1826". The amount involved is 8,283.15.0; however the financial statements show the full civil establishment as costing 62,554.18.2 ½. The British Government must have decided that the cost of supporting the full civil establishment was too expensive and that it would only contribute to the salary of selected personnel. The details as listed in the 1826 statement do not allow us to decipher how the 8,283 pound is made up, We can only assume that the Governor, the chief justice, and possibly the chief medical officer are covered. The reason we cannot identify the amount is that individual salaries were no longer being shown in the records, but rather the Governor and his establishment received a grant of 4933.06.5 ¾, whilst the judicial establishment receive a grant of 13,462.02.8 1/4.

f. The reference above to the 'notes' incorporated into each statement to the effect that 'the total is exclusive of the value of articles of colonial produce delivered to the commissariat from the convict agricultural establishment' stood until 1825 when the military chest received and deposited receipts from "the sale of articles of colonial produce delivered to the commissariat from the several convict agricultural establishments and coal mines". The first ever recognition that the production of convict labour should be shown as a 'crown receipt'.

g. The 1826 Financial Statements from the 'Blue Book' of that year record the consignment of specie as being 50,000.09.0 pound. Butlin "Foundations of the Australian Monetary System" refers to the copper coins sent to the colony at the instigation of Governor King in 1805, together with a second consignment in 1806 to Governor Hunter. Hunter recommended that the coins be circulated at "a greater value . . . . than their intrinsic worth."

h. Butlin suggests that the progress of government finance in the colony goes along these lines:

- the earliest coins arrive in the pockets of the first Fleeters
- Phillip's Bills & Dollars—bills on the English Treasury & Spanish dollars
- The 'Rum' Currency and Barter
- Promissory Notes—personally pledged
- Commissary's Store receipts and Bills of Exchange
- Paymaster's Bills & Notes—Copper coins of 1805

- Legal Tender & Colonial Currency
- 'Holey' dollars
- Macquarie's Bank & exchange rates

Butlin concluded that, between 1788 and 1803, the 'Colony had no treasury', but this omission was not to last long. The earliest funds were controlled out of England with even the colonial commissary operating purely on a barter system for the first fifteen years. The first colonial accounting was commenced in 1802 (through the Goal & Orphan Funds) with revenue amounting to 900 pound. The Colonial Fund commenced with the 'Blue Books'. The Land Fund according to the 'Australians: Historical Statistics' opened in 1833, although the 1833 financial statements do show the balance at the end of the year, in the Military Chest was 22,719 pound. It is logical, subject to further verification, that the Land Fund was the successor to the Military Chest; the main evidence being that, in 1834, the 'Receipts in Aid of Revenue' was changed to 'Revenue of the Crown' and included the proceeds from the sale of crown (waste) land, and other crown assets of the colony.

The names of the various funds changed at different times between 1802 and 1834, including:

- Gaol Fund
- Orphan Fund
- Police Fund
- Orphan School Fund
- 'Blue Books' & The Colonial Fund
- Military Chest
- Commissary Fund
- The Colonial Fund
- Land Fund

This was the story of how the Military Chest which became, during the Blue Book era, the holder of large balances in the Colony; became the main lender to an malnourished colonial treasury; and the beneficiary of the 'profitable' commissariat trading and discounting of bills drawn on the English Treasury. Its successor was termed the Land Fund, but we have little official recognition of this fund, other than what we learn from some of the economic historians.

The second THE LAND FUND

The military chest, as an account style for the colonial treasury was identified in the financial statements contained in the 'Blue Books', and we can readily identify the revenues credited to that account as well as the expenditures charged against the military chest.

However the Land Fund is without mention in the 'Blue Books' at least through the end of 1838, and the origin of this nomenclature must be accepted as 'untraceable' without proper basic evidence. We know only of its existence in firstly, the Australians: Historical Statistics P112, and then its mention in the works of economic historian, S.J. Butlin:

We find the following table in Historical Statistics of NSW

New South Wales Public Finance
Land Fund 1833-1850

Revenue '000   Expenditure '000

Year	Land	Other	Total		Immign	Other	Total
1833	**	26.1	0.1	26.2	9.0	17.2	26.2
1834		48.2	42.9	60.8	7.9	52.9	60.8
1835		88.9	121.3	131.9	10.7	121.2	131.9
1836		131.4	121.1	263.3	11.8	251.5	263.3
1837		123.6	202.6	254.9	44.4	210.5	254.9
1838		120.2	185.8	353.8	108.0	245.8	353.8
1839		160.8	148.8	321.8	158.3	163.5	321.8
1840		325.3	283.6	480.0	148.0	332.0	480.0
1841		105.8	21.4	386.5	331.6	54.9	386.5
1842		44.1	51.7	117.2	112.0	19.7	131.7
1843		29.3	49.3	56.5	11.6	44.9	56.5
1844		16.9	126.0	127.5	69.0	58.5	127.5
1845		38.0	131.0	127.9	20.0	107.9	127.9
1846		38.8	153.5	146.5	1.2	145.3	146.5

1847	51.7	109.7	212.3	1.0	232.6	233.6
1848	51.7	109.7	212.3	113.8	98.5	212.3
1849	109.0	237.4	296.0	138.5	157.5	296.0
1850	158.5	104.8	373.1	166.2	206.9	373.1

** Receipts in aid of Revenue (ie. paid into military chest—no record of land sales)

This table extracted from Historical Statistics can only be verified by reference back to the Blue Book Financial statements for those years, provided we make a generous assumption.

That assumption must be as follows:

a. If the 'military chest' is accepted as a predecessor to the 'Land Fund' then its purpose must have been essentially the same. The military chest took its revenue from the proceeds of sale of crown lands, sale of stores sent from England, sale of produce from the Convict Establishments and sale of crown livestock. In other words, only material items possessed by the crown; and that is most probably why the notations on the Blue Books changed from 'Receipts in Aid of Revenue' to 'Revenue of the Crown'. This important change occurred in the 1834 financial statements.

b. Obviously the Land Fund was so designated either officially or by Australian Economic Historians to be the account into which official 'crown' revenue is deposited and from which crown reserved expenditures are drawn. The crown reserved its use of portion of the funds for conveying selected immigrants into the country, and for (15%) aboriginal welfare. We will return to the official sanctioning of these funds later.

c. S.J. Butlin in his masterwork "Foundations of the Australian Monetary System 1788-1851" makes several passing references to the 'Land Fund' without fully identifying its source or use.

Butlin writes that "in February 1838, William Rucker, a Melbourne storekeeper, announced the opening of a Derwent Bank agency, to 'receive deposits and discount bills and orders for account and under the responsibility of the Derwent Bank Company in Hobart. He fixed the discount rate at 20%, letting it be known that Hobart rates would apply when a court was established in which debts might be recovered. Attempts were made, with what success it is not clear, to secure the accounts of the Customs Officer and of the Land Fund for the agency. But the agency met with considerable difficulty."

In 1846 there was a squabble between Stuart Donaldson, NSW Treasurer, Murray MHR and Dr. Bland MLC as to where certain colonial debentures were to be funded. Donaldson wanted the subscription to come from the public; Murray thought the Trust and Loan Bank should do the funding, but "Dr Bland wanted the loans to come from the Land Fund"

P 490 "Because of its late settlement and mining boom, land purchase in South Australia was heavy in the late 'forties and the local accumulations in the Land Fund were more than the local commissariat required. The practice developed, with English blessing, that any surplus in the Fund was paid to the commissariat which shipped the specie to other colonial commissariats in need, especially that in New Zealand, the amount being credited to the colony's account with the Land and Emigration Commissioners in London"

P539 Grey, in South Australia, decided to use, contrary to official directions from London, to use any bank he chose for Government business, and he used the Bank of South Australia. Being contrary to official direction, this action permitted a penalty. The Land Fund, which was a transient deposit remitted to England for immigration payments, was divided between the Bank of Australasia and the Bank of South Australia, but all other government business was given to the Australasia."

P540 n "In 1851, the SA Treasury decided to require banks to hold cash at least equal to the government deposit, and to insist on this for the Land Fund."

Some of these references through doubt on the strict governmental use of the Land Fund. Other quotes come from 'Historical Records of Victoria—Volume 7'

P35 "It was Lord John Russell's opinion in 1840 that the general revenue ought to provide for the general expenditure, leaving the Land Fund, apart from 15 percent to be used for expenditure on Aborigines, free for immigration purposes as originally intended"

A. Coghlan in his extensive work "Labour & Industry in Australia "helps place some of these matters in relation to sale of crown land & immigration into perspective.

It was upon emigration from England at the cost of the land revenue that the colonial authorities finally placed their confidence. They offered in 1822 to set aside 10,000 pound from the Land Fund for emigration purposes; of this sum they desired that about two-thirds should be devoted to promoting the emigration of unmarried women, as the proportion of men in the colony was excessive, and that about one-third should be used in loans for the emigration of mechanics. The colonial office objected vigorously but the British Treasury agreed to the proposal with the proviso that no further sum should be expended upon immigration until the money received from the sale of land had reached 10,000 pound.

"It had been Edward Gibbon Wakefield's philosophy that the idea of land disposition in the colonies was adopted . . . . If the land was sold, the proceeds of the sale might aptly be applied to transferring labour from Britain to the colony without which labour the land would be of very little value. In 1831 the English Government resolved to alter the land system of Australia with the view of throwing open the country more freely to settlement, and thereby increasing immigration. In the first four months of 1832, 103 mechanics reached the colony but were disappointed to find pay rates considerably less than those promised in England. The female emigrants all found ready employment, chiefly as domestic servants. Considering its resources, the colony went into the immigration business in a big way. The estimated expenditure of 1838 was 120,000 pound of which 80,000 was spent in chartering 26 ships, and 40,000 expended on bounty immigrants. With the overall success of the program it was decided that the whole of the rapidly increasing land revenue of New South Wales should be devoted to immigration and in 1837. 3093 immigrants arrived of whom 2688 were sponsored and 405 arrived under the bounty regulation of the colonial government.

COUNTING THE PENNIES

PUBLIC FINANCE IN THE COLONY OF NSW
1788-1855

PREFACE

The purpose of this study is to expand the existing knowledge of how the colonial economy of NSW grew in terms of the use and provision of public finance.

Public Finance, at least in relation to the colonial economy embraces multiple concepts including the appropriation and use of British Treasury funds, the raising of colonial revenues by way of import duties and other taxations and the recording and reporting of these funds, and the contribution to the colonial funding of economic growth and development by the Commissariat. The study of capital formation in the early economy has to-date been based on massive assumptions but not reliably measured until N.G. Butlin commenced his research for the year 1861. Preliminary assessment is now made for the pre-1861 period Capital formation in the form of public and private funds as well as the human capital can, in fact, be broadly assessed for the period 1802 to 1861.

This study runs for the period from the formation of the penal settlement in 1788 to the transfer to self-government in 1856, but obviously references to economic events outside those parameters must be referenced, and these references will also include mutually exclusive topics such as economic drivers for the period and special economic events for the period. Nine economic drivers of varying importance have been identified as have five special economic events which fuelled the growth of identifiable sectors of the colonial economy, such as growth in and from the pastoral industry; the introduction of formal education which contributed to the drop in illiteracy from over 75% to under 25%, over a period of less than a quarter of the 19th century.

Linked with the analysis of capital formation in the colonial economy, is the important question of British Foreign investment into the colony. This too came in multiple ways, including immigration, speculation, direct investment, government borrowing in Britain, availability of loan funds through new financial institutions and, of course, the introduction of the first bank and the subsequent development of a fully fledged banking and financial services industry. The Pastoral houses provided export funding and then rural mortgage loans, and there came about this special link between the land grant companies, the pastoral houses, the pastoral industry, foreign investment and massive speculation in livestock and rural land holdings.

Possibly the second most significant economic driver, after capital formation, was the growth of population. This was sourced from immigration from Britain and natural increase within the colony. The population history of the colony is rather short because of the circumstances of the colony, but is measured in terms of the transportation program (convicts dominated the labour market until the 1830s), the immigration program funded from revenues generated by crown land sales and the land grants program which encouraged settlers (ex-military as well as professional farmers and pastoralists in exchange for land grants and labour—convict—concessions).

The story of public finance in the colony is an exciting one, but sources are limited mainly to the official records (such as HRA, HRNSW, AJCP) and only two economic historians have formerly contributed to the literature—Butlin, S.J. in *Foundations of the Australian Monetary System* (1953) and Butlin. N.G in *Forming a Colonial Economy* (published posthumously in 1994 from earlier notes). Specialty sub-texts have been assembled by other economic historian's e.g. *One million pound & a million acres*—Damaris Bairstow and her story of the AAC Company(2003); Frank Broeze, *Mr Brooks & the Australian Trade* (1993) and Margaret Steven *Merchant Campbell* (1965).George Linge made a large contribution in his *Industrial Awakening* (1994).

This writer has concentrated to-date on the main symbols of the colonial economy by studying *The Economic role of the Commissariat **and** The Role and growth of the office of Treasurer and Auditor-General in the Colony,* as well as preparing *An Economic History of the Van Diemen's Land Company (1824-1899)*. The literature is slowly being added to but this present work is the first to complete a review of the public finance of the colony between 1788 and 1856

Five chapters in the study cover the period 1788 to 1856 whilst they also cover the contents referenced above. A sixth chapter attempts to summarise the results and conclusions from the study.

The Treasurers of the Colony knew only the advantages of balancing the books each year—there was no deficit financing undertaken until after 1856 when overseas borrowing commenced with the financial houses in the City of London, who had accepted the credit worthiness of the Colony and hastened to use this new outlet for surplus funds available for investment by Britain. The use of bank drafts for export commodities had commenced with the large wool exports to Britain and led to the creation of the Union Bank of Australia and the Bank of Australasia[1]. This period also saw the rise of the great pastoral and financing houses—Brooks and Younghusband, Dalgety and Goldsbrough Mort. Shipping fleets grew rapidly after 1792 for transporting convicts and then free immigrants and returning with wool[2], and other commodities. The P & O operators, with their One million pound of paid up capital won the lucrative mail contracts from the British Government and commenced regular monthly trips from London to Australia[3].

The published public accounts reflect an annual cumulative surplus (of revenue over expenditures) each year from 1822 to 1900[4]. What this meant was that the Colonial Treasurers and their advisers had the flexibility of running into temporary deficit, for instance in 1838 (-£164102) and 1839 (-£121464) knowing that the cumulative surplus of £314,517 (as of 1837) would allow them to do so without having to borrow long-term. In this instance the cumulative surplus was reduced to only £28951[5]. The

---

[1] Butlin, S.J. *Foundations* P.449
[2] Farrer, T. *Free Trade versus Fair Trade (1886)*
[3] Farrer *ibid*
[4] Ginswick statistics quoted by Butlin, N. G. in *Forming a Colonial Economy*
[5] Butlin, N. G. *ibid*

habits of recording in the various periods varied and opened the way for considerable mistakes and misinterpretation, as will be seen.

For the purposes of this study, there are five significant public finance periods during the 19th Century: the first is the goal and orphan fund period 1802-10, the second is the Police and Orphan Fund period 1810-21, the third covers the 'Blue Book' period 1822-55; the fourth is the post self-government period 1856-89, and the fifth will be the pre-Federation period 1889-99.

Governor Macquarie had appointed Darcy Wentworth and Reverend Samuel Marsden to be Treasurers of the Police and Orphan funds and we find their monthly reports published in the *Sydney Gazette* of the period 1810-1821. From 1822 clerical staff within the Colonial Secretary's office recorded the Blue Book even though William Lithgow as Colonial Auditor-General was held responsible for its compilation, audit and transmittal to London[6]. Prior to self-government public service lines of demarcation between the offices of the Colonial Secretary, the Colonial Accountant and the Colonial Auditor-General were unclear. From 1856, all accounting and reporting functions came under the Treasury, whilst the Colonial Secretary's department was responsible for the more routine 'housekeeping' functions of colonial government. The main difference in recording between the Orphan & Gaol Funds and the Blue Books is that the Funds were original records, whereas the Blue books were transcriptions of other records. There was, in fact, nothing in the Blue books that had not been collected in another record.

The Blue Books contains the comprehensive (albeit delayed and information of doubtful accuracy) recording system of the times whilst the Consulting Accountant to the NSW Treasury (James Thomson) introduced a new system after self-government, which was burdensome, intricate, and open to much abuse. It was as if the NSW Treasury, following self-government went out of its way to develop a singularly complex system to justify its continued existence. After self-government, the ledgers were kept in an 'open' condition until all of the funds appropriated to each line item in

---

[6]   Beckett, G.W. *The first Colonial Auditor-General—William Lithgow, a biography*

the budget were spent. This system had become even more complex after the introduction of Appropriation Bills in 1831. The system of keeping accounts 'open' sometimes meant the ledgers could not be closed for upwards of three years, by which time the trail was cold in trying to keep track of annual revenues and expenditures. This problem was corrected in 1885, when a return was made to annual statements based on cash inflow and outflow[7].

Observations on early Reporting Systems

Many of the Marsden and Wentworth funding transactions created major conflict of interest situations. It is interesting to muse how a Reverend gentleman who was paid from the Civil List at the rate of £150 per annum, could afford to operate 4,500 acres of pasture land (about 1/3rd received in grants, and 2/3 rds in purchased freehold land) and build up a flock of 3,500 sheep in a span of less than twenty years. Even allowing that some of the land came about from grants, all the sheep were purchased and although the convict labour assigned to him was unpaid, they had to be kept, with sleeping huts, food and clothing furnished. A close check on the built up of flock numbers shows that the computed rate of natural increase was physically impossible Marsden was obviously adding to his flock by other means. As was noted earlier, Marsden was Treasurer of the orphanage fund. We might also ask why its monthly meat bill ran to over £60 even though it owned and operated a sheep grazing operation, which sheep were regularly sold 'on the hoof' and then bought back as dressed meat[8]. For its annual sale of livestock in 1811-1812, the orphanage received only £127, but from the same source purchased over £700 of dressed meat. The means were easy to share the spoils between those who could help him gain wealth and reach his target of becoming a large landowner and successful grazier. Marsden's orphanage housed only female orphans aged from 5 to 14. On an average month, Marsden paid the butcher over £60, being for an average of 2,500 lb of meat (the average price per pound was 6 pence). By the 30th September 1818, Marsden held £3,033 in the orphanage account, and on average disbursed £550 each month from that

---

[7]   Thomson, James *Financial Statements of the Colony 1856-1886*
[8]   The Orphanage accounts reflect this policy but Yarwood in his biography of Samuel Marsden also confirms the practice.

account. Marsden's chief biographer, Alexander (A. T.) Yarwood makes no reference to any financial irregularities during Marsden's period as Orphan Fund Treasurer, but a careful audit of the quarterly published accounts shows errors in addition, and funds accounted for.

The only 'admonishment' that Macquarie made, if one can imply an act of admonition from a minor regulatory change, was that a lesser percentage of revenue from tariffs and duties was to be directed to the Orphan Fund. Macquarie, in 1817, chose to modify the basis of the Orphanage Fund revenue and deleted an item by redirecting that revenue to the Police Fund. In 1818, Macquarie then directed that £3,000 of the balance in the Orphan Fund be deposited with the new Bank of New South Wales[9].

Macquarie made no objection to the fact that Marsden was misdirecting funds from the Orphan Fund for the repair of St. John's Church, Parramatta, in July 1811 to the extent of £56, nor to paying the Matron of the Orphanage a monthly stipend of £5 when the going rate would have been only £1 per month, nor of paying £4.5.0 for a bonnet for his wife from the fund[10]. Macquarie personally approved each quarterly statement submitted by Samuel Marsden, as Treasurer of the Orphan Fund, when presented to the Lieutenant Governor for 'auditing', obviously without proper 'auditing' procedures being used. The 'auditing' function could not have been taken very seriously because numerous of these approved statements included arithmetic errors[11].

The Orphan Fund, as published in the *Sydney Gazette*, quarterly between 1811 and 1820, showed numerous arithmetic errors, always on account of a shortage, and one may wonder why, with numerous others handling the accounts, such as the other Trustees, the Governor's secretary, or the Judge-Advocate, no-one ever picked up these quite substantial errors.

---

[9]   HRA 1:10:169 Macquarie letter to Marsden as attached to a despatch to Lord Bathurst

[10]   The Orphanage accounts show this purchase

[11]   The writer recreated each quarterly report on a spreadsheet by categories and having identified an arithmetic error, checked with the source documents to verify who, in fact, made the error

During the course of the years 1812-1818, the amount of shortage or error in addition came to a total of £997[12].

Wentworth, as Treasurer of the companion 'Police' Fund, also had his dubious methods. He built up large surpluses of cash and bills receivable rather than spend funds on road and bridge or wharf construction; he did expend large amounts by using military men for 'repairs' to the streets of Sydney and other questionable contracts, which were never commented on publicly by Macquarie, and never checked as to quality or indeed, the work being actually carried out[13]. Macquarie's 'blindness' to any inconsistencies or abuses in the accounts, made it appear that he was only interested in outcomes, regardless of how they were achieved.

Wentworth was also the town Magistrate and Superintendent of Police responsible for fines, both positions being an important source of revenue to the Police Fund. Two items of regular expenditure open to abuse, and which appear to be inordinately high were purchase of firewood and lamp oil and payment for the capture of absconding convicts[14]. The Military personnel were fleecing the Government stores, operating the importation of consumption goods and the barter system in the Colony and were obviously monopolising the ample rewards in cash available if one found favour with Wentworth[15]. These fiscal irregularities persisted until 1822, when the 'Blue Books' were introduced and commenced the following year.

Members of the NSW Legislative Council, after its formation were always considering new means of raising local revenues, as the British Treasury was far from flexible and open in offering funding to the colony for other than civil list and commissariat expenditure items. The British treasury for those early years had its funds committed almost exclusively to the

---

[12] This shortage was identified by this writer
[13] Macquarie makes this admission by stating to Bathurst that his time was better spent that following behind Darcy Wentworth.
[14] This analysis follows from the spreadsheet by categories referred to in Footnote 20
[15] This analysis also follows from the spreadsheet by categories referred to in Footnote 23

European and French wars, and the colony was never considered a priority in allocating working funds, and Britain saw an excellent opportunity to cut its own expenditures in the colony and use local revenues and taxation instead. Once local revenues reached the level of £10,000 per annum, being about 10% of the total required from the Treasury to operate the colony, the Treasury relied on this taxation to replace British funds.

Legislative Councillor, Robert Campbell, recommended to the Governor on 25th August 1835 that the British Treasury should consider paying a flat rate of £10 per head for each of the 20,000 convicts in the colony at that time by way of maintenance and support to the local treasury. He suggested that 'because the accumulated balances in the Treasury are evidences not of superabundant revenues but of defective financial arrangements whereby public buildings have fallen into disrepair or become unfit for the required purposes'. Campbell suggested that 'because the large revenue raised is not the result of industry or creation of wealth but proof of the improvident and vicious habits of the community'. He noted that '3/4 ths of the revenue of £157,300 arises from duties on spirits'. This whole proposition was rejected by Governor Sir Richard Bourke, but associate Councillors, John Blaxland wrote a letter also on 23rd August, 1835, suggesting that the British Treasury had saved over £1,000,000 by using New South Wales as a penal colony—he represented that £1,913,462.17.0 had been saved if hulks had been used or £1,008,837.5.6 if prisons had been built. He was basing his numbers on a saving of £30 per head per annum for the 20,207 convicts in the colony at that time.

In response to this disagreement between Bourke and the Councillors, Bourke announced that 'the revenue of last year has been unusually productive. We are able to provide for such objects as tend to improve the morals, augment the wealth and procure the comfort and convenience of all classes of the community. These include supporting Public Schools and places of religious worship, the formation and improvement of roads and the repair and erection of public buildings'[16].

---

[16]   Votes & Proceedings NSW Legislative Council 1835

Conclusions for Chapter One

This work is the study of colonial Finance in NSW from 1788 to 1855, in order to reach an understanding about both Public Finance and Private Finance—its source and usage in the colony.

Associated with this study will be a reflection on the creation of Capital—private and public, human and financial. This is one area that Timothy Coghlan, Colonial NSW Statistician and author of *Labour & Industry in Australia* (four volumes—1917) and the series *Wealth & Progress of NSW between 1886 and 1902* excels in. In future chapters the formation of capital in the colony will be studied, as will the method and policy of recording and reporting financial affairs in the colony.

Professor S. J. Butlin, the pre-eminent portrayer of Australian Economic History in his work 'Foundations of the Australian Monetary System 1788-1851' (1953 Edition), wrote, "Australian Economic History is the major part of all Australian history;—from the beginning, economic factors have dominated development in a way that should gladden the heart of any Marxist. What is true of any particular strand of economic growth—land settlement, labour relations and labour organisation, immigration, secondary industry—is also true of each major stage in the development of the community as a whole: each is characterised by economic changes which conditioned political, social and cultural change.'[17]

To explore the most important of the economic events in the Colony from 1788 to 1855 is to inexorably intertwine our history, both social and political, with the growth of wealth and the growth of the people from the commencement of the original penal settlement to the age of self-government.[18]

These economic events don't fall naturally into the same level of importance as do tragedies such as floods or wars, earthquakes or unnatural dramas such as social riots. These events were awakened by the wonderful aura of discovery. The exploration over the mountains to open up a new land,

---

[17]   Butlin, S.J *Foundations* op cit
[18]   Beckett, G.W. *A Population History*

and unfold the story of the rivers; the discovery of gold, and the unfurling of the workers flag and untold riches; the amazing growth of the pastoral industry; the development of the great 'iron horse' and the opening of the vast inland to settlements; the unfolding of the education system to all young Australians 'free, compulsory and secular' with the relief of seeing illiteracy drop from 75% to under 20% in the decade;

The development of communications, from bush telegraph to the electric telegraph around the world, but mostly the natural advance of democracy leading finally to full self-government.

All these marvellous events had a major impact on the economy of the day. Revenue grew from £72,000 in 1826 to £13,000,000 less than 40 years later, without diminishing the peoples will to work and the acceptance of the government's right to fairly tax its people and create a strong social infrastructure. Revenue per head rose only from £2.08 to £3.79 over the 40 years, whilst the standard of living, by whatever measure, expanded exponentially

Export earnings kept pace with imports, so we did not buy overseas at the expense of the local ability to make new and worldly goods. By 1850 our exports, due to wool and gold, had out run imports, for the first time, but always the numbers grew. Exports grew from £3.08 per head in 1826 to £14.55 per head in 1860. Imports grew from £10.39 to £21.57 in the same period, seldom with imports less than exports during that time.

In 1850, in anticipation of full self-government, the Governors began playing with 'temporary' borrowing in order to meet monetary policy obligations and expectations, and to keep the budget in balance. Gold and wool exports came as immigration burgeoned and railways and other infrastructure capital expenditure came into sight. The impeccable relationship between the Colony and the 'City' of London, allowed attractive and relatively easy borrowing of capital in Britain.

The financial establishment and the workings of the first Commissariats are both to be considered, along with a consolidation and summary of the first Public Accounts in the colony, being the Gaol, Police and Orphan Funds. The first appropriation bill was brought down in 1832, long after the 1823

161

reforms to appoint an advisory council to the Governor. Both moves were small steps on the path to responsible Government. Full self-government in 1855 continued the slow reform of the treasury system and prompted further parliamentary reforms of financial statements prepared for the New South Wales Legislature. Finally, the Parliament received, in 1856, full control of its financial destiny and was able to increase and diversify sources of revenue and allocate funds for expenditure with only the local population watching over their shoulders.

Each of the five distinct financial periods will be analysed and examined, together with the economic and historical events, which so strongly shaped the life and future of the 'Mother' Colony.

Marjorie Barnard in her study [19]of the Macquarie Administration offers an insight into the economic planning by Macquarie for the colony. 'He was a road-builder and grasped what has remained a first principle in the colony—that roads must pioneer the country. The colonial Office thought otherwise. If those who would benefit by roads and other public works could not pay for them, said Lord Liverpool, it was an indication that they did not need them. Nevertheless Macquarie went ahead with his plans.'

The Colonial Office also opposed the concept of trade within and by the colony. Barnard comments[20] 'since the colony considered itself civilised it must have a monetary convention. That the colonial Office did not think so is an epitome of its whole conception of the colony. In theory it was to remain in a state of balanced simplicity, a penal settlement in which the convicts, at the end of their sentences, became peasant farmers, supporting themselves and the town with their produce, and, if possible, exporting some commodity to England that would reimburse the Home Government for its expenditure. Such people could live by barter. There would be no foreign imports. A little change for officials to jingle in their pockets was all that would be needed'.

---

[19] *Macquarie' World,* Marjorie Barnard *(1946)* p. 45
[20] *Macquarie' World,* Marjorie Barnard *(1946)* p. 56

Towards Self-Sufficiency

<u>Early Intentions, Policies & Plans</u>

It was British policy to retain the concept of a prison settlement but only if the colony could pay its own way. Such dual desires were in conflict. Autocracy (as in being necessary to operate a prison) would destroy any freedom of enterprise, which in any other circumstances was essential to the growth of colonial income. Would social and political progress come with economic advances?

Wealth would increase continuously between 1802 and 1850, not due to any industrialisation, but due to an entry into a cycle of investment in pastures and sheep—'the golden age'. Wealth was measured in purely tangible forms—Coghlan in '*The Wealth & Progress of NSW—1886*', computed the wealth of the colony at that time, in terms of the value of rural holdings, the value of residential town developments, the value of government buildings, of roads and other infrastructure, plus the value of all usable plant and equipment. Needless to say, this measurement got unwieldy and did not last as a statistical guide to the success of the colony. Probably Coghlan was being forced to compare the colony of NSW with other colonies in Australia as well as with similar countries overseas, for political purposes. Coghlan produces a table comparing the NSW wealth per head with that of numerous overseas countries, with little point except to comment that measuring standards were different elsewhere.

The cycle rolled forward—opening up new land, adding the grazing of sheep, adding to 'national income' followed by more investment—and the cycle rolls around again. Diversification of the economy soon followed and led to an ever-increasing standard of living, which, in itself sustained further growth.

<u>Capital formation</u> followed, mostly in agriculture but increasingly in manufactures[21]. Such steps usually relied on borrowing externally, but such borrowing must have been accompanied by development of financial institutions.

---

[21]   Butlin—Forming the Colonial economy

A society, which cannot by its own savings finance the progress it desires must strive, in the alternative, to make itself credit worthy and will only succeed if it follows market opportunities and adopts comparative advantage.

Because future prospects depend so much on present imports, the colony must look for profitable export industries[22]. It must also offer prospects of gain to people of enterprise.

Let me restate the salient points of the above synopsis.

The main characteristics of the colonial economy in transition[23](before 1832) are

- The Colonial Government adopted the policy of free enterprise and free trade, during and following the administration of Lachlan Macquarie.
- Out of necessity there was a dominance of agriculture in the economy—this was a social phenomena because of the needs and availability of convict labour.
- Social problems with bad treatment of aborigines and convicts curbed the otherwise 'clean' image of a successful economy.
- Lack of catalysts for British private investment prevailed until Macquarie converted the colonial image in the 1810-1820 period with new buildings, cleaning up the slums of the 'Rocks' area, and encouraging new enterprise.
- Wealth creation was taking place through capital investment and speculation.
- The growing need for financial institutions came with the commencement of borrowing and capital migration.
- The need for private borrowing overseas occurred because of the lack of savings, wealth and financial institutions in the economy before 1830.

---

[22]   Based on Hainsworth—The Sydney Traders
[23]   Beckett, G 'The economics of Colonial NSW' (colonial press 2003)

On the other hand the key factors of the (gradually) maturing colonial economy changed slightly (after 1832)

- Transportation and the convict labour program was the catalyst for growth until growth plateaued and transportation became more of an economic burden that could not continue to be tolerated
- The importance of the on-going British treasury support payments was that there was a steady flow of funds arriving in the colony, not only as support payments for the convicts, but they also had a flow-on effect through the commissary into the pockets of small farmers, pastoralists and vegetable growers as well as to the numerous cottage industries springing up throughout the settled areas of Sydney, Parramatta, Liverpool, Newcastle and the Hawkesbury.
- The role of free immigration and the accompanying capital contributions was essential to the constant demand for labour, enterprising operators and the capital formation within the colony. They brought capital goods, capital ideas and just plain capital to the colony.
- The role of land sales[24] was that it provided the colony with the funding boost it required to diversify the colony. Land revenues provided the direct funding for immigrants, aboriginal support, and a small amount of supplemental discretionary funding for the governor.
- The rise of the pastoral industry was crucial for trade, attracting immigrants, British investment and then to the attracting of manufacturers associated with the agricultural industries, including the extraction industries.
- The growth of manufactures[25] closely followed the growth of the agricultural sector and attracted another source and variety of capital and direct investment
- British capital investment and speculation was encouraged by the creditworthiness of the colonies, by direct investment of landowners from Britain and by migrant flow. British newspapers gave many column inches to events in the colony and there was a

---

[24] Butlin 'Forming the colonial economy'
[25] Hainsworth 'The Sydney Traders'

constant stream of books being written about life and exploits and successes in the colony.

- Population growth[26] was constant and fast and was supported by emancipated convicts, and convicts whose sentences had expired, by free immigrants and even by British ex-Military personnel attracted to the colony from India and post-Napoleonic Europe.
- The importance of education cannot be overstated. The illiteracy rate between 1788 and 1802 was high, but Marsden led the movement for schooling young people as well as creating literacy programs for the mature aged worker[27].
- Statistics collected for the period come from a variety of sources such as 'The blue books' original records held by the (NSW) State Records Office, from the HRNSW and the HRA. Some of the pre-1822 statistics are questionable but with nothing better, they offer a limited picture of life in the colony. Coghlan was the official collector of statistics for over 30 years and his 'Wealth & Progress' provides a vital contribution to our understanding of fiscal events, trends and achievements within the colony as well as a graphic comparison of the six colonies.

Each of these elements contributes to the growth of the colonial economy.

Thus, this is 'how' the economy grew[28], the 'why' is another matter. The why was, in reality, to further the goals of British colonial policy—to create a strategic base for defence and foreign policy rationales, as an investment outlet, as a source of trade, both with raw materials being exported to Britain and British goods being imported—a Navigation Act scenario, and mostly, in practice as a transference of some of the worst social ills in Britain to a colony' out of sight'. Wrapping all these aspects together was the goal of self-sufficiency and self-support.

---

[26] Hartwell 'Economic Development of VDL'
[27] Abbott—Chapter 3 in Economic Development of Australia
[28] Beckett 'The Economics of Colonial NSW' Chapter 3—Policies & Planning

As in any modern economy, the colonial economy had practical and physical limitations[29].

- The trade and economic cycles in the colony were influenced by events overseas, as well as local.
- Droughts and floods, insect plagues and livestock disease.
- Grazing land had limited availability until explorers found a way across the Blue Mountains in 1816.
- The Depressions of 1827 and 1841-1843 were man made and largely the result of British speculators, but the negative effects were largely offset by the boom times which attracted the investors and speculators, improved the trading between the two countries and improved the overall standard of living at a rate far greater than if there had been no cycles.

To offset these limitations[30], there were a number of positive aspects within the economy

- There was a continuous and growing flow of convicts between 1820 and 1842. In all over 160,000 convicted souls found their way to the colonies in Australia.
- Ever increasing physical and fiscal resources were provided by Britain to the colonial economy.
- There followed the creation of basic capital accumulation by individuals.
- Sustained higher living standards were underpinned by British fiscal support.
- The growing population was underpinned by the progressive freeing of prisoners, as well as by sponsored immigration, which in turn brought a constant social change.

Other commentators and writers comment on the source of growth in the colonial economy. Abbott and Nairn[31] introduce a number of specialist

---

[29] Based on Beckett, G 'The Public Finance of Colonial NSW' (colonial press 2002)

[30] Based on Butlin, S.J. 'Foundations of the Australian Monetary System 1788-1851'

[31] Abbott & Nairn (eds) Economic Development of Australia

economic historians in their edited version of 'The economic Growth of Australia 1788-1820' Hartwell[32] writes of the Economic Development of VDL 1820-1859, and Fitzpatrick[33] offers another opinion in 'The British Empire in Australia'.

Butlin, N.G[34] suggests his own formula of economic growth factors in 'Forming the Colonial Economy'.

However, Abbott in his Introduction[35] points out the dearth of any written treatment of the early phases of Australian economic development in publication between 1939(Fitzpatrick) and Shaw's Convicts and Colonies[36] in 1966. Abbott & Nairn try to fill that gap through a collection of short papers, usually an abbreviated version of the author's full account elsewhere in print. They believe (as stated in their Introduction) that the 'economic advantages to the colony included the resources made available by Britain, although the convicts provided merely the means, not the end of settlement'[37]. They also insist that the economic and strategic motives ascribed to Britain in the settlement of the colony must include the 'examination of the decision to transport convicts to Botany Bay in terms of British colonial policy before 1786, and of the prevailing social and economic conditions in Britain and their possible relation to crime[38].

Having considered the how of the equation seeking to determine the contribution to growth of the colonial economy, now we need to consider the reasons why.

The economic growth of the colony was but one of the considerations necessary to meet the defence, foreign policy, economic and social goals of the British settlement plan. An undeveloped colony did not gain the British any credibility in meeting their goals, and it was the transfer of the convicts to this alternative penal settlement that provided the workhorses

---

32 Hartwell 'Economic Development of VDL'
33 Fitzpatrick 'The British Empire in Australia'
34 Butlin, N.G. 'Forming the Colonial Economy'
35 Abbott & Nairn 'The Economic Growth of Australia'
36 Shaw, A.G.L. 'Convicts & Colonies'
37 Introduction to Economic Development of Australia 1788-1821
38 Abbott & Nairn (eds) 'The economic Growth of Australia 1788-1821'

of development to meet their full objectives. In addition, at least in Governor Phillip's settlement implementation plan, the convicts would be used to develop the infrastructure whilst at the same time encouraging the extraction and utilisation of available raw materials ready for shipping back to Britain.

We will now consider the key factors set down above, within the space constraints of this exercise. Each one would be the subject of a broad study in chapter length[39], under a number of category headings viz. Colonial Economic Statistics; Capital Formation in the Colonial Economy; Sequencing the Growth (an Abbott concept); The Patterns of Growth and The Cottage Industries.

A. Statistics

The statistical[40] summaries[41] show numerous highlights of the colonial economy and can be listed as follows:

o   The population growth[42] was regular and challenging, although the surplus of males over females was disparate and potentially detrimental. We should be mindful of the number of children and their specific needs. The nexus between total population and those 'on the store' was broken and reduced year by year. This progress affected the role, influence and operation of the commissary. Two other observations on the population growth can be made. Firstly, the growth rates in the Town of Sydney followed similar trends to those later found in Parramatta, Liverpool and Windsor. This means that selected decentralisation locations were attractive to new settlers and met the needs of these settlers. Secondly, as the earliest settlement outgrew its natural boundaries (of the Blue Mountains, the Hawkesbury to the north and the Nepean to the south), the new expansion settlements of Bathurst (ten (10)

---

[39]   Refer Beckett who includes chapter length discussions in 'The Economics of Colonial NSW'

[40]   Sourced from Beckett, G 'Handbook of Colonial Statistics' (colonial press—2003)

[41]   Reproduced in the appendix to this study

[42]   Source HRA, *passim*

small land grants were initially made 1815-1818) and Newcastle (twenty-three (23) small agricultural grants were made in 1821) supported Lord Bathurst's policy of large-scale land grants to be a catalyst to growth.

o   The number of convicts[43] arriving in New South Wales made a big difference to the colony in transition

o   The volume of treasury bills[44] drawn by the colony, especially in those first important 30 years, reflected two facts—the amazingly low cost to the British Treasury of operating the colony (that Treasury goal was being achieved) and of just where the 'capital formation' in those early years was coming from.

o   The return of livestock[45] shows the successful pasturing of sheep and cattle and the quality of management, climate and husbandry proffered this burgeoning industry.

o   Trade statistics[46] (imports) shows the source of such imports and the need for securing the Asian trade routes, for the majority of imports arrived from India and China and only in 1821 were the majority of imports from Britain.

o   From as early as 1810, private farming[47], based on evidence to the Bigge enquiry as contained in his subsequent report, was dominant, successful and essential to the needs of the colony. The accuracy of some of the statistics is questionable but they are the only statistics available. The total acres appear to be well balanced between grazing (sheep, cattle and hogs all grew rapidly with little sign of breeding loss or slaughter for food) and grain, with wheat and maize sharing the farming land.

o   By reviewing the prices obtained at the London auctions of NSW Wool between 1818 and 1821[48], we can understand Bathurst's goal of growing 'fine' wool, which he thought would have averaged 12s per pound rather than the 2s 10p it actually achieved.

---

43   Shaw, A.G.L. *Convicts & the Colonies* pp363-8
44   Bigge, J.T.—Appendix to Report III (1823)
45   Source: Select Committee of the House of Commons on Transportation 1838
46   Wentworth, W. C. 'History of NSW '
47   Bigge evidence
48   Macarthur Papers Vol 69

o   Wool shipments[49] soared between 1807 and 1821 and grew from 13,616lb to 175,433lb annually during that time.

o   An early 1821 map of Sydney[50] shows the location of the emerging manufactures of the colony. The second slaughterhouse had opened, a sixth mill was opened and we find the locations of boat-building, tanneries, salt works, furniture, candles, earthenware, tea and tobacco and a brewery, all serving the colony. Manufacturing was not the largest employer but in terms of import replacement goods, was the most important employer. Agriculture won the export stakes and supported the colonial local revenue base by allowing imports to match exports, and supporting a duty and tariff on all imports. This local discretionary revenue started off small and convenient, but grew rapidly into a major government source of revenues to cover every expenditure apart from the direct costs of the convict system.

o   A listing of major Public Works[51] helps us understand the benefits to the colony of the free settlers, the convicts, the contractors and the entrepreneurs. In summary, the period between 1817 and 1821 witnessed the development of 6 main roads, of major government buildings, of churches, of military barracks and growing infrastructure. Mostly the period witnessed the success of the Macquarie administration and his major contribution to the colonial economic growth.

o   This writer's assembling of raw colonial economic statistics[52] (refer appendix) suggests a positive balance of payments growth during the 1826-1834 period with growth, but sometimes negative balance of payments at other times. Imports took a dip in the depression years of 1827 and 1828 but grew dramatically until the next depression of 1842-1844. Local revenues, which the British treasury relied upon to replace contributions from Britain, also grew as a reflection of the burgeoning colonial economy. If we use 1826 as a base year then growth to 1834 became a cumulative factor of 280% over those 8 years or a remarkable 4% per annum.

---

[49]   ibid
[50]   NLA Map Collection—Sydney Map published 1822
[51]   Cathcart, L—Public Works of NSW
[52]   Beckett 'Handbook of Colonial Statistics (colonial press 2003)

All in all, the statistics acquaint the reader with a fairly comprehensive picture of 'how' (much) the colony was growing, especially during those important formative years. The colonial establishment had laid the basis for a successful colony and for supporting the future rounds of convict transfers.

Public Expenditure in the Colony

If the statistical summary shows how progress was made in the colonial economy then a brief study of the mechanics of 'capital formation' will evidence the fiscal factors underpinning that progress.

Capital formation in the colony during these early years can be focused on the massive building and construction program. In the new colony, there was a demand for convict and military barracks, housing and government buildings, storehouses for the commissary, docks, wharfs, draining programs, fresh water, and so on. The support services required a supply of bricks, tiles, timber, furniture, roads, boats, agriculture and farming for food production. *The core of government practical economic management between 1788 and 1830 was The Lumber Yard*[53], *which included The Dockyard, the Stone Quarries, the Female Factory, and various timber harvesting, land clearing and road making enterprises.*

The capital for these government enterprises had been provided by the British Treasury, and certainly in greater quantities than originally estimated. Matra, in his 1776 submission to the British Government estimated an outlay of £3,500 for the first year and from then on self-sufficiency and no further cost to the British Treasury.[54] This estimate was not only optimistic but did not allow for adequate infrastructure once the colony was settled. Matra's plan was for a small convict contingent by the shore of the deep water mooring, with a fresh water stream close by, level ground for building log barracks and store buildings. No weather disturbances, no wild animals, no deleterious convicts, and a plentiful supply of wild

---

[53] Refer Beckett' The Public Finance of NSW' where a full discussion is made of the Commissary and convict management including the various enterprises of the commissary operations.

[54] I IRNSW—Copy of Matra's letter to the British Colonial Secretary detailing the costs of establishing the new colony

animals and fruit and vegetables, good soils, and no interference from any natives. Matra's dream world was far from realistic and practical but his projections suited the senior government and parliamentary officials who approved a small impractical budget for the expedition.

The basic economic problem within the growing economy, and thus one of the early limitations to solid or speedy growth, was the provision of savings to sustain the army of unskilled and semi-skilled workers engaged in this construction and development work—this in turn, hindered private construction for other than settlers who had ready money to invest in such work, and thus most early residences were supplied and furnished by the government. However, in the absence of an adequate local supply, the greatest part of these 'investment' funds was to be drawn from outside Australia, in the form of imported British capital. This flow of British capital helps our understanding of the aggregate capital formation in the colony. British capital was important in inducing the smooth expansion during the first four decades of the colony, and it was a key factor in the subsequent economic declines in 1827 and in 1842-1844. For most of this period, prices and wages rose slowly if not persistently and inflation was imported on the back of speculative activities.

Obviously public authorities played an important role in capital formation[55] and the public sector seems to have contributed a declining portion of the aggregate from 100% to approx 50% during these first four decades. Four components dominated overall aggregate capital formation. These are ranked in terms of volume: Infrastructure such as roads, buildings, barracks etc; agriculture such as government farms, grain growing and livestock grazing; residential construction, and finally manufacturing. In broad terms, we can see that manufacturing investment in workshops and offices matched each other, and it is interesting to note that manufacturing investment did contribute to what was perceived as a dominant agricultural, pastoral and farming economy. It is also noteworthy that the British Government continued to pay for and thus contribute the convict and transportation system, the colonial defence and the 'civil list' for the colonial use.

---

[55]   Based on Hartwell 'Economic Growth of VDL'

C. The Role of the State[56]

If capital formation reflected the engine of growth and the statistics reflected the multifarious facets of growth, then the State became the conduit for growth[57]. Competent government policies, capable administration and sound conditions for enterprise were the essential ingredients for colonial economic growth, and even the dichotomy within the colony of 'free enterprise' or 'government enterprise' could not slow the clamour for better living conditions, jobs and a controlled haven for entrepreneurs.

Fitzpatrick in *The British Empire in Australia* reminds us of the transition in 1834 from the point 'where the earliest community was primarily a state-supported establishment to the next point (after 1834) when imported capital applied to wool growing and associated or derivative industries rapidly endowed the community with the character of British private enterprise instead of public enterprise, and appointed the pastoral sector as a field for investment into a profitable colonial territory'[58]. The Forbes Act (by the Legislative Council) in 1834 offered inducements to British capitalists to invest in New South Wales, and as a result the colony of NSW, with three million people, had received twice as much British capital as the Dominion of Canada, with a population of nearly 4.5 million. There are obviously two distinct stages of state intervention in reaching out to overseas investors. Before 1834 the role of the state was to provide British capitalists with free land and labour in the colony, then came the development of sheep-raising of fine wool, and the sequel was, having facilitated the importation of capital for investment, its role was to provide services which would facilitate the earning of dividends on the capital invested. However, even though initial dividends were sent 'home' in ever-increasing quantities, the time came when local people and institutions were the recipients of these dividends and great enterprises were part owned within the colony.

---

[56] Based on Fitzpatrick 'The British Empire in Australia

[57] Based on Beckett—Chapter 5—'William Lithgow' where capital formation and the role of government is discussed

[58] Fitzpatrick 'The British Empire in Australia

The state had, according to Fitzpatrick[59], four main functions:

o   Firstly, to take the responsibility for adjusting claims when the economic system reached crisis, as in 1827 and 1842, although Governor Gibbs acted reluctantly and belatedly in the latter crisis.

o   Secondly, the state is to administer essential services, in the operation of which private investors could not derive normal profits.

o   Thirdly, the state must nurture enterprise, including well-capitalised undertakings, by means of tariffs, bounties and other concessions.

o   Fourthly the State is to take responsibility for restoring to private capital, power, which has been taken away from it.

Fitzpatrick can be challenged on, at least, this last point. It surely cannot be the role of the state to supplant, supplement or fiscally support private capital lost within the colonial economy. If private investment criteria is invalid or faulty, then within a free enterprise economy, even one adopting an extended use of government enterprise, private capital must be supported by or subjected to market forces and not 'restored' by the state.

The introduction of the railways, just outside our time-line is such an example. The British were strongly urging private operators to install and operate in-town rail services. The *Sydney Railway Company* was empowered by the Legislative Council to build a private line with the support of 'government guarantees', with the right of the government to resume operations with minimal compensation to shareholders if the enterprise collapsed. The enterprise did collapse, was taken over by government planners, financially restored to health and the railway system moved on to be become a successful government enterprise[60]. The role of the State, in this typical case, was not to guarantee speculators, but to protect the suppliers and contractors who placed their trust and faith

---

59   ibid Page 347
60   Beckett 'The Public Finance of the Colony of NSW' (colonial press 2002)

in the free enterprise system. Fitzpatrick is confusing a touch of Marxist policy with a shackled government enterprise.

We can deduce that the state had an important role in the development[61] of the colonial economy and filled this role with supportive mechanisms and policies—especially guidance for financial institutions following overseas borrowing, overseas investment and land speculation.

D. Sequencing Economic Growth[62]

I come now to a brief study of 'in what sequence' did the economy grow, and as N.G. Butlin, in the Preface to *Investment in Australian Economic Development* writes "I have found no guidance on this question from the few essays which examine the early economy in identifying the sequence of economic growth in terms of both aggregate behaviour and the performance of major investment components".

One must fear to tread where Butlin finds weakness or gaps. This essay may still not fully satisfy the larger Butlin type questions but the immediate concern is about the 'hows' and the 'whys' of the colonial economic growth between 1788 and 1850 and as such there is an obligation, albeit ritualistic, to outline the main sectors of investment contributing to that growth. Since this study may cover many areas, methodology and circumstances of sequential development may not matter as much as first thought.

Some facts should perhaps be stated first as the basis for future conclusions:

o Government enterprise towered above private enterprise[63] at least between 1788 and 1821 because the government had the sole access to capital, land and labour, and government enterprise met the needs of the colony and its community of free settlers.
o Government enterprise was based on two facts—survival and self-sufficiency of the colony. From Phillip's livestock and building

---

[61] See also Butlin, N.G. 'Forming the Colonial Economy' for a discussion of these factors leading to changes in financial institutions
[62] Based on Butlin, N.G. 'Investment in Australian Economic Development
[63] A concept of Marjorie Barnard in 'Macquarie's World'

materials imported with the first fleet (including his 'portable' government house), government had undertaken to be the planner, the contractor, the financier and the provider of all labour and material resources in this new penal colony. That essentially was the nature of a penal settlement[64]. Then King decided he wanted a little 'spending money' outside the purview of the British Treasury, and this was a development unknown in normal prison or penal colonies but became the first step in the transition to a semi-autocratic free settlement. If this is an anachronism, then substitute 'planned economy' into any government encouragement of free enterprise. Then add Governor Macquarie, who as a free spirit, developer extraordinaire and ego driven creator of entrepreneurship[65]. Macquarie's contribution is in itself extraordinary. He applied, wisely, firm private enterprise principals to planning and development and set his sights on bettering the colonists' standard of living, changing the reliance on government hand-outs (the colony had to stand on its own feet, which is subtly different to being entirely self-sufficient, but is a good first step to self-sufficiency) and encouraging entrepreneurship in the colony. In Macquarie's mind, the role of his administration was to reduce British Treasury support payments, increase discretionary local revenues, build desirable government buildings and infrastructure, and create the atmosphere for manufacturing in the colony.

o   Obviously agriculture was the main objective of economic planning. It could use most of the convicts arriving in the colony[66]; it was minimalist in skills requirements, and relied more on natural events than most other colonial activities, but was mainly the most important of labour intensive undertakings. Agricultural operations would be extended to government farming, land clearing, timber harvesting and much of the work of the Lumber Yard. Its success was essential to maintaining the colony and making it self-sufficient As was pointed out above, agriculture contributed to more capital formation in the colony than did manufacturing but the rise of manufacturing mostly during and

---

[64]   Based on Ellis Chapter 11 'Lachlan Macquarie'
[65]   Concept from Barnard 'Macquarie's World'
[66]   Refer Shaw 'Convicts & Colonies'

following the Macquarie administration created balance within the economy and created a support structure internally and an import replacement opportunity

o The growth of government enterprises such as the government farms, the Lumber Yard,[67] which in turn included the stone quarries, and the timber forests, the Female Factory and the Dockyard, encouraged rather than damaged any move to free enterprise operations. The earliest private enterprises, other than pastoral establishments, were government contractors. Little capital was required, only limited skills (other than a nose for making money) were necessary, and there was plenty of work available and not a lot of competition.

o British private capital was uncertain and untried in the colonial context; investment within Britain or in the tropical colonies was considered more profitable and safer; of the hundreds of companies floated in the United Kingdom between 1820 and 1850, only five important companies were formed for investment in Australia. The Land Grant Companies—these were the three (3), plus two banks, within the Australian context—The Australian Agricultural Company (AA Coy), The Van Diemen's Land Company[68] (VDL Coy), The South Australia Coy (SA Coy), Bank of Australasia and The Union Bank of Australia—filled a role as catalyst for attracting new investment and even offered some official sanctioning and support parameters for colonial investing[69].

o A question should be posed, at this point, as assistance for understanding the sequence of development. Was the colonial NSW economy in 1830 a capitalist economy[70]? It was, as we learnt earlier, an economy in transition before and after that date. In so far as capitalism implies a rational, and acquisitive society, then NSW had been capitalist (urged along by Macquarie) ever since it had broken the bonds of being the self-contained

---

[67] Refer Beckett 'The Economics of Colonial NSW'

[68] Refer Beckett, G. 'The economic circumstances of the Van Diemen's Land Company (colonial press 2003)

[69] Hartwell refers to similar factors in 'The VDL Government 'Historical Studies ANZ, Nov 1950

[70] Butlin, N.G. in 'Forming the Colonial Economy states that the colonial economy was 'capitalistic' This portion of the essay is examining this claim

prison promulgated in 1788. Capitalist techniques, as opposed to traditional techniques of economic planning, assisted with the transition from a penal to a free economic society. The transition included the organisation of production by the capitalistic entrepreneur for profit, by the combining of labour and materials into a marketable product. The capitalist enterprise portrayed itself in the banks, the insurance companies, merchant houses and the large-scale pastoral farms—all institutions, which were rationally organised for the pursuit of profits. The most important means of production—land—had fallen by the 1830s into relatively few hands—trade and finance were highly concentrated, most of the population were without ownership of property, and worked for a wage determined by the market. West, in *A History of Tasmania*[71], offers us a quotable insight into the settlement progression "The dignity and independence of landed wealth is ever the chief allurement of the emigrant. Whatever his rank, he dreams of the day when he shall dwell in a mansion planned by himself, survey a wide and verdant landscape called after his name and sit beneath the vineyard planted by his own hands"

o   Another brief quote may also be in order. Hartwell, writing in *The Economic Development of VDL 1820-1850* thinks "it is impossible to study the trade cycles without reference to general economic development, and the existing economic histories of Australia did not answer the kind of questions I was asking"[72]. His point is that he offered, in his work, a specialist account of economic development, as will this account try to be in relation to the growth of the colonial economy in New South Wales.

E. Patterns of Economic Growth[73]

Although Butlin raised an interesting question on sequences of growth, any reference to sequences can also be raised in terms of 'patterns'.

---

[71]   West,' History of Tasmania—edited by Shaw in one volume
[72]   Hartwell 'Economic History of VDL' P.251
[73]   A Beckett concept developed in The Economics of Colonial NSW

The highlights of any 'pattern' can be traced to the foundation of the colony. This will also serve to identify some of the 'whys' in the essay topic.

The colony was founded for the multiple purposes of creating an intermediate stopping point for British ships travelling to India and China, of provisioning them, offering some form of back loading for the return trip to Britain, after unloading goods at this Port of Botany Bay. It was also considered to be of strategic value in limiting the expansion of Portuguese and Dutch interests in the sub-Asian region. Bonus reasons were considered to be that the East Coast region could be a source of raw materials for British industry[74], which was at that time coming to the implementation stage of the industrial revolution, and that any future colony would utilise British shipping and be an outlet for future investment and finally but almost as an after-thought any colony in so isolated a region could be a suitable location for a penal settlement.

Thus the growth in the colony followed first the formation of capital, then the importation preferences of capital, then the needs of the colony and finally the desires and preferences of the entrepreneurs and traders. This cycle continued right up to the discovery of gold, but it was not the traditional boom and bust cycle. It was a trade and investment cycle of designating an investment opportunity, bringing together the capital required, filling the opportunity and recommencing the cycle by starting all over.

The pattern changed somewhat in the mid-1830s (the colony was by now almost a mature 50 years of age) when the pattern of growth suddenly had a new spoke—local wealth, local ownership, locally retained dividends and the need for reinvestment. This change in pattern broke into the overseas raising of capital, and the overseas distribution of dividends and the overseas domination of manufacturing in the colony.

Local traders were gaining prominence in sealing, whaling, exporting and importing, merchant financing and the commencement of local auctioneering. Traditionally the Sydney markets had favoured enterprising

---

[74]   Proposed by Sir Joseph Banks (HRNSW—Vol 1)

practitioners who had surplus livestock or cottage industry manufactures, and these pursuits often led to more than the public markets as their distribution point. Simeon Lord, the master trader, bought a hat manufacturer in Botany whose rise had been exactly along those lines, cottage industry production, public markets distribution, rented premises, paid labourers, advertising, then buy-out and take-over.

Government policy fitted largely into this pattern and we have covered already the encouragement of business enterprise, however, the main role of government was to create the climate and the environment for entrepreneurs, borrowers, lenders and a satisfactory circumstance for making a profit and the return of capital. This came by way of successful business ventures, in both the agricultural and industrial enterprises. Because the skill levels within the colony were only gradually expanding and refining, there was official encouragement of British industry expanding with branch operations. Agricultural enterprise was encouraged by offers of land grants and then the cheap sale of land, and later the provision of either cleared land or convict labour.

Abbott[75] discusses the 'constituents' of the New South Wales colonial economy, and lists six. Agriculture; The Pastoral industry; Manufacturing; Trade within the colony; Exports other than wool; Government Works and Services.

Let me turn to some 'constraints' on the growth of the colonial economy; these include[76] Government policy; land, labour and capital.

There was an implied constraint to local colonial growth imposed by the Westminster parliament. The last of the series of Navigation Acts was in 1696 but stood unchanged until after the recognition of American Independence in 1783[77]. In general, until the legislation was passed,

British colonists had been free to trade with any country and to use ships of any nationality, and accept the cheapest freights. Following the passage

---

[75]   Abbott & Nairn 'The Economic Growth of Australia
[76]   Abbott & Nairn 'The Economic Growth of Australia
[77]   Discussed in Hainsworth 'The Sydney Traders'

of the legislation and the numerous amendments, they were obliged to use only British (including colonial) ships, to send all their exports direct to Britain and to import all their overseas goods direct from Britain. In this way, writes Abbott in *Economic Growth of Australia 1788-1821*, the colonists were virtually insulated from direct contact with the world economy.

Growth of Public Service 1800-1825

It is not unexpected that the public service for colonial NSW from 1800 revolved around the growth of the settlement, firstly as a penal colony and then changed as its role required transition into a market-driven economy.

The Governor's establishment changed little before Brisbane and Darling came Ion the scene. Its staffing was hierarchal and was based on the head of state being the governor, his deputy (Lt-Governor), and his heads of nominal departments. Darling referred to this group as his 'kitchen cabinet' or Board of General Purposes, but whatever the name, the role and participants remained the same—the chief judge, the chief surveyor or surveyor-general, the commissary-general, the chief surgeon, the chief chaplain and soon the Auditor-general (appointed 1825 under Darling)

Each governor had appointed a private secretary, and in 1822, this position was re-classified with its role expanded, and its own establishment created. Sub elements included the Colonial Treasurer and the Colonial Auditor-General and their expanding staff. The combined duties included issuing land grants, issuing land titles, collecting and accounting for all revenues, recording expenditures, completing feasibility studies for the expanding government services and handling all official correspondence into and from the colony.

Typical of the growing bureaucracy was the roads department. As treasurer of the Police Fund, Darcy Wentworth had been responsible for repairing roads, the Superintendent of Convicts was responsible for their formation and the Police Fund and its treasurer were responsible for payment of all associated costs. The British Treasury did not see the need for significant expenditure on road making, so the making and repairing fell to be supported by local revenues and convict labour. Macquarie increased this expenditure enormously when he designed and constructed the Great North Road (to the Hawkesbury), the Great West Road (to Parramatta and Bathurst) and the Great South road (to Goulburn). Within the colony, such road making was essential if new lands and settlements were to be opened up, and livestock moved around the colony. To raise revenue for the colony and to maintain the new roads, tolls were imposed on users of the road system, and these tolls eventually funded ferries and bridges, where rivers and streams had to be crossed.

This review of the growth of Public service is designed to embrace not on the coming 'Public Service 'system with its teams of public servants, but also the role of serving the public with official services. Obviously what springs to mind is the necessity for hospitals, coal for heating, fresh food, transport and communications, livestock, ferry services (initially between Sydney Cove and Parramatta), building materials, and most importantly, labour for hire.

Macquarie expanded this role by initialising a local manufacturing industry, essentially serving as an import replacement opportunity. He encouraged local entrepreneurs, who turned their hand to consumer imports, dressmaking, hats and apparel, shoes and furniture making.

Macquarie also co-ordinated the burgeoning government convict numbers into specialty trade teams for expanding government services.

The timber-cutters, carpenters, sawyers, bricklayers and blacksmiths were moulded into the full-service mini-manufacturing operation named the Lumber Yard. The boat-builders, boat unloaders and wharf-workers and ferrymen were moulded into the Dockyards, the brick and tile makers were pulled into the Brick Yard, whilst new activities included carriage making, cooper workers, whilst the commissariat grew with its own range of livestock herdsmen, slaughter men, storemen and clerical assistants. The commissariat also managed until 1817, the large government farm operations, used for the growing of government grain, vegetables, and fruit, for the colony as a whole.

The interest in the commissariat operating a more general store was too overwhelming and would have failed if the Treasury had not rejected the concept. The initial approach was along the lines of a catalogue service, whereby consumers ordered and paid in advance, and the commissariat placed the import request and added a sufficient margin to cover shipping, handling and clerical services.

Policing services were commenced under Macquarie band these numbers grew rapidly as the settlement grew in Sydney and outlying areas. Macquarie also appointed the first government printer, who used imported presses to publish official government regulations and orders.

The analysis of Accounts extracted from the 'Blue Books' of 1822 through 1828 allows a number of conclusions to be drawn.

f. The initial claim by the author that the cost to the British Treasury of establishing and operating the Colony, was NOT the millions of pounds claimed by other historians, is born out by examination. The accounting records as maintained by Governor Macquarie from 1822 leads to a statement of 'net revenue and expenses' which purports to offset all revenues against all expenses, and includes as revenue certain convict maintenance charges. Even in 1822 the Colony was showing a small operating surplus. This surplus grew through 1828 until, other than for transportation of convicts to the Colony, the charges on account of the British Treasury were under One Hundred Thousand pounds for protecting, feeding and housing nearly 5,000 fully maintained convicts. Against this cost, the charge for housing, feeding and guarding this same number of prisoners in Britain would have been substantially higher, since in addition to the 5,000 gully maintained convicts there were a further 20,000 being paid for by free settlers and used as supervised labour. Britain surely had found a cheap source of penal servitude for at least 25,000 of its former prisoners, and found a very worthwhile alternative to the American Colonies as a destination for its prisoners.

g. Revenue from Crown Land sales and rents was used to offset Civil (Crown) salaries and expenses.

h. It is probably incorrect, at this stage, to say that it cost Britain nothing or at best, very little, to establish and maintain the Colony, but it can be said that from 1842 the costs were limited to maintaining fewer and fewer convicts. But from these convicts great value in terms of agricultural produce, coal and other minerals extraction was derived. Just in terms of coal for lighting, heating, the cost to the government of purchasing these items commercially would have been substantial. The 'Blue Book', however, reflects the use of the coal as a cost rather than a gain as would be the accounting standard today.

i. A final conclusion could be given that there are much more known records available for this period (the first One Hundred Years) than the author originally thought. The reproduction of the 'Blue Book' by the State Archives Office is a major step forward in understanding the economic challenges faced by settlers and convicts in the early Colony. The sourcing of material from the Blue Book unveils the financial statements and conditions of these early years. It is still considered that finance records of the period 1788 to 1822 are not re-constructible, but the author feels that a deep search through the microfilms forming the Joint Copying Project will provide information on the two Colonial operating funds of the period—the 'Police Fund and the Orphan Fund'. This is a challenge for another time.

j. An interesting observation is found in 'The Constitutional History of Australia' by W. G. McMinn (1979).

P 33 records "Subject to the need for a vice-regal message, accepting that any locally (Australian Colony) initiated legislation of a money bill nature requires The Sovereign's ratification, the New South Wales Legislative Council was to have a general right to appropriate revenue from taxation, except for an amount of £81,600, the expenditure of which was to be in accordance with 'three schedules' to the Act; £33,000 for the salaries of those on the civil list eg Governor et al, the superintendent of Port Phillip and its judges and for the expenses of administering justice; £18,600 for the chief civil officers and their departments, for pensions and expenses of the council; and £30,000 for the maintenance of public worship. Land and casual revenues were also reserved.

The Sale of Waste Land Act raised the minimum reserve price of crown land to one pound per acre, except that large remote areas might be sold at a lower price, and established a formula for the use of the land revenue; fifty percent was to be spent on immigration, the rest was to be expended by the Governor in accordance with British Government directives from time to time. The Governor was to continue to have power to issue depasturing licences and to make regulations for the use and occupancy of unsold lands, but the existence of the Sale of Waste Lands Act placed an important restriction on the colony by implying a prohibition against the Legislative Council legislating on these matters. The first directive on how the Governor was to spend a portion of the fund, enjoined the Governor to spend a proportion on Aboriginal protection and another on the roads; he was left free to hand any surplus over to the Council for appropriation; but it was made clear that the whole of the fifty percent was to be considered as an emergency reserve if the Council proved difficult". McMinn sheds some further light on the Crown Lands mystery by there still remains the question of how, year after year, were these funds fully used or were they just included as a contribution to general revenue. It would appear that somewhere there is a firm directive from the British Treasury that the revenues from Crown Lands sale was to be used to 'offset' British costs of maintaining the Colony. The 'Blue Book' is evidence that as general revenues, these funds were already being used to pay for the costs of feeding, clothing, housing convicts, and we know they were specifically used to pay for 'sponsored immigrants', aboriginal 'protection', and now roads. The costs of the military establishment were charged against general revenues so in the quite large 'pot', nearly all Colonial expenditures were subsidised or offset by revenues from the Sale of Crown Land. Britain put its hand in the till only, it seems, to pay for the shipping and supplies costs of getting their prisoners to the Colony. After 1828, we know that convict production—both agricultural and mineral—went a long way to paying their expenses, so perhaps the British Treasury did in fact get off very lightly indeed, especially fort the benefits it derived.

The vexing question of Crown Lands revenues still remains. It is apparent from the 'Blue Book' notations that this revenue was 'reserved' for specific allocation by the Crown and remained in the Colony as an offset against British Government fiscal obligations (eg Civil List salaries)until self-government in 1855. A relevant quotation from the 1887 Financial Statements of the Colonial Treasurer of New South Wales, follows:

"Prior to the passing of the Constitution Act, the Territorial Revenues of the Colony belonged to the Crown, but upon that coming into operation in 1855, they were placed at the disposal of the local Parliament, and together with the taxes, imposts, rates and duties were formed into one fund, under the title of the Consolidated Revenue Fund. In lieu of the Crown Revenues thus given up to the Colony, an annual Civil List of £64,300 was made payable to Her Majesty out of the Consolidated Revenues of the Colony." What this means is that the British Treasury allowed the offset of all direct British payments made on account of the Colony against revenues raised by the sale, rent or lease of Crown lands.

Bigge in his first report to Lord Bathurst recommended that 'the number of convicts employed by the Government on public works should be reduced, both in the interests of economy and because it was argued that these men, especially if working in Sydney, were usually idle, and prone to misbehaviour in town. As far as possible, Bigge's recommended, convicts should be assigned to public service in the interior. He did, however, approve of sending convict offenders to penal settlements for further punishment, and he suggested that the settlements be expanded.

After the departure of Macquarie, administration of convicts became more efficient. The number of convict clerks in government service was gradually reduced, although the Marine and Survey Departments, the hospitals and domestic service for government officials became a reward for good conduct, although convicts were often placed in government service for breaches of discipline or failure to work effectively for private masters. In some areas, government service tended to be arduous.

The majority of convicts were 'assigned' to private employment and provided the bulk of the work force of the colony. Those 'assigned' were taken off commissary support and were entitled to be clothed and fed by their master in proscribed quantities of food and garb.

Foreign Investment to the Rescue

Explaining the Colonial Drivers 1788-1856

In order to understand the growth of the colonial economy, we must understand the economic drivers that underpinned, sustained and supported the colonial economy. There are at least six, if not seven, such economic drivers. They include the factors of (a) population growth, the (b) economic development within the colony, the (c) funding sources such as British Treasury appropriations and the (d) revenues raised from within the local economy (for example, taxes and duties on imports) and (e) foreign investment (both public and private). The traditional concept of growth within the colonial economy comes from (f) the rise of the pastoral industry. A seventh driver would be the all-important Land Board, which played such an important role within the colonial economy The Land Board played an important role in co-ordinating crown land policy, controlling land sales, squatting licenses and speculators, re-setting boundaries of location, establishing set aside lands for future townships and for church and school estates, carrying out the survey of millions of acres of land transferred by grant and sale, and offering terms sales for crown lands and being responsible for the collection of repayments, rents, license fees, quit-rents

and depasturing fees. In addition the land board was vested with road reserves for hundreds of miles of unmade roads but important rights-of-way that would well into the future protect access to remote pastoral and farming properties. The main thrust of published material about the Land Board is in conjunction with crown land sales policy, but the Board had a much larger role and the overall Board policies sand performances are what are to be reviewed here.

Although an important factor it is no more important that our other five motivators of the colonial economy between 1802 and 1856. Why have I selected these two specific dates? 1802 was when Governor King first imposed an illegal, but justified and well-intentioned impost on the local free community to build a local gaol to replace one burnt to the ground through a lightening strike but which the British would not replace. The local residents thought a more solid and durable prison was a worthwhile community investment. At the other end, the year of 1856 signalled the first real representative and responsible government in the colony, and although it was not the end of the colonial era, it was certainly the end of Britain 's financial support of sand for the colony and as such the colony was expected to stand on its own two feet.

These six factors will be discussed as mechanisms for 'growing the colonial economy between 1802 and 1856'

One consideration that must not be forgotten is the externally enforced pace of colonial expansion, particularly through the organised rather than the market-induced inflow of both convicts and assisted migrants. What this means is that instead of market forces requiring additional labour and human resources, extra labour and resources were imposed on the colony and there was an obligatory process of putting these people to work, in many cases by creating a public works program and pushing development ahead at an artificial pace rather than at a time and rate suited to the local economy. In much the same way, the 'assignment' system in the 1810-1830 period forced landowners to create clearing and development programs in order to utilise the labour available rather than only develop land as demand required.

1. Population growth including immigration of convicts & free settlers

The reason the colonial society did not change very much in the 1820s is that relatively few immigrants arrived. During 1823, Lord Bathurst, Colonial Secretary, sent instructions to Governor Brisbane (Macquarie's successor) altering the administration of the colony of NSW in most of

189

the ways Commissioner Bigge had recommended in his reports.[78] One result of the Bigge Reports was that Macquarie was officially recalled to Britain even though he had canvassed his retirement before Bigge's arrival in 1819. Macquarie was distressed by the Bigge Reports and took very personally the recommendations made for change. Although there were many implied criticisms Macquarie considered that the public perception was that he had not acted properly in his role as Governor. Macquarie set to and compared the circumstances of the colony at the time of his arrival in 1810, with the great achievements he had made through 1821. In hindsight, Macquarie had accomplished much, mostly by means of arrogantly pursuing a series of policies without the pre-approval of the Secretary or the Government in London.

The arrival of only a few immigrants was because Bigge and the Colonial Office believed that only men of capital would emigrate. Labourers and the poor of England should not be encouraged and, as these people rarely had money to pay for the long passage to Sydney, few of them arrived.[79] Although the numbers were small, few of them came unassisted. In 1821 320 free immigrants arrived and this increased each year; 903 in 1826; 1005 in 1829, but slipping to 772 in 1830. Mostly they were family groups with some financial security.

In 1828, the first census (as opposed to musters) of white persons in NSW was taken. 20,930 persons were classified as free and 15,668 were classified as convicts. However, of the free persons, many had arrived as convicts or were born of convicts. In fact, 70% of the population in 1828 had convict associations. However, by 1828, one quarter of the NSW population was native born; 3,500 were over 12 years of age

---

[78] Commissioner J.T. Bigge had been sent by Bathurst to Enquire into the State and Operations of the colony of NSW in 1819; the House of Commons had demanded an inquiry into the colony and had threatened to hold one of its own; Bathurst pre-empted a difficult government situation by appointing Bigge with a very broad and wide-ranging terms of Enquiry. Bigge held two years of investigations in the colony and reported to the Commons in 1823 with the printing of three Reports.

[79] Australian History—The occupation of a Continent *Bessant* (Ed)

There was another side to this migration of unregulated souls. Shaw writes" The cost of assistance, the unsuitability of many emigrants, their ill-health, and the numbers of children and paupers that were sent—all these gave the colonists a source of grievance".[80] A large part of the problem was that the English wanted emigration—but those they wished to see emigrate were not welcomed in the colony. A growing opinion in the colony was that free migrants could not work with convicts; the convicts by themselves were too few and with growing expense; therefore transportation must stop and immigration be encouraged. However, immigrants of a good quality were not those the English wanted to send; its preference was for the paupers and the disruptive in the society. To stop transportation would be "attended with the most serious consequences unless there be previous means taken too ensure the introduction of a full supply of free labour". [81] In the next five years, the number of free immigrants increased so much that transportation could be stopped with little political backlash. Between 1835 and 1840, the colony was quite prosperous (it was a case of boom and bust—the great depression came in 1841); sales of crown land were large, and consequently the funds available for assisting immigrants were plentiful.[82]

In 1838, land revenue was over £150,000 and assisted migrants numbered 7,400; in 1839, land revenue was £200,000 and assisted migrants 10,000; in 1840 revenue was over £500,000 and assisted migrants 22,500.

Between 1832 and 1842, over 50,000 assisted and 15,000 unassisted migrants arrived in NSW; or they might have arrived as convicts, and over 3,000 arrived that way each year. Thus between 1830 and 1840 the population of the whole of Australia increased from 70,000 to 190,000, with 130,000 of those in 1840 being in NSW. Of these 87000 were men

---

[80]   Shaw, A.G.L. *The economic development of Australia* p.44

[81]   HRA Bourke to Colonial Secretary *Governor's despatches* 1835

[82]   The British Treasury had agreed to put 50% of land sale proceeds into assisting immigrants with shipping costs; a further 15% into assisting Aborigines' and the balance was for discretionary use by the crown. These percentages changed in 1840 when all sale proceeds were spent on immigration but the land fund still ran out of funds in 1842 and no further assistance was made to immigrants other than by the colonial government borrowing funds in the London market through its own credit.

and 43000 were women; 30,000 had been born in the colony; 50,000 were free settlers, 20,000 were emancipists and 30,000 were convicts.[83]

2. Foreign Private Investment

We need to make the distinction between foreign public investment, and foreign private investment. The British Treasury appropriated specific funds for infrastructure programs in the colony, such as public buildings, churches, gaols, roads etc.

One reason that local colonial taxes and duties were imposed on the colony was to give the governor the funding source for discretionary expenditures in order to improve his administration. There were many instances of expenditures which could not be covered by the British funds, such as a bounty to recapture runaway convicts, building fences around the cemeteries and whitewashing the walls of public buildings (for instance barracks) in the settlement. The British Treasury would have considered such items of expense as being unnecessary. Road repair and maintenance was intended to be covered from toll receipts but they were never sufficient to make necessary repairs. Governors Hunter and Bligh did little to improve public and community buildings, roads and bridges and by the time Macquarie arrived in the colony in 1810, there was a major backlog of building work and maintenance to be undertaken. Macquarie expanded the local revenue tax base in order to give himself more flexibility in pursuing improved conditions for the settlers and the population at large.

Although Macquarie did not specifically seek new free immigrants for the colony, word of mouth circulated that the colony was in a growth stage and worthy of being considered for either immigration or investment. Usually one accompanied the other. The first private investment came with the immigrants. Free settlers would either cash up in England or transfer their possessions to the colony, and this small level of private investment was the start of a major item of capital transfers to the colony.

---

[83] Shaw *ibid*

However, private capital formation took many forms; the early settlers, bought or built houses, they built or bought furnishings, they had carriages and often employed water conservation.

As the system of land grants was expanded and farming was encouraged the spread of settlement required a combination of public and private investment.

The government had to provide roads and townships, and the settlers had to provide pastoral investment. This pastoral capital formation consisted of five main types of assets:

Buildings—residence, outbuildings, wool shed or grain storage
Fences—stockyards, posts and rails
Water conservation—dams, tanks, wells
Plant—cultivators, tools
Stocks—food, clothing, household items, materials for animal care and general repairs—livestock

Stephen Roberts offers an interesting insight into the colony of 1835.[84]

"It did not need much prescience to foresee the whole of the country united by settlement—so much had it outgrown the coastal stage of Sydney town. It was a new Australia—a land of free settlement and progressive occupation—that was there, and the old convict days were ending.

Both human and monetary capital were pouring into the various colonies and transforming the nature of their population and problems. Convicts no longer set the tone; even autocratic governors belonged to a day that was passing, and instead, the country was in the grip of a strangely buoyant, and equally optimistic, race of free men".

As part of our private capital formation, we must remember the growth of human capital and the needs for specific labour. Capital requires labour with a specific role. The establishment and expansion of farming meant more than shepherding and ploughing. There was a considerable demand

---

[84]   Roberts, S.H *The Squatting Age in Australia 1835-1847 (published 1935)*

for building skills, for construction and maintenance of equipment such as drays and carts, harness making and repair, tool-making etc. It became important, in order to support and sustain capital growth and economic development to be able to employ labour with multi-skills. This was a new phenomenon for the colony, especially since Britain did not develop these types of broad skills and self-motivation in its criminal class. The Rev. J.D. Lang sought a temporary answer by specifically recruiting 'mechanics' in Scotland as immigrant for the colony.

3. British Public Funding transfers

Public Capital formation is obviously different to private capital formation. I have given an example of rural-based private capital formation elsewhere in this study and will do so again here, in order to demonstrate both types of capital investment.

Private capital formation took many forms; the early settlers, bought or built houses, they built or bought furnishings, they had carriages and often employed water conservation techniques, which included tanks or earthen dams.

As the system of land grants was expanded and farming was encouraged the spread of settlement required a combination of public and private investment.

The government had to provide roads and townships, and the settlers had to provide pastoral investment. This pastoral (rural-based) capital formation usually consisted of five main types of assets:

Buildings—residence, outbuildings, wool shed or grain storage
Fences—stockyards, posts and rails
Water conservation—dams, tanks, wells
Plant—cultivators, tools
Stocks—food, clothing, household items, materials for animal care and general repairs—livestock

Public capital on the other hand was a socio-economic based government asset, and included:

Roads, bridges, crossings, drainage, excavation and embanking, retaining walls

Hospital, storehouses, military barracks, convict barracks, Court-house, police posts, government office buildings

Market house, burial ground, Church, tollhouse, military magazines.

Obviously the list can go on and on.

Major Public Works in NSW 1817-1821

Roads
Sydney to Botany Bay
Sydney to South Head
Parramatta to Richmond
Liverpool to Bringelly, the Nepean and Appin
Buildings
Sydney
A military hospital; military barracks; convict barracks; carters barracks; Hyde Park
Toll-house; residences for the Supreme Court Judge, the Chaplain and the
Superintendent of Police; an asylum; a fort and powder magazines; stables for
Government House; a market house; a market wharf; a burial ground; St. James
Church
Parramatta
All Saint's church spire; a hospital; a parsonage; military and convict barracks; a
Factory; stables and coach-house at Government House; a reservoir
Windsor
St. Matthew's Church; military barracks; convict barracks
Liverpool
St. Luke's church; a gaol; a wharf; convict barracks

4. Economic Development

K. Dallas in an article on *Transportation and Colonial Income* writes, "The history of economic development in Australia is concerned with the transplanting of British economic life into a unique and novel environment. All colonial societies resemble each other in the problems of transplanting, but only in Australia was there no indigenous communal life vigorous enough to influence the course of future development"[85]

Dallas in the same article declares, "The economic effects of the transportation system are usually misunderstood. The real development of Australia begins with the pastoral industry and the export of wool in the 1820s. Until then, penal settlements were a base fore whalers, and made the pastoral possibilities known to English capitalist sheep farmers earlier than they would otherwise have known."[86]

Since this is such a major point on which much disagreement exists, an analysis of its merits is required. No less an authority than N.G. Butlin, J.Ginswick and Pamela Statham disagree, and they record in their introduction to 'The economy before 1850 "the history books are preoccupied with the pastoral expansion in NSW. It is reasonably certain from the musters that a great many complex activities developed and Sydney soon became not merely a port town but a community providing many craft products and services to the expanding settlement".[87]

The next section of this study outlines the remarkable contribution of Governor Macquarie between 1810 and 1821, most of the physical development taking place before the arrival of Commissioner J.T. Bigge in 1819. The table of infrastructure and public building development below confirms that the greatest period of economic development in the colonial economy took place under the Macquarie Administration and did not wait until the spread of settlement and the rise in the pastoral industry (which brought with it so many economic problems) in the late 1820s and 1830s.

---

[85] Dallas, Keith *Transportation & Colonial Income* Historical Studies ANZ Vol 3 October 1944-February 1949

[86] Dallas *ibid*

[87] The Australians: Statistics Chapter 7 'The economy before 1850'

British Investments into the Colony of NSW in the 19th Century

Classifn Type	PERIOD 1800-25	1826-50	1850-75	1876-85	1886-90	1891-1900	Total
Private							
Govt borrowings o/seas		2350000	3861000	5458000	16066000	14709000	42444000
Immigrant's capital	547000	875000	1250000	1983000	2719000	956000	8330000
Foreigner's Investment	2166000	2750000	3038000	8597000	13791000	11420000	41762000
land mortgages	-	5700000					5700000
S/Total	2713000	11675000	8149000	16038000	32576000	27085000	98236000
		14388000					
Public							
British Treasury Grants	9855000	13886000					23741000
Convict tranps/food	2074550	3977000					6051550
British Treasury Bills	2018584	3366000					5384584
Civil List	333858	555000					888858
Military	696170	8933000					9629170
Commissary	2968000	5166000					8134000
Public Works	41000	1224000					1265000
S/Total	17987162	37107000	0	0	0	0	55094162
TOTAL	20700162	48782000	8149000	16038000	32576000	27085000	153330162

IMPACT OF THE COLONIAL ISOLATION DURING THE 1800S

The question of isolation was of positive benefit to the British authorities because the concept of creating a *'dumping ground for human garbage'* was synonymous with finding a *'penal wasteland that was out of sight and out of mind'*.

However the disadvantages to the Colonial authorities were numerous

a. There was the tyranny of distance—the huge risks, of frightening transportation by sailing ship to a land hitherto unknown, uncharted and unexplored, promising huge risks and great loss of life.

b. Food preservation during the voyage and in the Colony was a challenge with no refrigeration or ice. The only preservatives being salt and pickling.

c. Communications between Sydney and London made exchange of correspondence, obtaining decisions and permission tiresomely long. It often occurred that the Colonial Governor wrote to a

{}

Colonial Secretary, who during the twelve months of round trip, had been replaced with another person.

d. Laws and justice, in the Colony, were to be based on British law, but in reality, local laws became a mix of common sense and personal philosophies eg Lt Governor Collins, as Advocate-General in the Colony desperately needed law books to practice, but they were never sent. Bligh, as Governor, ruled virtually as a despot and tyrannical dictator, knowing that a sea trip of seven months was between him and any admonishment or complaints being heard.

Factors Affecting British Investment in the Colony

A number of factors affected the level of capital investment into the colony—many were ill informed and relied on delayed newspaper reports on activity in the various settlements.

a. The offer of assisted migration
b. The failing economic conditions in Britain
c. Economic expansion for the pastoral industry due to successful exploration in the colony
d. The settlement at Port Phillip and the eventual separation of Victoria from New South Wales would promote great investment opportunities
e. The rise of the squattocracy
f. The crash of 1827-28 in the colony shakes British Investors
g. The Bigge's' Report of 1823 breathed new life into capital formation especially with Macarthur sponsoring the float of the Australian Agricultural Company
h. Further along, the good credit rating of the colonies (and there being no defaults on loans) encouraged larger investments and loans into the colonies
i. Shortage of Labour in the colony and the offer of land grants to new settlers became a useful carrot to attract small settlers bringing their own capital by way of cash or goods or livestock with them.
j. Two other steps had important consequences, one in the colony and the other in Britain. In 1827 Governor Darling began to issue grazing licenses to pastoralists, and the terms were set at 2/6d per hundred acres, with liability to quit on one month's notice.

From this movement grew, writes Mad wick in Immigration into Eastern Australia, the squatting movement and the great pastoral expansion, and the idea of the earlier Governors that the colony of New South Wales should be a colony of farmers was thus abandoned. The concurrent event was the floating of the Australian Agricultural Company in London. Development by the AAC and by the free settlers brought increasing prosperity. Exports tripled between 1826 and 1831.

k. There is a connection between availability of factors of production and the level of investment. In the early days of the colony, labour was present—bad labour, convict labour, but still labour. The governors had demanded settlers with capital to employ that labour and develop the land. They proposed to limit land grants in proportion to the means of the settler. Governor Darling declared (HRA ser 1, vol 8) that 'when I am satisfied of the character, respectability and means of the applicant settler in a rural area, he will receive the necessary authority to select a grant of land, proportionate in extent to the means he possesses.

Under Macquarie the colony had boomed with new buildings, new settlements, new investment and lots of convicts. Under Brisbane the needs for economic consolidation and new infrastructure would be addressed, together with an appeal for free settlers.

Some significant events took place during the Brisbane guardianship

- The British were intent on accessing every available trading opportunity with the colony, and formed in Scotland *The Australia Company*
- A road was built to connect the Windsor settlement to the new settlement at Maitland. This decision opened up the Hunter River district to new farming opportunities
- The responsibility for convicts was transferred from the Superintendent of Convicts to the Colonial Secretary, although this move was to be reversed within the next decade
- The first documented discovery of gold was made. It was hushed in the colony lest convicts run off to find their fortunes

- In Bigge's third and final report, he recommended extra colonial import duties and less British duty on imported timber and tanning bark

The most significant event of all was the confidence placed in Bigge's favourable opinion of the potential of the colonial economy by the London Investment community and the resulting subscription of one million pound for the Australian Agricultural Company. The subscription was accompanied by a grant of one million acres of land around Port Stephens and the allocation of 5,000 convicts, but also brought inflation to livestock prices and availability throughout the colony.

J.F. Campbell wrote about the first decade of the Australian Agricultural Company 1824-1834 in the proceedings of the 1923 RAHS.

"Soon after Commissioner Bigge's report of 1823 became available for public information, several enterprising men concerted with a view to acquire sheep-runs in the interior of this colony, for the production of fine wool.

The success which attended the efforts of John Macarthur and a few other New South Wales pastoralists, in the breeding and rearing of fine woolled sheep and stock generally, as verified by Bigge, gave the incentive and led to the inauguration of proceedings which resulted in the formation of the Australian Agricultural Company.

The first formal meeting of the promoters took place at Lincoln's Inn, London, (at the offices of John Macarthur, junior).

Earl Bathurst, advised Governor Brisbane in 1824 that . . . .

His Majesty has been pleased to approve the formation of the Company, from the impression that it affords every reasonable prospect of securing to that part of His Majesty's dominions the essential advantage of the immediate introduction of large capital, and of agricultural skill, as well as the ultimate benefit of the increase of fine wool as a valuable commodity for export.

The chief proposals of the company are:

i. The company was to be incorporated by Act of Parliament or Letters Patent.

ii. The capital of the company was to be 1 million pound sterling divided into 10,000 shares of £100 each

iii. A grant of land of one million acres to be made to the company

iv. That no rival joint stock company to be established in the colony for the next twenty years

v. That agents of the company would select the situation or the land grants.

vi. The shepherds and labourers would consist of 1,400 convicts, thereby lessening the maintenance of such convicts by an estimated £30,800 or £22 per head/ per annum.

The Royal Charter of 1824 forming the company provided for payment of quit-rents over a period of twenty years, or the redemption of the same by paying the capital sum of 20 times the amount of the rent so to be redeemed. These quit-rents were to be waived if the full number of convicts were maintained for a period of five years. No land was to be sold during the five-year period from the date of the grant".

Being important that the investment be seen to have the support of strong leaders in Britain, and democratic governance, the company operated with

- A Governor
- 25 directors
- 365 stockholders (proprietors)

Leading stockholders included

- Robert Campbell
- Chief Justice Forbes
- Son of Governor King
- Rev'd Samuel Marsden
- John Macarthur

- Each Macarthur son, John jr, Hannibal, James, Charles, Scott & William

John Oxley, the Colonial-Surveyor had recommended the area of Port Stephens as an eligible spot for the land grant. The local directors inspected and approved the site but John Macarthur was extremely critical of the selection, the management plan and the extravagance of the first buildings.

This venture was the first major investment into the colony and set the scene for later developments. In 1825 the Van Diemen's Land Company was chartered by the British Parliament and granted land on the northwest corner of the territory.

Both the A.A. Coy and the VDL Coy still operate today after nearly 180 years of continuous operation, a record beaten only by the operation of the Hudson Bay Company in Canada.

Sir Timothy Coghlan was the colonial statistician whilst he was involved in preparing the series 'The Wealth and Progress of New South Wales 1900-01'. He was later appointed as Agent-General in London before compiling the 4-volume set of 'Labour and Industry in Australia'.

Circumstances in Britain contributed greatly to the climate of 'greener pastures' over the seas.

Conditions were never more favourable for emigration than they were during the 1830s. The decade had opened with rioting in the agricultural districts in the south of England. This was followed by the upheavals of the Reform Bill of 1832, the Factory Act of 1833 and the Corn Laws, which kept wages low and unemployment high. The Poor Law of 1834 withdrew assistance from the poor and re-introduced the workhouse. The Irish rebellion was creating both upheaval and poverty

These conditions were met by the enthusiastic reports coming from Australia of the progress being made in agriculture, commerce and the pastoral industry. The assistance granted to emigrants as a result of Edward Gibbon Wakefield's reforms made possible the emigration of people who had previously been prevented by the expense. It is almost certain that free passage would not have been a sufficient enticement if conditions in Britain had not been unfavourable. It is significant that years of small migration coincided with good conditions in England accompanied by unfavourable reports from the colony.

4. Creating Opportunities in the Colony

Availability of land and labour to yield profit on invested capital is the constant decisive condition and test of material prosperity in any community, and becomes the keystone of an economy as well as defining its national identity.

British Government policy for the Australian colonies was formulated and modified from time to time. Policies for the export of British capital and the supply of labour (both convict and free) were adjusted according to British industrial and demographic and other social situations, as well as the capability and capacity of the various colonial settlements top contribute to solving British problems.

By the 1820s there was official encouragement of British Investment in Australia by adopting policies for large land grants to persons of capital and for the sale of land and assignment of convict labour to those investors. Then followed the reversal of the policy of setting up ex-convicts on small 30 acre plots as small proprietors. The hardship demanded by this policy usually meant these convicts and families remained on the commissary list for support (food and clothing) at a continuing cost to the government. It was much cheaper to assign these convicts to men of property and capital who would support them fully—clothe, house and feed them.

We can ask, what led directly to the crash of 1827?

a. Firstly, the float of the Australian Agricultural Company raised a large amount of capital, mostly from the City of London investment community, and this contributed to speculation and 'sheep and cattle mania instantly seized on all ranks and classes of the inhabitants' (written by Rev'd John Dunmore Lang) 'and brought many families to poverty and ruin'.

b. When capital imports cease, the wherewithal to speculate vanished; speculation perforce stopped; inflated prices fell to a more normal level, and wrote E.O. Shann in Economic History of Australia 'because those formerly too optimistic were now too despairing, and people had to sell goods at any price in order to get money; men who had bought at high prices were ruined, and perforce their creditors fell with them'.

c. In 1842, it was the same. The influx of capital from oversees, pastoral extension, and large-scale immigration, caused much speculation. The banks, competing for business, advanced too much credit. Loans were made on the security of land and livestock, which later became almost worthless; too much discounting was done for merchants (Gipps, HRA Vol 23) In the huge central district on the western slopes, along the Murrumbidgee and the Riverina, the squatters triumphed, as was inevitable. He had the financial resources to buy his run—especially after the long period of drought. Four million acres of crown land was sold for nearly £2.5 million. The confidence of British investors was waning. A crisis in the Argentine and the near failure of the large clearinghouse of Baring's made them cautious. Stories of rural and industrial strife in the colony were not inducements to invest: and wood and metal prices were still falling Loan applications being raised in London were under-subscribed, at the same time the banks were increasingly reluctant to lend money for land development, which was so often unsound.

5. Assisted Migration

The dual policy of selling land to people with sufficient capital to cultivate it, and keeping a careful check on the number of free grants was adopted after 1825. 'Yet the Colonial Office', says Madgwick, 'failed to administer land policy with any certainty (R.B. Madgwick 'Immigration into Eastern Australia'). There was no uniform policy adopted to encourage economic development in a systematic and rational way. The Wakefield system found new supporters. The principle had been established that the sale of land was preferred to the old system of grants. The dual system of sales and grants had failed to encourage local (colonial) purchases. They were willing to accept grants or even 'squat' rather than purchase land. Sales to absentee landlords and investors stepped up, and as can be seen from the following table, provided extensive revenue to the British Government to promote free and sponsored migration.

6. Successful exploration promotes new interest in the Colony

A period of rapid expansion followed the change in economic policy. Wool exports by 1831 were 15 times as great as they had been only 10 years earlier (in 1821). The increase in the number of sheep led to a rapid opening of new territories for grazing. It was the search for new land with economic value that underpinned most of the explorations. Settlers and sheep-men quickly followed exploration, and growth fanned out in all directions from Sydney town.

However, exploration was not the only catalyst for growth.

a. The growing determination to exclude other powers from the continent stimulated official interest in long-distance exploration by sea and by land and in the opening of new settlements. For instance, J.M. Ward in his work 'The Triumph of the Pastoral Economy 1821-1851' writes that Melville and Bathurst Islands, were annexed and settled between 1824 and 1827, whilst Westernport and Albany were settled in order to clinch British claims to the whole of Australia

b. When Governor Brisbane opened the settlement at Moreton Bay in 1824, it was to establish a place for punishment of unruly convicts and a step towards further economic development, and of extending the settlements for the sake of attracting new investment

7. Colonial Failures fuel loss of Confidence

The collapse of British Investment can be traced to one or two causes, or indeed both.

I. The British crisis of 1839 reflected the availability of capital for expansion by the Australian banks of that day—The Bank of Australasia and the Union Bank. These banks, three mortgage companies and the Royal Bank went into a slump due to shortage of available funds and deferred the raising of new funds until after the crisis. Stringency in the English Capital market had a serious impact on the capital raising opportunities in the colonies.

II. The second possibility is that the sharp decline was initiated by bad news of returns in the colonies, and that its role accentuated a slump with the dire consequences experienced in 1842-43. Recovery was delayed and made more difficult as there was 'no surplus labour in the colony'

It would be dangerous to imply or decide that every slump in Australia could be explained as being caused by economic evens. British investment was independent then, as it is now, and so the more valid explanation of the downturn in British investment in this period is that negative reports from the colonies disappointed and discouraged investors with capital to place.

Most facts about public finance in New South Wales lead to the conclusion that it was disappointed expectations that caused the turn down in the transfer of funds. At this same time Governor Gipps (Sir George Gipps) was being pushed by bankers and merchants to withdraw government deposits from the banks and thus this action caused a contraction in lending by the banks which in turn caused a slow down of colonial economic activity. The attached statistics of land sales, registered mortgages and liens on wool and livestock reflects the strong downturn in the agricultural economy, which naturally flowed on to the economy as a whole.

CHAPTER 4

THE NEED FOR
MANUFACTURING

Hainsworth in his Chapter Twelve 'Dawn of Industry' from _The Sydney Traders_88 guides us in a review of the growth of manufactures before 1825.

'Thanks to the initiative of Sydney traders, manufacturing and processing industries emerged very early and helped to transform NSW from penal settlement to colony'.

The traders supplemented government activity, often by carrying out similar activities, and sometimes launched various types of manufacturing in which the government was not concerned. It was natural that the government should play a dominant role at this early stage, for it had the responsibility of clothing, housing, feeding and working the convicts, both male and female. The government role was as the chief employer of the convicts, the chief provider of capital and of course, the chief consumer of their output. In a limited way, the government was prepared to foster industrial enterprise, though this encouragement was haphazard, capricious and oftentimes playing favourites. The government, itself, launched brewing, salt-making, milling and basic textiles, and operated a number of crude industrial processes before allowing them to be taken

---

88   Hainsworth, D.R. The Sydney Traders

over by enterprising colonists on favourable terms. Privatisation was not a deliberate policy, one more so of convenience.

Sealing[89] by 1800 was dominating the trading calendar. The official return for that year showed over 118,000 skins had passed through Sydney with Simeon Lord and his fellow ex-convicts, Kable and Underwood handling over 72,000 from just one source—Antipodes Island. By 1815, the *Sydney Gazette* was reporting the sealing industry was in decline. The intense harvesting of the seals had lowered their natural numbers, but the British Government was influenced by the 'whale lobby' to raise discriminatory duties against colonial oil, seal and whale. Spermaceti oil was to bear a duty of 15s 9d per ton for British ships but £24 18s 9d if obtained by colonial ships. Duties of £8 8s a ton were imposed on Black Whale oil from the Derwent estuary. Thus through these discriminatory tariffs, colonial oil was virtually barred from London.

Cottage industries were not only the preserve of the small home-based manufacturers. Coghlan[90] points out 'those who had the enterprise and industry to devote land to gardening were amply repaid'. The broad acre crops raised were chiefly wheat and maize, with a little oats and barley, some potatoes and other vegetables.

Excellent opportunities, for fresh fruit and vegetables, were provided by the weather, the climate and the generally good soil around Sydney, but gardening was not undertaken other than by the few conscious of home grown vegetables. They were able, says Coghlan, 'to grow almost all ordinary English vegetables, all the English fruits and some fruits, such as grapes, grew in abundance. Macquarie described his garden at Parramatta as 'full of vines and fruit trees and abounding in the most excellent vegetables'

Stock-raising was given impetus when, in 1805, the two Blaxland brothers arrived in the colony, bringing a considerable amount of capital and more than a little acquaintance with husbandry of cattle. In 1810, horned cattle numbers stood at 12,442. Ten years later, when Macquarie left, the herds

---

89   Based on Hainsworth 'The Sydney Traders Ch12 'The Dawn of Industry'
90   Coghlan, T.A. 'Labour & Industry in Australia' (Page 117—Vol I)

numbered 102,939, so that the annual increase was at the rate of 20.5%. The numbers were carefully guarded and there was no undue slaughtering, and salt beef was still being imported in 1814. Even so, the records show that beef was cheap with a herd selling at £8 per head. Horses, says Coghlan, 'throve'[91] in the settlement from the beginning although their numbers increased very slowly. In 1800 there were only 203 horses, but by 1810 the numbers had grown to 1134 and by 1821, the numbers totalled 4564.

Coghlan recognises the importance of the timber industry and writes "the export of timber became fairly considerable and in 1803, Governor King spoke of it as the only staple of the colony"—the inland forests could not be exploited because of the lack of any means of transport, and as a result 'numerous saw-pits were established on the inlets of Port Jackson, along the banks of the Hawkesbury, and later at Newcastle on the Hunter, where convicts were engaged cutting timber as well as in mining coal"

Occasionally cargoes were shipped to India, and in 1809 timber to the value of £1500 was sent to that country in part payment for a return shipment of rice. "The presence of so much valuable timber would in ordinary circumstances have led to the establishment of shipbuilding yards. Vessels were built for sealing purposes as early as 1791, but the presence of craft capable of going to sea was considered a menace to the safe-keeping of the convicts and the governor directed no boats were to be built of greater length than 14 feet". Hunter removed this restriction in 1798, and in fact encouraged the shipbuilding industry by permitting a vessel of 'thirty tons to be built to procure seal skins and oil in Bass Straits'.[92] Campbell then built a vessel of 130 tons launched in 1805[93].

There was considerable activity mostly through the *Dockyard* (attached to the Commissary) in boat-repairs, refurbishing and provisioning, but the stoppage of the fishery in 1810 was a serious blow to the industry.

---

[91]   This is an editor's change—the Coghlan text states 'shrove'
[92]   Coghlan, Labour & Industry Vol 1 Page 121-2
[93]   Steven, Margaret 'Merchant Campbell 1769-1846'

Immigration to the colony was mostly by way of assigned servants between 1821 and 1826, but the difficulty experienced in collecting the payments for the servants made the whole notion difficult. Coghlan tells "in the matter of indentured service many employers, principally those in the country districts were willing to advance £8-10 towards the cost of each immigrant labourer obtained by them and in February 1832 Governor Bourke despatched a list of 803 labourers who might be sent out on these terms. It was on immigration at the cost of land revenue that the colonial authorities placed their confidence. They offered to set aside £10,000 from the land fund for emigration purposes; of this sum they desired that about two-thirds be devoted to promoting the emigration of unmarried women, as the proportion of men in the colony was excessive and that one-third should be used in loans for the emigration of mechanics".

After 1836, it was decided that the whole of the rapidly increasing land revenue of NSW should be devoted to immigration[94] and in 1837 over 3090 immigrants were brought to the colony of whom 2688 were sponsored through the Emigration Commissioners in London and 405 were under the bounty scheme by colonial employers.

The need for manufacturing in the colony was created by local demand for tools, materials and supplies, in large demand for meeting general construction and housing needs. Manufacturing in the colony was catered by the private sector and the government sector. The private sector was sponsored by a handful of entrepreneurs or skilled settlers, who wanted to satisfy local demand for their product by creating a 'cottage industry', due to generally limited demand and a constantly changing market. The public/government sector became involved through the commissariat operations

in order to put convicts to productive work, reverse the long lead time for purchasing urgent materials from Britain, and more fully utilise the 'free' local resources such as timber and convict labour. Barnard observes[95] 'The colony was never wholly penal, like France neither's Devil Island, nor was it intended to be. It was, in due course, to be balanced by freed men,

---

[94] Coghlan 'Labour & Industry in Australia—Vol I Page 178
[95] Barnard, Marjorie *A History of Australia* 1962 (Page 304)

their children, and such other settlers, soldiers, seamen and the like who cared to take the reward for their services in land, of which the Crown had a superfluity. Actually, NSW suffered very little from being a penal settlement and was fortunate in that her first unpromising colonizing material was early swamped by infusions of new blood, that wool, land grants and then gold attracted free colonists. There were no foreign elements to arouse Imperial suspicion, no subject race to put what might have been considered a necessary brake on progress'. This statement by Barnard is a rewriting of history, but would be an ideal policy, if it were true. The settlement was designed to be a penal one, and every move made was designed to be about the convicts—their work, protecting them from themselves, feeding, clothing and maintaining them, providing them with tools, equipment and supplies. Laissez-faire might have been in vogue in London during the Phillip Administration but the settlement struggled whilst awaiting food and other supplies, and convicts were held tightly accountable for all their activities. Until 1823, the entire responsibility for the settlement rested on the Governor. Upon him was bestowed a power to control lawlessness, which he effectively exercised.

The diversity of manufacturing within the colony by 1821, at the end of the Macquarie Administration was far more impressive than could reasonably be expected from a former penal colony transforming itself into a free market economy. Macquarie's enthusiasm for free enterprise and 'cost saving' led to great production sponsored by the commissariat. Convict labour was considered to be without 'cost' and therefore without 'value', as was local raw materials, so much of the output of the commissariat business enterprises left without recognition of value, which well-suited Macquarie's purposes. Ass early as 1812, he had been sternly warned by Colonial Secretary Liverpool [96] that 'the burden of the colony of NSW upon the Mother Country has been so much increased since the period of your assumption of the government of it, that it becomes necessary that you should transmit a more satisfactory explanation of the grounds upon which the unusual expenditure has been sanctioned by you'. Liverpool admitted he had misgivings of this attack when he continued his letter to Macquarie in terms of 'I can't point out what expenses have been unnecessarily incurred, and the only ground I have for forming a judgement

---

[96]   HRA 1:7:476 Liverpool to Macquarie 4th May,1812

is by comparison of the total amount of bills by your predecessors and yourself'. Naturally enough, absolute total were progressively higher, but in terms of bills drawn per head of convict on the store' the comparisons declined. Macquarie was actively creating an investment for the future, and at some future point the colony could easily be self-supporting and outside the need for treasury appropriations. However, in philosophical terms, why should the local revenues be used to support any form of a penal colony for Britain. Surely the free settlers could grow in conjunction with the transfer of convicts to the colony; whilst Britain supported the convicts and the colony supported its own operations. One of Macquarie's goals in having the government business enterprises so active in the colony was to quickly achieve this self-sufficiency and be out from the clutches of Whitehall. Macquarie's thinking was only half right. He was so preoccupied with the economic and fiscal arrangements in the colony that he lost sight of the overall plan. Local revenues were first raised in 1802 and were designed for 'discretionary' expenditure by the governor of the day. The reason for this loose arrangement was that the Treasury appropriated funds for specific purposes such as convict maintenance, and civil establishment salaries, but did not see the need for maintenance works, repairs, infrastructure development and the like, so the money for these essentials had to come from local sources and be reserved for deployment by the government. Whitehall soon caught onto this stream of revenue and although the Treasury officials new it was illegal revenue, they restricted its use by withholding British funds to the amount of revenue raised within the colony. Thus in Macquarie's administration, private enterprise figured as a means of both import replacement and cost saving for the colony. Manufacturing filled the joint roles of availability of key/essential merchandise and of putting convicts to productive work.

Barnard records[97] that even the 'boys—some as young as eleven—were kept in Sydney at Carter's Barracks near Brickfield Hill and were working as a carpenter, shoemaker, stone-cutter, blacksmith, and other trades to which the boys were apprenticed. The product of their labour went into the public store, and a pool of much needed mechanics was created'. This observation is rather unique, is unsourced and does not have the ring of accuracy about it. Barnard is implying that these trades were carried out

---

[97] Barnard, M *A History of Australia* Page 237

at the Barracks, which means that materials and tools were brought daily to the barracks. With carts and bodies for hauling purposes being in very short supply, it seems unlikely that large lumps of stone or tree trunks would be hauled from Upper George Street (the Lumber Yard was at the corner of George and Bridge) all the way to Brickfields Hill for young boys to play with. The carter barracks were used for confinement and punishment, and there was little space for practicing wood craft or stone masonry. It is much more likely that the boys were released on a weekly basis, under supervision, and taken to the raw materials source—for instance the stone-yard and the Timber Yard, which were both on George Street North. This is a rare unsourced apparent contradiction by Barnard. She is probably incorrect when she states the apprentices' output went to the public store—it probably went to the Lumber Yard store—from where all building materials, supplies and tools were inventoried. The public store kept only dry goods, fresh foods or grain.

The extent of private sector manufacturing ranged from clothing, castings and carts to soap, silver-smithing, tanneries and tin-smithing. In addition government manufacturing covered an equally broad range—from nails to timber framing, bricks tiles and stone blocks, forged items and boot making.

The broad intent, because of the small local population, which by itself would not have supported such a sector, was two-fold—to replace imports and the timeframe of a year or two between ordering and receipt of goods, and to create an export market of sorts.

According to Jackson[98], the population in the colony during 1820 was only 34,000 and too small to create sufficient demand for private sector output and to establish economic development.

The early entrepreneurs and their activities raise numerous questions which to-date has not been studied in the literature. Hainsworth records[99] 'Simeon Lord cannot be described as a typical emancipist trader for his operations were too large and diverse, but he was a member of a numerous

---

[98]   R.V. Jackson *Australian Economic Development in the 19th Century*
[99]   H.R. Hainsworth *Sydney Traders* P.41

group. Another was Henry Kable, whose commercial beginnings are still more shadowy—an illiterate man transported in the first fleet, Kable was for several years a constable of Sydney and probably profitably plied with liquor the drunks he locked up'. What Hainsworth is by implication questioning, is how these two (of many) eventually became such successful traders? What was their source of start up monies? How did these emancipist traders get started? Hainsworth, later in his study concludes 'the capital they mobilised for shipbuilding and sealing in 1800 must have come from trading'[100] Other examples of early unexplained success include John Palmer and his associates, who as the third Commissary on 5/—per day, became the wealthiest man in the colony during the King Administration, and that was before his sister, Sophia, married the largest merchant in the colony, Robert Campbell. Palmer and his trading colleagues prospered in a colony whose commercial life was supposed to be monopolised by an officer clique.[101] Although the officer class is usually described by historians as having caste a large shadow in the early 1790s under Hunter, they could not stop an undertow of small dealers and emerging traders growing up around them. Rather the officers brought this about by allowing the retail trade to fall into the hands of 'ambitious and able (if uneducated) men with no gentility to lose'[102] In many cases because the wholesale market was officer controlled and these emancipist retailers wanted to continue to expand and grow, they moved into 'cottage' manufacturing—often working with the commissariat to supply finished goods or raw materials for further processing by the Lumber Yard or Female Factory (e.g. Tanned leather, scoured wool, and crushed grain). For many emerging entrepreneurs, this was the way they commenced their manufacturing activities—trader, marketer and then manufacturer. According to Hainsworth[103], Simeon Lord was typical of the early merchant traders. When a shortage of circulating notes occurred, Lord (amongst others) requested his creditor customers to liquidate their debts to him by any means possible. The result was that Lord accepted grain, (which he then put into the store on his own account), most of which he had bartered from his retail customers, payroll bills from military officers

---

[100] Hainsworth refers his readers, on this point, to his inserts in the ADB for Lord, Kable and Underwood Volumes 1 & 2
[101] ADB Volume 2—John Palmer (Hainsworth)
[102] Hainsworth *The Sydney Traders* Page 42
[103] Hainsworth *Sydney Traders* Page 83

with whom he was dealing on a wholesale basis, individual 'notes or bills' payable, which were freely circulating and classed as petty banking. Lord would consolidate these bills and exchange them for one large bill drawn by the Commissariat on the Treasury in London. This bill he would then release to his suppliers—usually visiting ship's captains, or transfer to his Indian or Macao (Hong Kong) suppliers. So obviously the greatest limitation to entrepreneurial activity in the colony was 'the medium of exchange: the lack of a mint and a Treasury, or even a private bank of issue. However with all its faults the system worked. It was the only system they had and the traders made the best use of it'.[104]

Thus private sector output was limited by government demand for food and materials.

The Jackson theory is that the sale of goods to the government store (commissariat) provided a major source of foreign exchange to the private sector because sale proceeds were made available in the form of Treasury Bills drawn on London.

Organisation of Government Business Enterprises.

Under the guise of controlling the activities and rehabilitation of convicts, Macquarie decided that placing all convicts on assignment, thereby removing any financial obligation for their maintenance, a percentage could be put to work on behalf of the government. This would be accomplished in two ways. Firstly, direct convict labour, rather than the preferred contractor program, would be used for infrastructure development and the other public works program, specifically government building.

So there became a great concentration of convicts in Sydney, employed in two big workshops, the lumber-yard and the timber-yard. Both were located on George Street, together with the stone-yard (across from the lumber-yard) and the three-storey Commissary Store, wharf and Dockyard, fronting the western side of Sydney Cove. The convicts worked on a task, or piece system. In the Lumber Yard, surrounded by an 8 foot high brick wall, for security purposes, forges were used for making nail,

---

[104]   Abbott & Nairn (*Growth*) Chapters 8 & 9

hinges, wheel irons and other metal products. Other 'sections' were set aside around the outside walls of the factory, for boot-making, cabinet and furniture-making, coopers for barrel making, course wool and cotton for slops and hat making. In the centre of the large factory the two saw pits were manned by up to 25 men, who cut the timber taken from the kiln after its drying process. In the timber yards, beams and floor-boards were sawn and prepared from the timber drawn from the lumber-yard. The brick and tile yard was built around a huge kiln (22 feet long by 18 feet high producing 24,000 bricks at one raking. The Stone-yard not only produced large building blocks from stone but also flagstones, hearth-stones and mantelpieces. Within the lumber-yard, was stored all the tools required within the various business enterprises as well as on each work site. Each item was recorded going out and coming in. Equally carefully, all materials—both raw material and finished product—were recorded at the clerk's office located at the main gate. The Superintendent of Convicts, Major Ovens had set a piece work productivity rate. For instance, the shoemaker's gang of about eight me, were supposed to produce a pair of shoes each day, each man from leather tanned at the government factory at Cawdor; likewise, the brass-foundry and the tailors' gang each had their own production goals; the carpenter's gang which was usually of fifty men, was made up of cabinet-makers, turners and shinglers; the bricklayers' gang was generally between five and ten men who were expected to lay 4,500 bricks each week; the Sawyers gang was usually twenty-five men. Other gangs based in the lumber yard were also sent out to garden, cut grass, dig foundations, and carry grain. The lumber yard was responsible for over 2,000 men in all.

The government business enterprises were a comprehensive and massive undertaking, and Macquarie took pride in their output and accomplishments.

Manufacturing is only part of the story included in any study of economic development of the period. Economic development drove public finance in the same way that population growth, pastoral growth and growth of decentralisation and land utilisation impacted on the source and use of public funds. Other factors to be considered include:

1. The commissariat established multiple stores and supplied foodstuffs and materials (at government expense) not only for convicts but for civilian and military personnel as well. In the early years, well over 50% of the entire population would have been victualled by the commissariat
2. The commissariat also established, work centres for convicts:

    i.   The Lumber Yard,
    ii.   The Timber Yard
    iii.   The Dockyard
    iv.   The Stone Quarry
    v.   The Boat Yard
    vi.   Timber-Cutting Camps
    vii.   Land Clearing Camps
    viii. The Government Farms
    ix.   The Government stores

These centres employed until 1820 over 50% of the convict population.

The output of these centres was directed at Agricultural output; Livestock supply;

Import Replacement manufactures; Materials required in the Construction and building industries; Materials required in the Public Works and Infrastructure Construction program, and Transport and storage requirements of the government.

Colin White[105] in has concluded that the colonial government controlled the local economic mechanism. There were three main elements to the mechanism:

> (1)The government provided the social infrastructure to mitigate risk to individuals, and further, (2) guaranteed a market, at fixed prices, for output of the private sector. This government action also provided (3) grants of free land, inexpensive credit

---

[105] *Mastering Risk—Environment, Markets and Politics in Australian Economic History* Page 52

and cheap labour with the return of any redundant labour to government service when needed.

Public Works

Public Investment in public works infrastructure was a major challenge. Britain essentially saw the settlement as little more than a tent town. These inhabitants were prisoners, under guard, transported 'out of sight and out of mind' and had no need of money or coins, public buildings or fancy housing or amenities. Early governors from Phillip to Bligh kept to the minimum work and therefore expense, and by the time of Macquarie's arrival, there was a deferred maintenance and construction schedule that dumped all of the expense and workload on his Administration. Commissioner Bigge recorded for his Enquiry that 76 buildings had been completed under Macquarie, some of which were extravagant for example the Governor's *Stables*, The Rum Hospital, and the toll booths on the Parramatta Road. Bigge directed they be revamped and put to alternate (less extravagant use). Bigge made no comment on the provision of water, sewer or drainage measures made for a town with a growing population. Macquarie had drained the marshes in the present Centennial Park as the water supply for the town—and outlawed the use of the Tank Stream for animal grazing, washing, and waste sewer.

Governor Darling, as part of his structuring of a public service for the colony, established in 1826 the first Office of Inspector of Roads and Bridges, with charge over the Engineer's office. From April 1827, his title was changed to Surveyor of Roads and Bridges, and the office remained active until 1830, when in an economy drive, Sir George Murray, Secretary of State for the Colony and War Departments passed these responsibilities to the Surveyor-General. In 1832 the Colonial Architect's Department was established in order to be responsible for the planning, repair and construction of public buildings. In 1833, in another economy drive, this department was also transferred to the Surveyor-General. Later the duties of colonial engineer for superintendence over roads, bridges, wharves and quays were added to those of the Colonial Architect and all planning came under the Surveyor-General. It was this concentration of work load in such few hands that led to an increasing public investment in public works.

Another effort by Governor Darling to centralise planning and control into a new public service bureaucracy, was the establishment of the Clergy and School Lands Department in 1826. The corporation was to receive a seventh in value and extent of all the lands in each county in the colony. Out of this land the corporation was to be responsible for the payment of salaries of clergy, schoolmasters, and for the building and maintenance of churches, school and minister's residences.

Governor Darling had centralised the planning for all public works into one department—the Land's Department which in turn employed the Surveyor-General and provided for the Lands Board. This balance assisted in prioritising and funding all public works and thus brought order to the former Macquarie chaos of building as he saw fit. A by-product of this new policy was that all convicts were now on assignment and 'off the stores', and a competitive contracting arrangement was used for tendering for all public works.

An Economic Model of the Colonial Economy GDP

The pre-1861 period has long been considered[106] too risky to assemble data for creating an economic model of the times. However certain elements of such a model can be identified and used for, in the least, a good indicative assessment of the economic growth between 1788 and 1860.

A practical example of an economic model which could be adapted for the period was found in McTaggart, Findlay and Parkin *Macroeconomics*.

The basis for the model is that 'aggregate expenditure equals aggregate income i.e. $Y - C + I$, where aggregate income (Y) equals aggregate expenditure $(C + I)$'. A corollary will be that aggregate production or GDP = aggregate expenditure = aggregate income'.

There is a circular flow which equates *inputs* and *outputs*

Inputs   Outputs

---

[106]   N.G. Butlin and T.A. Coghlan write of the inaccurate statistics and other data for this period.

Labour	Agricultural Production & Natural resource extraction
Public Capital	Public Infrastructure
Private sector subsidies by government	Manufacturing
Imports	Exports
Civilian/military payroll	Entrepreneurial Profits
Foreign Investment	Growth of Inventories
Local Natural Material	Foreign Ownership of Land & Capital
Trees	Import Replacement
Lime	Import Replacement
Clay	Import Replacement

Aggregate expenditure equals aggregate income.
Where:
Consumption expenditure is (C)
Investment is (I)
Government Expenditure on goods/services is (G)
Net Exports is (NX)

GDP = C + I + G + NX (where, NX =EX-IM)

Investment is financed by national saving & overseas borrowing

Disposable Income (consumption expenditure + savings) = Aggregate Income—Net Taxes

Colonial GDP	**Gross Domestic Product**	
Circular Approach		
Aggregate Expenditures **equals**	Aggregate Incomes	£
Consumption expenditures(C) £	Aggregate Income-Taxes = Disposable Income =	
Investment (I) £	Consumption exp + Savings	
Government expenditures (G) £		
Net Exports (NX)		

£

GDP = C+I+G+NX   £

Investment is financed by
National Saving AND Borrowing
Overseas

Colonial GDP
THE PRODUCTION APPROACH

| | 1820 |
	£
Agriculture, Fishery & Forestry	
Mining	
Water, lighting & heating	
Construction	
Wholesale Trade	
Retail Trade	
Hotels, Cafes	
Transport & Storage	
Communication services	
finance & insurance	
Gov't admin & defence	
education	
health & social services	
cultural & recreation	
taxes on products	
Total	
£	

The rise of manufacturing was a significant part of the economic growth in the early colony. Of all the sectors, agriculture (including whaling, sealing and wool) gave the most significant results in terms of manpower used, capital invested, export returns, and GDP. In second place would be the development of local natural resources followed closely by manufacturing outcomes. These observations can be made from individual statistics of employment, exports, convict work organisation and data about immigrants and their assets. However, the more reliable statistics will come from the assembly of a model using either the production approach, or the aggregate income/expenditure approach. Both methods will be attempted and compared, but as can be seen an understanding and assessment of manufacturing is essential to either methodology.

Hainsworth in the prologue to *The Sydney Traders* writes 'To study the 'entrepreneur' is to study the central figure in modern economic history—the central figure in economics'. The years 1788 to 1821 are the seed-time of Australian government'.[107]

Although it is difficult to connect the growth of economic development in percentage of contribution terms for any one sector, we know that the more important sectors must be

1. Growth of population
2. Government immigration policy
3. Foreign capital
4. The need for Import replacement
5. The need for foreign exchange through exports.

In each of these the commissariat had a role and an important government need.

The government had to grow the economy at the lowest practical cost, but offer official services which would attract growth, trade and population. This it achieved, at least through 1821, by using the commissariat as the quasi-treasury, the manager of government business enterprises, and the employer of government-sponsored convict labour.

The point here is that the economic model had to incorporate each of these 'input' factors and reflect them. Here in brief is the methodology used.

The commissariat influence over foreign exchange, imports and exports, and government-sponsored manufacturing and even over attracting foreign investment capital is without comparison, but measurable. The economic model for the period does not nor cannot parallel Butlin's measurement of post-1861 GDP, but does use basic ingredients like:

---

[107]   Hainsworth *Sydney Traders* prologue page 14

1. Computing working free population
2. Computing working convict population
3. Assuming a productivity adjustment for lower than expected convict output
4. Valuing productive labour at Coghlan suggested rates
5. Interpolating labour product to total output.
6. Comparing annual total production per head of population and per head of 'worker'
7. Estimating total output by industry and comparing this to underlying assumptions about labour output.
8. Extending the estimated GDP from 1800 to 1860 to ensure the recessions of 1810-1816, 1828-29 and 1842-45 as shown in the GDP figures were responsive to these downturns.
9. Comparing the growth of local revenues from 1801 and of trade, for the same period reflected changes to estimated GDP.
10. Announcing the adopted GDP figures for the period 1800-1860 and seeing how they blended in with the Butlin figures.

The results are assembled on a spreadsheet for each year, but a summary has been produced as an extract in order to evidence gains for each ten-year interval, and to show that the Beckett compilations and the Butlin compilations fit in with each other.

Table Estimates of GDP between 1800 and 1900

Year	GDP per head of popln	GDP per head of workforce
1801	13.61	35.1
1811	28.06	49.95
1821	33.54	59.70
1831	35.68	63.51
1841	39.66	70.60
1851	40.13	76.43
1861	46	85
1871	47	118
1877	57	139
1881	63	151
1889	67	158
1891	66	155
1900	57	132

Source: Beckett *Handbook of Colonial Statistics for period 1800-1860*

Butlin, N.G. *Investment in Australian Economic Development 1861-1900*

Certain conclusions can be reached about this table:

1. GDP in the colony grew in each ten year period because the components of that GDP grew eg population, manufacturing enterprises, convict numbers, exports and immigration. As the colony went through its transition from penal to free, especially a free market-based economy, so government investment in services and infrastructure also grew. Personal investment in housing increased and the individual wealth as well as the collective wealth of the colony grew. The down turn in 1900 was due to the recession in the mid-1890s, when many banks failed, unemployment increased and the previous land boom of the 1870-80s crashed, leaving many families and businesses in tough times.

    However certain questions remain: This model relates to restricted sectors of the colonial economy, but only touches indirectly on important sectors such as the pastoral industry, the whaling and seal industry. These sectors are indirectly reflective of a growing export market. A more detailed model with declared sub-elements would express the importance of these natural resource or primary production industries including timber, shipping, coal, minerals as well as wool and wool by-products

    There were some distractions from within the colony to Macquarie's aggressive enterprise policies. In a wave of perversion, William Charles Wentworth led an anti-Macquarie movement against local manufacturing in favour of importations.

    In January of 1819, Macquarie gave permission for a group of clergy, merchants, settlers, and other gentlemen to convene a meeting in the court-room of the new General Hospital, to prepare a petition. The petition was for a redress of grievances and essentially was to try and expand rather than restrict imports into the colony. Macquarie by trying to match exports with imports (in value terms), was restricting the type of imports authorised.

Macquarie, in a despatch to Bathurst of 22nd March, 1819 notates[108] the resolution

'1. That a regular demand exists in the colony for British manufactures of nearly all descriptions, greater than the established mercantile houses here have supplied or are likely to supply regularly.
2. Restrictions prevent merchants from employing ships of less three hundred and fifty tons burthen (under the *Navigation Acts)*
3. That this meeting requests Gov Macquarie to try and expand shipping between Britain and Australia for transporting Manufactures and colonial produce.'

The sentiments were laudable but the request baseless. The commissariat with its huge buying opportunities could have achieved the desired result. Merchants' collaborating into a buying group could have achieved the same result but the obvious solution was to encourage the local production of all imported items at a lower cost.

Macquarie made no recommendations to Bathurst, which meant that he had strictly fulfilled his role to the petitioners, and had left Bathurst with the opinion that the colonial manufacturers and merchants were ill-prepared to fight British exports

In over 300 pages of text, John Ritchie[109] reviews the submissions made in the colony to Commissioner Bigge, but does not recite any submission made by merchants or manufacturers. However in the Bigge reports, we find details of evidence submitted by Simeon Lord about his manufacturing activities. At his factory at Botany Bay, he employed between 15 and 20 convicts in the making of:

Blankets	Stockings
Wool hats	Trousers
Kangaroo hats	Glass tumblers

---

108 HRA1:10:52 Macquarie to Bathurst 22nd March, 1819
109 Ritchie, John *Punishment and Profit—The Bigge Commission in to NSW'*

Seal hats,	Kettles
Possum skin hats,	Thread
Boot leather	Shirts

Between 1810 and 1820 the number of sheep trebled in the colony, and many producers were finding it more profitable to sell carcasses instead of fleeces

Local manufactured items did not entirely replace imports. Items were still imported from India and China.

From India came
Sugar
Spirits
Soap
Cotton goods

From China came
Sugar candy
Silks
Wearing apparel

Colonial Exports included
Sandalwood
Pearl shells
Bache de mar
Whale oil and meat
Seal Oil

Trade exchange, on a barter basis, was made with a number of the Pacific Islands of 'coarse cotton' and ironware, for coconut and salt pork.

Among other evidence to the Bigge Enquiry were numerous complaints by manufacturers on the limited supply of materials, the high cost of buying from government business enterprises—for instance the cloth produced by workers at the government female factory was 2/5 1/4 d per yard, whereas at Mr Kenyon's private establishment it was only 11d. The Manager of the Robert Campbell merchant business complained to Commissioner

Bigge about the duties on whale and seal oil from the colony, arriving in England. He also criticised the port regulations which required captains to give 10 day's notice of intention to sail—he claimed this resulted in high wharfage charges.

Ritchie (*Punishment & Profit*) concludes that although Bigge wanted to encourage trade and certain manufacturing, he was reconciled to the fact that their promotion would not provide an adequate or proper solution to the question of convict employment, punishment and reform. [110]

Observations on Industry & Commerce in NSW

By 1820 Simeon Lord had turned the profits of fishing in the south seas and trade in the Pacific Islands into a manufactory at Botany Bay where he employed convicts and from 15 to 20 colonial youths making blankets, stockings, wool hats, kangaroo hats, seal hats, possum skin hats, all of them shoddy but cheaper than English imports of hats, boots, leather, trousers, shirts, thread, kettles and glass tumblers. [111]

The heavy influx of immigrants during the Darling Administration brought its own difficulties, especially when drought and depression closed down on the colony at the end of the 1830s. This period led onto the sever economic depression of 1842, which had been fuelled by a reduction of foreign investment, a cessation of the British speculators and absentee landlords, as well as local factors, partly sponsored by Sir George Gipps, the successor to Darling as Governor. Between 1831 and 1841, imports had increased by 518 percent to a total of over two and a half million pounds and exports by 1257 percent to a total of two million pounds.[112]

The severe drought of 1825-8 was unfairly blamed on Darling, as was the epidemic of 'hooping cough' which killed Darling's own son and of smallpox which afflicted the colony.

---

[110] Evidence of sundry manufacturers to Commissioner Bigge Enquiry)
[111] An quote extracted from Clark, A History of Australia sourced by Clark from 'An account of Mr Lord's manufactures, submitted to Commissioner Bigge, 1st February 1821
[112] Barnard, Marjorie *Sydney—A story of a City'* P.18

Between December 1831 and December 1832 325,549 gallons of spirits and 109,406 gallons of wine were imported and at least another 11,000 gallons of gin were distilled locally—all for a population of only 15,000.

As for prices, milk was 8 pence per quart, potatoes were fifteen shillings a hundredweight, beef had declined to one penny halfpenny a pound[113], mutton twopence halfpenny, veal five-pence, pork four-penny halfpenny. Fowls cost from 1/9d to 2/3d per pair, whilst butter varied from season to season between 1/—and 3/—per pound,; cheese sold at 4 pence per pound, Cape wine was 8d to ½ per pint and port was 1/45 to 2/—per quart. Respectable lodgings were a pound per week. And a horse could be hired for 10/—a day, and a gig for 15/—per day. Housing costs had risen to £530 for a six-roomed cottage

The depression that lasted from the late 1830s to 1842 but created a slow down in the colony until gold was discovered in 1852, caused an estimated 1638 bankruptcies. There was a glut of livestock such that sheep were selling for 6d per head. Land sales ceased and there was an oversupply of labour for the first time in 50 years. Almost a final blow to the struggling economy came with the discovery of gold in California, with estimates of 5757 houses being empty out of the 7100 houses in Sydney town.[114]

The economy in the period up to 1800 was based upon the limited trade monopolised by military men like John Macarthur as well as a steady expansion of government-financed agriculture to feed the growing number of convicts. This expansion could only continue until the colony became self-sufficient in food. Then an alternative product, of sufficient value to be exported would be required to generate the hard currency that in turn would pay for the increasing imports demanded by the growing economy. Only by developing such a staple export could the colony become economically viable and thereby partially believe the treasury of the burden of supporting it. With such a staple export attracting additional population, the colonists would also have some hope of eventually claiming the continent's wide interior.

---

[113] Beef during the Macquarie Administration was bought by the Commissariat at 5 pence per pound
[114] Barnard Marjorie *ibid*

By 1802, Governor King could report to London that seal skins were the way ahead in terms of exports. More than 100,000 skins were landed in and shipped from Sydney between 1800 and 1806, In 1804, 11 Sydney-based ships were engaged in the Bass Strait sealing trade, in addition to the large number of ships in pursuit of whaling.

By the early 1800s there were four main types of economic activity in the colony. Agriculture and grazing was making the colony almost self-sufficient in this product, and large landowners were undermining the governor's attempts to encourage yeomen farmers. Many of these large landowners also engaged in mercantile activities. A growing number of emancipated convicts became traders on their own account, with speculation in trade marked by gluts and scarcities. Many merchants also operated their own vessels, engaging in sealing and whaling. The number of whalers operating out of Sydney rose from 5 in 1827 to 76 in 1835. Between 1826 and 1835 the value of fishery products passing through Sydney reached £950,000. In 1849, there were 37 boats based in Hobart employing 1000 seamen.[115]

Sealing and Whaling were followed by exports of wool. Although only 29 sheep had arrived with the First Fleet, successive convict fleets added to the flocks and herds and the numbers quickly expanded by natural increase. By 1805, there were 500 horses, 4000 cattle, 5000 goats, 23000 pigs and 20000 sheep. The efforts of these large landowners, including John Macarthur resulted in a dramatic change in the export statistics, with the weight of wool being exported rising from just £167 in 1811 to £175,433 in 1821.[116]

By 1835, the supremacy of pastoralism was beyond dispute, with exports of fine wool dominating the trade figures. The success of the pastoral industry was at the expense of the British government's efforts to slow the invasion of the interior. The success was the result of a combination of factors—cheap land taken from the Aborigines; cheap labour in the form

---

[115] Day, David *Claiming a Continent—A new History of Australia.* Pages 49,50,51

[116] Day, David *Ibid pages 52,53*

of convict and even cheap Aborigine labour from those able to supervise large flocks over extensive unfenced grasslands in the interior.[117]

Not surprisingly the Europeans found the same attractive places to settle, as the aborigines also found most desirable—water sources and native grasslands.

By 1850 over 4000 pastoralists with their 20 million sheep occupied 400 million hectares (1000 million acres) of inland Australia.

The growth of population contributed greatly to the rise of manufacturing and the general economic growth in the economy. NSW grew from 76,845 Europeans in 1836 to 187,243 in 1851. Growth in Port Phillip and South Australia was even more dramatic. By m1841 more than half the male population of NSW was colonial-born or immigrant rather than convict, while convicts and emancipists comprised just over 1/3rd of the total population. However males still outnumbered females roughly two to one.

One aspect of trade is generally overlooked when it comes to identifying special and important exports. Wool exports began to sour in the early 1820s, and most historians claim wool dominates agricultural exports and that opinion clouds the real truth.

In fact from 1788 to 1828, if a reliable set of export statistics is compiled, it will be surprising if Australian-owned whaling and sealing vessels are found to be less productive than sheep in those first 49 years. The figures do exist for the next six years from 1828 and for Australia as a whole; whaling narrowly exceeds wool for that period, whilst as late as 1833 whaling is New South Wales' main export industry. However, after that time, 'wool races away, yielding in the last three years of the 1830s almost double the export value of Australia's whale products[118]

A secondary importance of this industry is that each vessel whilst in port is estimated to have spent an average of £300, not counting the

---

[117]   Day, David *ibid* page 74
[118]   Blainey, Geoffrey *The tyranny of Distance* Page 115

sovereigns the crew spent in the inns and elsewhere.[119] Then there was the work for the dockyards. Shipbuilding was probably the largest and most dynamic colonial manufacture before 1850, and Tasmania alone built 400 vessels from small cutters to ships of 500 tons burthen that joined the England-Australia run. Blainey also observes that the reluctance to put whaling into accurate perspective in importance to the colonial economy stems from apathy towards maritime history. He claims that 'except for ship-lovers, the sea and ships are still virtually banished from written history'.[120]

Bigge referred in his third report in 1823[121] to the high level of efficiency amongst the convicts assigned to 'task work' for the government manufactures. Commissioner Bigge discovered at the close of the Macquarie period that the significance of the Government Store as a market for colonial produce and a source of foreign exchange were greater than ever. The heavy increase in the number of convicts transported after the end of the Napoleonic wars had correspondingly increased the government's demand for foodstuffs. Thus Bigge reported, had retarded the growth of export industries by encouraging the growth of agriculture—farming as opposed to grazing. 'It is possible, given other circumstances the settlers might have turned their attention to the production of other objects than those that solely depended upon the demands of the Government'[122]

Bigge also refers to the high level of skills used in the Government Business Centre—the Lumber Yard—and to the benefit the colony derived from the local public sector manufacturing.

Summary

Of the nine economic drivers within the colonial economy, the role of manufacturing had the far reaching and desirable results.

---

[119] Coughlin, T.A. *Labour & Industry in Australia* Volume 1, Page 367

[120] Blainey *ibid* Page 116-7

[121] Commissioner Bigge's Estimate of the value of convict labour in Sydney for 1822

[122] Bigge, J.T. *Report on the Agriculture and Trade of NSW* 1823 Page 22

The Macquarie Administration decided to centralise and highly regulate the labour and output of the more than 50% of the convicts, who having arrived in the colony were assigned to private or government work. For those assigned to government labour, the broad range of activities required a smarter government store than had hitherto been the case. The store was to have on hand sufficient tools and materials to keep these people fully utilised in their allotted task. Those convicts assigned to land and road clearing needed grubbing tools and axes. They required hauling equipment, and food supplies. Those allocated to public building projects and public infrastructure required tools, bricks, blocks, tiles and a large array of sawn timbers.

The Governor ordered the commissariat to create a central facility for assembling and distributing these materials. Most items could have been ordered in from Britain or elsewhere in Europe. The lengthy purchasing and requisition procedures required a lead time of between fifteen months and two years. Thus Macquarie's charge to the Commissariat to employ convict labour in the manufacturing locally of as many imported items as possible created an import replacement program that created employment, led to private sector entrepreneurs, and generated a program of transition in local manufacturing from the public to the private sector.

Commissioner Bigge reported on the extent of the trades utilised in the Lumber Yard and it makes an impressive list[123]. The trades carried on in this government business enterprise [in this case, the Lumber Yard] are also reported on by Major Ovens, the former Superintendent of Convicts[124]

'In the Lumber Yard are assembled all the indoor tradesmen who work in the shops such as blacksmiths, carpenters, sawyers, shoemakers, tailors etc. The workmen, carrying on their occupations under the immediate eye of the Chief Engineer are probably kept in a better state of discipline than those, who working more remote, are dependent on the good behaviour of an overseer for any work they may perform. Whatever is produced from

---

[123] Bigge, J.T. *Report on the Agriculture and Trade of NSW* 1823 Page 22
[124] Report by Major Ovens to Governor Brisbane on reorganisation for the Lumber Yard HRA 1:11:655-7

the labour of these persons[125], which is not applied to any public work or fore any supply of authorised requisitions, is placed in a large store and kept to furnish the exigencies of future occasions'.

Growth in the colonial economy came in numerous guises, such as technological progress in industry and agriculture, transport and communication; the growth of population, and the accumulation of capital; the discovery of raw materials, and the spread of economic freedom.

The rise of a manufacturing sector relied on most of these areas, especially technological gains, supply of capital, immigration of skilled trades and Macquarie's sympathetic encouragement of entrepreneurs. Although not as vital as the agricultural sector, the manufacturing sector provided substantial employment, innovation, skills training, and the basis for potential decentralisation. Most importantly, during the Macquarie Administration, the manufacturing sector supported Macquarie's transition from a penal to free market economy. As the colonial economy stabilised, it became attractive for a large number of British based industries wanting to open branch offices in the colonies to invest in small scale activities, often transferring skilled labour from Britain to underpin their colonial operations.

Local industry also helped develop local resources, both human and capital. Both coal and timber became important exports for the colony, whilst the list of other natural resources being developed for both local use and exporting grew longer and longer.

New industry required new talents and skills. So a number of adjunct industries came into being—engineering design, equipment manufacturing and equipment maintenance. Not all new equipment was imported and particularly in agricultural equipment suitable for local conditions, local manufacture and assembly was the norm rather than the exception.

---

[125] Sawn timber for framing, roof battens, flooring, window frames, doors, nails, bolts, bellows, barrels, furniture—from Beckett *The Operations of the Commissariat of NSW 1788-1856*

Employment in the sector grew to an important level, with the number
of factories in NSW increasing from 37 in 1829 to 174 in 1850[126].
Exports increased during the same period from £79,000 per annum to
over £8,000,000[127]. Boatbuilding peaked in 1843 at 46 vessels for the
year, although the average size halved between 1841 and 1843. There were
102 vessels registered in the colony in 1841 disbursing 12,153 tons. By
1843, this number had declined to 77 and continued to decline until the
1900s.[128]

Even as late as 1827, the Colonial Office was still very suspicious about
the expenses of the convict establishment. Lord Bathurst wrote of 'the
difficulty I feel in reconciling the scarcity of assignable convicts . . . . with
the enormous and increasing expense with which this country is still
charged'[129] Every effort to trim convict maintenance expenses or expand
the assignment system impacted on the Commissariat business operations.
The Superintendent of Convicts would agree to the training of apprentices,
only to find them sent of 'on assignment' whilst the best workers in the
Lumber Yard were always in demand by private manufacturers, and
government building workers, were constantly in demand by the private
contractors.[130]

. . . .

---

[126] Butlin, Ginswick & Statham *The Economy before 1850* (Australians:
Historical statistics—p.108)

[127] Butlin et al *ibid*—P. 109

[128] Sourced by Beckett from original data in *Australians: Historical Statistics,*
Coghlan and Butlin

[129] HRA 1:8:221

[130]

FINANCIAL STATEMENTS FOR THE FIRST PERIOD—1800-1810

A reader may ask, why 1800 and why 1810. As we saw in the first chapter of this study on the rise of public finance and public accounting in the colony, 1802 was the first attempt to record either income or expenditure in the colony. The British Treasury had for the years between 1788 and 1801 recorded all of the expenditure in equipping and moving the first and second fleet, and for the provisioning and victualling the colony for this same period. However, with the necessary, but loose, mechanism of drawing Bills on the Treasury for most purchases, there is a great deal of doubt in the mind of Butlin, Shann and even Clark, that the published figures of the period are accurate.

For this study we are relying on the source documents—the hand-written documents prepared by Reverend Samuel Marsden and Asst Surgeon Darcy Wentworth, 'audited' by the Lieutenant Governors each quarter and then published for all settlers to read in the *Sydney Gazette*.

In a splendid work, edited by James Thomson in 1881, the resources of the Sydney Morning Herald were used (since the Hansard transcription service had not yet commenced in the New South Wales Legislative Chambers) to assemble the Treasurers statements between 1855 (the First Parliament) and November 1881 (the Tenth Parliament).

Thomson wrote in the Preface "Some years ago it was considered desirable that all the Financial Statements made since the inauguration of Responsible Government should be collated and printed for future reference, and for distribution amongst the Public Libraries, Schools of Arts and other literary institutions of the colony. The task of editing these Statements was entrusted to me, I presume, of the experience, which I had acquired, during a long course of years, of the financial affairs of the colony, and the practical knowledge which I possessed of its public accounts generally. Until recently (when Hansard commenced a reporting service in 1880) no authorised copy of any of the Financial Statements (by the Colonial Treasurers) was in existence, so that in the discharge of the duty imposed upon me I had to carefully revise the reports that were given of them in the *Sydney Morning herald*, which I found extremely accurate. In revising these statements I had to compare the Herald's figures with the published printed documents,—a labour which necessarily involved much trouble and occupied a considerable amount of time.

I have placed, as an Appendix to the Financial Statements, a memorandum explanatory of the financial system of New South Wales and an account of the rise, progress and present condition of the public revenue, as it is considered they may be found useful to those who take an interest in the financial affairs of the colony. I prepared these two papers in 1876 and 1879 for the information of the Imperial Government, who had it in contemplation at the time to publish some kind of official work on the defences, financial resources, and general condition of the several Australian colonies."

Why 1810? This was the year during which Lachlan Macquarie arrived in the colony, as the successor to William Bligh, whose failure to govern for all residents led to a slackness and sickness in the colony, which would take many pains from Macquarie to make better and allow the deep wounds to heal. Macquarie reformed the Commissary operation firstly, then 'reformed' the public finance and the public reporting of the colony, but tightening up the currency movement, creating a bank to assist both the traders and the colonial merchants, and 'regularising' the accounting mechanism of the 'Orphan Fund' and the 'Police Fund'.

The period between 1802 and 1810 was highlighted by a change of governor (King to Bligh) in 1806. This date marked a social decline in the colony, with Macarthur turning into a bitter enemy of the governor, followed by a re-alignment of the NSW Corps allegiances away from the governor and towards the rampant self-serving individually profitable trading activities of the military officers.

The colonial economy had been running in freefall. Little government support, a touch of entrepreneurial activity and a few governor declarations that urged the emancipists onto a self-supporting 30 acres and off the general stores. By the end of the King era, he could account for only 180,246 pounds in 'value' of assets as a 'credit against expenses'.

- The value of grain and supplies in the commissary stores of about 62,000 pound
- The value of buildings completed by King, could only account for 6,500 pound
- The value of public livestock owned by the governor would amount to 112,000 pound

The contribution of King to the colonial economy was little (especially when compared to Macquarie). He was not even the able administrator that Phillip had encountered in the time prior to 1792, and other than a few social welfare titbits, King managed to let the colony run without much interference by government. Many more persons were dependent on the government store in 1806 than when King accepted his appointment in 1800. Hunter had led the social decay during his years of 1795 and 1800, but much of his era was spent undoing the damage completed by the interim administrators (between Phillip and Hunter)—Captain Grose (upgraded from Lieutenant Governor for two years, and then Captain Paterson, acting as Lieutenant governor for the next year. These three years allowed the military officers to become dominant in the colony and run things on their own terms—the assignment of the convicts; the run-away trade in spirits; the use of spirits as the means of exchange; the absolute domination of the military in buying shiploads of goods for re-sale. It took the shipment of Macquarie's own regiment to the colony and the withdrawal of the NSW Corps to finally put a stop to the military occupation of spirits and trade. Bligh saw the problem but appeared powerless to intervene.

H.V.Evatt describes these years well in his 'Rum Rebellion'. In a forward to the 1938 edition, Hartley Grattan (a Carnegie Scholar 1937-38), and an American who became enamoured with Australian History wrote" the law can become a weapon in the social struggle and the courts a battleground of opposing class interests on which justice is weighed in favour of one side. This is inn response to Justice Evatt's assertion that 'the Courts were the true forum of the little colony . . . . there was no legislature, no avowed political association or party, no theatre and no independent press' but the major social issues are generally apt to be subverted to the interest of the dominant class in the community." This class struggle pitted Bligh against Macarthur even though the English Government's economic plan for the colony envisaged the strong establishment of a small-holding peasantry in the country, the bulk of the peasants in any future of the colony then visible would be limited to time expired and emancipated convicts. Grattan suggests this economic plan was merely the projection on virgin Australia of an economic pattern being disrupted by the industrial revolution, which plan was destroyed after Phillip's departure from Sydney by the military officers.

The military, in the period between Phillip and Hunter, manipulated their own plan into full operation. They wanted a trading monopoly which was a combined with land holding on an extensive scale along with the ruthless exploitation of convict labour. Rum became the established medium of exchange and it was monopolised to raise its price, whilst consumption was pushed to the limit, thus allowing the monopolists to make huge profits. The defence of the system became the Rum Rebellion' of 1808-09. The struggle over the rum traffic was merely symptomatic of a deeper issue. The small landholders only existed to be exploited until economically exhausted and then removed through inevitable bankruptcy.

Grattan records in his Forward that "since the officers held, in their hands, the military power, as well as such minimum civil as had been developed, whilst the Courts held the supreme economic power, the combined power made them masters of the community. They directed it in a fashion that benefited themselves, but allowed for no progress"

The 'brains' of the system was John Macarthur though he was far from being the sole initiator, beneficiary or protagonist. These monopolists broke three governors—Hunter, King, through complete lack of scruple and set a patter for any successor, even though Bligh had been instruction to break up the monopoly and return the small landholders to the place in the community originally planned for them. Setting about his orders, Bligh quickly fell foul of Macarthur and his associates

Macarthur came through this relatively unscathed, especially in latter-day public opinion, and his legacy, as muted through John Thomas Bigge in 1822 was to create a third economic program of foreseeing a broad acre pastoral industry, utilising the free labour of the convicts, but repaying the costs of the colony afforded by the British Treasury through the export of raw wool and the resulting strengthening of the woollen industry in England.

A review of significant events will show that the 'Rum Rebellion' was not the only big event that affected the colony.

When Phillip arrived in the colony in 1788 and established the penal settlement, he came with the authority to raise taxes. This was part of his instructions dated 2nd April 1787.

"Our will and pleasure is that all public monies which shall be raised be issued out of warrant from you and disposed of by you for the support of the government and for such other purpose as shall be entirely directed and not otherwise".

Phillip had been instructed to create a local commissary (he was provided with a commissary officer) in order to acquire, stock and furnish supplies within the colony to victual convicts, the military and the 40 military wives and families that had arrived with the Fleet. The commissary thus became the heart of the local economy for at least the first 20 years of settlement. The commissary was responsible for planning the rations required for the number of persons to be provisioned, based on the governor's decision on individual rations. The role of the commissary was to purchase supplies from visiting ships or, when available, local suppliers and pay a bill of exchange drawn on the British Treasury. This system provided the supplies needed but promoted great inaccuracies in the recording area, and thus, according to N.G. Butlin, the figures from the British Treasury for the tooling and victualling of the colony during the first few years are questionable and likely inaccurate. Phillip had been authorised to draw a bill at the Cape on route with the First Fleet, in order to purchase fresh supplies for the remainder of the voyage. It would have taken many months for this bill to be presented in London, and so, even if accurate, it is unlikely that the expenditures via bills presented would have reflected the correct time period.

There were many items that became short in the first few years and since there were no local persons to provide a source of supply, the governor stepped in and provided the labour within a government-inspired operation. The governor created his own vegetable patch and orchard in the 'governor's domain' and on 'Garden Island'. The governor organised a 'government farm' for watching over the livestock that had arrived and to grow grain that appeared to do well in the colony. It was to take a convict experienced in English style farming to cross grain strains and achieve a suitable local strain of wheat, barley, corn and maize. Clothing had become a major difficulty, with convicts going around in an advanced state of undress and shoeless. The answer was to establish a clothing factory in which the female convicts could be utilised. This answer would also segregate the male sand female convicts as already the fear of growing numbers of illegitimate children running around the colony occupied the governor's mind. Children meant education, as well as extra mouths to feed and this was a penal colony with growing numbers of convicts expected. Phillip's planning for the colony had not included social or political matters. He had not anticipated free settlers, other than military or civil officers needing to retire and wanting to remain in the colony. Phillip himself had planned only to return to England at the end of his official term.

There were many opportunities for small business in the colony. For a start, very quickly it became apparent that the tools and equipment supplied with the First fleet were neither entirely suitable or in sufficient quantity. The felling axes were of little use against the standard trees in need of clearing around Sydney Cove and the Rose Hill settlements, and naturally, each new 30-acre farmer required a set of tools if he was to clear his land and become a farmer supplying produce to the commissary. But the second most important need was that of transportation. Since there were no working horses there was no need for carts, but there was an urgent need for boats for fishing and movement of people and goods between Sydney and Rose Hill. It took until 1790 for the first locally made boat to be ready to cover the Sydney-Rose Hill (Parramatta) link.

The first mill assembled on Observatory Hill could only grind 6 bushels of wheat each day. Mills were to play an important role in the colony and from just one operating mill in 1795, the number grew rapidly so that by 1848, there were 220 operating mills of which 79 were steam powered, and the remainder were horse, wind or human driven. Mills accounted for over 50% of total industry by the middle of the 19th century.

New industry was to be the mainstay of the fledgling colonial economy. The growth of industry was slow but creative and ranged from road making and road repairs to boat building, whale and seal hunting to a broad range of farming—vineyards, brooms, clothing and linen (from locally grown flax).

Other developments that created work for convicts and a trading and export opportunity were the discovery of coal. Newcastle became a convict centre as well as the main provider of coal for export to South America, England and Calcutta. The discovery of seals in Bass Strait gave encouragement to a large sealing industry, which led to a dramatic growth of the local boat-building industry. Exporting commenced in 1800 with the first shipment of sandalwood, wheat and pork. Obviously trading was expected to grow and become quite important to the colony, because Governor King built the first Customs House on the edge of Sydney Cove.

Funding for the first twelve years of the colony had come from the British Treasury but keeping in mind that the colony was instructed to become self-sufficient as quickly as possible, and also that the governor had been given taxing powers, King decided to impose tariffs on spirits, wine and beer in 1800 to complete the new Sydney Gaol that could not be completed by subscription as originally planned by Hunter.

Thus, by 1800, the colony was finding a sense of direction. King was not the right man for the times and there was more neglect during the Bligh times until Macquarie arrived with enthusiasm and a resolve to build the colony into the giant economy that was expected by the British Treasury.

One of the last acts of Phillip before he left the colony for his home in Britain was to proclaim the hours of work to be adopted by the convict labourers.

Phillip set "from sunup to sundown, with a break of 2 ½ ours during the day". When food was particularly in short supply, Phillip had expected that the finishing hour would be 3 o'clock in the afternoon, which would allow time, before dark, to tend to a vegetable patch or such food sources (livestock) that was being set aside for nutrition apart from foodstuffs supplied by the Commissary.

Hunter era was unremarkable for any positive gains in the colony. He claimed at one time that the Combination act in Britain of 1799 would restrict economic activity in the colony, but this piece of legislation intended by Westminster to stop formation of unions and prohibit strikes, was of little, if any, interest to colonial settlers, who went on their own way building homes, farming, trading, protecting what little they had and being subjugated to the military officers. The only relief or release would come from orderly organisation of the convict work gangs but since the military decided it was not their role to supervise convicts the work supervision was left to independent supervisors, but mostly to other convicts. The system did not work well, at least until Macquarie came to the colony.

Both Hunter and King arrived in the colony with instructions from the British Government to break the trade monopoly by the military, but reform was slow to gain any foothold at all. Even King sought relief from the military activists. King decided to rebuild the government herd of livestock, which was a noble enough plan and designed to provide food in the event of another severe drought and food shortage, but in order to implement his plan, he purchased cattle from the very military officers who were rorting the system and King paid far in excess of their real worth. Lackadaisical supervision of both cattle and convicts saw the cattle escape and until near the end of the Macquarie years, build into a substantial herd worth a goodly sum to the settlers when finally recaptured.

King did introduce a ticket of leave system for the convicts who were in good stead with the military, their direct supervisors, the commissary, and the law. It was King's way of removing convicts who could be trusted to be good colonial citizens from the commissary ration list.

King's other contribution was to foreshadow the usefulness to the colony of a local vineyard, and upon receiving two Napoleonic War prisoners in 1801 put them to work in establishing a wine industry for the colony.

The Hunter River area received a boost when it was found that locally grown flax could be used to produce linen. It was not the best quality but the governor thought it could be of great interest to the English government. In this way King recognised the conflict he was in the middle of. He was the British representative in the colony, was paid (rather handsomely as it turns out) by the British Government from the Civil List, but was usually respected and befriended by the settlers to whom he felt a moral and ethical, if not a legal responsibility. In the event of a conflict between the colony and the crown whose side would he choose?

The flax exercise should have been beneficial to both sides, but King knew in his heart that the local product was not of a high quality and would not be accepted by the British public or the British manufacturers. Likewise in declaring in 1801 that all coal and mineral reserves in the colony were the property of the Crown, he knew that only lackadaisical convict labour would be used to extract, load and work the coal removed from the Newcastle coal—fields. King was a free enterprise man under his gubernatorial cloak and invited Robert Campbell (from India) to set up a warehouse and trading post in the colony.

Campbell brought immediate gain and benefit to the colony by shipping a load of colonial coal from Newcastle to Calcutta.

The British encouraged free enterprise in other ways. The English government was going through one of its phases of privatisation. After the second fleet was thought to be much more expensive that Matra had projected, the Colonial Office decided to ship via contractors future prisoners to the penal colony, for a fixed fee. Competition brought a high price for the privately transported prisoners. Savings were encouraged by the contracts on the ship's captains by cutting food (both quantity and quality), limiting appropriate clothing, eliminating exercise and generally creating deplorable conditions for the prisoners, not least being the overcrowding. As a result the death rate of prisoners between England and Botany Bay was nearly 50% in the third fleet. The Government was only mildly offended by the charges of unlawfulness by Wilberforce and his ilk. But the resolve was to make failure to deliver healthy humans instead of human misery hurt the contractor's pocket. Surgeons were included on each shipping manifest with a bonus of 10/6 for each convict landed in healthy condition and a bonus of 50 pound to the ship's captain for assisting the surgeon to land healthy convicts. The problem may not have been solved but was made much better by these incentives.

With the sealing industry showing great promise, the whaling industry was given new strength mostly by the arrival of American whalers into Sydney Harbour. The local industry got underway in 1802 with 7 ships operating from Port Jackson. The Bass Strait area was using half of the 22 ships operating by 1803. The others were successfully operating in New Zealand and South Australian waters.

The colony by this time was moving through turbulent times. The settlements were mostly rural in nature and relied mainly on produce grown with the assistance of assigned convicts. By governor regulation these assigned persons were to be fed, housed, clothed and generally maintained by the 'master'. This was not an inexpensive program for the masters, especially where smallholdings were involved. King ordered that the commissary purchase all produce from these landholders and set a minimum price at which wheat and other grains would be purchased. In this way the landowners could be seen to receive adequate compensation to meet their obligations to their convict workers. As the colony grew demand for 'luxury' items as well as a broader range of staples also grew and this attracted a growing number of 'speculative' ships into the port of Sydney. A price war developed between the traders, the military and those wanting to participate in the purchasing of imported goods. Governor King, having set the original tariff collections on only spirits, wine and beer, decided to impose a 5% ad valorem duty on all imports in 1802. This immediately created a steady revenue stream that needed accounting for. King assumed that this was discretionary income available to him to dispense, as he considered fair and not as an offset to what the British Treasury was providing to the colony.

King had identified a growing social problem as the one where street children were in large numbers, and decided to do something about it. King formed the female Orphan Committee, with the object of housing, feeding, clothing and educating these children until they could be put into service in the colony. The committee included the Reverend Samuel Marsden who had really been instrumental in recognising the problem and finding a partial solution. King appointed Marsden the Treasurer of the committee and decided to use certain Treasury funds to buy the house of the departing Lieutenant Kent, who made it known that he (Kent) had the finest residence in Sydney. Kent was leaving the colony to return to England and take up another posting and he negotiated with the governor for the government to buy his house at 'valuation'. The valuation was based on a replacement cost, whether or not another house like Kent's would ever be built again, and the valuation came to 1,700 pound. Kent received his money via a bill drawn on the British Treasury, which King prayed would be accepted by the Treasury. The bill was negotiated and the Female Orphanage got a residence for about 80 waifs off the streets, although a revenue-raising plan came about when Marsden accepted destitute children from single fathers for a lump sum of 5 pound. It was not as though Marsden or the Orphan Committee were short of revenue. With the growth tax imposed by King, the amount of revenue raised by the Harbour Master from imported goods, especially the alcohol trade, Marsden was constantly looking for ways to spend his money.

King sent Lt-Governor David Collins off to open a settlement at Port Phillip but Collins decided that the Mornington Peninsula was not an ideal place to commence a colony and crossed the strait and selected Hobart instead. Van Dieman's Land had been settled first in 1803, just as the *Sydney Gazette* newspaper was being founded by King as a means of keeping the settlers informed. He would make many proclamations to the free settlers as well as advertising that certain convicts had gone bush. The scourge of the importation of spirits could not be handled but King decided that 32,000 litres of rum brought to the colony from Bengal by Campbell should be returned and he accepted no counsel to the contrary although Marsden led a group to announce how great noble and strong the governor was becoming. It was at this time, with minimum imports transferring from the colony into Britain that the British Government decided to impose a tariff on all colonial imports. Sealskins had yielded either to the colony or to the British merchants over 100,000 skins between 1800 and 1806. This could be considered an ecological disaster or a trading triumph, depending on one's viewpoint, but then the British Government cashed in on the colonial 'success' by imposing this levy on all imports.

In the colony, prices were heavily influenced by local conditions including droughts and floods, and English economic conditions all affected events in the colony. The drought of 1804 for instance affected the wheat crop and thus the price of wheat within the colony. King decided to increase to price the Commissary would purchase private farm grain but even so the shortages were reflected in the price of bread. A settler could buy a loaf of bread for 4p or barter it with 2 ½ pound of wheat.

By 1805 Macarthur could see the writing on the wall for his days as a military officer and accepted his grant of land available to all military who intended to settle in the colony and opened his estate at the Cowpastures, probably the best grazing land within the 1805 limits of the colony.

King's next contribution to the social needs of the convicts was to proclaim a 56-hour workweek for all assignees in return for bed and breakfast, tobacco and tea. The convict rations from the commissary would meet their needs for lunch and dinner.

The first free settlers were wealthy Britains who were enticed into relocating by the offer of free land grants, convict labour to work the land and an allocation of government livestock. The Blaxland brothers responded to this enticement in 1805. In that same year the first colonial built whaler was launched so that greater local participation could be realised.

Pressure on the colony was coming not only from outside the territory but inside as well. We have accounted for King's sudden interest in the growing orphan numbers in Sydney town, but the cause of the problem raises concerns as to the type of society the colony could develop into. Two measures offer some indication of the underlying movement.

- In 1805, there were 1400 women in the colony but there were only 360 married couples
- Of the 1800 children, under 18, over half were illegitimate
- The crime rate in the colony was by 1807, 8 times the rate in England.

The 1806 drought made the wheat crop fail, and the grain became scarce. The price of wheat rose from 1/1/—to 3/14/—per bushel and the price of bread rose 12 fold from 4p to 4/—per loaf. The new governor, sent to replace Phillip Gidley King arrived in Sydney. Tales of the Bounty mutiny and its remarkable voyage of skill and endurance had foreshadowed William Bligh's arrival across the Pacific

Having outlined the many events, which both curtailed and encouraged the colonial economy, it is time to review the impact on the financial situation brought about by these economic conditions.

N.G. Butlin reports in *Forming a Colonial Economy*

"British decision makers were far from consistent in their attitudes to fiscal obligations to and from the colonists. All governors to 1821 left with at least his fiscal reputation tarnished. Intermittent and at times irascible and condemnatory intervention in colonial expenditures reflected, in part, British ignorance and suspicion. In fact, complex colonial fiscs operated almost from the beginning of the settlement. By 1830, local revenues were offsetting expenditures for everything except convict and defence functions.

"The transfer of prisoners was, from a colonial Australia view, a capital transfer, even if, from a British perspective, the human capital involve had a negative vale. Britain was determined to constrain the British contribution to the colonial operations and to narrow the range of support. It sought ways of ever reducing, to the British taxpayer, the per capita costs of prisoners landed in the colony and to limit the total budgetary costs of sustaining colonies. One way, they decided to achieve this was through auditing public accounts and criticising local behaviour. Other ways was the adoption of a policy of private development of the country, and make the country no longer dependent essentially on convict transfers. A second they decided would be to encourage the emergence of a freed society from a freed population. Thus part of the funds could be diverted from the convict population to the funding of public activity.

"The question remains is the extent to which the colonists could be encouraged to enter the colony and how much of the burden could they bear".

A study of the types of public and private British Investment in the colony is the subject of another exercise, but it can be said here that a wonderful model could be constructed of the formation of a colonial economy.

Consider the inputs: British investment of capital and goods, the transfer of industry—the branch office in the colony, the use of the colony as a source of raw materials—the colonial garden, ripe for the picking. British ships transferring people and goods.

Consider the restraints of population to adopt and utilise the investment

Consider the ultimate limitations of human personality—the convicts forced to labour, when their colleagues back 'home' were lounging in a prison cell. Why should they work in exchange for a limited freedom?

If all this sounds far fetched let us consider the role of free trade and its benefits to Britain.

This is a piece by Sir T. H. Farrer (Bart) from his 1887 book 'Free Trade versus Fair Trade'. The notation on the front-piece of the book shows the Cobden Club emblem with the words 'free trade, peace, goodwill among nations'. We will discuss Cobden a little later when we review the work of the Federation Senator Edward Pulsford—another outspoken supporter and devotee of the Cobden philosophy, and free trade and open immigration.

"The amount of English capital constantly employed abroad in private trade and in permanent investments, including Stock Exchange securities, private advances, property owned abroad by Englishmen, British shipping, British-owned cargoes, and other British earnings abroad, has been estimated by competent statisticians as being between 1,500 and 2,000 million pounds, and is constantly increasing. Taking the lower figure, the interest or profit upon it, at 5 per cent, would be 75 million pounds, and at the higher figure it would be 100 million pound."

Farrer then equates this income figure to the spread of imports over exports and finds that the two compare. But then he argues there is the question of freights. "A very large proportion of the trade of the United Kingdom is carried in English ships, and these ships carry a large proportion of the trade of other countries not coming to England. This shipping is, in fact, an export of highly-skilled English labour and capital which does not appear in the export returns of the 19th century, and considering that it includes not only the interest on capital but also wages, provisions, coal, port expenses, repairs, depreciation and insurance; and that the value of English shipping employed in the foreign trade is estimated at more than 100 million pound per annum, the amount to be added to our exports on account of English shipping, must be very large". But he goes further, "add to this the value of ships built for foreigners amounting to over 70,000 ton per annum, worth together several millions, and all these outgoings, with the profits, must either return to this country in the shape of imports, or be invested abroad—I believe 50 million pound is too low an estimate of the amount of unseen exports. In addition there are the commissions and other charges to agents in this country, connected with the carriage of goods from country to country, but each of these items do not appear in the statistics of exports. I can only assume that we are investing large amounts of our savings in the colonies, such as Australia".

The Farrer argument in favour of 'free trade' then turns to the 'fair trade' objections to foreign investments.

Farrer writes "When we point to the indebtedness of foreign colonies to England as one reason for the excess of imports, they tell us that we have been paying for our imports by the return to us of foreign securities; and at the same time they complain bitterly that, instead of spending our money at home, our rich men are constantly investing their money abroad, and thus robbing English labour of its rights here"

But we know that is not the whole story.

If England investors remit capital to the colonies, it is not only in the form of cash (which would come from savings) but it is more often in the form of capital goods. England sends iron; the shipbuilders who make the ships that carry the goods, and the sailors who navigate them. When they reach the colonies, what happens then. They return with grain, or coal, or wool, or timber, and that makes those commodities cheaper in England. The investor receives the interest or profits on that capital invested which would generally be greater than what could have been earned if the capital had been invested in England. Now that return can be spent on luxury goods, invested locally or re-invested overseas to commence the whole cycle again. That return will be employed in setting to work English labour, earn a return and so on.

It remains true that on the whole, based on the Farrer argument, the transfer of English capital from an English industry that does not pay to a colonial industry which does pay, is no loss to England generally, and causes no diminution in the employment of English labour. There are at least two drawbacks to colonial investment by a maritime power; one, in the event of a war, the returns would be open to greater risk, and two; the investors can more easily evade taxation by the English Government.

Obviously since 1886, when Farrer constructed this argument, the world has changed, investment opportunities have changed, England has fallen from its pinnacle as a world power and international commercial leader and the improved collection of statistics now recognises movements of goods and investments on both current account and capital account. But the concept helped put the Australian colony on the map and attracted enormous amounts of private capital into the colony to make it grow and prosper.

Farrer concludes his argument with this observation.

"The desire to make profitable investments, however valuable economically, is not the only motive which governs rich men; it's the love of natural beauty; interest in farming and the outdoor life; personal and local attachments; all of which are quite sure to maintain a much larger expenditure on English land than would be dictated by a desire for gain. Let these other motives have their way, as these investors still contribute to the welfare of the toilers and spinners who produce the goods, and make a good return that in the end makes England wealthier"

If Farrer really believes his wholesome argument, then the theory of developing a colony economy as espoused by the British Government took on great validity, and if it had been followed through fully, the colony may have developed faster and been self-sufficient long before 1830, but on the other hand, it may or would have emulated the British economy much more than it did.

A closer examination should be made of the original intention of 'local' revenue raising. Phillip's instructions had included the right to raise local 'taxation', however Butlin, in *Forming a Colonial Economy* writes that

"At least as early as 1892, Phillip had sought approval for introducing indirect taxation. The British officials approved the raising of charges but not as 'revenue' for disposition by the governor. It took until 1896 for such charges to be put into operation, when Hunter imposed a charge on access to imports, not a duty on the goods themselves".

Hunter's action, writes Butlin appears devious when put into the context that the British reserved the sole right to raise revenue from duties, tolls, and licences.

Again, in the context of the British policy to make the colony self-sufficient and self-regulated, it does not make sense to have firstly included in the official instructions to Phillip the right, if not the obligation to raise local revenues, to then impose restrictions on the governor by limiting the area, range and amount of taxes, but by 1800 King was raising duties and tariffs, with any restriction on amount, disposition or accounting. Butlin may, himself, have misinterpreted the role and intent of the local efforts and the British policy.

Far from being able to privatise development in the colony and rely on private development, the British Government had to take account of the recommendations of the Select Parliamentary Committee on Transportation, which reported in 1810 on the need, and benefits of continuing with transportation of prisoners to the colony. This policy would continue to provide workers and population for the colonial economy, since by the time the Committee reported, less than 33% of the population were convicts at this date.

On the other hand, four statistics provided to the Committee should have persuaded the Committee to terminate transportation

- The cost of convict maintenance rose to a high of 120 pound per convict per annum. This had risen from the previous average of less than 32 pound
- Marsden took the first wool for weaving to England and received a very positive reception
- The Commissary was able to buy fresh beef and mutton from farmers for rations, and replace salted imports
- The port duties in 1810 had risen to 8,000 pound annually and were making a good contribution towards local discretionary revenue for the governors.

The colony was finally finding its feet. A solid base had been set, one from which Macquarie could build and use a building program with investment opportunities relying on free enterprise. The economy was on the move.

The financial statements for the colony during this period come to us via the *Sydney Gazette* each quarter. The newspaper published the quarterly statements of the Orphan Fund and the Police Fund (the successor by name change) to the Hunter-sponsored Gaol Fund.

FINANCIAL STATEMENTS for the period

CHAPTER 6

THE SECOND PERIOD 1811-1822

The Macquarie years are the most special period—they were dynamic in every respect—economically, socially and politically. After the years of torment during the Bligh era, Macquarie was like a breath of fresh air, arriving in the colony. His role was an important one, and he brought with him, not only a new regiment which would further assist in ridding the colony of the vestiges of the 'Rum Corp' and all it stood for, but the hopes and aspirations of the British Government for Macquarie to complete the transition and transformation of the heavily subsidised colonial operations but the possibility of the colony feeding the British manufacturers with resources of raw materials and grow into a recipient of British manufacture. Wakefield foresaw the British Treasury reaping rich harvests from the sale of pastoral land, whilst the free traders saw the colony as an opportunity for being the outlet for British machinery and in so many ways, the branch office for British manufacturers.

A.T. Yarwood states that Marsden's name once again came to the fore during the early Macquarie years. He writes in 'Marsden of Parramatta'

"During the first few years the relations between Marsden and Macquarie deteriorated steadily, for Macquarie identified him as the leader of wealthy colonists who opposed his policies of self-interested and unworthy motives. Involved in the dispute was Macquarie's vision of the colony as a place where convicts had the chance, on proven good behaviour of regaining freedom and aspiring to social recognition and even official positions.

We will set down some of the major economic highlights of the Macquarie era—those very special 11 years between 1810 and 1821. Obviously the one highlight not to be overlooked is the massive contribution to the economy and the future of the colony made by his building program.

Macquarie told Bigge, in a very understated way that he decided the colony could justify a major building program because it would lift the tenor of the colony, lift the spirits of the residents, set the tone for future generations, use local materials (timber, bricks and tiles, lime and, mortar—all of these items were made by convict labour) and use an ex-convict as designer / supervisor (Francis Greenway). The equivalent value of the labour, using 3/—per day as a base rate is 500,000 pound, whilst the value of materials is approx 420,000 pound. Although Bigge agreed that it was a good use of convict labour, and the results cost very little in cash terms to the British Treasury, the benefits were enormous to the morale and the social well-being of the settlers—they were given a boost that might not have come in ordinary circumstances for another few generations, in fact not until the discovery of gold sand the resulting gold rush.

Macquarie began his administration with a goodly amount of economic passion. He talked about establishing a bank. He discussed with his senior officials the expansion of private enterprise and expansion of local industry. Immigration of free settlers was not high on his list of things to do, since he considered the economy needed lots of attention. In this area Macquarie made good progress. The naval boatyard was carrying out building and repair work. The sealing and whaling industry had established a viable export business and was bringing a regular supply of goods and supplies into the colony with every foreign boat that arrived. Blaxland advertised his locally grown salt for sale at 2p per pound. Thus, in addition to the milling operations, boat building, clothing and boot manufactures; the colony could boast a salt manufacturer.

It is only when things are starting to go right that the Government wanted to make change. The second committee on Transportation recommended in 1812 that fewer ticket-of-leave convicts be created. This would affect the commissary operations as well as expanding the cost of maintaining convicts on government rather than assigning them to private 'masters' and taking their clothing, feeding and housing costs off the government.

1812 also saw a second credit/liquidity crisis due to credit withdrawal by British investors.

The next major event with long-term ramifications was the crossing of the Mountain range (the Blue Mountains) that was boxing in the pastoral and farming prospects of the colony. In 1813, Blaxland, Lawson and W.C. Wentworth proudly advised Governor Macquarie that they had found a way across the mountains and witnessed the open panorama on the other side.

Locally, another drought in 1813 created a scarcity of corn and wheat and drove prices higher. Wool was catching on both at home and abroad. The significance of the crossing of the mountain range west of Sydney can be seen in the record quantity of wool being grown and thus the number of sheep running in the colony. In 1814 the Female factory at Parramatta used over 35,000 pound of wool, rising to 40,000 pound by 1818. In the same year the colony exported 30,000 pound of wool to Britain. Macquarie sent Surveyor-General Oxley and Mitchell to mark the route taken across the mountain and explore the open land on the west side of the range. After the 'explorers' returned Macquarie determined to establish Bathurst as the first plains settlement. Wool exported to England was not only a boon to the colony; it raised revenue for Britain as well. Britain decided to impose a duty on wool. Before 1819, the rate of duty was 6p per pound, during 1819 the rate was halved to 3p. During 1819 a new industry was introduced to the colony. In spite of the tariff, the woollen mills could not buy enough colonial wool and asked the British Government to do whatever it could to lift production.

Local industry demonstrated the capacity for innovation which resulted in productivity gains as reflected in total output increases without accompanying increases in labour input. This gain in productivity led to a mini 'business' boom. New settlements were still in demand and a penal settlement was established at Port Macquarie on the north-coast of New South Wales. For every door that opens another closes. Having supported the concept and operation of private enterprise and having encouraged new industry as well as a favourable setting for progress in the colony, Macquarie was confronted with his adversary Commissioner Bigge recommending the privatising of the coalfields. Consolidation in the pastoral expansion meant that in 1821, 80 owners controlled 60% of all land in the colony. Another sign of the times arose from the coal-mines being placed into private hands. The first free labour was used in the coal-mines in 1821. Settlement was now taking place along the south-coast of the New South Wales colony.

The paper used for the *Sydney Gazette* was now locally produced

The credit squeeze of 1812 was the first time economic hardship or stress had reached the colony since 1788 and was the first occasion that the withdrawal of British investment scrambled the comparative gains being made steadily in the colony. Of course, Macquarie tried to counter the effects of the credit squeeze by encouraging trade, creating the atmosphere for entrepreneurs and encouraged local business to establish and grow. This was an unusual credit squeeze and an even more unusual impact on the new and fledgling economy. Since there was little employment, as we know it today, there was little unemployment created as a result of the downturn. The main impact in the colonial economy was in the level of confidence. After the Bligh years and the constant warring between the governor and the military, Macquarie went out of his way to keep the military in its place. Having come to the colony as head of his own regiment he expected and received strong and loyal support and little distraction from the military officers. As a way of reversing the troubled mindset of the population away from the turbulent Bligh years, Macquarie commenced his four-fold program of

- A building program of fine buildings that would make the people proud
- A local revenue raising program that would provide a significant amount of discretionary revenue to support his local and almost all unapproved activities
- A social revolution whereby convicts who had served their time and returned to the regular community were welcomed into society and seated at his table. Simeon Lord was even appointed a Magistrate by Macquarie much to the consternation of leading citizens including Rev'd Samuel Marsden
- Encouraging free enterprise and new businesses, privately capitalised and operated.

The withholding and withdrawal of investment capital had only marginal impact. Mostly the traders lessened their level of speculation, which slowed the introduction of new supplies and stocks of new goods into the colony. The export trade still continued but prices sat their destination were lower and in spite of lower wholesale prices demand was reduced in Britain. For once the Keynesian laws of supply and demand did not work.

Governor Brisbane arrived in 1821 to replace Macquarie who had returned to Britain and his home in Scotland.

FINANCIAL STATEMENTS for the period

CHAPTER 7

THE THIRD PERIOD 1823-1840

These are the years leading up to the great recession of 1842. The foundations of the causes of the recession lay in the British influence on and over the colonial economy.

Naturally 50 years from the founding of the first penal settlement produced more than just one recession, although the term of the day referred to the economic collapse as being a depression. Gipps, as governor of the senior colony, found it difficult to ascribe more than partial blame on the British situation, but modern economic historians including Brian Fitzpatrick, Noel Butlin and A.G.L. Shaw place much if not most of the blame on the withdrawal of British Investment from the colony. The depression of 1842 was a follow-on event from the hiccup of 1827. The credit squeeze of 1812 was the first time economic hardship or stress had reached the colony since 1788 and was the first occasion that the withdrawal of British investment scrambled the comparative gains being made steadily in the colony. Of course, Macquarie tried to counter the effects of the credit squeeze by encouraging trade, creating the atmosphere for entrepreneurs and encouraged local business to establish and grow.

Brisbane's arrival in the colony in 1821, marked the end of the successful Macquarie years, and reduced the growth of activity in the colony to a more normal level.

One of the first steps taken by Brisbane was to approve of and encourage the spread of settlement along the south coast from Sydney. The coast to the north of Sydney had been successfully settled for some time, sponsored by the coal fields around Newcastle, the fertile soils of the Hunter River region and the convict settlement in Port Macquarie.

New investors were showing interest in the colony following the publication in England of the three Bigge Reports. One such investment company was being formed in Scotland to exploit trading opportunities between Scotland and the colony. The Australia Company was formed in 1822 in Scotland to take advantage of the coming investment opportunities in the colony. By 1830 over 33% of all landowners in NSW were Scots born.

To further assist the growth of the settlements, Brisbane built a road from Windsor to Maitland and opened up more of the Hunter River district.

The organisation of the convict labour was consistently a problem in the colony, and although Macquarie had taken a personal interest in the convicts by receiving the convict ships into Sydney Harbour and by directing the assignment of convict labour to public projects, Brisbane chose to transfer responsibility for convicts from the Superintendent of Convicts to the Colonial Secretary.

Brisbane suppressed the first recorded discovery of gold from the Bathurst District in 1823. He was concerned his convicts would be tempted to escape the assignment provided and head for the hills of gold. Thus it took a further 30 years for the official find to be publicly announced.

Upon leaving the colony, Commissioner Bigge recommended to the British Treasury that extra import duties be placed on all colonial products except wool, timber and tanning bark. On these goods he recommended lower duties.

1823 also saw the formation of the NSW Legislative Council authorised by the New South Wales Judicature Act (UK legislation) which also extended the role of the Supreme Court in the colony.

In 1824, William Charles Wentworth commenced *The Weekly Australian Newspaper*. The challenge thrown before Brisbane in the newspaper columns brought about the first threat of censorship to the new publication. This followed Brisbane heavy censorship of the *Sydney Gazette* and forbidden to report on local politics.

A giant boost to the development of the colony and the spread of settlement and the attraction of new investment from abroad came with the formation of the Australian Agricultural Company in 1824. The establishment of the AAC is described in more detail later on.

Another new and promising industry was established, when, in 1824, sugar was produced from local sugar cane.

Brisbane opened the Morton Bay settlement in 1824 and moved to further explore the Brisbane River.

Brisbane was recalled without having achieved much of what he was sent out to do. The post—Macquarie years had witnessed the decline of growth and the decline of British interest in the colony.

General Sir Ralph Darling arrived as Governor in 1825 (Brian Fletcher has written a comprehensive biography of Darling's life—*Ralph Darling—A Governor Maligned*)

The first of Darling's proclamations restored the supervision of convict labour to the Assignment Board.

When the question of legitimacy of import duties imposed under former governors was raised Darling moved to ratify their legality through the new Legislative Council

The AAC utilised their exclusive access to the coal-fields of Newcastle and even though the company was the recipient of both a grant of land (one million acres) and an assignment of many convicts, the company decided to modernise coal hand and laid a tramway in Newcastle to carry and move coal from the fields to the wharf.

We noted a first liquidity crisis in 1812 when British investors withdrew credit from the colony. A second liquidity crisis took place in 1827 and was due to a decline in export prices in Britain and cuts in foreign investment.

Darling introduced the concept of pastoral and commercial land leasing in 1828 just as a significant boost in convict numbers arriving inn the colony was creating further investment opportunities and demand for labour. The arriving convicts were mostly assigned to pastoralists and farmers. This boost in transported convicts increased the convict element of the overall population from 29.8 to 46.4

'Bay whaling' was commenced at Twofold Bay on the south coast of the colony in 1828, whilst VDL boasted 5 bay whaling stations.

The only way Darling could try to control squatters and pastoralists was to impose 'limits of location', and by 1829 the limits of location was limited to 219 counties in New South Wales.

Extending the settlements embraced the new colony of South Australia and Edward Gibbon Wakefield published his plan for land reform and the colonising of Australasia.

Labour organisation was underway in Sydney now that the restrictive UK labour laws on association and organisation of workers had been repealed. The Sydney Shipwright's Association was formed as a trade society in 1829. Later, in 1833, the Cabinet Maker's society was formed to maintain piece rates for workers.

New industry attracted many interested entrepreneurs. With over 3 million lb of tea being imported annually from China, tea plantations were first experimented with in northern NSW.

Darling's last acts as governor saw the implementation of the Rippon Regulations which approved crown land sales at 5/—per acre; the Molesworth Committee's recommendation that transportation be suspended, and the funding of immigration into the colony from the Land Fund

Upon the return of Darling to England, Sir Richard Bourke was appointed governor of the colony in 1831.

The colonial governors were still under heavy influence from Britain with Bourke being faced with action being required on the recommendations of the Committee on secondary punishments. Due to the growing crime rate in the colony (it was 8 times the rate in Britain) the UK House of Commons committee recommended more convict discipline and harsher treatment. The crime rate, especially amongst convicts had reached startling levels. In 1835 there were 28,000 convicts and over 22,000 summary convictions against convicts.

Bourke didn't agree with this action but was aware that if free migrants and investment were to be attracted to the colony then the people of Sydney and Parramatta were not to be scandalised by convict misbehaviour, a high crime rate and chain gangs of convicts being paraded through the streets of the principal town.

Due to growing land sales revenue and a strong interest in migration from Britain to the colony, an Immigration Commission was established in London and funded by the Land Fund. Land sales were not the only growth revenue increasing. In 1833 the import duties into the colony exceeded 100,000 (108,466) pound for the first time With the ad valorem duty being set at 5%, this revenue indicated that over 2 million pound of goods were being imported into the colony. With the total population set at 60,794, this level of imports meant that every man, woman and child, civil servant and convict, was importing nearly 33 pound of goods per year. With exports matching imports in value, trade had reached a remarkable level of 65 pound per head per annum in less than 45 years from the original settlement.

The recommendation to cease transportation to the colony was generally welcomed by the town people, but pastoralists bemoaned the fact that they would lose future access to assigned free labour. It was decided that all prisoners convicted to less than 7 years punishment would in future be handled within Britain.

The pastoralists had plenty to be concerned about. The convicts constituted most of their labour, and few free workers were available in the colony to replace them. All this at the same time that wool exports from the colony reached record levels in Britain and replaced whale products as the colony's main export.

They were not welcomed but the first Chinese labourers arrived in the colony in 1837. Plenty of local opposition stopped any large scale transfers of Asian workers to the colonies.

Workers were an important ingredient missing in the colony and that is why the Land Fund was being used to sponsor free settlers into the colony, but they could not arrive fast enough.

The census of 1839 (Sir George Gipps arrived as the new governor in 1838) showed that NSW had 2 distilleries, 7 breweries, 12 tanneries, 3 brass foundries, 77 flour mills, whilst single factories were producing hats, salt, sugar, tobacco and other goods. Bread had become a good barometer of changing prices and cost of living in the colony and in drought or in times of shortage, wheat would rise in cost, and the price of bread would react accordingly. In 1839, the reverse was happening. Good conditions led to a favourable harvest and a good crop so wheat prices fell from 1/2/—per bushel to 2/9 and bread dropped from 4/—per loaf to 1/3p.

By the end of this third period, the colony was making giant strides in growing and acting like a town that was there to stay. Food was plentiful. Jobs were available for everyone wanting to work. The Military was loyal top the Governor and the Legislative Assembly appeared to be acting responsibly. In 1832 the first Appropriation Bills had been provided to the Legislators and it was shown that the colony was in good shape financially. Social problems were being addressed, convict transportation had ceased and less than 1,000 convicts were still under maintenance.

Investment from overseas was being attracted to the colony and there were lots of opportunities for investors and new settlers. There was a cloud on the horizon in 1842 but until that time the colony was under good management.

Factors Affecting British Investment in the Colony

A number of factors affected the level of capital investment into the colony—many were ill informed and relied on delayed newspaper reports on activity in the various settlements.

a. The offer of assisted migration
b. The failing economic conditions in Britain
c. Economic expansion for the pastoral industry due to successful exploration in the colony
d. The settlement at Port Phillip and the eventual separation of Victoria from New South Wales would promote great investment opportunities
e. The rise of the squattocracy
f. The crash of 1827-28 in the colony shakes British Investors
g. The Bigge's' Report of 1823 breathed new life into capital formation especially with Macarthur sponsoring the float of the Australian Agricultural Company
h. Further along, the good credit rating of the colonies (and there being no defaults on loans) encouraged larger investments and loans into the colonies
i. Shortage of Labour in the colony and the offer of land grants to new settlers became a useful carrot to attract small settlers bringing their own capital by way of cash or goods or livestock with them.
j. Two other steps had important consequences, one in the colony and the other in Britain. In 1827 Governor Darling began to issue grazing licenses to pastoralists, and the terms were set at 2/6d per hundred acres, with liability to quit on one month's notice. From this movement grew, writes Mad wick in Immigration into Eastern Australia, the squatting movement and the great pastoral expansion, and the idea of the earlier Governors that the colony of New South Wales should be a colony of farmers was thus abandoned. The concurrent event was the floating of the Australian Agricultural Company in London. Development by the AAC and by the free settlers brought increasing prosperity. Exports tripled between 1826 and 1831.
k. There is a connection between availability of factors of production and the level of investment. In the early days of the colony, labour

was present—bad labour, convict labour, but still labour. The governors had demanded settlers with capital to employ that labour and develop the land. They proposed to limit land grants in proportion to the means of the settler. Governor Darling declared (HRA ser 1, vol 8) that 'when I am satisfied of the character, respectability and means of the applicant settler in a rural area, he will receive the necessary authority to select a grant of land, proportionate in extent to the means he possesses.

Under Macquarie the colony had boomed with new buildings, new settlements, new investment and lots of convicts. Under Brisbane the needs for economic consolidation and new infrastructure would be addressed, together with an appeal for free settlers.

Some significant events took place during the Brisbane guardianship

- The British were intent on accessing every available trading opportunity with the colony, and formed in Scotland *The Australia Company*
- A road was built to connect the Windsor settlement to the new settlement at Maitland. This decision opened up the Hunter River district to new farming opportunities
- The responsibility for convicts was transferred from the Superintendent of Convicts to the Colonial Secretary, although this move was to be reversed within the next decade
- The first documented discovery of gold was made. It was hushed in the colony lest convicts run off to find their fortunes
- In Bigge's third and final report, he recommended extra colonial import duties and less British duty on imported timber and tanning bark

The most significant event of all was the confidence placed in Bigge's favourable opinion of the potential of the colonial economy by the London Investment community and the resulting subscription of one million pound for the Australian Agricultural Company. The subscription was accompanied by a grant of one million acres of land around Port Stephens and the allocation of 5,000 convicts, but also brought inflation to livestock prices and availability throughout the colony.

J.F. Campbell wrote about the first decade of the Australian Agricultural Company 1824-1834 in the proceedings of the 1923 RAHS.

"Soon after Commissioner Bigge's report of 1823 became available for public information, several enterprising men concerted with a view to acquire sheep-runs in the interior of this colony, for the production of fine wool.

The success which attended the efforts of John Macarthur and a few other New South Wales pastoralists, in the breeding and rearing of fine woolled sheep and stock generally, as verified by Bigge, gave the incentive and led to the inauguration of proceedings which resulted in the formation of the Australian Agricultural Company.

The first formal meeting of the promoters took place at Lincoln's Inn, London, (at the offices of John Macarthur, junior).

Earl Bathurst, advised Governor Brisbane in 1824 that . . . .

His Majesty has been pleased to approve the formation of the Company, from the impression that it affords every reasonable prospect of securing to that part of His Majesty's dominions the essential advantage of the immediate introduction of large capital, and of agricultural skill, as well as the ultimate benefit of the increase of fine wool as a valuable commodity for export.

The chief proposals of the company are:

   i.   The company was to be incorporated by Act of Parliament or Letters Patent.
   ii.   The capital of the company was to be 1 million pound sterling divided into 10,000 shares of 100 pound each
   iii.   A grant of land of one million acres to be made to the company
   iv.   That no rival joint stock company to be established in the colony for the next twenty years
   v.   That agents of the company would select the situation or the land grants.

viii. The shepherds and labourers would consist of 1,400 convicts, thereby lessening the maintenance of such convicts by an estimated 30,800 pound or 22 pound/per head/ per annum.

The Royal Charter of 1824 forming the company provided for payment of quit-rents over a period of twenty years, or the redemption of the same by paying the capital sum of 20 times the amount of the rent so to be redeemed. These quit-rents were to be waived if the full number of convicts were maintained for a period of five years. No land was to be sold during the five-year period from the date of the grant".

Being important that the investment be seen to have the support of strong leaders in Britain, and democratic governance, the company operated with

- A Governor
- 25 directors
- 365 stockholders (proprietors)

Leading stockholders included

- Robert Campbell
- Chief Justice Forbes
- Son of Governor King
- Rev'd Samuel Marsden
- John Macarthur
- Each Macarthur son, John jr, Hannibal, James, Charles, Scott & William

John Oxley, the Colonial-Surveyor had recommended the area of Port Stephens as an eligible spot for the land grant. The local directors inspected and approved the site but John Macarthur was extremely critical of the selection, the management plan and the extravagance of the first buildings.

This venture was the first major investment into the colony and set the scene for later developments. In 1825 the Van Diemens Land Company was chartered by the British Parliament and granted land on the northwest corner of the territory.

Both the A.A. Coy and the VDL Coy still operate today after nearly 180 years of continuous operation, a record beaten only by the operation of the Hudson Bay Company in Canada.

Sir Timothy Coghlan was the colonial statistician whilst he was involved in preparing the series 'The Wealth and Progress of New South Wales 1900-01'. He was later appointed as Agent-General in London before compiling the 4-volume set of 'Labour and Industry in Australia'.

A review of the Coghlan account of Public Finance includes references to

- Loan expenditure
- Government Services
- Public Debt
- Colonial Debt Rating
- Land Grants versus Sales
- Treasury bills
- Assets of New South Wales
- Private Finance

The Coghlan analysis on each of these points will now be given analysis.

i. Loan Expenditure

The Loan Account was not established until 1853, although the system of raising money by loans commenced as early as 1842. The first ten loans of the colony were raised on the security of the Territorial Revenue, which fund was the proceeds of Land sales and used for the benefit of assisted immigration. Prior to 1842, capital expenditure was made from normal revenue and no differentiation was made between expenditure on capital account and expenditure on current account. All funds flow into and from Consolidated Revenue. From 1853, after the securing of funds through the Loan Account, all proceeds of loans were paid into Consolidated Revenue fund, without being separated into specific capital or current account allocations. So those funds that were raised for specific capital projects had to rely on available surpluses in Consolidated Revenue if the project was to proceed and be fully funded.

The use to which loan funds were generally put was capital works such that the citizens of the settlements would have running water, sewerage, tramways, and telegraphic services. docks, roads and bridges, public works and buildings, fortifications and military works, immigration, public instruction and school buildings, lighthouses and improvements to harbours and rivers.

Coghlan states that 'a vigorous works policy was usually the order of the day'. This, put simply, meant that 'the opportunity engendered the desire, and the open purses of the investors tempted the colonies to undue borrowing and lavish expenditure'. It is Coghlan's opinion that 'the plethora of money has been harmful in many ways, but is most apparent in the construction of a few branch railways in outlying and sparsely-settled districts which do not even pay their working expenses, with the consequence that interest on loan capital has to be paid out of general revenue. Overall, it will be found that the proceeds of loans has been well expended.' The attached loan expenditure table reflects the growing debt per inhabitant. The table shows two interesting facts

a. The annual loan expenditure per inhabitant varies from 18/9d to 4/4/-, and
b. The accumulated debt per inhabitant grew, in twenty years, from 17/0/6d to 44/17/6d

ii. Public Borrowing and Public Debt

It was after 1831, when the system of free land grants was abolished, and the auction system of land disposal was introduced, that it was decided to pay these auction proceeds into the Land Fund. It was from this fund that that charges relating to the assistance for migrants was to be paid. From 1831 to 1841, this fund was adequate, but in 1841 the fund was insufficient and it was decided to borrow on the security of the Land Revenue. Thus on the 28th December 1841, a notice was placed in the Gazette to the effect that 49,000 was to be raised by way of a debenture loan with interest at 5.25%. This was the start of public debt in the colony, and the first ever raised by Australian Government. A further 10 loans between 1842 and 1850 quickly followed, amounting in total to 705,200 pound, the proceeds of which were allocated exclusively to furthering immigration.

At 1850, when responsible government was underway, the public debt was 1,000,800 pound. Of this amount, 640,500 had been raised on the security of land revenue. The balance of 360,300 pound was raised on the security of general revenue.

Of the total, railways accounted for 474,000, water and sewerage 82,900, public works 21,000 and immigration was 423,000. Of the total 1,000,800 only 47,500 was redeemed out of general revenue, the balance being rolled-over into new loans.

The Public Debt balances for this period are shown on the attached table

Nothing quite engenders confidence in an investor like the thought of a new bank opening for business.

Less than three months after his arrival in the colony, Macquarie foreshadowed his plan for a bank on the South African model, as a 'remedy' to 'be speedily applied to this growing evil' of private promissory notes. With some exaggeration he explained that there was 'no other circulating medium in this colony than the notes of hand of private individuals' which, as he said, had 'already been productive of infinite frauds, abuses and litigation'. He accordingly announced his intention to' strongly recommend the adoption here of the same system of banking and circulating medium as is now so successfully and beneficially pursued at the Cape of Good Hope'.

By June 1810 Macquarie had developed his plan for 'The New South Wales Loan Bank' as a government institution 'as nearly as possible on the same system and principles as the Government Loan Bank at the Cape of Good Hope'. There, he explained the government issued notes by way of loan on the security of mortgages at 6 per cent per annum. He also pointed out that in England the government borrowed on exchequer bills at 5 %, so that the Cape was 11% better off. 'It appears to me' was his conclusion, 'the most perfect model in all its parts that could be possibly adopted here' By October 1810, he was willing to accept any alternative form of bank which Liverpool (Secretary for the Colonies) might believe to be 'better calculated to effect the desired object'.

Obviously a Bank would form the foundation for a monetary policy in the colony, and stop the use of Commissary receipt (store receipts) as an exchange mechanism, promote a currency and an official exchange rate for traders and cease to rely on bills drawn on the British Treasury to pay for goods and services.

3. The British Scene

Circumstances in Britain contributed greatly to the climate of 'greener pastures' over the seas.

Conditions were never more favourable for emigration than they were during the 1830s. The decade had opened with rioting in the agricultural districts in the south of England. This was followed by the upheavals of the Reform Bill of 1832, the Factory Act of 1833 and the Corn Laws, which kept wages low and unemployment high. The Poor Law of 1834 withdrew assistance from the poor and re-introduced the workhouse. The Irish rebellion was creating both upheaval and poverty

These conditions were met by the enthusiastic reports coming from Australia of the progress being made in agriculture, commerce and the pastoral industry. The assistance granted to emigrants as a result of Edward Gibbon Wakefield's reforms made possible the emigration of people who had previously been prevented by the expense. It is almost certain that free passage would not have been a sufficient enticement if conditions in Britain had not been unfavourable. It is significant that years of small migration coincided with good conditions in England accompanied by unfavourable reports from the colony.

4. <u>Creating Opportunities in the Colony</u>

Availability of land and labour to yield profit on invested capital is the constant decisive condition and test of material prosperity in any community, and becomes the keystone of an economy as well as defining its national identity.

British Government policy for the Australian colonies was formulated and modified from time to time. Policies for the export of British capital and the supply of labour (both convict and free) were adjusted according to British industrial and demographic and other social situations, as well as the capability and capacity of the various colonial settlements top contribute to solving British problems.

By the 1820s there was official encouragement of British Investment in Australia by adopting policies for large land grants to persons of capital and for the sale of land and assignment of convict labour to those investors. Then followed the reversal of the policy of setting up ex-convicts on small 30 acre plots as small proprietors. The hardship demanded by this policy usually meant these convicts and families remained on the commissary list for support (food and clothing) at a continuing cost to the government. It was much cheaper to assign these convicts to men of property and capital who would support them fully—clothe, house and feed them.

We can ask, what led directly to the crash of 1827?

a. Firstly, the float of the Australian Agricultural Company raised a large amount of capital, mostly from the City of London investment community, and this contributed to speculation and 'sheep and cattle mania instantly seized on all ranks and classes of the inhabitants' (written by Rev'd John Dunmore Lang) 'and brought many families to poverty and ruin'.

b.   When capital imports cease, the wherewithal to speculate vanished; speculation perforce stopped; inflated prices fell to a more normal level, and wrote E.O. Shann in Economic History of Australia 'because those formerly too optimistic were now too despairing, and people had to sell goods at any price in order to get money; men who had bought at high prices were ruined, and perforce their creditors fell with them'.

c.   In 1842, it was the same. The influx of capital from oversees, pastoral extension, and large-scale immigration, caused much speculation. The banks, competing for business, advanced too much credit. Loans were made on the security of land and livestock, which later became almost worthless; too much discounting was done for merchants (Gipps, HRA Vol 23) In the huge central district on the western slopes, along the Murrumbidgee and the Riverina, the squatters triumphed, as was inevitable. He had the financial resources to buy his run—especially after the long period of drought. Four million acres of crown land was sold for nearly 2.5 million pound. The confidence of British investors was waning. A crisis in the Argentine and the near failure of the large clearinghouse of Baring's made them cautious. Stories of rural and industrial strife in the colony were not inducements to invest: and wood and metal prices were still falling Loan applications being raised in London were under-subscribed, at the same time, the banks were increasingly reluctant to lend money for land development, which was so often unsound.

5. Assisted Migration

The dual policy of selling land to people with sufficient capital to cultivate it, and keeping a careful check on the number of free grants was adopted after 1825. 'Yet the Colonial Office', says Madgwick, 'failed to administer land policy with any certainty

(R.B. Madgwick 'Immigration into Eastern Australia'). There was no uniform policy adopted to encourage economic development in a systematic and rational way. The Wakefield system found new supporters. The principle had been established that the sale of land was preferred to the old system of grants. The dual system of sales and grants had failed to encourage local (colonial) purchases. They were willing to accept grants or even 'squat' rather than purchase land. Sales to absentee landlords and investors stepped up, and as can be seen from the following table, provided extensive revenue to the British Government to promote free and sponsored migration.

6. <u>Successful exploration promotes new interest in the Colony</u>

A period of rapid expansion followed the change in economic policy. Wool exports by 1831 were 15 times as great as they had been only 10 years earlier (in 1821). The increase in the number of sheep led to a rapid opening of new territories for grazing. It was the search for new land with economic value that underpinned most of the explorations. Settlers and sheep-men quickly followed exploration, and growth fanned out in all directions from Sydney town.

However, exploration was not the only catalyst for growth.

a. The growing determination to exclude other powers from the continent stimulated official interest in long-distance exploration by sea and by land and in the opening of new settlements. For instance, J.M. Ward in his work 'The Triumph of the Pastoral Economy 1821-1851' writes that Melville and Bathurst Islands, were annexed and settled between 1824 and 1827, whilst Westernport and Albany were settled in order to clinch British claims to the whole of Australia

b. When Governor Brisbane opened the settlement at Moreton Bay in 1824, it was to establish a place for punishment of unruly convicts and a step towards further economic development, and of extending the settlements for the sake of attracting new investment

7. Colonial Failures fuel loss of Confidence

The collapse of British Investment can be traced to one or two causes, or indeed both.

I.   The British crisis of 1839 reflected the availability of capital for expansion by the Australian banks of that day—The Bank of Australasia and the Union Bank. These banks, three mortgage companies and the Royal Bank went into a slump due to shortage of available funds and deferred the raising of new funds until after the crisis. Stringency in the English Capital market had a serious impact on the capital raising opportunities in the colonies.

II. The second possibility is that the sharp decline was initiated by bad news of returns in the colonies, and that its role accentuated a slump with the dire consequences experienced in 1842-43. Recovery was delayed and made more difficult as there was 'no surplus labour in the colony'

It would be dangerous to imply or decide that every slump in Australia could be explained as being caused by economic evens. British investment was independent then, as it is now, and so the more valid explanation of the downturn in British investment in this period is that negative reports from the colonies disappointed and discouraged investors with capital to place.

Most facts about public finance in New South Wales lead to the conclusion that it was disappointed expectations that caused the turn down in the transfer of funds. At this same time Governor Gipps (Sir George Gipps) was being pushed by bankers and merchants to withdraw government deposits from the banks and thus this action caused a contraction in lending by the banks which in turn caused a slow down of colonial economic activity. The attached statistics of land sales, registered mortgages and liens on wool and livestock reflects the strong downturn in the agricultural economy, which naturally flowed on to the economy as a whole.

ii. Government Services

Sources of Revenue for each colony was generally classified under four (4) headings—taxation, land revenue, receipts for government services rendered and miscellaneous revenue. Prior to 1850, the 'Blue Books' were compiled annually for circulation to the Colonial Office in London, the Colonial Governor, Colonial Treasurer and Legislative Council. After self-government a new system of public accounting was introduced which reflected the four headings mentioned above. Annual comparisons are best made on a per inhabitant basis, and whilst 'taxation' remained fairly constant at a rate per head of 1/17/6d to 2/4/2d, land revenue and government services ranged widely. Land revenue grew from 1/9/7d per head to 2/6/0d; government services naturally grew from 1/11/11d to 3/15/1d, obviously reflecting the growing demands for government to provide all manner of assistance to the settlers and growing population. Services included:

Railways
Tramways
Postage
Telegraphs
Money orders
Water supply
Sewerage
Public school fees
Pilotage and harbour fees
Mint fees

Coghlan confirms that 'the income derived by the government from services, has, been steadily increasing; this is only what would naturally be expected in a growing community, but income per head has been fairly well sustained, holding in a 12 year period from 3/9/11d to 3/17/11d. This result is in spite of the fact that the railway system rarely made a 'profit' with earnings generally being around 3.81%, with the average interest payable being 3.61%. As the revenue from services naturally depends upon the amount of production, the rate per inhabitant will not only cease to increase, but will ultimately decline.'

Government services were supposedly being conducted on commercial principles; except that in the case of providing most services, receipts are less than expenditure meaning that these services were generally subsidized from general revenue. The gap appears to have increased exponentially year after year.

Conclusion

Our period starts in one of two ways depending on your viewpoint.

"Macquarie's arrival was the beginning of a new system of administration in Australia, says Jose in '*The History of Australasia*'. Marjorie Barnard, on the other hand writes in '*A History of Australia*' With Macquarie an old order ended. The colonial office changed its mind and its policy. It no longer wanted a community of peasant farmers' Macquarie however, spoke his own epitaph "I found New South Wales a gaol and left it a colony; I found a population of idle prisoners, paupers and paid officials, and left a large free community thriving in the produce of flocks and the labour of convicts".

Our period ends with the threat of recession, which we will review in the next period in 1842

Since the funding of the colonial operations is our main interest it is of value to listen to N.G.Butlin in '*Forming a Colonial Economy*'

"The local contributions were typically less than 5% of British Expenditures, and even at the end of the Macquarie Administration, they were not over 10%. The scale of the local contribution

THE FOURTH PERIOD 1841-1855

Two interesting discoveries emerge from the table on Page 219-British Investments in to the Colony 1800-1850.

We have noted above that T.A. Coghlan, that doyenne of all things statistical, especially in relation to the colony, states very strongly and without qualification that 'the private capital invested in the colony prior to 1871 was 16 million pound.

Coghlan provides no supporting evidence to substantiate this statement, but having broken the actual verifiable figures down into components, that Coghlan figure sounds quite plausible. This writer's estimates of private capital invested in the colony between 1800 and 1850 are 14,388,000 pound. The components include Government borrowings overseas; immigrant's capital; foreigner's investment, and I have included the amount of land mortgages recorded under the Deeds Registration Act of 1843. Although land mortgages after 1843 would normally have been recorded, there was provision in the Act for re-registration of earlier mortgages and many lenders, both private sand corporate, took advantage of ratifying their previous lien rights. Since my figures relate to the period to 1850, it is more than likely that between 1851 and 1870, a further 1.7 million pound was invested privately. So Coghlan is essentially. Correct.

However it is the N.G. Butlin assumptions that trouble me, and I would like to restate an earlier conclusion that the British accepted an excellent return on their investment in the colony, and this is really what the opening of the colony was all about.

The Table of British Public Investment in the colony shows from the inception of the colony, through to self-government, the British 'invested' nearly 70 million pound in capital works or their equivalent. What this means is that I have included the cost of shipping and transporting the convicts to the colony and the cost of food and provisioning. Professor Butlin, at one point, refers to the level of British investment for this same period as being 74 million, but the components are not described. However, it is a not unreasonable figure to work with. It includes the early grants to the colony from the British Treasury; it includes the transportation of the convicts and their food en route; it includes the treasury bills drawn by the colony on the British Treasury for materials and contract labour, purchases from trading ships coming into the Harbour; it concludes payments made for civil list and military salaries, and it includes the verified public works expenditure. Each of these figures has been drawn from the 'Joint Copying Project of Historical documents' and 'historical statistics'.

The essential point of this assembly of public investment is to put into perspective the original investment by the British Treasury and compare it with the level of 'return' the British, as a whole, were to receive.

So, before we assemble the figures into a table of investment and return, let's review again the elements of what constitutes a 'return'.

Each of the elements of the return, and we might even say the expected return, for it was James Matra's submission to the British Government that first identified that the colony would be self-supporting within two years of commencing and provide advantages to Britain. It was Arthur Phillip in a letter to Lord Sydney in July 1788 who wrote ' . . . nor do I doubt but that this country will prove the most valuable acquisition Great Britain ever made . . . . '

The elements of this 'opportunity cost' include:

a. The opportunity cost of housing, feeding and guarding prisoners in England. This is set at the rate of 20 pound per head per annum, but does not take into account any offset for work undertaken by prisoners.

b. The use of convict labour for construction work on colonial buildings. This is set at 35 pound per annum for 2/3rds of the convicts (Macquarie employed about 70% of the male convicts in this way.

c. The balance of the male convicts were used on road construction, wharves, barracks etc and had an equivalent value, net of support payments, of 35 pound per annum (The James Matra letter of October 1784 stated that the contract price for maintaining prisoners on the hulks was 26/15/0 per annum). In the early years, we can also include in this figure, the convict labour used for land clearing, farming and food production, and the convict labour used for maintaining the supply of building materials, timber, bricks, tiles etc

d. The Molesworth Committee concluded in their Report to the House of Commons that there were significant savings in food costs for these convicts

e. Another benefit to the British by way of opportunity cost is the value of the land grants to the Military officers by way of fringe benefits as civil payments. On average, the land had a value of 1 pound per acre and we know that land grants were in the order of 5228015 acres

f. An as yet economically unquantifiable gain to British industry was the value of the import wool trade, and the export purchases of tobacco and spirits for the colony. In addition timber, coal, whale oil, skins and fur were all important imports by British Industry, and assisted Britain by making them less reliant on Europe.

g. It is assumed that the private investment received a return on capital equivalent to an interest and super profit.

So out Summary Table can now be assembled

TABLE
British Investment & Returns from the Colony of NSW

Public Investment

Treasury grants	23741000
Convict transport/food	6051550
Treasury Bills	5384584
Civil List	888858
Military	9629170
Commissary	8134000
Public Works	1265000

Total Public Investment 69,482,162

Benefits & Gains to the British

Opportunity Costs	–	a.	84000000
Convict labour	–	b.	70000000
Convict labour	–	c.	21000000
Food savings	–	d.	7000000
Land grants	–	e.	5228015

Total estimated Returns 180228015

This fourth and last period commenced with the big recession of 1842. Existing studies by Brian Fitzpatrick suggests there are 5 main contributing factors to the 'depression'. Other writers (eg N.G. Butlin) have relied on Fitzpatrick's conclusion. My research has provided many more contributing factors, and the whole episode is worth understanding in depth.

Contradictions in the Causes & Effects of the Depression of 1842

In recent examinations of:

- The Economic impact of the introduction of railways in the colonies, and
- The Boom and Bust of the 1842-1845 period,

Certain events were presented which supposedly led to the depression of 1842.

These events included

1. The fall in English Wholesale prices 1839-1843
2. The gradual fall of NSW export prices
3. The economic crisis in England of 1839
4. The severe drought in NSW in 1838-1841
5. The setting aside of crown land sales revenue to fund the Government immigration program
6. The reduction of investment capital from England to the colonies, which undermined the continuing land boom of the late 1830s.
7. The dramatic increase in the wool cheque of the 1830s could not be sustained into the 1840s
8. The impact of Colonial Isolation during the 1800s, wherein the colony became a 'dumping ground for human garbage' and thus became a 'penal wasteland that was out of sight and out of mind'
9. The introduction of the *Forbes Act* that declared English money laws to be inapplicable in the colony and undermined the focus of English absentee investment in the colony.

Against these truly economic events, we can set a number of more 'political' events which by rights should have equally impacted the depression of 1842, and caused a more minimalist effect on the colonial economy. These contradictions include:

a. The political arguments relating to the development of railways in the colony were ones of 'private enterprise' (as strongly recommended by the British Secretary of State) versus 'government sponsorship of public enterprises' (as made necessary by the vast territory to cover with tracks. The cost, even at the most optimistic cost estimate of 1,500 per mile of track, was beyond the resources and ability of private entrepreneurs in the colony.

b. The use of revenues derived from sales of crown land for sponsoring free immigrants into the colony was a supposed (Fitzpatrick suggests) negative influence on the local economy and contributed to the depression of 1842. However over 50,000 immigrants arrived in the colony between 1837 and 1842, and brought with them a great variety of personal wealth, both tangible and intangible, and far from taking cash out of the economy, contributed many valuable assets to their new home. It is beyond doubt that immigrants brought with them goods and coinage of far greater value than the 15 pound it cost for each immigrant to be sponsored to the new colony. It is more likely that of the funds allocated to the immigration program, a significant portion was used to cover bureaucratic overhead, in addition to meeting the costs of passage for these selected immigrants.

c. The movement towards self-government commenced occupying the minds of the politically influential, in the colony, with the formation of the Australian Patriotic Association in 1835. These deliberations led to the first Australian Constitution Act of 1842. The British Parliament created amendments, which led to the second Constitution Act of 1850. This second Act gave power to the four colonies (NSW, Vic, VDL and SA) to create for themselves bicameral legislatures. The exception was that they could not access revenues from crown lands, nor change the civil list salaries. Such reservations were not acceptable to either of the two leaders of the Legislative Assembly—James Macarthur and William Charles Wentworth. Before the challenge based on control over all the colony's wealth, could be made to the British Parliament, a third Act was received in the colony.

It is to be considered that the movement towards political independence and self-government distracted the politicians and governor from dealing promptly with matters of economic moment. It is likely, even in the days when economic management was of little moment, that political attention to matters relating to the economy could have changed the boom & bust syndrome in the colonial economy of the 1835-1845 period.

d. The immigration process itself must have been an influence on the economy leading to the depression of 1842. By 1830 it was clear that the Government had granted more land than could readily be cultivated wit the available convicts and emancipist labour. Settlement was widely dispersed and there was an acute labour shortage. The remedy seemed to be to restrict land grants. In 1831 under the Ripon Regulations, land grants were prohibited and land grants were substituted. This step, it was considered, would prevent settlers from taking up too much land, for they would now have to pay for it; also if the land revenue were devoted to assisting immigration, the labour shortage would be relieved. This was the Wakefield theory. The scheme was a partial success. Between 1832 and 1842 over 70,000 immigrants arrived in the colony. Free labourers, together with the free native-born, effectively diluted the convict element and helped to diversify the population and to stimulate the economy. But the expansion of settlement was not checked because the pastoralists, when unable to get their land by grant, simply squatted on it, and the labour shortage remained unabated.

e. *The Slump of 1842-44*

We have been discussing firstly the apparent economic causes of the depression of 1842, and secondly, some political distractions which affected the depression and which should have and did minimise the impact of factors on the economic scene of the early 1840s. The acute depression lasted only three years, but after those years, the pastoral expansion slowed. Lack of transport made settlement in the interior expensive, and the explorations of Eyre and Sturt suggested that the interior was largely an arid and waterless desert.

Drought, a fall in wool prices, the increasing costs of squatting farther out, and the higher cost of labour after the ceasing of transportation and the stopping of assignment in 1840 combined to make wool-growing temporarily uneconomic, and brought widespread bankruptcy to the colonies. The slump stopped all land sales; and without land revenue to assist migration, British migrants found it cheaper and easier to cross the Atlantic than to come to Australia.

The point here is that the slump of 1842 had a variety of economic causes—both internal and external events; however there are also a limited number of political events which also influenced, probably equally favourably and unfavourably.

Two of these events are now discussed in further detail—the advent of economic growth from the coming of the railways, and the impact of immigration.

f. On one hand, the colonial economy had underlying strength, and gave encouragement to special economic events that partway compensated for the external effects on calming the boom-times. On the other hand, political events played a role of growing importance in influencing the colonial economy.

g. The large increase in the population of the colonies in the 1835-1845 period, gave emphasis to the demand for better communications between the port cities with the interior of each colony, and gave support to the numerous projects for railway construction. In January 1846 Gladstone, the British Secretary of State, sent a despatch to each colony containing instructions relative to the introduction of railways

    He referred to

    i.   The initial securing of capital
    ii.   The right of the government to provide railway regulations
    iii. The carriage by railways of postal articles, and troops,
    iv.   The right of each colony to legislate themselves in railway matters

    Thus in 1846, the first encouragement of economic growth sponsored by a colonial government was seen. The context of such encouragement was also seen as a positive step towards self-government

    Prior to any gold discoveries, the government of the colony of New South Wales had been content with providing and maintaining only four main roads leading out of Sydney, each extended as the settlements advanced. Subsidiary roads were essentially uncared for. Thus the railways were initially discussed as a means of both communication and transportation links, although following English tradition, the government leaned towards private enterprise for railway construction and management. In 1848, the Legislative Council passed a series of resolutions offering land grants to any company undertaking the business of railway construction. In addition the colony would subscribe 20,000 pounds to the cause and guaranty interest on 100,000 pounds. Thus the *Sydney Railroad & Tramway Company* was formed with a capital of 100,000 pound and set as its object, the building of a line between Sydney and Parramatta. Liverpool and Bathurst were to be later links to this system. The Legislative Council in October 1849) contradicted the request, to keep railway development in the hands of government, by the then current Secretary of State, Earl Grey, by passing an Act incorporating this first private rail company along with a guaranty of a 4% return on the stock of the company. When work commenced in mid-1850, the wages of the labourers employed was increasing as many responded to the call of the gold discoveries outside Bathurst. By 1852, the government had assumed responsibility for funding and completing the construction work

The prospectus of the *Great New South Wales Railway Company* claimed that in 1853, a planned line in the Hunter Region of the colony could be laid for a cost not exceeding 1,500 pound per mile. This claim was justified by the directors' claim that:

"It is intended to apply for Articled Labourers from China or other parts, at reasonable wages, and under the customary legalised regulations"

Coghlan ('Labour & Industry in Australia') writes that 'the construction of both the Sydney and the Hunter Region lines languished, held back by want of capital and by the high price of wages and materials, following the gold discoveries. A New South Wales Legislative Council Report in June 1854 declared that "the government had already gone too far in carrying out the guarantee principle and it seemed that private companies could not succeed in constructing railways without government aid on a scale which ought not to be conceded'. These principles were incorporated into a Bill introduced in December 1854, which authorised the government to carry out state construction of works of large public utilities, and assume the lines already constructed. In the years following gold discovery, private enterprise was again given a free hand in developing public utilities and infrastructure when the 'paternalism of the preceding years became very much out of favour' (Coghlan).

The need for railways as a means of economical transportation was urgent. The cost of sending goods by team from Sydney to Goulburn, a distance of 134 miles, was 12 pound 5 shillings, and the time taken was 17-18 days. The same journey to Bathurst, a distance of 145 miles, took 23½ days and cost 15 pound 10 shillings per ton. These rates reflect an approx. per ton-mile cost of 1s 10p.

The demand for rail may have been great but real progress was slew. 16 miles of track were opened in 1855 and by 1861 the total was only 70 miles. There was little capital in the colony for public enterprises and what little was available came with high interest rates (more than 5% per annum). This was unfortunate, since the railways earned in New South Wales less than 2% on the capital outlay for the first twenty years of operation.

The contradiction here is that after the bust of 1842 the British investors were wary of lending into the colonies, but theirs was the only capital suitable for use in constructing the railroads. The shipments of unrefined gold going steadily to England from June 1851 helped change the mindset of British investors. British flagged ships charged ½ % for shipping and bought the gold FOB at 3:8:6 an ounce. The bill discount rate also increased from the traditional 1% to 2-½%. By February 1852 the discount rate had grown to 12%, which slowed the amount of business in advancing money against gold. This trend of allowing cash advances against

GORDON BECKETT

shipments to England troubled the Legislative Council in New South Wales, which recommended that a mint be established in Sydney, in order to counter the 'enormous exactions imposed on the producers of the colony, by the various banking institutions'. Coupled with the effect of the Forbes Act, which declared that *English money laws were not applicable in the colony'* this high discounting rate made interest rates an effective 40% pa.

2. Another contradiction in the boom to bust syndrome of the 1840s can be seen in the movement towards 'independence' or self-government of the late 1840s.

Alan Atkinson, writing in *Australian Historical Studies*, suggests that a large part of the foundation of independence in New South Wales was laid by the remarkable demographic changes of the 1830s. The system of assisted immigration which was set up in 1835 led to the arrival of 50,745 free men, woman and children between 1837 and 1842. This was to be a fraction of the numbers to arrive during the gold-rush immigration period. For the colony of New South Wales, the white population grew by 70%, with men and women fairly balanced in their numbers, as compared to the 4:1 ratio of men to women during the gold-rush period'.

These immigrants brought with them a number of social influences

- A much higher level of literacy that came with the convicts
- A Christian faith drawn 'from the deep fund of British popular religious tradition (Atkinson)
- A more avant guard willingness to experiment with a new moral order

Dark Days

Governor Gipps wrote, in 1842 "From a system, indeed, of nearly unbounded credit, the transition has been sudden to an almost total denial of it: and consequently persons, who can no longer get accommodation from the banks are obliged to dispose of such property as they may be possessed of at very depreciated prices"

Sheep which had sold at 25s each during the boom, now sold at 5s or less. One settler wrote that 'insolvency was almost universal and confidence in mercantile affairs lost entirely—the whole community seems horror-struck and nothing that can now be foreseen can avert general bankruptcy'. (Hobler) About 600 insolvency petitions were filed in 1842 and almost as many in the following year. As Gipps pointed out 'for a man who purchased his sheep in money borrowed at 10 to 15 percent, there is no hope but in the Bankruptcy Court'

Investors in Britain, alarmed by reports of the difficulties in the colony, stopped exporting their capital and recovered earlier investments as best they could. NSW was sinking deeper into a morass of falling prices and incomes, unemployment and bankruptcies.

Several banks failed in the depression, and others were in difficulties. The major failure was that of the Bank of Australia, the 'pure Merino' bank established in 1826. The final blow to the bank came from a trading firm—Hughes and Hosking—which had borrowed 200,000 pounds from the bank and been unable to repay.

Gipps had raised the minimum price of Crown land in 1839 and 1842. This, it can be believed, was a primary cause of the great fall in land sales and it deterred, no doubt, the immigration of capitalists willing to enter the pastoral industry, to the extent that the bottom fell out of the livestock market.

The availability of land privately owned and available for sale at below the crown land minimum price, was evidence that the subsequent Gipp's suggestion to drop crown land prices would not assist the economy.

The banks responded to pressure from W.C. Wentworth to ease the economic hardship by dropping interest rates. The banks cooperated by dropping their lending rates but also took interest on deposits away.

At the turning point to the depression in 1844, wool production was still marginally profitable, whilst wages had fallen.

Gipps finally observed that 'no-one had any real solution to offer other than to allow the depression to work itself out, but that observation did nothing to make the Governor less unpopular.

Brian Fletcher in his biography of (Governor) Ralph Darling that 'financial problems which beset the colony in 1826 were aggravated by the collapse in December of 1825 of an English speculative boom, which forced merchants and financiers to recall cash from colonial entrepreneurs. A quotation by Hartwell in his JRAHS article—*Australia's First Trade Cycle*—reveals that "the most horrible revolutions have taken place in the mercantile affairs in England and upwards of 100 banks and a large portion of the best mercantile houses in the commercial world have failed. A simultaneous drop in the price of wool, averaging 50% was witnessed in 1826 (as compared to 1825 prices).

Other than wool—the colonies main export—the price of timber (the third main export of the colony, also fell and Governor Darling observed 'the exports of Blue Gum and similar timber have been almost entirely discontinued in consequence of the low prices obtained for them in England' (HRA Darling to Huskisson)'. He went on to say that 'only fisheries fared well, with the export value of whale oil and seal skins consistently exceeding that of wool'. However few colonists were employed in the fisheries industry and their success did not compensate for the setbacks experienced by pastoralists. Stock prices also declined, on an average of 400% between 1826 and 1830. Leading this tend was the highly speculative prices generated by the Australian Agricultural Company before prices tumbled 'to a degree never seen in any other community in such a short period' (Darling). These problems were exacerbated by the severe drought between 1825 and 1829. 'The long continuing drought', said Darling, 'which is currently being experienced has subjected the colony to suffer materially from the want of rain'.

Exploring the Period

A. The economic Scene

The period of our focus 1825-1845 is a fairly interesting period, and is worth a closer examination.

Our main sources are

- An Epitome of the Official History of New South Wales from 1788 to 1883—compiled from the official records
- Shann 'Economic History of Australia' (1930)
- T.A. Coghlan 'Labour & Industry in Australia' (1918-1969)

As Shann sets out the record "There were two bad stumbles, the booms of 1826 and 1838-39, and the financial crises which followed them. Each arose through the failure of the leaders of the free community to justify their leadership by a single-minded activity in developing the pastoral industry".

The opening operations of the Australian Agricultural Company also led much weight to the boom & bust syndrome. J.D. Lang records the scene at the weekly livestock auctions.

"The AAC commenced operations in 1826. Cattle of colonial breed were actually sold to the company's agent for twelve guineas and sheep for 4 or 5 guineas per head. Barristers, attorneys, military officers, clergymen, medical men, merchants, dealers mingled at the weekly Thursday auction and outbid each other for the purchase of every scabbed sheep, scarecrow horse or buffalo cow in the colony that was offered for sale".

Shann moves on to 1830 and relates precursor to an economic downturn prompted by the rising interest rates—"although the rate of interest allowed by law was only eight percent, the market accepted 12,15, 20, 25 and even 30 percent interest, to meet the necessities of individual settlers".

Shann records the second period of speculation, in 1838,—"seen through a period of increase in livestock and land values. The population was increasing rapidly (it reached 68795 in 1838); new colonies in VDL and SA were expanding and new pastoralists were buying up flocks and herds without the experience necessary to calculate the income they could expect to yield. The proceeds of government land sales at Port Phillip and at Sydney were being used to bring out numbers of assisted immigrants. There was a fever to buy stock and equip stations. Speculators put about that land values must rise still more".

The resulting downturn commenced with the price of land being raised to 12 shillings an acre. Auction sales of Melbourne allotments reached 313000pound in the first ten months of 1840. Private resales were made on credit (some lots sold in 1837, were resold in 1840 at 80 times their original price). Others financed by borrowing on the collateral security of land at the inflated prices. Two banks were competing for this business. The Banks of New South Wales and of Australia (the latter floated in 1826 with a paid capital of 400,000 pound). Numerous other banks followed from 1834 . . . London merchants fuelled the fire by consigning huge quantities of luxury goods to the Sydney and Melbourne markets, whilst the banks held over 80% of their total assets in discounted bills. A scourging drought from 1838 to 1840 accentuated the mistrust felt in England about the future of the colonies. The financial stringency in London in 1839 checked the flow of capital to Australia. Governor Gipps had to withdraw earlier deposits of land sales funds from the banks and banks suddenly stopped all 'cash credits'. Merchants were paralysed by auction sales without reserves. Pastoralists bartered for goods and cash by offering livestock or wool at a sacrificed price into an already glutted market".

The second downturn had arrived with gusto. The event gave rise to a new industry. 44 boiling-down plants rendered 350,000 sheep into 48,000 cwt of tallow earning the equivalent of 6 shillings per sheep. Coghlan thought that 'the value of this discovery lay more in its effects upon men's minds than in the actual use to which it was put'

Shann confirmed our reckoning on the economic events of the period including two cycles of surging and downturns in the colony economy.

The Epitome of Official Records offers a variety of views of a political nature of the same period.

B. The Political Scene

Governor Sir Thomas Brisbane 1821-1825 was an eminently suitable man for the British Government to be able to manipulate whilst he was filling the post—Macquarie seat of government. The last days of Macquarie had seen fewer free immigrants into the colony and even fewer grants of land. Macquarie was reversing the old habits of giving grants to those who came freely to the quasi-penal colony. However the capabilities of the colony were being exposed in England and becoming better known and understood. Commissioner Bigge had not been so unkind in his observations of the colony to dissuade a steadily increasing stream of free immigrants, expecting grants upon arrival. It was Bigge who recommended new settlements along the north coast, especially Port Macquarie. Oxley led an even more northerly expedition and discovered the Brisbane River where a penal settlement was formed in 1823. Brisbane encouraged Stirling to uncover the treeless plains of the Monaro, whilst Hume & Hovell made their way overland from Lake George to Bass Strait, passing by Port Phillip in December 1824. Cunningham, a botanist discovered the Liverpool Plains. In this same year of 1824, the *Sydney Gazette* reported that George IV was arranging an appointed Legislative Assembly to advise the governor. The first council included the Lt-governor; the chief justice; the colonial secretary; the surveyor—general and the principal colonial surgeon. The purpose of this 1824 council was to advise the governor who shall have 'power and authority to make laws and ordinances for the peace, welfare and good government of the colony'.

Trial by Jury was also conceded by this same Act of George IV (Act 4 Geo. IV cap. 96), as was the formation of the Supreme Court of New South Wales (Francis Forbes—Chief Justice). The censorship over the *Sydney Gazette*, previously exercised by Macquarie, was removed by Brisbane and led to the establishment shortly after of the *Australian* and the *Monitor* newspapers under the control of W.C. Wentworth, Dr. Wardell and E.S. Hall. With the establishment of the A.A.C, Brisbane transferred to the company, on very easy terms, the coalmines at Newcastle along with the plant and equipment. The company by 'virtue of this transfer was possessed of a very lucrative monopoly'

The Brisbane move to revalue the colonial currency brought great embarrassment and led to his recall in December 1825.

The seventh Governor of the still fledgling colony was Ralph Darling (1825-1831). His first act was to appoint new Legislative Council, which included a number of prominent freemen in the colony—John Macarthur, Robert Campbell and Charles Throsby. The journal records that one by-product of the surge and decline of livestock prices (due mainly to the buying spree by the AAC) was that the 'pursuit of agriculture (farming and cropping) was almost abandoned during the pastoral mania, and also to the drought destroying most of what wheat and maize was planted'.

The official records details other significant events of the Darling administration.

- 'Australian geographical discovery made considerable progress under Darling. An outcome from the drought of 1812 was the crossing of the Blue Mountains and the discovery of fertile plains beyond. An outcome of the drought of 1826 was the discovery of the Darling River by Capt. Sturt, and subsequently of the future province of South Australia
- The influx of free immigrants had received a check from the financial reverses of 1827 and 1828, in the consequence of the sheep and cattle mania. But Dr. J.D. Lang brought with him from England 60 Scotch mechanics with their wives and families.
- The Sydney Water Supply was commenced during Darling's administration. Up to this time the inhabitants of Sydney were wholly dependent upon the 'Tank Stream' a small watercourse, which ran midway between George and Pitt Streets. Darling had entrusted to James Busby a mineral surveyor, the task of creating a permanent water supply for Sydney, and he recommended that the swamps between Sydney and Botany Bay (now the Centennial Park) should be tapped by tunnel. Prison Labour was employed to complete the project and the supply of water 'proved to be of

excellent quality, and of sufficient quantity to meet the demands for many future years'.

- The first conveyance of mail was commenced, and the first colonial-built steamer was launched—in 1831. The first colonial steam company was formed—*The Australian Steam Conveyance Company.*
- On August 2, 1831 the *Sydney Gazette* announced that crown lands would in future only be disposed of through auction sale, at a minimum of 5 shillings per acre. Terms of a 10% deposit and the balance in 30 days were available.
- VDL was officially separated from NSW and provided with its own Legislative Council and Governor.
- The governor was recalled in October 1831.

The five Darling years saw population, official revenue and exports increase.

1. Population went from 35000 (1826) to 51200 (1831)
2. Government revenues grew from 72000 to 121000
3. Exports grew from 106600 to 324200

There was nothing dramatic during the Darling days but the colony grew in wealth, reputation and a positive mindset, giving strength to the next administration—that of Sir Richard Bourke (1831-1837)

. The highlight of the Bourke period was the First Appropriation Bill in 1832. To the first Legislative Council meeting in January 1832, the new governor announced that 'An abstract of the Revenue and expenditure would be submitted later in the year, also an Estimate of the Probable Expenditure of the current year and of the Supplies by which the expenditure was to be defrayed. The Revenue of the last year had been unusually productive, Bourke advised his Council, and a considerable balance remained in the treasury after discharging all demands upon it'.

'After the Estimates had been discussed (by the Council), Bourke advised, an Act of Appropriation would be submitted. Provision would be made for the financial support of public schools and places of religious worship, the formation of roads, and the repairs and erection of public buildings

Bourke intended to include in the estates the probable amount of rents and sales of crown lands together with a considerable portion thereof being appropriated to bring free labourers from England under the direction of the Emigration Commissioners sitting in London. The first Appropriation Bill was passed—and assented to—on 21st March 1832. One of the items appropriated was 6,400 pound to defray the expense of bringing out female farm-servants from England at the cost of 8 pound per head.

Bourke instituted the *New South Wales Government Gazette* to be issued every second Wednesday and to contain all official notifications. In September Bourke tabled the directions from the King, declaring that estimates for the next year should be tabled before June of that year—thus setting the government fiscal period as July to June (it hitherto having been promulgated as January to December).

The Abstract of Revenues and Expenditures for the year 1832 showed an improving state of the public revenue since Customs Duties had reached a sum never before reached. The economy appeared to be in sound shape with buildings rising rapidly in all settlements, cultivation extended, and investment capital attracting a high return; new roads were in course of construction; and a steady flow of immigrants—free and unassisted—were welcomed to the colony. The number of immigrants in this category between 1829 and 1832 was 2544, whilst sponsored immigrants numbered 792 with a cost of 5256.3 pound. For the year 1833 the number of unassisted immigrants numbered 1432 and those assisted numbered 1253. This brought the total in both categories between 1829 and 1833 to 6021.

Bourke used his new financial measures with a passion. In a three year period, the members of the Legislative Council and readers of the Government Gazette were literally 'bombarded;' with estimate and estimate, projection and projection and Appropriation of revenues of every imaginable proportion. The economy was recovering and getting stronger. Its openness was enthralling to settlers who wanted to follow the ways & means of the colony in detail.

The 1836 Session was summoned for 2nd June 1836, and in a "Speech, Bourke announced the increasing prosperity of the colony. In no former year reported the SMH had the revenue equalled the amount of the last, nor had the exports and imports been so large. The influx of foreign capital had been considerable. Collegiate and Educational institutions had been established; and a taste for fine arts was beginning to show itself. To extend the blessings of wholesome education to the poorer classes, it was necessary to introduce a system of general instruction. Improvement had been made to the great lines of road throughout the colony Receipts from sales of crown land during 1835 was 89380 pound with an end balance, after expenses for the purpose of immigration, of 120858.

Before the Estimates were presented on the 5th July, Bourke introduced a Bill on 28th June to restrain unauthorised occupation of Crown Lands. He claimed a number of pastoralists had complained that there was indiscriminate occupation of these Waste Lands by 'squatters'. Bourke's response was to require licenses, renewable annually, to persons of good repute to depasture sheep and cattle beyond the limits of location. The cost of these licenses was to be set based on the cost of administering the Act.

Bourke recalled that the expenses of the new settlement at Port Phillip had 'been hitherto defrayed from the revenues of the sale of Crown Lands' but that he was considering the possibility of the new settlement being self-funding'.

Bourke had 'fitted out' the Major Mitchell (Surveyor-General) expedition of 1836 which had 'discovered a splendid tract of country which he named Australia Felix, which now constitutes the colony of Victoria or Port Phillip, equal in size to the whole of Great Britain, fascinating in its general aspect, traversed by numerous perennial streams, and equally adapted to agricultural or pastoral pursuits". Major Mitchell was knighted for this service.

Bourke's recall in 1837 brought to an end a most successful period of economic activity in the colony.

- Population rose from 53500 (1832) to 85250 (1837)
- Revenues went from 135800 to 354800
- Exports gained from 384000 to 760000

Governor Sir George Gipps (1838-1846) likewise made a major contribution to the colony and both its fiscal and political operations.

Gipps, upon assuming office 24th February 1838 had the need to fill the local Treasury. He took a deliberate policy of limiting the amount of available land for sale (especially in Port Phillip). Consequently, the price of land, especially in the Port Phillip district, 'became enormously high', and the settlers were therefore 'heavily handicapped by having to part with so much of their capital in purchasing the land'. (Epitome of official history)

'The extensive immigration which took place was attended by a large influx of British Capital. There were a number of financial institutions in existence:

Local Banks:
- Bank of New South Wales
- Bank of Australia

'Mammoth' Banks (Branches of overseas banks):
- Bank of Australasia
- Union Bank of Australia

Other Colonial Banks:
- Sydney Bank
- Commercial Bank

Monetary Institutions:
- The Loan Company
- The Trust Company
- Aberdeen Loan Company

The government was in the habit of depositing large amounts, the proceeds of land sales, in the different banks, at 4% interest, but Gipps insisted on 7-7.5 %. In order to pay this high interest the banks had to enlarge their discounts, and in doing so they crossed the line of safety.

'The rage for speculation now seized the colonial public with even greater vehemence than during the sheep and cattle mania of Governor Darling's time; the unbounded extravagance of living was indulged in; everyone bought land and livestock at enormous prices, until with the obligations to the Banks and Loan companies coming due, land and stock, costly equipages and property of all kinds, were forced upon a falling market and the inevitable crash came. The Bank of Australia was the first to fall'. (Epitome)

As a result of Gipps forcing squatters to buy a minimum amount of land periodically, and the great outcry that followed, a society called he Pastoral Association of new South Wales" was formed to secure the due protection of the pastoral interests.

In addressing the first session of the Legislative Council on 29th May 1838, Gipps informed the members that 'it was the intention of Her Majesty's Government to propose a new bill for the government of the colony; but it would follow an inquiry by a Select Committee into the State of the Colony.

Gipps' reported another increase of revenues; the land account held a balance of 254881 pound, whilst the Immigration Fund held a balance of 197326 pound. Revenues into the Colonial Fund (excluding crown land sales) were 202960 pound, whilst projected expenditure was 295000 pound, forcing a shortfall of 92000 pound. 'Economy is therefore necessary!—An economy of a sort designed to call forth the energies of the people, rather than repress them'

Amendments to the Crown Lands Act included establishment of Border Police and Stock Inspectors, both groups paid for from higher rents on land. The winter rains of 1840 brought an end to the drought and provided improved prospects for the colony. A rise in the price of all provisions had caused all public contracts to greatly exceed the approved expenditure for the current year, and 'had it not been for this circumstance, the expenditure for the current year would have been with the estimates sanctioned by the Council. Returns of the colony showed that in the previous year, 7580 migrants had reached the colony of which sponsored migrants were 4480, bounty 1622 and unassisted 1478. In the following year of 1839, these numbers had increased to 11368 migrants, of whom 2802 came unassisted, the remainder being assisted by the government.

The Gipps' papers show that in 1840 he had extended the laws of New South Wales to the territory of New Zealand, since the British Government had treated the natives of that territory very differently to those in the colony of Australia. In New Zealand, a treaty between the British Government and the New Zealand chiefs, the chiefs agreed to forgo their right of selling land to any but the British Government, thus giving to Her Majesty the right of pre-emption. The epitome records that 'Up to the time that new Zealand was taken under the protection of the British Crown, the sovereignty of the chiefs as ruling over an independent people had been admitted, and their flag was acknowledged in such ports as their vessels had visited; the declaration of independence by the confederated chiefs had been approved, and ordered to be printed as a State Paper by the Home Government'.

Opening the 1841 session, the governor reported, "The colony continued to advance in a gratifying and encouraging manner. Steam navigation had greatly increased, immigration had been continued in a copious stream, and the streets of Sydney were lighted by gas. Although land sales were still running at record levels, pecuniary difficulties under which many interests in the colony were still suffering might naturally be expected to affect the revenue of 1841especially since the falling off was as yet to be felt in the sale of public lands".

Two most interesting bills were brought forward in the 1842 session. Firstly the government sought the approval of the Council to issue debentures to the extent of 160000 pound to meet the payment of immigration bounties, secured by the Land Fund and bearing interest at the rate of 8%, with the option of using the bonds at any time for the purchase of land.

The second bill was to incorporate the principal towns of the colony by means of letters patent (with the exception of Sydney and Melbourne—both to be incorporated without the issue of a charter). Gipps argued that "so long as the expense of police, public buildings, roads, bridges, and other works were defrayed centrally, there would be wastage and extravagance, whereas when each town defrayed its own expenses, it became the evident interest of each to avoid extravagance, and to spend no more of its money than was absolutely necessary". Gipps' intention was not to make each town fully responsible for police but to provide assistance based on the sums raised locally. Gipps also announced that although the revenue of the colony for 1841 was the largest ever collected, the land fund had dwindled to a remarkable extent. In 1840 land sales produced 316000 pound but in 1841, they only produced 90000 pound and the first quarter of 1842 only produced 4000 pound.

The governor was so concerned about this turn of events that he asked the Council for advice on the continued importation of immigrants. When the advice was followed, the result was (a) an additional subsidy by the British Government; (b) a reduction in the borrowing in London for the Immigration Fund, and (c) a surge of labourers arrived into the colony—26546 'souls' arrived at a cost of 468,000 pound.

Gipps recorded that "An apprehension, happily unfounded, had been created in England that the large emigration going on from the United Kingdom would occasion a heavy demand for subsidy from the British Treasury, but in fact, the whole of the 468000 pound had been paid out of the revenues of the colony. The chief exciting cause of the late mania for speculation was that for several years preceding 1840, capital was poured into the colony faster than, for want of labour, it could be safely employed; consequently it passed into the hands of persons willing to engage in hazardous speculations".

'The abundance of money provided by the new banks', reported the SMH in May 1842 'from English depositors caused a rapid price rise to take place in almost every species of colonial property. These speculations were at their height during 1839 and 1840. They were first checked in 1841 by revisions to the insolvency laws. Since the speculations were checked before the big increase in immigration, the idea prevailing in England that the commercial depression was led by the increased immigration, is clearly incorrect'. Despite the fears of a commercial depression, the colonial treasury reported a small surplus of 6932 pound for 1842. Land sales had swung back to 120,000 pound and total revenues reached 763000 pound. Of the 23,200 new immigrants, 8548 were landed at Port Phillip in 1841.

Again, in spite of the commercial depression, the 1843 estimates showed a surplus of 32733 pound. Immigration sponsored by the government from the Land Fund had been suspended in 1843

In opening the new and expanded Council in 1844, Gipps announced that 'although the decrease in the Revenues of 1843 had been quite large, the ordinary expenditure for the whole year had not exceeded the ordinary revenue and that it was the territorial revenue of the Crown alone which was encumbered with a debt'. 'This debt had been necessarily increased by the late, partial renewal of the immigration program'. Gipps' concluded that "notwithstanding the pecuniary distress which had so long prevailed in the colony, *there was nothing in the state of finances to create alarm*'.

In 1844 the Imperial Parliament denied and refuted any responsibility for payment on behalf of the Police and Gaol funds, and ruled that the proceeds of fines and penalties inflicted in the colonial law courts also belonged to the Crown.

The census of 1841 gave the population at 130856; by 1846 the official population had risen to 189609, more than double the population at the close of the Bourke administration. Revenues between 1838 and 1845 had grown from 335000 pound to 366000 but had peaked at 683,000 in 1840. Exports had grown from 802000 in 1838 to 1555986 in 1845, and imports had fallen from 1579000 to 1233854.

Summary & Conclusions

We can draw some conclusions at this point having considered the official records of political actions and inactions during the period 1821 (Sir Thomas Brisbane); Sir Richard Bourke (1831-1837) to 1845 (Sir George Gipps).

The first and main conclusion should be that there are many more factors in the lead-up to the Depression of 1842-44 than the 5 that Brian Fitzpatrick had enumerated and which were supported by N.G. Butlin in his incomplete work 'Forming the colonial Economy' which expands the scene leading to the depression but also misses the point with some of the essential economic and political events in the picture.

Here are the 5 nominated events by Fitzpatrick & Butlin, and some further events researched by this present writer. These will be followed by a summary of outcomes.

a. The fall in English wholesale prices
b. The fall in NSW export prices
c. The economic crisis in Britain of 1839
d. Severe drought in NSW 1838-1840. Moving funds from land sales to support assisted migration
e. The reduced investment from England

(In this writer's opinion, factor 2 and factor 1 are linked and should be associated directly. Factor 4 should not have led to a cyclical downturn as most immigrants brought with them sizeable capital and assets, even though they received assisted passage)

Offsetting or mitigating factors

It is essential that we consider the 'depression of 1842-1844' in the context of the day. By definition, a depression is a downturn and stalling of the economic, where in economic growth is at best zero and at worse, in the negative. A depression brings about wholesale unemployment, business failures and a severe drop in government revenues.

If we analyse the events in the political arena, set out above, especially during the administrations of Governors Bourke and Gipps, we do not appear to find the economic savagery usually accompanying a 'depression'. Government revenues dipped slightly but remained in balance or in surplus, usually, with official expenditures; it was the change to the insolvency laws that essentially brought about the increase in insolvency filings; the increase in land prices brought a temporary stop to large land sales but within two years they were back over the 120,000 pound per annum level; the migration levels peaked in the middle of this 'depression' and Gipps repeatedly claimed more labourers were needed; the livestock market boomed for at least two reasons before falling back, once those two needs were met (the stocking of the AAC land grant and the stocking of the large land sales in the Port Phillip settlement, both meant higher prices for New South Wales sheep and cattle). Low wool prices in the English market made many leveraged pastoral interests in the Colony uneconomic; however, the pastoral industry was still the only outlet for employment and investment in the colony and was essentially unsinkable. The withholding of investment funds by the City of London 'speculators' led to a slowdown in the colony, but as with any economic cycle, investors pursued areas offering the best rewards at optimum returns. The English banks were furnishing large amounts of credit and deposits to their colonial branches as well as to their correspondents in the colonies; so English Investors using English banks as a front, achieved safety and a high return in this period without the attendant risks of finding investment opportunities and monitoring their investments in the colony 12,000 miles away.

The political scene in the colony had problems and disparity between the ambition of self-government and fighting for equitable access to crown funds.

It is possible that this cyclical downturn could have been prevented if Britain had funded the full cost of keeping their prisoners in the colony, but the members of the Legislative Council claimed the British Treasury owed them over 800,000 pound on account. That debt was disputed and never paid, either in cash or in kind, and we'll never know if the downturn might have been avoided if the government had changed its fiscal policies and removed the temptation for international speculation. Speculation by the very people he British Investors) who 'owed' the colony reimbursement for assisting their own economy.

The economic slowdown was therefore largely externally sponsored as Fitzpatrick points out, but in economic terms the impact of the cycle was far from that of a serious 'depression' as both Butlin and Fitzpatrick claim.

A.C.V. Melbourne in the biography of William Charles Wentworth writes of two events that changed the colony and possibly influenced the period of this 'depression'. The first we have discussed above—"Wentworth, as the leader of the 'popular party', and James Macarthur as leader of the 'exclusives', were united in opposing the attempt made by Britain to compel the colony to assume the cost of police and gaols. They were also united in demanding that all land revenues should be used for immigration purposes and in trying to secure for the colonial legislature the right to appropriate all colonial funds. The second event was that the affairs of New South Wales were being influenced by events taking place in the new province of South Australia—the new territory was established by the supporters of Wakefield in order to give a practical application to his theory of colonisation'

The Wakefield theory was being undermined by the sale of land in New South Wales at less than a 'sufficient' price, the funds so gathered were not being exclusively used for immigration of free labour, but the ignoble frustrating point was that transportation of convicts had not been stopped and assignment still supplied employers with cheap labour.

Other factors of interest include:

a. The statement of Gipps that there was *nothing in the state of finances of the colony to create alarm*. This statement appears to be truthful and realistic based on the numbers, and must support the contention that only limited sectors of the economy were suffering this downturn.

b. There colony had no debt, except for the debentures raised on account of the immigration subsidy and that 21,600 pounds was covered by the Commissioners of Colonial Lands and Emigration from its own resources.

c. Representative Councillor Charles Windeyer introduced a bill on 24th August 1843 (right in the middle of this downturn), which was based on a report by the Select committee on the 'monetary confusion' of the day. The Bill is referred to in detail in Appendix A. Windeyer introduced his 'monetary confidence' bill, believing that the current 'depression;' was aggravated by a decrease of currency in circulation as well as a lack of confidence and credit. He proposed a solution based on the Prussian *Pfandbrief* scheme. The bill passed the Council, but Gipps withheld consent.

d. The free trade movement was influencing the British scene and the changing identity of old style-trading merchants. David McIntyre in his work 'Colonies into Commonwealth' describes these changing patterns as being led by Adam Smith who wanted to sweep away the threefold monopoly of export, import and transit, as described in his 1776 book 'The Wealth of Nations'. Adam Smith was incensed about the navigation acts (which boosted British naval power), and restrictions on colonial industry (this was 'a manifest violation of the most sacred rights of mankind). One stage of the reduction of these monopolies occurred in the 1820s. British traders sought a reduction of restraint of trade. The Board of Trade lowered customs duties on many items and offered a reciprocal reduction of the shipping regulations to foreign nations. By 1840 the main core of the protection system had crumbled. The campaign of the Anti-Corn Law League combined with the Irish Potato Famine combined to convince Sir Robert Peel to abandon his land-owning supporters and repeal the Corn Laws and the Navigation Acts. This allowed the Australian colonies to levy a non-discriminatory tariff and established the *Free Trade Movement* leading to Cobden's treaty with France, when customs duties were removed from all but 48 articles.

e. The group of colonial reformers including Molesworth and Wakefield were pushing for more self-government for the colonies, the creation of new colonies, reform of emigration from Britain, a new land settlement system. This 1830s movement preached the doctrine that 'colonial freedom and self-government was not incompatible with loyalty to the Empire'. After the American Revolution, the fear in Britain was that all colonies, if 'let loose' would go the way of the USA. The British scene influenced events in the colony.

f. Thus the local terms referring to the cyclical downturn included
   • 'Monetary confusion'
   • 'Commercial recession'
   • 'Monetary confidence' (The Windeyer Plan)
   No-one in public life (particularly the governor was referring to a general economic depression during this period of 1842 to 1844. In fact the Governor asserted with confidence that "At no time during the period of his administration had the general affairs of the Colony been in a more healthy state than at present"

g. The Year 1843 showed a surprisingly strong surplus of revenue over expenses in spite of the survey department expenses of over 80,000 pound having to now be drawn from the colonial fund because there were insufficient funds in the Land Fund.

h. A dispute between the governor and his council over expenditure for 1844 resulted in district councils again being stripped of responsibility for police and local services. The problem arose over the inability of many District Councils to implement the governor's arrangement that council's should subsidise the operations of the local services, with only a top-up from the central government. The plan failed when local funds were not sufficient to maintain regular services.

i. A move by Dr. Lang to complete the legal separation of Victoria from NSW was defeated 19 to 6 with 5 abstentions. Lang's purpose was to make the southern settlements self-supporting financially. However the governor's financial statements to the Council showed that in fact the Port Phillip settlement was contributing to the colony of New South Wales.

j. The Cowper sponsored report to the Council recommended the abolishment of both the Squatting regulations and the license fee for squatters. This was strongly supported by the Pastoral Association, and it was hoped that the price of crown lands would be restored.

k. The Cowper committee also recommended the repeal of the Edward Gibbon Wakefield sponsored legislation of bounty emigration being paid from ½ of the revenues of land sales. The other ½ of the revenues was meant to defray the expenses of the Police and Gaol costs. To-date the expenses of the Police & Gaols had been made from the Military Chest until transferred with limitations (of 25000 pound pa) to the responsibility of the General Revenue. Since then the general fund had annually used 45000, 135000 and 85000 pounds to meet outlays. The outlay from the Colonial Funds of such amounts for the 'coercion and punishment' of British criminals was deemed as unfair'. The Council demanded from the British Treasury the sum of 793,034 pound to meet the arrears of expenditure for the goal, judicial and police operations, and a further sum of 74000 pound to cover the costs of convict administration in the colony **or** (as an alternative) 59,788 migrants were to be sent free of charge to the colony, together with a loan of 500000 pound raised in London for public works in the colony to support the migrant intake.

l.   Another Councillor, Charles Windeyer moved to enact a free general system of primary and religious education into the colony. This move led to formation of the Board of Education.

m.   1844 saw a marked increase in the value of colonial wool and the improvement in the general condition of the colony. The governor informed the council that for the first time in the history of the colony, exports had exceeded imports. The falling of revenues for 1843 and 1844 had been offset by the decrease in expenditures, so that ordinary revenues were free from encumbrance or debt and deposits with banks were currently higher than at any time since 1841.

Highlights of the Fourth Period

Although it was not the most active period in terms of establishing a solid base for future gains in the colony (the Macquarie era took this prize), it is obviously that in a colony with population growth averaging 10.5% many significant events took place and these events (such as the imposition of protective tariffs between colonies in 1841) affected the colonial economies.

- Ben Boyd's Company formed in Twofold Bay
- The suspension of immigration slowed the demand for shipping
- The first navigation by sloop on the Murray River
- The first shipment of silver-lead from the Adelaide Hills and copper from Kapunda set underway the first mineral boom. Tin was to be shortly discovered in South Australia
- 123 foreign whaling ships call in at Hobart between 1840 and 1846
- The colonies report 479 manufacturers in operation of which 220 are flour mills
- 67,000 tons of coal were exported to South America
- Mineral exports exceed those of wool
- The first meeting of the Sydney Rail Coy in 1846 with James Macarthur as Chairman
- The united tradesmen of Sydney began acting as the peak labour council

- The first steps are taken in 1843 towards representative government
- The recession of 1842 sees cuts in wages

Of course in this fourth period, the biggest event of all and the one that brought both good and bad effects on the colony was the discovery of gold in 1851 in both New South Wales and Victoria

The negative effect of gold discovery was the pressure place on labour and commodity prices. The manufacturing industries were growing at a steady rate and were looked upon as providing the balance to the very cyclical pastoral industry. However, manufacturing often requires some element of skilled labour, and as soon as the gold discovery was announced the 'waged' workers were the first to travel to the goldfields. Naturally many farm and agricultural workers also travelled to the gold fields. However the effect on the rural sector was rather beneficial. With no herdsmen available, the pastoralists looked to fencing as an alternative and a new industry developed. The timber industry was in boom times, with the huge need for sleepers for the coming of the railways and now cut fence posts, local forests were being cleared at a rapid rate. But timber workers wanted to also join the procession to the goldfields and this placed upward pressure on the price of timber as well as most domestic products.

The Chinese population on the goldfields grew to 20,000. Higher labour than planned caused major cost blowouts on the private rail construction in New South Wales and the colonial government took over the Sydney Rail Company and Hunter River Rail. The British Government was pushing very strongly for private rail, in the colony, on the strength of them having been successful in Britain. However, due mainly to the distances involved in the colony, and even though at about 1,500 pound per mile, the colony was producing one of the lowest installation costs in the world, the overall level of investment required was far too great for private investors, and the government stepped in with Loan Funds.

This was a sensible and brave move for a number of reasons. It was directly contrary to the British requirement; it obligated the colony to officially borrow in the London money market—a move which held the colony to ransom with British Investors who manipulated interest and discount rates but having locked the colony into a borrowing and re-borrowing pattern, gave the City of London some monopoly powers over the colony's financial needs. With labour being in temporary short supply, the government had, and used, this perfect opportunity to relocate disenchanted gold miners back into a waged job. The railways provided the opportunity for decentralisation of workers and families through the country areas. The railway system peaked at over 10,000 employees, which was a useful way of controlling unemployment and many aspects of the economy. Small industries were springing up not only in Sydney but around the rural areas as well. A building boom was underway with construction of the railway stations, some of which (Albury, Goulburn, Orange, Forbes and Armidale) were magnificent buildings, more in the Macquarie line of over-design than in the context of the penny-pinching days of the late 1850s and 1860s (post self-government).

The cleanest news of the 1855 days was the opening of Lever Brothers soap factory in Melbourne.

CHAPTER 9

SPECIAL ECONOMIC EVENTS

A number of 'special' events that influenced the course of the early economy and impacted on the extent and rate of economic growth have been selected and outlined. The list of events is not extensive but indicative of sometimes obscure events which can impact on economic growth eg education.

Although it may be suggested that the Report by Commissioner Bigge did not largely influence the Colonial economy, it must be stated that his recommendations to continue with the new Bank of New South Wales, which had been chartered incorrectly by Governor Macquarie, moved the economy along, as did his support for the continuation of the transportation of convicts to the Colony. His lack of support for land grants and early release of convicts may have slowed the economic growth until the consequences of his recommendation that the sale of Crown land be made, is considered. The revenue from the Sale of Crown land was considerable and kept the economy afloat, even if it was being badly managed, until 1810 and the arrival of Macquarie, in terms of food production.

Other special events fed on each other. Exploration across the mountains and uncovering the mystery of the rivers opened up huge pastoral areas and fostered the growth of the sheep and wool industries. The continued growth of the pastoral industries all through the 1800s was eclipsed as the prime exporting commodity only upon the 'official' discovery of gold. The discovery of gold once again filled the Colonial coffers and set into motion the most remarkable of special events, the expansion of the rail system across the Colony and inter-Colony. Instead of relying on sea transport, the very reason that the major cities were located on harbours and bays, the cities were connected by rail. The senior colony of New South Wales, could now diversify its population, move livestock and produce from Tamworth to Albury. The most powerful benefit of the advent of the rail system is the most simplistic one. The Colonial labour-force learned how to engineer bridges (the Hawkesbury); how to construct gradients (crossing the Blue Mountains); and engineer the iron horses themselves for local conditions. This new knowledge led directly to the coming engineering shops and the likes of business adventurers such as Thomas Mort, whose remarkable drive, ingenuity and entrepreneurial ability led to the Mort Dry Dock & Engineering complex in Balmain, NSW Fresh Food & Ice, refrigeration and abattoirs in remote locations rather than in Sydney town. We cannot overlook the value of education to a largely illiterate economy. Finally the growth of the free trade movement brought to the fore the likes of Parkes, Reid, Wise and Pulsford—politicians who stood for a sound policy and formed the first 'party' ticket in the country. Federation took centre stage in the second half of the century and changed the face of the country and our analysis of the fiscal considerations of Federation and the post-Federation relations between the Commonwealth and the States will set the stage for review as to whether the Federation movement was successful.

There may well be more 'special events 'than those discussed but it seems, at least to this writer, that these interlinking events boosted the Colonial economy in a remarkable way:

- the crown land policy and reform
- the growth of education
- the Report by Commissioner Bigge
- exploration
- pastoral expansion
- the expansion of the rail system
- the Fiscal impact of Federation
- Commonwealth-State Financial Relations

The Report of the Select Committee on Transportation-1812 pages 11-12-records that 'The convicts who were distributed amongst the settlers, were clothed, supported and lodged by them; they either work by the task or for the same number of hours as the Government convicts; and when their set labour is finished, they are allowed to work on their own account. The master has no power of corporal punishment over them as this can only be inflicted by the interference of a magistrate. The convict, if he feels abused by his master, can complain to a magistrate who, if justified, can deprive the master of his servant.

It is to be found in the evidence of Mr Commissary Palmer that the expense of each convict in the service of the Government was about 40 pound per annum, and that a free labourer at Sydney could be hired for about 70 per year, but would do twice as much work. Palmer reports the annual expense of a convict is 30 pound, compared with the cost of holding them in a prison hulk on the Thames at 24 pound, with the value of their work being about 8 pound or $1/3^{rd}$ of the cost of keeping them."

The system was fundamentally changed in 1836, and the 2nd Select Committee in 1837-38 P669 recorded that" All applications for convicts are now made to an officer—'Commissioner for assignment of Convict Servants' who is guided by Government Regulations. Settlers to whom convicts are assigned, are bound to send for them within a certain period and pay the sum of 1 pound per head for their clothing and bedding.

Each assigned convict is entitled to a fixed amount of food and clothing—in NSW of 12 lb of wheat, or equivalent in flour and maize meal, 7 lb of mutton or beef or 4 ½ lb of salt pork, 2 oz of salt and 2 oz of soap each week. 2 frocks or jackets, three shirts two pair trousers, 3 pair shoes and a hat or cap, annually. Plus one good blanket, a palliasse or wool mattress which remain the property of the master. Obviously they are well fed well clothed and receive wages of between 10 to 15 pound per annum."

The 2nd Select Committee also heard evidence on convicts who have been emancipated or their sentence has expired.

"These people find no difficulty in obtaining work at high wages; and having acquired experience in the Colony are generally preferred to new arrivals. They fill many positions of trust for instance as constables, overseers of pastoral; properties and road or building gangs, as superintendents of estates, clerks to bankers, lawyers and shopkeepers, and even as tutors in private families. Some have married free women and have become prosperous."

LAND REFORM IN AUSTRALIA

The Problem

By 1860, the need for new land legislation in the eastern colonies became urgent because the leases of the squatters issued under the authority of the Order in Council of 1847, expired in 1861.

The attempt to pass new land legislation was one of the immediate causes of conflict between the Legislative Assemblies and the Legislative Councils of the colonies.

The two new NSW Acts did provide for other forms of land tenure, other than 'conditional purchase' and 'leasehold' eg purchase by auction, timber reserves, stock reserves, etc These acts dealt exclusively with the disposal of crown lands, and do not affect private sales of land.

The author of the Alienation and Occupations Bill (leading to the above mentioned Acts) in NSW, John Robertson, insisted that the interests of the squatters and selectors be safeguarded. The Bill made ample provision for the obtainment of lands by those who really desired to settle upon the land and improve it, whatever might be attempted to be done for the advancement of the masses of the people, the squatter's interests were by no means overlooked.

An editorial in the SMH of 8th October 1860 set out the record

> "the origin and basis for our colonial prosperity has been pastoral occupation of the waste (Crown) lands. For a time it was the only thing possible, and it answered excellently its purpose of creating a valuable export, and spreading civilisation over the interior. But the growth of society requires modification to the system. Experience seems to point out that the advantages it has offered are too much confined to a particular class—that

the scope offered to the agriculturalist and the small squatter is too limited, and a demand has arisen that greater freedom and opportunity should be given to those who are willing to invest their industry and their savings in rural pursuits. It is natural that those who feel, and who have perhaps felt for some time, the pressure of restrictions, should be prompted to advocate rather violent rearrangements—to sweep away, not only without compunction, but with a certain grim satisfaction, all the vested interests that have grown up, without sufficient considering the evils that would result even to themselves and their friends from such an iconoclastic policy."

The SMH of 10th October, 1860 had reported some of the speeches in the Legislative Assembly:

"The moral argument for the squatters was presented by a squatter, Mr O'Shanassy: 'Within a few days of the end of the year, would it be thought fair to say 'Here, you pastoral tenants, whose rights have been recognised under law for the past twenty years,—you who opened up the wilderness, risked all your invested capital—and after all your pains and trouble, you are fourteen days of losing your tenure. Go about your business. No man in the community would deal in this way with slaves, let alone men of character and respectability.'

Some background

A Member of the NSW Legislative Assembly—Mr Jenkins—spoke during the debate:

'It has been said that the produce of the pastoral districts did not stand so high on the list of exports as those of the gold districts. Now I do not wish to deprecate that interest, but I can show that a mistake was make in those statements, for the pastoral exports are far greater over a period than those of gold (the amount of gold dust exported annually is between 2 & 3 million; and the pastoral exports are between 3 & 4 million pound. But which industry employs the most labour.

The amount of grain imported into the Colony has practically declined to zero, whilst the local production was fast overtaking demand.'

Alternatives

Following the earlier acts, an inquiry into 'Public Lands' was completed by Morris and Rankin, which roundly condemned the entire system and concluded that the 'most noteworthy matter that has come to light, and the most ominous for the future well-being of the Colony (of NSW), is the class contest for the possession of its lands which has covered five-sixths of the surface. the huge area of 86 million acres has provided a field on which every form of abuse has been carried out in defiance of the public interest. It needs little argument to prove the vice of a policy which of its very essence divides the rural population into two hostile camps; and it would be superfluous top state that the personal virtues of veracity and honourable dealing have been tarnished by the daily habit of intrigue, and the practice of evading the law and by declaration in defiance of fact universally made.'

The most radical solution to the Land Reform Movement was adopted in New South Wales, where it was called 'Free selection before survey'. The essential feature of this system of selling Crown, was not the sale price of the land, but its immediate release to homesteaders; they paid one-quarter of the price as a deposit, and received their title deeds after three years and completion of the payment. John Robertson successfully piloted two Bills through both Chambers incorporating these principles., after a political crisis involving strong opposition from squatters with seats in the Upper House. The Two Acts gave adequate protection to squatters by granting them long leases of Crown Land in pastoral areas, but allowed selectors to take up Crown land in agricultural or mixed farming and grazing areas with the minimum of delays and with only a low deposit. They could then begin cultivation immediately, and wait for the government surveyor to arrive later. However, they could get their freehold only if they made improvements.

The new system worked!

A Brief History of the Crown Land Disposal

The practice of recording money derived from the sale of crown land was common to all colonies and formed one of the largest items of their annual income. Auction sales raised significant income before being suspended in 1883, when 'it became evident that this indiscriminate sale of the public estate and its alienation was threatening to endanger the true interests of the country" (Wealth & Progress of NSW 1886-87-P385). This alienation was due to rivalry between the two principal classes of settlers—the pastoral tenants and the free selectors, and the fact that the sales were concluded without conditions relating to use, improvement or settlement. Sales were temporarily suspended by auction and it was decided to sell only limited area during any one year.

Under the Crown Lands Act of 1861, the Governor was empowered to sell crown leasehold lands (upon which improvements had been made) to the owners of the improvements, without competitive bids, at a price determined by valuation, the minimum price being fixed at One pound sterling per acre. The area of land able to be purchased in this way was increased from 320 acres to 640 acres. This privilege of purchasing, without competition, Crown Lands held under lease did not extend merely to the pastoral tenant of the crown but to leaseholders in general including goldfield leases. Broad acre Pastoral leases could also be freeholded in lumps of 25 square miles. All conversions of crown land generated revenues of two hundred and ten thousand in 1871 and two hundred and sixty thousand pounds in 1886. The Government entered into 'conditional' or terms sales which in 1862 amounted to twenty-five million acres and generated a total of eleven million five hundred thousand pounds. Interest accrued on such terms transactions and in 1886 amounted to two million 605 thousand pounds.

Pastoral leases generated generous revenues but a significant element of default occurred. In 1886 revenue obtained from these leases amounted to only 374 thousand pounds, but lease payments in default amounted to over 500 thousand pounds.

Revenue from Government services was the largest sector of overall Government revenue.

In 1886, the percentage breakdown was as follows:

Services	40.7
Taxation	34.4
Land sales etc	21.6
miscellaneous	

THE CONSEQUENCES OF TRANSPORTATION TO THE COLONY OF NEW SOUTH WALES

a. Economic Consequences: During the time convicts provided the principal source of labour for government purposes and private enterprise, the consequences of transportation appeared to be measurable. One of the indirect consequences was the 'opportunity' cost to both Britain and the Colony of the transportation program. The Molesworth Committee in 1838, believed that their definitive opinion on the value of transported labour could only justify the continuation was an obstacle to economic growth. An advocate* of transportation, some twelve years later produced figures to show that just the opposite was true. (*Archibald Atchison—Crime and Transportation—Lndon 1850).

b. Social Consequences:

   The transfer of so many male convicts led, by 1841, to 'a dearth of females', a situation named as alarming by Ralph Mansfield 'Analytical view of the census of 1841 in New South Wales'—1841.

c. Political Consequences:

   The nature of the penal settlement required a 'peculiar form of government'
   The Molesworth Committee Report—Some Conclusions
   (British Parliamentary Reports 1838)

"Some persons contend that the pecuniary interests of the penal Colony require the continuation of transportation; that as the extraordinary commercial prosperity of these colonies was occasioned by the constant supply of convict labour, if that supply be cur off the colonies would be ruined, from great wealth be reduced to great poverty; and that this change in the fortune of inhabitants, especially if it were sudden, would necessarily produce the worst moral effects upon their character, and still further demoralise the already demoralised.

"The extraordinary wealth of these colonies was occasioned by the regular and increasing supply of convict labourers. The convicts were assigned to settlers as slaves, they were forced to work in combination, and raised more produce than they could consume; for this surplus produce Government provided a market, by maintaining military and convict establishments, which have cost this country above 7,000,000 pound of the public money.

"Labour is in short supply whilst capital has amazingly increased. The flocks of sheep are double the size they ought to be; a vast number perish for want of care; labour must be furnished from sources, other than convicts, if the colonies are to continue to flourish"

Analysing the Benefits to the United Kingdom

Although the consequences of transportation of British convicts to the Colony of New South Wales may have been both economic and social, the consequences of transportation of transportation of British convicts out of the United Kingdom are numerous and quantifiable.

The essential question becomes—Would the United Kingdom have pursued a Colonial expansion policy if there had not been a need to transfer convicts from the Americas elsewhere?

The answer is of course, a simple—'yes'. The trade, defence and colonisation policies, in place, and under discussion, made territorial acquisition essential. The British Navy needed supplies of masts and spars to maintain its fleet in sailing condition. The British Trade tsars wanted to see further expansion, after a successful entrance into the Caribbean area, and the eyes of the East India Company were wanting to spread further across the Asian region. Terra Australis—the great south land—was an obvious desire.

So, it is fair to say that the gains to Britain were enormous in economic terms, especially in terms of opportunity cost in dealing with the housing, feeding and guarding of the great surge of prisoners between 1750 and 1850.

Some of the advantages to Britain include:

a. The build-up of trade by the East-India Company
b. The advantage of a secure, in-house, supply of raw wool, to keep the spinning mills occupied
c. the opportunity cost of housing, feeding and guarding prisoners
d. The use of convict labour in the new Colony
    • land clearing, farming, food production
    • for road construction
    • public wharves
    • barracks
    • Public Buildings
    • for Materials supply eg brick & tile production.
    • as unpaid day labour for the pastoral & agricultural industry
e. We can assume that Land grants, in the Colony, to men on the military and civil list was a form of 'fringe benefits' and should be quantified as an alternative to paid remuneration for these people. Even land grants to emancipists were used as an incentive to increase food production.
f. We can quantify items C, D and E into a 'value of direct gain to the British economy of nearly 140,000,000 pound(refer details in 'Statistics'), compared with the publicly recorded expenditure on transportation, supplies, and military personnel of 5,600,000 pound, between 1788 and 1822.

The purposes of trying to quantify these benefits is to challenge to traditional concept that 'the British invested millions of pounds in the Colony of New South Wales'.

It is obviously only the case when the outlay is shown and not the on-going benefits for over fifty years, and indeed two hundred years. It is still arguable that the Continent of Australia is, in Captain Arthur Phillip's words 'the best investment Britain will ever make'.

THE PASTORAL SYSTEM AND LAND REFORM

Edward Pulsford, the doyenne of Free Trade wrote in a learned work on 'Trade & Commerce in NSW'(1892) that

"New South Wales is not great in agriculture, unless the term be used in the wide sense accepted in Great Britain and the United States, where it includes the pastoral industry. It is difficult to say why the distinction should be made in Australia, but at all events it is made. 'Agriculture' in Australia is divided into (1) the pastoral industry (2) agriculture, and (3) the dairying industry

Agriculture in New South Wales has yet (as of 1892) to achieve great distinction, but steady progress is being made. In 1871 only 417,000 acres were under cultivation; by 1881, it had increased to 710,337, and by 1891 it had grown further to 1,241,419 acres; about ¼ of the area is under artificially grown grasses. During the last harvest it little over 10 million bushels of grain was grown in the Colony. Maize was the largest grain at 5 million bushels, a little more than sufficient to meet local needs and so a small inter-colonial export trade has commenced; wheat stood at 4 million bushels; hay at 210,000 tons; potatoes at 62,000 tons, and the rest of the acreage is in sugar cane and a small acreage in tobacco.

There is potential for great diversity and the future should hold plenteous bounty for the inhabitants of the Colony and certainly self-sufficiency in food production."

Wool remains and should continue to remain, wrote Pulsford, 'the backbone of our commerce'. Since 1871 the number of sheep has risen to thirty-six million, from sixteen million in that earlier year. in 1871 one-third of the sheep were in NSW, in 1881 there was one-half, in spite of bad seasons. The losses from 1876 to 1885 were twenty-eight million, not including the lambs not realised. The year 1884 was a horror and the biggest drought year seen since the Colony began. In 1871 wool production stood at 65 million lb.

Wool Production 1871-1891

year	wool/lb	wool—pounds	sheep numbers
1871	65,000,000	4,748,000	16,000,000
1881	139,600,000	7,149,000	
1886	174,000,000	7,028,000	
1891	340,691,382	11,312,980	50,000,000

Up until 1890 the whole of the wool clip had been shipped to London, and dispersed there by public wool sales. Since that time, a growing percentage of the clip is being sold in Sydney to representatives of English, German, French and Belgian wool-spinning firms. This trend is both to the advantage of the producer and the buyer. It is noteworthy that as of 1895 there were no American, Chinese or Japanese buyers in the Sydney markets. The former situation, that of the missing American buyers was of particular concern to the Government of New South Wales, as imports were increasing from that country but without any increase in exports. The Premier of the day, Cowper declared 'trade cannot attain its natural development unless it is conducted on a basis mutually satisfactory to the countries engaged in it; and it cannot be mutually satisfactory if one of the countries finds its products excluded from the markets of the other.'

Agriculture lost some of its gleam during the gold rush years. Being labour intensive and with labour more attracted to the riches under the ground, farmers waited to plant crops until labour was more readily available and a little less expensive. For example the acreage under crop in 1851 was 153,000 but for years 1852-55 the acreage fell to 134,000, but in 1869 it was 469,000 and 1871 fell further (because of the drought) to 417,000. On the other hand, in Victoria during the 1850s agriculture was almost 'extinct'. During this time wheat was being imported from America, Chile, Brazil and Britain, whilst even butter was being imported from Britain. Any farmer who had stayed with agriculture during this time, must have struck greater riches than on the gold field.

In the same way gold excitement delayed agriculture, it also delayed manufacturing, due to the large number of artisans seeking gold in the fields. Yet in the end many new arrivals chasing the gold fever in the Colony, and then returned to paid employment, used their lifelong skills to advance many industries with rapidity that would not otherwise have been possible.

Squatters had first grazed the coastal belt until following the explorers they ranged further and further with their flocks into the inland.

Although the pastoral industry is principally restricted, in the Australia of pre-1901, to sheep and cattle grazing, our objective is to examine the growth of the sheep and wool industry.

However, we find in the 1874 edition of W. H. L. Ranken's The Dominion of Australia' a keen observation of the cattle industry.

"In the earlier days, before gold was thought of, as herds of cattle increased beyond the capability of their pasturages, they used to be sent out to the nearest unoccupied good country. Thus, the western streams of New South Wales became stocked, and the country occupied. This system arose when cattle were decreasing in value, and when it was therefore indispensable to breed them, at least cost, so that these herds were inferior, often became wild and unmanageable, and only rose into value when the crowds of gold-diggers arrived and paid any price for meat. But these cattle proved how good all the interior was for stock, and convinced people that the land, which seemed a desert, was the most fattening pasture. They discovered 'salt bush' and gave a character to the eastern portion of the great plain which, as the Riverina, it has ever held since. The Riverina became the fattening ground for Victorian meat, and the outlet for squatting enterprise.

History of Sheep Breeding in Australia

From humble beginnings a magnificent industry rose, to lead the way in opening new districts, to creating great wealth to stumbling when droughts and floods and plagues of pests transformed the landscape periodically and challenged the strength and commitment of the squatters and pastoralists.

Included in the humble beginnings were 29 sheep brought with the first fleet. Although the great flocks had not sprung from those humble few alone, it is important to set the scene as a witness to a triumph over adversity. Between 1788 and 1800 there were imports of some sheep from India, and in 1823-25 imports came in from Spain. By the end of 1792 there were 105 sheep and by 1796 the numbers had increased to 1,531 sheep; in 1800 there were 1,044 sheep; and 1803 there were 10,157; 1825 there were 237,622 sheep and in 1842, the number was 4,804,946.

year	sheep numbers
1788	29
1792	105
1796	1531
1800	6124
1825	237622
1842	4804946
1850	13059324*
1861	5615054
1871	16278697
1881	36591946
1891	61831416
1900	40020506**

*The transfer of the Colony of Victoria dropped sheep numbers in NSW by 6,589,923

** The 1893 and 1897 drought and the 1894-95 depression accounts for the dramatic decrease in flock numbers in all regions but in the Riverina and Western Plains a decline of 7 million.

The average rate of increase for the period was 4.8 %.

It was John Macarthur's breeding for wool types and yield rather than meat that led to a most profitable industry in fine merino wools, readily marketable to English and European manufacturers.

Heavier fleeces came about by an increase in density and length, both leading to a continued improvement in quality. By 1891 it was obvious that the pastures were overstocked and this led to a push for exploration.

As well, many sheep were boiled down for tallow and killed for export, with the advent of refrigeration and freezing. Thus in 1894-95 of the decline of 9 million sheep, half was due to the drought and the balance to export and rendering.

The size of flocks took a strange turn towards the end of the century. In 1891 there were 73 holdings carrying more than 100,000 sheep, while in 1897 there were only 21 and in 1900 only 14.

LAND REFORM IN AUSTRALIA

The Problem

By 1860, the need for new land legislation in the eastern colonies became urgent because the leases of the squatters issued under the authority of the Order in Council of 1847, expired in 1861.

The attempt to pass new land legislation was one of the immediate causes of conflict between the Legislative Assemblies and the Legislative Councils of the colonies.

The two new NSW Acts did provide for other forms of land tenure, other than 'conditional purchase' and 'leasehold' eg purchase by auction, timber reserves, stock reserves, etc These acts dealt exclusively with the disposal of crown lands, and do not affect private sales of land.

The author of the Alienation and Occupations Bill (leading to the above mentioned Acts) in NSW, John Robertson, insisted that the interests of the squatters and selectors be safeguarded. The Bill made ample provision for the obtainment of lands by those who really desired to settle upon the land and improve it, whatever might be attempted to be done for the advancement of the masses of the people, the squatter's interests were by no means overlooked.

An editorial in the SMH of 8th October 1860 set out the record

"the origin and basis for our colonial prosperity has been pastoral occupation of the waste (Crown) lands. For a time it was the only thing possible, and it answered excellently its purpose of creating a valuable export, and spreading civilisation over the interior. But the growth of society requires modification to the system. Experience seems to point out that the advantages it has offered are too much confined to a particular class—that the scope offered to the agriculturalist and the small squatter is too limited, and a demand has arisen that greater freedom and opportunity should be given to those who are willing to invest their industry and their savings in rural pursuits. It is natural that those who feel, and who have perhaps felt for some time, the pressure of restrictions, should be prompted to advocate rather violent rearrangements—to sweep away, not only without compunction, but with a certain grim satisfaction, all the vested interests that have grown up, without sufficient considering the evils that would result even to themselves and their friends from such an iconoclastic policy."

The SMH of 10th October, 1860 had reported some of the speeches in the Legislative Assembly:

> "The moral argument for the squatters was presented by a squatter, Mr O'Shanassy: 'Within a few days of the end of the year, would it be thought fair to say 'Here, you pastoral tenants, whose rights have been recognised under law for the past twenty years,—you who opened up the wilderness, risked all your invested capital—and after all your pains and trouble, you are fourteen days of losing your tenure. Go about your business. No man in the community would deal in this way with slaves, let alone men of character and respectability.'

Some background

A Member of the NSW LA—Mr Jenkins—spoke during the debate:

> 'It has been said that the produce of the pastoral districts did not stand so high on the list of exports as those of the gold districts. Now I do not wish to deprecate that interest, but I can show that a mistake was make in those statements, for the pastoral exports are far greater over a period than those of gold (the amount of gold dust exported annually is between

2 & 3 million; and the pastoral exports are between 3 & 4 million pound. But which industry employs the most labour. The amount of grain imported into the Colony has practically declined to zero, whilst the local production was fast overtaking demand.'

Alternatives

Following the earlier acts, an inquiry into 'Public Lands' was completed by Morris and Ranken, which roundly condemned the entire system and concluded that the 'most noteworthy matter that has come to light, and the most ominous for the future well-being of the Colony (of NSW), is the class contest for the possession of its lands which has covered five-sixths of the surface. the huge area of 86 million acres has provided a field on which every form of abuse has been carried out in defiance of the public interest. It needs little argument to prove the vice of a policy which of its very essence divides the rural population into two hostile camps; and it would be superfluous top state that the personal virtues of veracity and honourable dealing have been tarnished by the daily habit of intrigue, and the practice of evading the law and by declaration in defiance of fact universally made.'

The most radical solution to the Land Reform Movement was adopted in New South Wales, where it was called 'Free selection before survey'. The essential feature of this system of selling Crown, was not the sale price of the land, but its immediate release to homesteaders; they paid one-quarter of the price as a deposit, and received their title deeds after three years and completion of the payment. John Robertson successfully piloted two Bills through both Chambers incorporating these principles., after a political crisis involving strong opposition from squatters with seats in the Upper House. The Two Acts gave adequate protection to squatters by granting them long leases of Crown Land in pastoral areas, but allowed selectors to take up Crown land in agricultural or mixed farming and grazing areas with the minimum of delays and with only a low deposit. They could then begin cultivation immediately, and wait for the government surveyor to arrive later. However, they could get their freehold only if they made improvements.

The new system worked!

A Brief History of the Crown Land Disposal

The practice of recording money derived from the sale of crown land was common to all colonies and formed one of the largest items of their annual income. Auction sales raised significant income before being suspended in 1883, when 'it became evident that this indiscriminate sale of the public estate and its alienation was threatening to endanger the true interests of the country" (Wealth & Progress of NSW 1886-87-P385). This alienation was due to rivalry between the two principal classes of settlers—the pastoral tenants and the free selectors, and the fact that the sales were concluded without conditions relating to use, improvement or settlement. Sales were temporarily suspended by auction and it was decided to sell only limited area during any one year.

Under the Crown Lands Act of 1861, the Governor was empowered to sell crown leasehold lands (upon which improvements had been made) to the owners of the improvements, without competitive bids, at a price determined by valuation, the minimum price being fixed at One pound sterling per acre. The area of land able to be purchased in this way was increased from 320 acres to 640 acres. This privilege of purchasing, without competition, Crown Lands held under lease did not extend merely to the pastoral tenant of the crown but to leaseholders in general including goldfield leases. Broad acre Pastoral leases could also be freeholded in lumps of 25 square miles. All conversions of crown land generated revenues of two hundred and ten thousand in 1871 and two hundred and sixty thousand pounds in 1886. The Government entered into 'conditional' or terms sales which in 1862 amounted to twenty-five million acres and generated a total of eleven million five hundred thousand pounds. Interest accrued on such terms transactions and in 1886 amounted to two million 605 thousand pounds.

Pastoral leases generated generous revenues but a significant element of default occurred. In 1886 revenue obtained from these leases amounted to only 374 thousand pounds, but lease payments in default amounted to over 500 thousand pounds.

Revenue from Government services was the largest sector of overall Government revenue.

In 1886, the percentage breakdown was as follows:

Services	40.7
Taxation	34.4
Land sales etc	21.6
miscellaneous	3.3

Early Land Disposition

In the early days of colonisation the Governor had the sole power of granting lands, which he did under prescribed conditions, such as the payment of an annual quit-rent, the cultivation of a certain proportion of the area granted, and other services specified in instructions received from the Secretary of State.

Coghlan in 'Wealth & Progress of New South Wales' (1900-1901) writes about the early legislative disposition to the settlers, and said (P425) "The first instructions issued to Governor Phillip on 25th April, 1787, authorised him to make grants only to emancipated prisoners, in the following terms:—'to every male shall be granted 30 acres of land, and in case he shall be married to 20 acres more: for every child who may be with them at the time of making the said grant, a further quantity of 10 acres, free of all fees, taxes, quit rents, and other acknowledgments for the space of ten years. 'The annual quit rents to be paid on these grants and afterwards to be fixed at 6d for 30 acres.

The first settler was a prisoner named James Ruse, who having completed his sentence, entered on his farm of 30 acres at Parramatta on the 25th February, 1789. Additional instructions were issued by the Secretary of State on 20th August, 1789, extending the privilege of obtaining grants to such of the non-commissioned officers and men of the detachment of marines serving in New South Wales as were desirous of remaining in the territory following their discharge. The Governor was further requested to facilitate the settlement of free persons who might be disposed to emigrate with the view of becoming settlers in New South

Wales, by giving them grants of land not exceeding the maximum area granted to non-commissioned officer, viz., 100 acres, subject to the same quit-rent, the annual amount of which was 1s for every 50 acres, payable at the expiration of five years after the issue of a grant. In thew original instructions no mention was made of grants to officers, but this omission was afterwards rectified. These early grants were made on condition that a certain proportion of the land should be cultivated, and although this condition was not always complied with, no grant was ever withdrawn.

Commissioner Bigge reported to the British Parliamentary Committee on the Colonies that under Governor Macquarie, no quit-rents were collected between 1809-1823.

With regard to settlement in the town of Sydney, grants were not made until 1811, when the necessary authority was given to Governor Macquarie to do so, and allotments were granted on lease for periods of only 14 or 21 years. Prior to building regulations issued by Macquarie on 18th August, 1810, no attention was paid to the boundaries of town allotments or to the formation of streets. The town lots were subject to quit-rents of between 2s 6d and 20 s. per annum."

The following table shows the amount of land granted and sol between 1788 and 1823.

Table
LAND ALIENATION 1788-1823

Area granted by Governors up to 1810	177,500 acres
Area granted by Governor Macquarie 1810-23	400,000 acres
Area granted and sold 1824-1831	3,386,250 acres
TOTAL	3,963,750 acres

Introduction of Land Sales

Under a general order by the Governor on behalf of Viscount Goderich, Secretary of State for the Colonies, dated 14th February, 1831, it was notified that no Crown Lands were to be disposed of, other than by public competition, the minimum price being fixed at 5s per acre. Settlers were allowed to select within the settled districts only, and the land thus selected was submitted to auction and sold to the highest bidder, the selector generally being the purchaser. In 1839 the upset price was raised to 12s. per acre. This price was raised to 20s. per acre for the Port Phillip District on 22nd June, 1842. Under this arrangement, the lands applied for were to be surveyed first before being placed into the quarterly sale. A new regulation was made at this time, that blocks of 20,000 or more, could be sold, in one lot, by private contract at not less than the minimum price.

The Imperial Act of 9th March, 1847, made further changes to the regulations and set a one year lease denying long term tenure, and it was these regulations which the Robertson's Land Acts of 1861 (referred to above) changed to meet the needs of squatters and selectors.

The Act of 1861 was superseded by the Acts of 1884 and 1899, which consolidated the many amendments to the 1861 legislation passed during the intervening 23 years, which had seen the conditional sale of 23,470,140 acres and 15,572,001 by auction(without conditions). Because of harsh conditions and poor selection, over 7,000,000 million acres of the original 39,000,000 acres was abandoned and reverted to the Crown.

that extensive land grants were provided to many people, until it was seen that this was a potential source of revenue. The British Parliament first legislated in 1823 (59 Geo III c.114) to designate revenue from Crown land sales, Crown land leases and the associated financing charges to the account of the British Treasury. This was confirmed in two successive and related pieces of Colonial legislation under George IV. Obviously in the mind of the British Colonial Office, revenue from Crown Land (initially Waste Lands) was of great potential and was to be reserved for British Treasury use.

TABLE
NEW SOUTH WALES—LAND GRANTS 1789-1850

Year	No.	Acres	Year	No.	Acres
1789	1	30	1801	2	348
1790			1802	45	82820
1791	36	1620	1803	87	27587

1792	46	2225	1804	118	20230
1793	34	2250	1805	18	9630
1794	248	9050	1808	24	15064
1795	181	5526	1809	344	66641
1796	37	2114	1816	215	44862
1797	83	2116	1823	568	199294
1798	40	2417	1831	246	55091
1799	117	12816	1839	418	310250`

Table
LAND SALES & MORTGAGES 1832-1850

Year	NSW	Vic	Town & Country Mtges
1832	20861		
1833	29026		
1834	91394		
1838	277467	38694	248891
1839	234272	38347	348818
1841	30591	337	1098741
1850	11473	40043	142022

N. G. Butlin in the introduction to Chapter 7 of Historical Australian Records—Statistics—'The Economy before 1850', suggests there is a great deal of statistical data available on the new settlement before the discovery of gold. 'It represents some indication of the nature of the workforce of the settlements, the arrivals of convicts and free settlers, the economic activities they developed to support themselves and the heavy expenditure by the British Government to make the settlement a success. The Colony was supposed to support itself, increasingly so as pressures for public economy grew in post-Napoleonic Britain. The tables on Colonial Fund and Land Fund Revenues show this increasing shift to local self-support'. Butlin, by implication, is suggesting the financial pressures on Britain by the Colony would have caused the use of Crown Land sales to become a relief in the homeland Budgets.

Special Grants

Instructions to Governor Brisbane directed the reservation of one-seventh of the Crown lands in each county for the purpose of church and school establishments, but these instructions do not appear to have been carried out in full. Ten counties listed by Coghlan show a total survey of 443,486 but only show grants making less than 8% of the total.

These lands were administered by the Clergy and school Lands Corporation, until 1833 when they were reverted by order to the Crown until under the Church and School Lands Act of 1897, they were once again vested.

The Australian Agricultural Company was incorporated by an Act of the British Parliament on 21st June, 1824 with a promise of One million acres, and a grant of 1,027,538 acres was recorded at Port Stephens, Peel River and Warrah Estate. In addition the company obtained leases of coal fields at Port Hunter for 31 years.

Accessing the Pastoral Lands

Larcombe's 'The Origin of Local Government in New South Wales 1831-1958' (Vol 1 of a 3 volume work) records that the Report of the Select Committee on Roads (1847) stated "The 29 counties in New South Wales, could not be expected to construct roads for the whole of the Colony and therefore ought to be constructed by means of the contributions of all, in other words, out of general revenue." His report was adopted and general road construction commenced under the supervision of a Colonial Trust, with two full-time executive officers, and the authority to impose tolls where appropriate."

The Main Roads Management Act of 1857 provided for three lines of roads, south to Albury, west to Bathurst and north to Armidale.

Administration of these roads was undertaken by a Commissioner for Internal Communication, rather than a trust. Trusts recorded revenue of over 20,000 pound(which defrayed more than 60% of the cost of road construction on 800 miles of road constructed in the period) in tolls between 1860 and 1890 when tolls were abolished.

W. C. Wentworth in his 1817 volume 'A Statistical Account of the Colony' wrote of his impressions on road development (P32) "The roads and bridges which have been made to every part of the colony, are truly surprising, considering the short period that has elapsed since its foundation. All these are either the work of, or have been improved by, the present governor (Macquarie); who has even caused a road to be constructed over the western mountains, as far as the depot at Bathurst Plains, which is upwards of 180 miles from Sydney. The colonists, therefore, are now provided with every facility for the conveyance of their produce to market; a circumstance which cannot fail to have the most beneficial influence in the progress of agriculture. In return for these great public accommodations, and to help keep them in repair, the Governor has established toll-gates in all the principal roads. These are not farmed out to the highest bidder, and were let during the year 1817, for the sum of 257 pound."

The Financial Statements
Of the Colony
Of
New South Wales
1800-1855

INTRODUCTION

It is always exciting to discover something new. Well, at least new for the writer.

This study must fit into that context. To this writer, the subject is new and indeed, quite novel. Not in the literal sense, however, but in the sense that it is an unusual hobby. The two key words here are unusual and hobby. This refers to the fact that for more years that one can remember, the writer has been a practicing accountant, by way of being a provider of management advisory services. This role has taken me around the world and supported living in three states of Australia and overseas in the United Kingdom and the United States of America. That is not to say that this hobby has been continuous during that time.

High School in Sydney resulted in Matriculation with honours in English, History and Economics. College studies were in Accountancy (Commerce) and Economics. This background sets the scene, one would think handsomely, for a latter day interest in Economic History in general, and the financial statements of the early years in particular.

This preoccupation with the colonial period of our Australian History came about when a set of 'Financial Statements of the Colony of New South Wales 1855 to 1885 'came to hand from a second–hand bookshop. Being published in 1885, the book held a fascination because of its age, its title and its contents.

But the nagging question remained. Why 1855? Why not 1788? And that's when the research commenced into discovering more about those early years of the colony. Who paid for all the development? Who paid for the convicts? When and how was the first local revenue raised and how did it grow? So many questions but, in reality, so few answers.

This was obviously not the stuff of best sellers. Few writers or historians, let alone Economic Historians explored through the Sydney Gazette from 11803 to 1822, and then through the 68 volumes of the *Blue Books* from 1823 to 1855. However this exercise for a student historian and accountant was exciting, educational and lead to many new journeys. Having read and considered the financial statements of the colony from 1800 to 1855

Australia's history is a proud record of entrepreneurial ability, after being given a 'leg-up' by Britain. This is the story of just a sample of our colonial history from the records—the record of Financial transactions in the colony 1800 to 1855

PREFACE

Professor S. J. Butlin, the pre-eminent portrayer of Australian Economic History in his splendid work 'Foundations of the Australian Monetary System 1788-1851' (1953 Edition), wrote, "Australian Economic History is the major part of all Australian History;—from the beginning, economic factors have dominated development in a way that should gladden the heart of any Marxist. What is true of any particular strand of economic growth—land settlement, labour relations and labour organisation, immigration, secondary industry—is also true of each major stage in the development of the community as a whole: each is characterised by economic changes which conditioned political, social and cultural change."

To explore the most important of the economic events in the Colony to 1899 is to inexorably intertwine our history, both socially and economically, with the growth of wealth and the growth of the people.

These events don't fall naturally into importance by the tragedy of the circumstances like so many historical events can lay their focus to (such as like floods or wars, earthquakes or unnatural dramas such as social riots). These events were awakened by the wonderful aura of discovery. The exploration over the mountains to open up a new land, and unfold the story of the rivers; the discovery of gold, and the unfurling of the workers flag and untold riches; the amazing growth of the pastoral industry; the development of the great 'iron horse' and the opening of the vast inland to settlements; the unfolding of the education system to all young Australians 'free, compulsory and secular' with the relief of seeing illiteracy drop from 75% to under 20% in the decade; the development of communications. From bush telegraph to the electric telegraph around the world, but mostly the natural advance of democracy leading finally to full self-government.

All these marvellous events had a major impact on the economy of the day. Revenue grew from 72,000 pound in 1826 to 13,000,000 pound less than 40 years later, without diminishing the peoples will to work and the acceptance of the government's right to fairly tax its people and create a strong social infrastructure. Revenue per head rose only from 2.08 pound to 3.79 over the 40 years.

Export earnings kept pace with imports, so we did not buy overseas at the expense of the local ability to make new and worldly goods. By 1850 our exports, due to wool and gold, had out run imports, for the first time, but always the numbers grew. Exports grew from 3.08 per head in 1826 to 14.55 per head in 1860. Imports grew from 10.39 to 21.57 in the same period, seldom with imports less than exports during that time.

In 1850, in anticipation of full self-government, the Governors began playing with 'temporary' borrowing to meet monetary policy obligations and expectations, and to keep the budget ever in balance. Gold and wool exports came as immigration burgeoned and railways and other capital expenditure came into sight. The impeccable relationship between the Colony and the 'City' of London, allowed attractive and relatively easy borrowing of capital in Britain.

The financial establishment and the workings of the first Commissariats are both to be considered, along with a consolidation and summary of the first Public Accounts in the colony, being the Gaol, Police and Orphan Funds. The first appropriation bill was brought down in 1832, long after the 1823 reforms to appoint an advisory council to the Governor. Both moves were small steps on the path to responsible Government. Full self-government in 1855 continued the slow reform of the treasury system and prompted further parliamentary reforms of financial statements prepared for the New South Wales Legislature. Finally, the Parliament received, in 1856, full control of its financial destiny and was able to increase and diversify sources of revenue and allocate funds for expenditure with only the local population watching over their shoulders.

Each of the five distinct financial periods are analysed and examined, together with the economic and historical events, which so strongly shaped the life and future of the 'Mother' Colony. The next step was obvious—explore the events which shaped the colony—events that influenced an economy were both internal (domestic) and external (mainly

British induced). These facts were gathered year by year, mostly from the records—the HRNSW and the HRA.

Overall, there were eight major events, which underpinned the Colonial economy, and each of these was pursued in some detail for further 'financial' evaluation. In each instance, the impact on the colonial economy was measured and noted. This surely was the excitement that comes once in a lifetime!

My reader may be wondering what were these 8 events that created such excitement and made such a major contribution.

- The Macquarie Building Program
- The Bigge Reports to the Westminster Parliament
- The Pastoral expansion
- Crown Land Sale and Reform
- The Recession of 1842
- The Discovery of Gold in 1851
- The Growth of the Railways
- The Movement for education and Free Migration

Of course, there were many other minor events such as exploration, the story of the river system, decentralisation, river transportation, overseas trade and the regular economic cycles. These are all examined and are reflected in the financial affairs of the colony.

We are bound to remember the highlights of the Financial System

- The first colonial revenue in 1800
- Marsden as Treasurer of the Orphan Fund
- Darcy Wentworth as Treasurer of the Gaol Fund and then the Police Fund
- The myriad of funds that grew from just these two
- The opening of the Bank of New South Wales
- The 'Blue Books' that formalised the commencement of public accounting in the colony
- The operations of the quasi-treasury 'The Commissary', until the real Treasury was established in 1823

- The appointment of the first Auditor
- The introduction of 'Appropriation Accounts' in 1832
- The modification to accounting policy after self-government

Borrowing Overseas and the Raising of first Foreign Debt

FOREWORD

This work is entitled 'Public Finance in the Colony of New South Wales 1788-1899'. Its purpose is to follow the five main stages of public finance recording and reporting during this period and review the eight special events, which, during the 1800s shaped, promoted and guided the Colonial economy like no others. The economy, like most unplanned economies in the New World went through its two paces—boom and then bust. But the busts were essentially limited to two periods, the 1840s and the 1890s. The boom times came with the discovery of gold; exploration followed by the growth and expansion of the pastoral industry and the rise of the squattocracy. As the momentum gathered for Federation, Free Trade policies in the Colony of New South Wales set it aside from the protectionist and restrictive policies of Deakin, and his champion, David Syme of the Age newspaper, in the Colony of Victoria. However with the discovery of gold in the 1850s came other side effects such as the termination of transportation, introduction of self-government, along with further land reforms, a rise in wages, prices and rents due mainly to the shortage of a general labour supply.

The railway system underpinned the economic gains from the 1850s and set the pastoral industry onto a more comfortable plain. But mainly the railways allowed the policy of decentralisation to be formally adopted. The regions of Newcastle and the Riverina grew and developed rapidly. Newcastle had been an ideal of Macquarie but it developed slowly until the rail system allowed coal extracts from the region to be moved quickly and cheaply to Sydney and then onto Victoria, which area became a major user of New South Wales coal.

The Treasurers of the Colony knew only the advantages of balancing the books each year—there was no deficit financing undertaken until after 1856 when overseas borrowing commenced with the financial houses in the City of London, who had accepted the credit worthiness of the Colony and hastened to use this new outlet for surplus funds available for investment by Britain. The use of bank drafts for export commodities had commenced with the large wool exports to Britain and led to the creation of the Union Bank of Australia, the Bank of Australasia. This period also saw the rise of the great pastoral and financing houses—Brooks and Younghusband, Dalgety and Goldsbrough Mort. Shipping fleets grew rapidly for transporting convicts, and then free immigrants and returning with wool, and other commodities. The P & O operators, with their One million pound of paid up capital won the lucrative mail contracts from the British Government and commenced regular monthly trips from London to Australia.

The published public accounts reflect an annual cumulative surplus (of revenue over expenditures) each year from 1822 to 1900. What this meant was that the Colonial Treasurers and their advisers had the flexibility of running into temporary deficit, for instance in 1838 (—164102 pound) and 1839 (—121464) knowing that the cumulative surplus of 314517 pound would allow them to do so without having to borrow long-term. In this instance the cumulative surplus was reduced to only 28951 pound. The ways of recording in the various periods varied and opened the way for considerable mistake and misinterpretation, as we will see.

Governor Macquarie had appointed Darcy Wentworth and Reverend Samuel Marsden to be Treasurers of the Police and Orphan funds and we find their monthly reports published in the Sydney Gazette of the period 1810-1821.

Clerical staff within the Colonial Secretary's office period recorded the Blue Book.

The Blue Book contains the comprehensive recording system of the times and the Consulting Accountant James Thomson introduced a new system after self-government, which was burdensome, intricate, and open to much abuse. After self-government, the ledgers were kept open until the funds appropriated to each line item in the budget were spent. This sometimes meant the ledgers could not be closed for upwards of three years, by which time the trail was cold in trying to keep track of annual revenues and expenditures. This problem was corrected in 1885, when a return was made to annual statements based on cash inflow and outflow.

Some Observations of Interest

The Marsden and Wentworth transactions created major conflict of interest situations. It is interesting to muse how a Reverend gentleman who was paid from the Civil List at the rate of 150 pound per annum, could afford to operate 4,500 acres of pasture land and build up a flock of 3,500 sheep in a span of less than twenty years. Even allowing that the land came about from grants, the sheep were purchased and although the convict labour assigned to him was unpaid, they had to be kept, with sleeping huts, food and clothing furnished. We might also ask why the monthly meat bill for the orphanage ran to over 60 pound even though the Orphanage owned and operated a farm, which regularly sold 'on the hoof' and then bought back, dressed meat. For its annual sale of livestock in 1811-1812, Marsden received only 127 pound, but from the same source purchased over 700 pound of dressed meat. The means were easy to share the spoils between those that could help him gain wealth and reach his target of becoming a large landowner and successful grazier. Marsden housed only female orphans aged from 5 to 14. On an average month, Marsden paid the butcher over 60 pound; being for an average of 2,500 lb of meat (the average price per pound was 6 pence. By the 30th September 1818, Marsden held 3,033 pound in the Orphanage account, and on average disbursed 550 pound each month from that account. The only 'admonishment' that Macquarie made if one can imply an act of admonition from a minor regulatory change, was that a lesser percentage of revenue from tariffs and duties was to be directed to the Orphan Fund. Macquarie, at this time, chose to modify the basis of the Orphanage Fund revenue and deleted an item by redirecting that revenue to the Police Fund. In 1818, Macquarie also directed that 3,000 pound of the balance in the Orphan Fund be deposited with the new Bank of New South Wales.

Macquarie made no objection to the fact that Marsden was misdirecting funds from the Orphan Fund for the repair of St. John's Church, Parramatta, in July 1811 to the extent of 56 pound, nor to paying the Matron of the Orphanage a monthly stipend of 5 pound when the going rate would have been only 1 pound per month, nor of paying 4.5.0 for a bonnet for his wife from the fund.

Macquarie wrote approved on each monthly statement, when presented to him by Marsden, obviously without proper 'auditing' procedures being used.

The Orphan Fund, as published in the Sydney Gazette, quarterly between 181 and 1820, showed numerous arithmetic errors always on account of a shortage, and one may wonder why, no-one handling the accounts, such as the other Trustees, the Governor's secretary, or the Judge-Advocate, ever picked up these quite substantial errors. During the course of the years 1812-1818, the amount of shortage or error in addition came to a total of 997 pound.

Wentworth, as Treasurer of the companion 'Police' Fund also had his dubious methods. He built up large surpluses of cash and bills receivable rather than spend funds on road and bridge or wharf construction; he expended large amounts through the military for 'repairs' to the streets of Sydney and other questionable contracts, which were never commented on publicly by Macquarie. Macquarie's 'blindness' to any inconsistencies or abuses in the accounts, made it appear that he was only interested in outcomes, regardless of how they were achieved.

Wentworth was also the town Magistrate and Superintendent of Police responsible for fines, which were an important source of revenue to the Police Fund. Two items of regular expenditure open to abuse, and which appear to be inordinately high were purchase of firewood and lamp oil and payment for the capture of absconding convicts. The Military personnel were fleecing the Government stores, operating the barter system in the Colony and were obviously monopolising the ample rewards in cash available if one found favour with Wentworth.

Legislative Councillor, Robert Campbell, recommended to the Governor on 25th August 1835 that the British Treasury should consider paying a flat rate of 10 pound per head for each of the 20,000 convicts in the colony at that time by way of maintenance and support to the local treasury. He suggested that 'because the accumulated balances in the Treasury are evidences not of superabundant revenues but of defective financial arrangements whereby public buildings have fallen into disrepair or become unfit for the required purposes. Campbell suggested that 'because the large revenue raised is not the result of industry or creation of wealth but proof of the improvident and vicious habits of the community. He noted that 3/4ths of the revenue of 157,300 pound arises from duties on spirits'. This whole proposition was rejected by Governor Sir Richard Bourke, but associate Councillors, John Blaxland wrote a letter also on 235th August, 1835, suggesting that the British Treasury had saved over 11000,000 pound by using New South Wales as a penal colony—he represented that 1,913,462.17.0 had been saved if hulks had been used or 11,008,837.5.6 if prisons had been built. He was basing his numbers on a saving of 30 pound per head for the 20,207 convicts in the colony at that time.

In response to this disagreement between Bourke and the Councillors, Bourke announced that 'the revenue of last year has been unusually productive. We are able to provide for such objects as tend to improve the morals, augment the wealth and procure the comfort and convenience of all classes of the community. These include supporting Public Schools and places of religious worship, the formation and improvement of roads and the repair and erection of public buildings'.

A. T. Yarwood in his biography of 'Samuel Marsden—the great survivor' writes that Marsden opened the female orphan house on Sunday 12th August, 1801 with a sermon followed by a visit through 'the best house in all Sydney (Rowland Hassall), and a feast. 'Thirty-one girls had been received into the house for learning, clothing, bed and board—and protection from parents and their associates (Yarwood)

At the other end of the time scale in 1899, the Federation debates also warrant a closer look at the figures furnished to Convention delegates. As the official Colonial Statistician for New South Wales, Timothy Coghlan was trying to make a name for him in the Commercial world and was in regular disagreement with the Premiers and Treasurers of the Colony. He had been publicly accused by Edward Pulsford, the leader of the Free Trade Movement of 'playing games' with his statistics, but the greatest self-serving abuse must have come with the request to furnish official statistics to the Federation debates in general and the Financial Sub-committee in particular.

He provided, in 1892, statistics for the year 1889 knowing that the figures were out of date, and were to be used until 1899, and as such capable of misinterpretation and misuse. But these figures became the guiding hand for the Finance Committee's recommendation on the structuring of the financial clauses for the Constitution. The 1889 figures remained in use until 1899 even though Coghlan delayed the scheduled collection of new statistics (which was scheduled for 1896) until 1902. Revised interim figures would have changed the course of Australian history, especially the fiscal nature of the Federation debates. A set of figures which should have formed the basis of the Federation debates and the Constitutional clauses is included in the Appendix to this work and the reader may judge for himself whether Coghlan's self serving submissions made sense. That New South Wales, being a free trade state, got great benefit from the incorrect figures being used is not questioned but the three smaller colonies—South Australia, Tasmania and Western Australia, were all significantly disadvantaged, although Western Australia was the only Colony to get preferred treatment under the Constitution. One example is with the Colonial debt in New South Wales. In 1890 the debt was only 16 million-pound, but by 1900 the debt had burgeoned to over 150 million pound. This appeared to be a carefully planned exercise by the Premiers and the Treasurers to manipulate the proposed constitution for the benefit of that colony.

By also manipulating the figures presented to the Convention delegates, Coghlan's hoped to get appointed as Commonwealth Statistician and get recognition as a great Australian. Neither happened, but he did manoeuvre a knighthood in spite of a poor showing as Agent-General for NSW in London. His writings, especially the four-volume work of Labour and Industry Growth in New South Wales are illuminating, mischievous in their conclusions, and self serving and misguided. His was a life spent on serving two masters. Himself and to a lesser extent the Government that paid him handsomely for many years.

CHAPTER 1

INTRODUCTION TO THE PUBLIC FINANCE & THE REPORTING SYSTEM IN THE COLONY

BACKGROUND TO THE COLONIAL ACCOUNTING

Colonial Origins of Public Accounts

One goal of the Governor of the Colony of New South Wales in 1788 was to achieve self-sufficiency for the colony even though it was a penal Colony. By 1823, the British Government had taken the approach it would be limiting its direct expenditure to the transportation of the convicts and they're travelling food and supplies. The Colonial Administrators would be responsible for the convict's security, food, clothing and accommodation in the Colony. The proceeds from the sale of Crown land were to be the exclusive reserve of the British authorities, and not that of the colonists. The Governors commenced working the convicts for creating food, minerals (eg coal production), roads, housing and public buildings, and generally paying their own way. By 1796, other convicts had been assigned to landowners on a fully maintained basis, thus saving the British Treasury a great deal of money.

Such policy, of the Government maintenance of convicts, created the need for an accounting by the Colony to the British Parliament with the appointment of a Treasurer acting as a Financial Controller, who could prepare monthly and annual despatches to the British Colonial Secretary. Following self-government in 1856, the procedures changed, as the Colony became fully responsible for their own economic planning and fiscal management.

Colonial Accounting in New South Wales

The Colony went through two stages before adopting the standards recommended in the 1823 'Blue Book', which replaced the 'gaol' and orphan funds. These two phases were the Gaol and Orphan Funds pre-1810, and the Macquarie promoted Police and Orphan Funds of 1811-1821, which results were published quarterly in the Sydney Gazette. The 'gaol' fund was a record of funds raised by a surcharge on the citizens of Sydney town, as a means to complete the construction of the Sydney 'gaol'. The voluntary collections fell far short of the funds needed and a part-completed gaol required official support. Customs duties were imposed on imports, and the gaol was completed with Government monies, the fund was renamed the police fund. The orphan Fund started in 1802 accepted as its revenue the customs duties on spirits and tobacco and was later (1810) named the Orphan School Fund with the intention of creating a fund to erect the first school building in Sydney town. The advisory Legislative Council were appointed in 1823, and the first Appropriation Act was passed in 1832, even though, in the interim, the Governors were passing 'messages' of the financial condition of the Colony to the members of the Council.

Upon self-government in 1855, the government accounting procedures were again revised, since the Colony was now fully responsible for all its fiscal matters.

About this time, gold was discovered and license fees, duties on exports of gold and duties on the domestic conversion of gold were applied and helped fill the Treasury coffers.

This was a major step forward in Government economic planning. A limited deficit budgeting commenced at this time. Deficits were short term and recovered usually within 5 years, although the Colonial debt, mainly to overseas bondholders was kept very much in check after the surge of investment in railways and telegraph services.

The formal Federation debates commencing in 1888 were based around the role and adjustment to individual Colonial tariffs, their discussion in the Finance Committee of the National Debates, and their incorporation into the final Constitution of 1901. These trends from 1856 are to be discussed and analysed

Federation installed a new system within the structure of the new Commonwealth Treasury whilst the States revised their reduced revenue collection procedures and accounted for the grants (return of surplus) of revenue from the Commonwealth.

Federation brought further changes to the raising of revenues, whilst the largest expenditure of the Commonwealth became the return of centrally collected funds to the States. The advent of the Commonwealth Treasury improved once again the quality of recording keeping and brought into being the first Commonwealth estimates and National budgets. By 1901, the public finance mechanism had grown from a colonial exercise by appointed settlers to a fully charged Government instrumentality.

From the earliest records (HRNSW), certain conclusions can be drawn, and these can be set out as follows:

p. There was a wide range of duties and taxes imposed on the early settlers, especially on alcoholic beverages. The general rate of duty on spirits was 10 shillings per gallon, and on wine it was 9 pence per gallon. On tobacco the rate was 6 pence per pound, while timber attracted a rate of one shilling per solid foot. General Cargo attracted an ad valorem duty at a flat 5% rate.

q. There were also licenses and tolls. Hawker's Licenses sold for 20 pound, and it cost a settler 2 pence (tuppence) to go from Sydney town to the settlement of Parramatta. A country settler (in the Hawkesbury) paid One penny to cross the Nepean River Bridge at Windsor.

r. References to crown land sales were recorded in the 1825 'Blue Book', and based on the decree by George 3rd in a Proclamation on 25th March, 1825, that there was to be imposed a new charge on crown lands at the rate of One shilling for every 50 acres, to commence 5 years after the date of the original grant. To that date all crown lands had been disposed of by way of grants, and this rent was a form of back door compensation to the crown. In the official grant documents, the receiver of the land grant was given notice that further costs may attach at some future time to the land, and it was this opportunity that provided the Crown to raise this 'rent' charge on the land in 1825.

s.   There was to be a Land-holders fee of Fifteen shillings per 100 acres of crown land reserved for each three years for free settlers, followed by a two shilling fee per 100 hundred acres redeemable after twenty years from purchase.

t.   On the 18th May 1825, the 'rent' was changed, by order of Governor Sir Thomas Brisbane, to a flat rate of 5% of the estimated value of the grants, without purchase (as opposed to purchased land), to commence 7 years from the date of grant. 'Rents' on any 2nd and subsequent grants were payable immediately, without the benefit of the 7 years grace period.

u.   The Table of Land Grants between 1789 and 1850 shows the substantial number of acres granted to settlers and we can conclude that the revenue sourced from 'rents' on Crown land grants could build into a considerable sum for the Crown in the future.

v.   By Proclamation, also dated 18th May 1825, George III authorised the sale of crown lands at the rate of 10 shillings per acre, to a maximum of 4,000 acres per individual or a maximum of 5,000 acres per family. Payment was by way of a 10% deposit and four equal quarterly instalments.

w.   The title pages to the 1822 'Blue Book' are entitled 'Abstract of the Net Revenue and Expenditure of the Colony of New South Wales for the Year 1822', which indicates (and as the detailed records also reflect) that all Colonial revenue and expenses were consolidated in the 'Blue Book'.

x.   The Table of Civil List Salaries for 1792-1793 sets out the Governor's Salary at One Thousand Pounds. But in the 1822 statement of expenditures on the Civil Salaries, the Governor's Salary had increased to Two Thousand Pounds. By 1856 the Governor's establishment was costing 15,000 pounds per annum.

y.   In fact, the total of Civil List salaries in 1792 was only 4,726.0.0 pounds, but by 1822 the total had increased to 9,828.15.0

pounds, due to both individual salary increases as well as more people being placed on the Civil List.

z. The official 'Observations upon revenue for the Colony in 1828' (written by the Colonial Treasurer of New South Wales) makes an interesting point. It observes that the 'net colonial income' of the year 1828, as actually collected, is exclusive of sums in aid of revenue, which cannot be viewed in the character of income. This item is further defined as 'the proceeds of the labour of convicts, and establishments connected with them, being applied to the reduction of the amount of parliamentary grants for their maintenance'. In subsequent reports, 'receipts in aid of revenue' included items such as—'sale of Crown livestock; sale of government farms produce; sale of clothing and cloth made at the Female Factory at Parramatta; sale of wheat, sugar, molasses and tobacco produced by the convicts at new settlements such as Port Macquarie.

aa. The total quantity of alcohol imported into and thus consumed in the Colony, even in 1828, and with a population in 1828 of only 37,000 people, of which adult numbers would be less than 25,000, was 162,167 gallons of spirits and 15,000 gallons of Colonial distilled spirits (distillation from sugar was prohibited in 1828, however, the high price of grain and the higher taxing of locally manufactured spirits became a natural deterrent). A final observation was made in the 'Blue Book' compilation of 1829 that the only duties imposed on spirits in that year was upon spirits imported directly from H. M. Plantations in the West Indies. So the British authorities received a double benefit in trading and duties.

ab. The quantity of dutiable tobacco in 1828 was 136,748 pounds (compared to 91,893 pounds in 1825). The Government experimented with locally grown tobacco at establishments in Emu Plains and Port Macquarie with the result being 51,306 pounds produced. So the total consumption of tobacco in 1828 was over 4 Lb. Per head of adult population.

ac. Shipping companies also paid lighthouse charges, along with wharfage. The growth of shipping, into the Port of Sydney, was so great that it meant that by 1828, the revenue from lighthouse dues, harbour dues and wharfage was over 4,000 pound.

ad. In 1828, the postage of letters attracted fees, for the first time, and the official Postmaster collected 598 pounds for general revenue. This revenue grew rapidly so that by 1832 the amount of postage collected was 2,00 pound. Each colony imposed its own postage and printed its own stamps until Federation.

The commencement of sales of both crown lands and crown timbers increased general revenues to the extent that in 1828, the amounts realised were:

Sale of Crown Lands	5004.19.2
Sales of Cedar cut on crown land	744.15.11
Sales of other Timber	9365.11.4

The Governor imposed a fee of one halfpenny per foot for all cedar cut on crown lands. The 'Blue Book' makes the further observation that this charge 'has checked bushrangers and other lawless depredators by depriving them of ready means of subsistence by the absence of all restraint from cutting Cedar upon unallocated lands'.

q. There was a major improvement in record keeping and reporting after self-government in 1855. The "Financial Statements of the Colonial Treasurers of New South Wales from Responsible Government in 1855 to 1881" provide a detailed accounting mechanism for recording classifications and compilation of budgets and reporting to the Authorities. They contain 'explanatory memoranda of the financial system of New South Wales, and of the rise, progress and present condition of the public revenue'.

The interest in this period (from 1822 to 1881) is that these records, of the 'Blue Book' and the printed Financial Statements of 1881, provide the first identification of the items included in the revenue and expenditures for the Colony. This historical data is relevant to understanding the social conditions in the Colony, the application of duties, tariffs, tolls and fees which embraced the essential revenue of a Colony that was designed to be self-sufficient and which was being given minimal economic support by the British Government, even though the opportunity cost of housing 'prisoners' in the Colony was a fraction of the cost of housing them in England.

Colonial Accounting in Victoria

The new settlement of Port Phillip adopted the standards set out in the Governor George Gipps Report on Government Accounting and Reporting after 1836 Public Finance following separation from New South Wales to form the Colony of Victoria. The Blue Book was more accurately kept in the new settlement (than in the colony of New South Wales) and full records are available concerning the commencement of the settlement and leading to the separation from New South Wales.

Table A
New South Wales Public Finance
Orphan, Gaol & Police Funds 1802-1821
Revenue

Year	Opng Balances	Customs	Total	Works Outlay
1802			490	
1803			5,200	
1804				
1805			3,100	
1806			1,900	
1807			1,200	
1808				
1809				
1810	1,384	3,272	2,194	
1811	769	7,872	10,939	2,965
1812	5,016	5,579	13,494	3,259
1813	4,502	5,228	14,621	4,426
1814	6,016	4,529	13,325	4,993
1815	1,681	13,197	17,994	6,350
1816	3,327	11,200	17,782	5,582
1817	5453	16,125	24,706	7,048
1818	9363	17,739	31,008	6,219
1819	18900	22,579	42,968	17,131
1820	10725	27,891	44,507	14,700

<u>Commentary on Table A</u>

In 1876, the Colonial Financial Officer (the Treasurer—James Thomson), acting for the Colonial Secretary of New South Wales, wrote, in a report to the Imperial Government that "From the foundation of the Colony in 1788 to 1824, the records of local revenue and expenditure are too imperfect to render them of much value for statistical purpose, or for comparison with subsequent years."

However these figures, from Table A above, have been collated in the 'Historical Records of Australia—Statistics' from reports by the Colonial Governor to the British authorities and go someway to telling a story. The claim made by historian N. G. Butlin in his introduction to the Historical Records of Australia series—'The economy before 1850'—"that the British Colonial Office spent millions of pounds to start up the Colony"—does not seem to be verifiable. In fact exactly the opposite.

The British expected their colonies to pay their way

We know that the British authorities had the choice of building new prisons in Britain and housing, feeding, guarding and clothing these prisoners, or relocate them to a 'penal colony'. The previous penal colony in America was no longer available because of the American Wars of Independence and the British were no longer welcome there. The recommendation of Sir Joseph Banks, after his voyage to the southern oceans with Captain James Cook, was to use the land and resources available in the newly charted East Coast of 'Australia'. The favourable opportunity cost of this arrangement was enormous. Britain was fighting wars in a number of areas and had numerous Colonies to administer, and one more Colony; supposedly rich in potential rewards and able to be converted to self-sufficiency was most attractive. So, the opportunity cost was became one form of savings.

By 1824 the convicts were also paying their way (in opportunity cost terms) by removing coal from the ground in the Maitland area and using it for heating purposes. No value was ever placed on this work, nor on the use of convicts as builders of roads, housing, barracks, storage sheds, port wharves, churches and government buildings. It would appear that the convicts earned their keep whilst the Colony paid its own way very quickly. The 'Blue Book' of 1828 states that there was revenue from the sale of convict produce such as 'coal, wheat, sugar, molasses and tobacco' but the value of convict labour was to remain unreported. Historians should recognise the value of the convict work as well as the opportunity cost of having transported the prisoners offshore, when an assessment is made of the 'investment' made, and the benefits gained by Britain in the new Colony of New South Wales.

The original estimate of direct gains by the British authorities from the original and continuing investment in the Colony of New South Wales was based on 5 (five) identifiable and quantifiable events, even though the convicts were assigned jobs on the basis of 'full keep'.

2.   The opportunity cost of housing, feeding and guarding the convicts in the Colony compared with the cost of doing the same thing in Britain.

The original estimates, in this category, were based on an estimated differential of ten pound per head—an arbitrary assessment of the differential cost.

However recent and more reliable information has come to hand which gives further validity to a number of 20 pound per head per annum, compared with the original 10 pound per head per annum.

A letter to Under Secretary Nepean, dated 23rd August 1783, from James Maria Matra of Shropshire and London assists us in this regard.

It was Matra, who first analysed the opportunity of using the new Colony as a Penal Colony; only his estimates were incorrect and ill founded. He had advised the Government that it would cost less than 3,000 pound to establish the Colony initially, plus transportation cost at 15 pound per head and annual maintenance of 20 pound per head.

In fact the transportation was contracted for the second fleet at 13 pound 5 shillings per head and Colonial revenues from 1802 offset annual maintenance.

However, Matra made a significant statement in his letter to Nepean, when he pointed out that the prisoners housed, fed and guarded on the rotting hulks on the Thames River were being contracted for in the annual amount of 26.15.10 per head per annum. He also writes that 'the charge to the public for these convicts has been increasing for the last 7 or 8 years' (Historical Records of NSW—Vol 1 Part 2 Page 7)

Adopting this alternative cost (of 26.75 pound) as a base for comparison purposes, it means that the benefit to Britain of the Colony over a twenty-year period increased from 140,000,000 pound to 180,000,000 pound. This calculation assesses the Ground 1 benefit at 84,000,000 pound.

7. Benefit to Britain on Ground Two is put at 70, 000,000 pound (again over a 20-year period) which places the value of a convict's labour at 35 pound per annum. Matra had assessed the value of labour of the Hulk prisoners at 35. 85 pound.

8. The valuation of convict labour in the new Colony should reflect the convicts not only used on building sites, but also on road, bridge and wharf construction. This would add (based on 35 pound per annum) a further 21,000,000-pound.

9. The Molesworth Committee (A House of Commons Committee investigating transportation) concluded that "the surplus food production by the convicts would feed the Military people and this, over a period of 10 years, would save 7,000,000 pound for the British Treasury.

10. The benefits of fringe benefit grants of land to the Military etc can be estimated (based on One pound per acre) at over 5,000,000 before 1810.

11. We learn from Governor King's Report to Earl Camden (which due to a change of office holder, should have been addressed to Viscount Castlereagh as Colonial Secretary) dated 15th March 1806 that the Convicts engaged in widely diverse work. The Report itself is entitled

"Public Labour of Convicts maintained by the Crown at Sydney, Parramatta, Hawkesbury, Toongabbie and Castle Hill, for the year 1805

Cultivation—Gathering, husking and shelling maize from 200 acres sowed last year—Breaking up ground and planting 1230 acres of wheat, 100 acre of Barley, 250 acres of Maize, 14 acres of Flax, and 3 acres of potatoes—Hoeing the above maize and threshing wheat.

Stock—Taking care of Government stock as herdsmen, watchmen etc

Buildings—
- At Sydney: Building and constructing of stone, a citadel, a stone house, a brick dwelling for the Judge Advocate, a commodious brick house for the main guard, a brick printing office
- At Parramatta: Alterations at the Brewery, a brick house as clergyman's residence
- At Hawkesbury: completing a public school
- A Gaol House with offices, at the expense of the Colony
- Boat and Ship Builders: refitting vessels and building row boats
- Wheel and Millwrights: making and repairing carts

Manufacturing: sawing, preparing and manufacturing hemp, flax and wool, bricks and tiles

Road Gangs: repairing roads, and building new roads

Other Gangs: loading and unloading boats"
(Historical Records of NSW—Vol 6 P43)

Thus the total benefits from these six (6) items of direct gain to the British comes to well over 174 million pound, and this is compared to Professor N. G. Butlin's proposal that the British 'invested' 5.6 million.

However, one item of direct cash cost born by the British was the transportation of the prisoners to the Colony, their initial food and general well being. Although the British chartered the whole boat, some of the expense was offset by authorising private passengers, 'free settlers' to travel in the same fleet. A second saving was the authorities had approved 'back-loading' by these vessels of tea from China.

Only limited stores and provisions, tools and implements were sent with Captain Arthur Phillip, the appointed first Governor, and his efforts to delay the fleet until additional tools were ready was met with an order to 'commence the trip forthwith'. This turned out to be a mistake as the new Colony could only rely on minimal farming practices to grow a supply of vegetables and without the tools to scratch the land, remove the trees and vegetation, little progress was made. A potential big cost to the fledgling Colony.

iii. The 'Blue Book' accounting records as maintained by Governor Macquarie from 1822 includes a reference to 'net revenue and expenses' which suggests an offset of all revenues against all expenses, and would include as revenue certain convict maintenance charges, to be reimbursed by the British Treasury. Such reimbursement was accounted for and reported only once—in 1825, when it is recorded as a 'receipt in aid of revenue' that an amount of 16,617 pound 'the amount of the parliamentary grant for the charge of defraying the civil establishment'. Prior to and since that date, there are only reports of payments and outgoings to the civil establishment, military and other personnel, without offset from reimbursement.

iv. Other notations in 1825 include revenues from rentals of government assets (Government outsourcing and privatisation obviously started back in 1825) such as;

Ferries	1584 pound
Toll gates	6554
Gardens	1835
Mill	1749
Canteen	910
Church pews	1296

The hire of 32 convict 'mechanics' raised 6853.27 pound

Slaughtering dues contributed 975.54 whilst duty on colonial distillation reaped 4901.30 pound.

The biggest revenue earners were duty on imported spirits (178,434 pound) and duty on imported Tobacco (21,817 pound)

ii. Even in 1822 the Colony was showing a small operating surplus. This surplus grew through 1828 until, other than for transportation of convicts to the Colony, the charges on account of the British Treasury were less than One Hundred Thousand pounds for protecting, feeding and housing nearly 5,000 fully maintained convicts. Against this cost, the charge for housing, feeding and guarding this same number of prisoners in Britain would have been substantially higher, since in addition to the 5,000 gully maintained convicts there were a further 20,000 being paid for by free settlers and used as supervised labour. Britain surely had found a cheap source of penal servitude for at least 25,000 of its former prisoners, and found a very worthwhile alternative to the American Colonies as a destination for its prisoners.

m. Revenue from Crown Land sales and rents was used to offset Civil (Crown) salaries and expenses.

n. It is probably incorrect, at this stage; to say that it cost Britain nothing or at best, very little, to establish and maintain the Colony, but it can be said that from 1822 the costs were limited to maintaining fewer and fewer convicts. But from these convicts great value in terms of agricultural produce, coal and other minerals was derived. Just in terms of coal for lighting, heating and power, the cost to the government of purchasing these items would have been substantial. The 'Blue Book' reflects the use of the coal as a cost rather than a gain as would be the accounting standard today.

o. A final conclusion could be given that there are much more known records available for this period (the first One Hundred

Years) than the author originally thought. The reproduction of the 'Blue Book' by the State Archives Office is a major step forward in understanding the economic challenges faced by settlers and convicts in the early Colony. The sourcing of material from the Blue Book unveils the financial statements and conditions of these early years. It is still considered that finance records of the period 1788 to 1822 are not re-constructible, but the author feels that a deep search through the microfilms forming the Joint Copying Project will provide information on the two Colonial operating funds of the period—the 'Police Fund and the Orphan Fund'. This is a challenge for another time.

An interesting observation is found in_'The Constitutional History of Australia' by W. G. McMinn (1979), referring to the post 1855 financial arrangements. On P 33 he records "Subject to the need for a vice-regal message, accepting that any locally (Australian Colony) initiated legislation of a money bill nature requires The Sovereign's ratification, the New South Wales Legislative Council was to have a general right to appropriate revenue from taxation, except for an amount of 81,600 pounds, the expenditure of which was to be in accordance with 'three schedules' to the Act; 33,000 pound for the salaries of those on the civil list eg Governor et al, the superintendent of Port Phillip and its judges and for the expenses of administering justice; 18,600 pound for the chief civil officers and their departments, for pensions and expenses of the council; and 30,000 pound for the maintenance of public worship.

The Sale of Waste Land Act of 1828 raised the minimum reserve price of crown land to one pound per acre, except that large remote areas might be sold at a lower price, and established a formula for the use of the land revenue; fifty percent was to be spent on immigration, the rest was to be expended by the Governor in accordance with British Government directives from time to time. The Governor was to continue to have power to issue depasturing licences and to make regulations for the use and occupancy of unsold lands, but the existence of the Sale of Waste Lands Act placed an important restriction on the colony by implying a prohibition against the Legislative Council legislating on these matters. The first directive on how the Governor was to spend a portion of the fund, enjoined the Governor to spend a proportion on Aboriginal protection and another on the roads; he was left free to hand any surplus over to the Council for appropriation; but it was made clear that the whole of the fifty percent was to be considered as an emergency reserve if the Council proved difficult". McMinn sheds some further light on the Crown Lands mystery but there still remains the question of whether, year after year, these funds were fully used or just included as a contribution to general revenue. It would appear that somewhere there is a firm directive from the British Treasury that the revenues from Crown Lands sale was to be used to 'offset' British costs of maintaining the Colony. The 'Blue Book' is evidence that as general revenues, these funds were already being used to pay for the costs of feeding, clothing, housing convicts, and we know they were specifically used to pay for 'sponsored immigrants', aboriginal 'protection', and now roads. The costs of the military establishment were charged against general revenues so in the quite large 'pot', nearly all Colonial expenditures were subsidised or offset by revenues from the Sale of Crown Land. Britain put its hand in the till only, it seems, to pay for the shipping and supplies costs of getting their prisoners to the Colony. After 1828, we know that convict production—both agricultural and mineral—went a long way to paying their expenses, so perhaps the British Treasury did in fact get off very lightly indeed, especially for the benefits it derived.

The vexing question of Crown Lands revenues still remains. It is apparent from the 'Blue Book' notations that this revenue was 'reserved' for specific allocation by the Crown and remained in the Colony as an offset against British Government fiscal obligations (eg Civil List salaries) until self-government in 1855. A relevant quotation from the 1887 Financial Statements of the Colonial Treasurer of New South Wales follows:

"Prior to the passing of the Constitution Act, the Territorial Revenues of the Colony belonged to the Crown, but upon that coming into operation in 1855, they were placed at the disposal of the local Parliament, and together with the taxes, imposts, rates and duties were formed into one fund, under the title of the Consolidated Revenue Fund. In lieu of the Crown Revenues thus given up to the Colony, an annual Civil List of 64,300 pound was made payable to Her Majesty out of the Consolidated Revenues of the Colony." What this

means is that the British Treasury allowed the offset of all
direct British payments made on account of the Colony against
revenues raised by the sale, rent or lease of Crown lands. A
theory promoted by the writer but hitherto before unable to
be officially verified.

GOVERNANCE OF PUBLIC FINANCE

Included in the appendix to the 'Financial Statements of 1887' is the record (by the Colonial Treasurer—James Thomson) that:

> "The Financial System of the Colony of New South Wales is regulated chiefly by the Constitution Act of 1855 and the Audit Act of 1870, and in matters relating to Trust Funds and Loans by special Appropriation Acts of the local legislature.
>
> The Imperial Act granting a constitution to the Colony of New South Wales was assented to on 16th July 1855, and became effective on the 24th November 1855. This Act provides for a Legislative Council (Upper House) and a Legislative Assembly. The Upper House members were to be nominated by the Governor, while the Lower House members were to be elected by inhabitants of the Colony.

"Prior to the passing of the Constitution Act, the territorial revenues of the Colony belonged to the Crown, but on that Act coming into operation in 1855, these revenues were all placed at the disposal of the local Parliament, and together with the taxes, imposts, rates and duties, were formed into one fund, under the title of the Consolidated Revenue Fund. In lieu of the Crown Revenues thus given up to the Colony, an annual Civil List of

64,300 pounds was made payable to Her Majesty out of the consolidated revenues of the Colony.

The Constitution Act also provides that the legislature of the Colony shall have power to make laws for regulating the sale, letting, disposal, and occupation of the wastelands of the Crown within the Colony; and also for imposing taxes and levying customs duties. All Money Bills must, in the first place, be recommended to the Legislative Assembly by message from the Governor, and no part of the Public Revenue can be issued except on warrants bearing the Governor's signature, and directed to the Treasurer of the Colony.

The Audit Act of 1870 was passed to regulate the receipt, custody and issue of public monies, and to provide for the audit of the Public Accounts. The Treasury is the Department entrusted with the collection and disbursement of the revenues and other public monies of the Colony. It is under the control and general management of the Treasurer and Secretary for Finance and Trade. The permanent head of the Department is responsible to the Minister for the efficient conduct of its business.

The revenue of the Colony is now to be classed under the following general headings:

1. Taxation
2. Land Revenue
3. Receipts for services rendered
4. Miscellaneous receipts

The main elements of the these four categories items consist of:

a. Taxation
    1. Customs duties
    2. Excise duties
    3. Duty on gold exported
    4. Trade licenses

b. Land Revenue
    1. Proceeds from land auctions

    2. Sales of improved lands
    3. Rents and assessments on pastoral runs
    4. Quit rents
    5. Leases of mining lands
    6. Miner's rights

  c. Services receipts, include:
    1. Railway & telegraph revenue
    2. Money orders
    3. Mint charges
    4. Gold escort fees
    5. Pilotage & harbour fees
    6. Registration of cattle brands
    7. Other fees of office

  d. Miscellaneous
    1. Rents
    2. Fines
    3. Sale of government property,
    4. Interest on bank deposits
    5. Other general revenues

The revenue and expenditure of the Colony is increasing year by year in proportion to the prosperity of the people and the increase of population. This is naturally to be expected for as new lands are taken up and outlying districts occupied, demands upon the government for all those services which tend to promote the well-being of a community are constantly being made; and although these services when granted create an additional expenditure, there generally follows an augmentation of the revenue both from the sale and occupation of the waste lands of the Colony, and the larger consumption of dutiable articles"

When responsible government was established in 1855, the revenue amounted to 973,178 pounds (or 3.51 pound per head) and the population was then 277,000. In 1875, exactly twenty years after the introduction of responsible government, the population had increased to 606,000 and the revenue to 4,121,996 (or 6.80 pound per head)."

From the Government Gazette of 2nd January 1879, this condensed statement is taken:

REVENUE, 1878

Taxation

Customs Duties		44,220
Duty on gold		6,898
Licenses		109,851

Land Revenue

Sales		1,915,466
Other		410,254
Services		1183,582
Miscellaneous		172,907
TOTAL REVENUES for 1878		4,991,919 pound

An interesting observation on latter day government finance and government involvement in entrepreneurial activities is made by Trevor Sykes in his book, 'The Bold Riders' 1994-Chapter 14, Page 438:

> "The Savings Bank of South Australia was formed in 1848 and the State Bank of South Australia was formed in 1896. By 1984 they had led stolidly blameless lives for 136 and 988 years respectively. In 1984 they merged to form a new, larger State Bank of South Australia.
>
> The chairman of Hooker Corporation, Sir Keith Campbell, headed the Campbell Committee, set up by Federal Treasurer, John Howard, in 1979. The Committee delivered its report in March 1981. The Report recommended deregulation of the financial system, a part of a worldwide trend, leading to deregulation in the federal sphere in 1984 by Paul Keating. The Campbell Report recommended that, once the banking system had been deregulated to make it more competitive, there would cease to be any justification, on efficiency grounds, for continued government ownership of banks, so that if government banks were to remain, should be no more fettered or subject to government interference than private sector institutions undertaking similar activities."

The State Savings Bank of South Australia foundered and failed in 1989, only 5 years after deregulation and 140 years after its opening.

GOVERNANCE OF PUBLIC FINANCE IN THE COLONY

GENERAL OBSERVATIONS

On the origin and nature of the New South Wales Colonial Revenue:—

"The Revenues collected within the Colony of New South Wales, from its establishment until the commencement of the administration of Governor Macquarie in 1810, were raised in support of the 'Gaol' and 'Orphan' Funds respectively. The Revenue thus levied for, and appropriated to the Gaol Fund consisted of a Duty of 1s. per gallon on Spirits, 6d per gallon on wine, 3d per gallon on beer, together with a wharfage duty of 6d on each cask or package landed. These duties appear to have been first established upon the authority of Governor John Hunter R.N. during his administration in 1795-1800 and were the earliest sources of local revenue in the Colony.

The Revenue raised for the Orphan Fund was derived from fees on the entry and clearance of Vessels, and for permits to land and remove spirits—both first levied in 1800; from licenses to retail liquor and from a duty of 1.5% on goods sold by auction (first collected in 1801); from a duty of 5% ad valorem on all articles imported, the produce of countries to the eastward of the Cape of Good Hope (first imposed in 1802); from fines levied by the Courts and Magistrates; from fees from grants of lands and leases, and quit rents on crown lands (Quit rents ceased in 1805). Other than quit rents and crown land fees, all revenues were levied upon Colonial authority.

The following is revenue raised in 1805 (James Thomson reports that the records from 1805 to 1810 are 'imperfect')

1805 Revenues in Gaol and Orphan Funds:
Duties on Spirits   1569.11.3
Fees on Vessels, licenses   595.13.7
Ad valorem duty   531.10.3

| Fines by courts | 86.5.8 |
| Revenue raised in 1805 | 2783.0.9 |

In 1810, Governor Macquarie changed the designation of these two funds to 'Police Fund' and Orphan School Fund. The designated revenues were split 3:1 into each fund. The Act 3 Geo IV c.96 of 1822 gave further powers of taxation to the Governor.

UNDERSTANDING THE PUBLIC ACCOUNTS OF 1810-1818

In preparation for understanding the Public Accounts of the Colony as printed by the Sydney Gazette between 28th August, 1810 and the 28th November 1818, and published under the authority of the Governor (Lachlan Macquarie), we must understand firstly the nature of the two Treasurers.

The Orphan Fund, whose official nomenclature is 'The Female Orphan Institution Fund' (a successor by name—change to the Orphan & School Fund) was administered by the Reverend Samuel Marsden, an Anglican churchman, who, as an official (principal) chaplain was on the Civil List for receiving an annual stipend or salary, as well as being the principal trustee and administrator of the Orphanage, the rector of St. John's Church, Parramatta, livestock trader, a marriage celebrant, a large land and livestock owner and a pastoralist, as well as self-appointed moral censor of the Colony. Marsden was also a magistrate at Parramatta—'the hanging preacher'.

That a conflict of interest is perceived is acceptable but the nature of the accounting process allowed the distinct possibility of misappropriation of funds. For instance the orphan fund was designated as being used for the operation of the Female Orphanage within an existing building in Sydney town, with a larger building to be constructed at Parramatta. However, we find that the orphanage farm sold produce in the amount of less than 1,000 pound during seven years. Marsden also 'sold' the labour or services of orphans for 310 pound during that period, and deposited that cash as revenue to the fund, instead of either dropping fees from people having to place children in the orphanage (usually 3 pound per head) or giving the money (or its equivalent in goods) to the Orphans themselves. The governor shared the import duties between the two funds so that the Orphan Fund received 17,649 pound and the Police Fund received 77,600 in funds or bills receivable during this period.

But Marsden acted with impunity in expending over 1,000 pound on expenses, repairs and improvements to St. John's church. At least this amount was recorded.

The frightening thought is that some of the higher, unexplained expenditures could well have been going into the Marsden personal fund and assisting with the expenses of operating his 4,000 head herd of sheep and cattle or of paying farm expenses for his 4,500 acres. The small 30-acre farm attached to the Orphanage cost 1,268 pound to run for seven years so it is reasonable to expect that Marsden's broad acres were costing a goodly amount to operate. His stipend of 150 pound per annum would not have stretched to paying farm expenses, especially with a wife and 5 children, 5 servants and 10 'assigned' convicts. He eventually became the largest sheep owner before 1819.

Without proper authorisation, the new orphanage building had cost 4,000 pound to construct. The original estimate to Macquarie (HRNSW) was 500 pound. This is just another example of Macquarie's extravagance, which could not be reined in, not even by Lord Bathurst. It demonstrates the deviousness that Marsden could show when he craved something badly enough.

It is questionable, as well, that the 45 orphans housed in the original buildings could consume a monthly average food bill, for meat (of 70 pound) or of flour (of over 50 pound). With meat selling at about or below 6d per lb, the supposed quantity of meat was unmanageable, in infants. It is possible that during the period, the butcher was being paid for extra sheep on the hoof going to the Marsden farm. The amount of firewood purchased was 278 pound, regardless of the available wood on the orphanage farm and the surplus labour available to the farm. Shoes and clothing, in the amount of 600 pound during the period from 1825, for the orphans suggests frequent new clothing items, whilst the monthly 'donation' to the orphanage matron of 5 pound made her the highest paid female in the Colony.

There were five 'charity' schools operating until Macquarie decided to bring them under the umbrella of the governor, leave the administration to Marsden but now using paid and supervised teachers and other staff. These schools paid over 2,000 pound in salaries to its staff plus a further 187-pound in school supplies, books during the period.

Darcy Wentworth's fiduciary responsibilities, as Treasurer of the Police Fund were marginally better but this is mainly due to his handling over 120,000 pound during his eight years as Treasurer. His areas of revenue raising were hotel and spirit licences, road tolls (mainly Sydney to Parramatta), auction and marketing licences, and the bulk of import duties.

Wentworth also had ample opportunity to salt some revenues away to his own use, although in the main his financial statements did not contain too many arithmetic errors. His main areas of expenditure were repair work and new work on the many streets and roads within the Sydney and Parramatta areas.

Wentworth was the Treasurer of the Police Fund as well as a Police Magistrate for the town, and the 'Commissioner' of Police, it was not surprising to find that all of his repair work was carried out by soldiers and police officers. The recapturing of escaped convicts was paid for handsomely and Wentworth again made most of these payments to police officers and soldiers. It may be questioned whether they were being paid more to guard to convicts or to re-catch them, after they escaped. So, if 'trading' was not the military people's forte, Wentworth remunerated them well with extra pay for services and assistance from within his bailiwick. Road repairs and minor new construction came to over 15,000 pound whilst new wharves came to 2,000 pound. His largest single item was for salaries to those many people not on the civil list. This amounted to over 53,000 pound during the period

For full details of revenue and expenditure of these two funds between 1810 and 1821, refer to the appropriate table of statistics, in the appendix.

The Funds available to Wentworth and the Governor from the Police Fund, at the end of 1818 was nearly 17,000 pound. Macquarie directed in 1818 that this amount be placed on deposit in the new Bank of New South Wales.

Macquarie's policies of improving the Colonial operations did work, as can be seen from the 'investment', from Wentworth's account, in new buildings and other contract work of over 25,000 pound.

In terms of revenue, the Colony increased its costs of living by over 173,000 pound in just 7 years. In terms of pounds per head per year, it is estimated that amount is equivalent to at an impost of nearly two pound per head per year of additional duty, tolls, fees etc.

That Macquarie's successor, Sir Thomas Brisbane, as well as Commissioner Bigge, demanded full, proper and regularised accounting of all revenue and expenditures is reflected in the transfer to the 'Blue Book' system in 1822 and the appointment of a full-time salaried financial officer, for the Colony, in the same year.

THE ROLE OF THE COMMISSARY

(In The Operations of the Colonial Government)

Planning for a Commissary for the new Penal Colony was well under-way by the 1795, and was to be operated and managed along the lines of a naval purser's office. The Commissary was to be responsible for all purchasing, storage, payment and distribution of goods. Its purpose was to provision the convicts, civil employees, the military personnel, and their families.

However for a new colony, which had decided not to adopt a currency, the Commissaries role was made especially challenging. A currency is the traditional means of exchange. There would be no buildings initially available and only convict labour to work the stores in Sydney, Parramatta and the Hawkesbury area—'always unreliable and untrustworthy', said John Palmer the third Commissary.

The first supply ships arrived with the rest of the first fleet on the 26th January 1788 in Port Jackson. The unloading of bare essentials, such as tents and a few tools and minimal food was completed that day, but the balance of the supplies would be left aboard the Sirius and the Golden Grove until a storehouse was available.

Every carpenter available was busy with the building of barracks for the soldiers and military personnel, followed by a facility for the Governor and only then a storehouse. But first the land had to be cleared of trees and timber cut for the first makeshift buildings.

The first Commissary, Andrew Miller, had been hand picked by Governor Arthur Phillip, based on Phillip's past experience with Miller (as a seaman), rather than Miller's experience as a Commissary chief. Phillip had provided detailed instructions of how he wanted the operation performed. Phillip, in turn, had been given his instructions by the Lords of the Admiralty and the Colonial Secretary, and the most important of these were the overall goals:

- Keep the cost per head per day for supplies as low as possible
- Keep the number of fully victualled persons as low as possible
- Establish the Colony to be self-supporting as quickly as possible
- Put the convicts out to work to earn their keep (although this was a new and untried policy)
- Assign convicts to non-government masters on a full support basis (again, this policy was untried and untested—but one strongly supported by Phillip)

Phillip had transported the first One thousand convicts and military without loss of life or loss of property. He had brought the first animals for breeding into the Colony, all healthy and was assigning duties by the 28th January 1788 (2 days after arrival in Port Jackson or Sydney Harbour) for the general unloading of the animals, convicts and material supplies ready to commence his Colonial operations.

Convicts were set to clearing the ground for vegetable plantings and building sites.

Phillip decided that instead of relying on stores transported on an irregular basis from Britain, that he would commence a planting program to provide fresh vegetables and grain; fresh meat, fish and game and make it a happy colony in which to live and work. He did not plan, nor was prepared for the harsh climate and the periodic droughts and flooding rains, or the unhappy natives.

His goal of victualling the whole Colony for less than 14p per day was going to be difficult, but he could do it if some level of self—support could be accomplished. He had brought quantities of seed for planting, but his fears were that northern hemisphere soils and climate would be very different from local 'New Holland' conditions and his crops would fail or yields would be minimal. His first corn crop, however, returned his planting twenty times over (HRNSW), and he was pleased and hopeful of the future returns being plentiful. In fact, he wrote to the Lord Commissioners stating that 'this Colony will become the greatest investment ever made by the British'.

Phillip planned for other possible ways to reduce costs; such as reducing imports, commence an export trade, establish settlers on farming ground, establish remote settlements, establish jobs and trades and build the necessities and Phillip thus went about his work, putting these plans into practice. He assumed, incorrectly, that the convicts and the military shared his enthusiasm and commitment to hard work.

However, his experiment with tobacco planting, and grains, other than corn and wheat, and even sugar was encouragingly successful.

He planned for another new settlement at the head of the harbour, near fresh water, and with boat access at high tide. Rose Hill, soon to become Parramatta, was to be established with convict and military quarters, a church, and some emancipist settlers. To this end he released convicts for good conduct, who were willing to marry, and provided them grants of good land, usually 30 acres, and an admonition to become self contained and sell their surplus to the Commissariat store. He did allow the emancipists to retain access to the Government store for a period of two years. He would, in the future, exchange settler's grain for Government—owned cows, to enable a breeding program to commence and further expand the likelihood of a successful colony.

His building and construction priorities changed. He saw the priority need for a hospital building, especially since he had a surgeon in his midst, and some of his convicts had been speared and even killed by the natives. So the barracks were completed and then the hospital and finally the storehouse were ready by early April 1789. Phillip wrote in his journal that 'the timber has one very bad quality, which puts us to great inconvenience; I mean the large gum tree, which warps and splits in such a manner, when used green, to which necessity obliges us, that a storehouse boarded up in this wood is rendered useless' (HRNSW)

David Collins, a military Lieutenant and Phillip's Private Secretary, wrote on the 5th April, 1788, 'As the winter of this hemisphere is approaching, it becomes absolutely necessary to expedite the buildings intended for the detachment, so, every carpenter that could be procured amongst the convicts was sent to assist, since as many as could be released from the transports were employed working on the hospital and storehouses.'

Collins recorded on the following day, the 6th April, 1788 'worship was moved indoors as divine service was performed in the new storehouse. One hundred feet by twenty-five feet were the dimensions of the building, constructed with great strength and covered in with thatching. But we were always mindful of fire since no other materials could be found and we became mindful of accidental fire.'

Obviously, the hospital was finished, the storehouse was complete, some female convict huts had been completed and the military barracks were well under way. Phillip's plan was now in full swing.

This first and temporary storehouse was built somewhere around the Sydney cove (at the top end of High Street, now George Street), where a landing wharf had been constructed and where the camp was getting into working order. Subsequently permanent storehouses were built nearer the hospital, using roof tiles instead of thatching, and connected from the landing area to the hospital past the storehouses via a convict constructed 'road'.

Andrew Miller, the first Commissary, grew sick and frail (during 1788), in the service of Phillip and asked to be returned to England. He died on route but was replaced as Commissary by his former assistant, Zachariah Clark, who had come from England originally as agent to Mr Richards the shipping contractor.

Collins reported on the 12th April, 1788 that the 'issuing of provisions, was in future, under Mr Clark, to be once a week.'

Lieutenant John Hunter, soon to be Lieutenant Governor of Norfolk Island, recorded in his diary for 5th September 1788, that 'because of some failed crops, rotting food, and a plague of rats in the storehouse, that the colony would need more stores and provisions than any Pacific island could supply, and he would dispatch the Sirius to the Cape of Good Hope, in order to purchase such quantity of provisions as she might be capable of taking on board; and that she should be made as light as possible for that purpose. In consequence, eight guns and their carriages were removed together with 24 rounds of shot for each gun, 20 barrels of powder, a spare anchor and various other articles. These were all put on shore at Sydney Cove. I was also directed to leave the long boat behind for use by the Colony. The master of the Golden Grove store-ship was also ordered to get ready for sea to take supplies, convicts and some military personnel to Norfolk Island.'

Phillip was obviously panicking about the shortage of supplies and the empty storehouse. The proposed settlements at Rose Hill and Norfolk Island and a ship to the Cape had almost emptied the first settlement at Sydney Cove, of people as well as provisions.

A number of storehouses had been established. The first, a temporary one at the Cove, now the permanent one near the hospital on the first Sydney town street—High Street (now George Street), the lumber yard store, the military detachment store and the naval store. Clarke was nominally in charge of all stores but was also assigned other duties with the Governor, and with the hope of cutting rations even further by only opening the regular store once each week, was obviously in charge of only empty buildings.

In October, 1788, Warwick Tench observed, in his diary that 'we have now been here over half a year and are becoming acclimatised, even if we lack the shelters thought necessary. Since our disembarkation in January, the efforts every one has made was to put the public stores into a state of shelter and security and to erect habitations for the hospital, convicts and ourselves. We are eager to escape from tents, where only a fold of canvas was between us and the hot beams of the summer sun and the chilling blasts of the winter wind from the south. Under wretched covers of thatch lay our provisions and stores, exposed to destruction from every flash of lightning and every spark of fire. A few of the female convicts had got into huts but almost all of the officers and all the men, were still in tents.'

In February 1789, the only free immigrant, James Smith, who had procured a passage from England on the Lady Penrhyn was placed in charge of the new storehouse at Rose Hill and was also sworn in as a peace officer, or special constable. Claiming to be a 'practical farmer', Phillip gave him a number of convicts to assist him in exercising his abilities. This was the first trial of the assigned convict system.

On the 18th March 1789, Collins recorded the first major theft of stores and provisions from the secured commissary. There were seven of the military, convicted of theft, undertaken over a period of some weeks, robbing the store of liquor and large quantities of provisions. Phillip made an example of these men, but to little avail, as later that same year another six soldiers were convicted and hung for doing exactly the same thing.

The Economic Role of the Commissary

Over time Phillip increased and improved the operations of the Commissary and planned to offset the effect of having no currency in the Colony by creating a barter economy. To aid in this plan, Phillip arranged that all goods received into the Commissary would be recognised and accepted by 'store receipts'. Payment for goods arriving by ship or purchases made from other ports and brought to Sydney town was done via official 'bills' drawn for payment upon presentation on the British Treasury.

By 1790 store receipts and the related official government bills formed the basis of the currency in the colony. The settlers would lodge their grain, wool, or meat with the store and receive an official receipt in exchange.

The receipt stated the recipients name, type and quantity of goods and the price paid. Because they were backed by the Government, the receipts became an increasingly popular instrument of exchange. They could be transferred between parties in payment for a debt, exchanged amongst settlers in the course of trade and for products from the Government stores, redeemed for the equivalent in coin and banknotes, and through the commissariat, exchanged for government bills drawn on the English Treasury". Eventually when colonial banks became established, store receipts and government bills were accepted as deposits. In these early days, a store receipt was as good as cash and for many people, a lot more convenient." (Encyclopaedia of Australia)

The Final Volume (# 7) of Historical Records of Victoria (Vol 7-Public Finance) sets out some background of what was happening in New South Wales whilst Victoria was still part of the Port Phillip colony.

"New South Wales was one of only three of the Empire's colonies established at the expense of British taxpayers. Most British colonies were begun by trading companies or settlement associations, and were expected to be self-sufficient. The British Government was usually prepared to provide a civil administration and military protection, but wherever possible, these were to be funded from local sources. The commissariat was responsible for many of the early financial arrangements in New South Wales. From the beginning, practices had been highly unsatisfactory and allowed much corruption. The first fleet brought with it in 1788 only the most meagre of supplies of coin. This shortage of a circulating currency became increasingly acute. In the short term, the government used promissory notes, government store receipts, treasury bills, spirits and shipments of coins of various denominations and currencies to which varying values were assigned. All were part of a volatile and unstable money market."

Britain had, prior to the first fleet invoked its right to tax its dependencies. The loss in the 1770s of its valuable American colonies, the previous dumping ground for convicts, was directly attributable to these taxes.

The Napoleonic Wars (1793-1815) almost beggared Britain, and ruthless experiments with new taxes and duties was tried in a desperate effort to meet national debts. Income tax was introduced in 1798, modified in 1805 and 1807 but discontinued in 1816. The unpopularity of direct taxation resulted in wider nets of indirect taxation, such as customs duties. The New South Wales experiment echoed some of these developments. But it became Governor Gipps' opinion (1838-46) that nowhere else was so large a revenue raised from so small a population." And this opinion is born out by the official Treasury reports of the time (refer attached Statistics).

Marjorie Barnard in her fine work—'A History of Australia' (P327) reflects on the early workings of the commissary and the financial dealings it accommodated.

"The commissariat had charge under the Governor of all stores and provisions. It acquired locally produced supplies, but the importation of food, clothing and other necessities from overseas was the responsibility of the home office, or in emergency, of the governor.

The commissariat was the colony's store and it also became the financial centre of the colony, where all transactions were by barter or note of hand. The only note in which there could be universal faith was that issued by the commissary as a receipt for goods received into the store. This department was the quasi-treasury, so that when a colonial treasury was set up, the commissary remained for provisioning of the convicts and only withered away at the end of transportation. Large sums could only be paid by the commissary's notes, for these alone had credit behind them, and they had to be eventually redeemed by bills on the treasury."

R. M. Younger in his work 'Australia & The Australians—'

writes (P78) "The only market for produce was the government store in the various farming districts, run by the commissariat under the ultimate control of the superintendent of public works. The governor fixed the price of grain, and it was left to the storekeepers to decide whose grain should be bought and who's refused. David Collins, former secretary to Governor Phillip wrote of this operation:

'The delivery of grain into the public storehouses when open for
that purpose was so completely monopolised that the settlers
had but few opportunities of getting full value for their crops.
The ordinary settler found himself thrust out from the granary
by a man whose greater opulence created greater influence. He
was then driven by necessity to dispose of his grain at less than
half its value. He was forced to sell it to the very man who had
first driven him away and now whose influence was the only
available way to get the grain into the public store.'

Such incident evidenced a fundamental weakness in the economy. Farming
had to be expanded so that the community could become self-supporting;
but since the demand was in fact small and inelastic, and since there was
no export, a glut or a shortage could easily occur. Because of strictly limited
demand the wheat acreage could not be expanded too greatly, yet when
two bad years occurred, there were dangerous shortages, and the colony
had to revert to imports.

The commissary store continued to be the centre of the colony's economy.
A great number of the population were still victualled from the store; these
included the military and civil list people and their families, together with
settlers receiving land grants, whether expirees or free, for the first two years
on the farm. And convicts unassigned or working for the government.
The requirement that the military officers clothe, feed and house assigned
convicts was not strictly enforced and so in 1800 Hunter's record must
show that 75% of the population was victualled by the government."

The anomaly was that by 1813 a few Sydney merchants were exporting,
even though the NSW Corps still dominated local business. Exporting had
begun in 1801 with Simon Lord, selling coal, whale oil and seal-skins to
the American boats visiting Sydney for the purpose of two-way trade; they
brought moderately priced cargo for general sale as well as provisions and
supplies for the commissary. Campbell, the biggest trader got around the
British support of the East India Company having a trade monopoly with
China by using French or American ships. Campbell had built a warehouse
in 1800 supplying wine, spirits, sugar, tea, coffee and tobacco and a wide
range of household articles However Campbell was additionally soon
selling livestock, grain and merchandise to the commissary and private

buyers, with the government spending several thousand pounds with his firm each year. He then entered the whaling and sealing trade and sent a trial shipment of each to England. This caused a dispute between the East India company on one side(pushing for exclusion), Sir Joseph Banks on the other (encouraging freedom of trade)and Simon Lord, whose cargo had now been seized in Britain as contraband."

One of the charges made to Justice Bigge when he was sent to Australia to investigate and report on the Macquarie governorship, was to review the cost of operating the colony in terms of its original charter. It was of great concern to Lord Bathurst that the British Treasury in 1820 was still paying so much of the colonial operations.

So Bigge reviewed and commented on the high number of persons still victualled from the government store as late as 1823. An extract from his third report (dated January 1823) into 'The Nature of the Expenditure in the Colony' sets out his observations.

. He writes that in 1821 the Civil list salaries amounted to 8,474.17.6 but those paid from local revenues, being the 'Police Fund'_amounted to 9,824.05.0. So it is confirmed that within 22 years of the Colony being established, it was substantially on course to paying its own way. In fact Bigge writes, that "some of the salaries included in the parliamentary estimate (the Civil List) have not been drawn in this, or in some of the preceding years but have been defrayed by the police fund of NSW, including two government school masters, six superintendents and the clerk to the judge advocate, all amounting to 500 pound.

The clerks in the commissariat generally consist of persons who have been convicts and also of persons who are still in that condition (being ticket-of-leave individuals) They are paid variously from 18d to 60 d per day, plus lodging money. They also receive the full ration. And a weekly allowance of spirits. Bigge recommended that to reduce the fraud on the commissary, along with the high cost to the public purse, that (a) all bread be baked by a variety of contractors in lieu of convicts, and (b) that contracts for the supply of hospitals with bread, meat and vegetables be also let. He likewise recommended that all meat to the King's stores be furnished by contract from the settlers at the price of 5d per lb. He reports that the number of provisioned convicts is constantly changing. For instance, the total number of people provisioned from the Sydney store on 30th December, 1820, was 9326, of which only 5135 were convicts unassigned."

Author's Note: As can be seen from the following table, the number of victualled convicts (and others) is surprisingly high, especially at the end of the last two periods (1810 & 1820). The Governor's were directed to assign convicts to settlers or military officers for assistance with farming operations; the intention was for the colony to supply its own provisions and stores. The settlers and officers were directed to house, clothe and feed all assigned convicts and take them off the public stores. However, by virtue of being in a special position in the colony, most civil list persons and military were still being supported by the public stores. Even emancipists or free settlers that carried out special duties (eg police constables) became entitled to support from the stores.

Number of people on Rations (number victualled from public store) between 1795 and 1820 were:

1795	1,775
1793	1,682
1799	1,832
1800	3,545
1804	2,647
1810	5,772
1820	9,326

(compiled from individual records in vols 1-7 HRNSW)

As Bigge's concluded "some rations were issued in higher allowance than decreed because of extra work or hard labour.

Government owned livestock is held at the Cow Pastures, Parramatta and Emu Plains. These facilities are operated by a Superintendent and 3 oversees, all paid by the police fund. In addition 75 convicts are employed as stockmen and general labourers. All these people in total draw 122 daily rations from the public stores. The cost of daily rations were estimated by Bigge at 4s 8d or 56 pound per annum, or nearly 4 (four) times the targeted cost.

There were also 451 head of wild cattle which had over the previous year run off from the holding areas, but were recovered in 1820 and used for public meat supply. In total, with slaughtered sheep and cattle from government herds, over 237,000 lb of fresh meat was supplied at a savings of 5,000 pound to the government. This still left 6,000 animals in the government herd, but the settlers were increasing their pressure on the Governor to buy only meat from the settlers and not use government herds for slaughtering.

Of the total colonial expenditure in 1820 of 189,008 pound, the cost of rations for troops, civil list and convicts amounted to 143,370 or 75%. Bigge did report that the general expense of erecting buildings in the Macquarie years in the colony of New South Wales is lessened by the use of convict labour and locally found timbers and locally made bricks, tiles and stone. He suggested that the cost of local funds used for buildings would be better spent on clothing, and feeding the convicts and taking them off the public stores.

Reviewing the Official Records on the Commissary

The HRNSW contains numerous references to original records reporting the instructions on how to operate, or the anecdotal reports on how the commissariat operated.

Phillip wrote that 'It is planned that a quantity of provisions equal to two years consumption should be provided (written 1786), which will be issued from time to time, according to the discretion of the Superintendent, guided by the proportion of food which the country and the labour of the new settlers may produce.'

'Clothing per convict was estimated to cost 2.19.6 including jackets, hats, shirts, trousers, shoes'. Phillip further wrote that 'the type of clothing was not always suitable for the climate, and should be ready made rather than relying on the convicts to sew their own.'

He noted that 'The Sirius brought seed wheat and barley and four months supply of flour for the settlement, together with a year's provisions for the ships company,'

and, 'Supplies of grain or flour from England will be necessary to maintain the colony until there is sufficient local crops in store rather than 'in the ground', because of grub, fire, drought and other accidents.'

and 'I have directed the commissary to make a purchase (9th January, 1793) and have thus augmented the quantity of provisions in the colony to 7 months at the established ration.'

On 6th January 1793, Phillip recorded his opinion that the expense for the settlement projected for 1794 was 25913 for 5,500 person. With 3000 convicts this cost translated into a per head cost per annum of 13.14.0,(or approx. 9p per day) which he pointed out 'this sum cannot increase, but must gradually diminish.' This converted within the officially targeted allowance of 14p per head per day.

'Whitehall reported on 9th November 1794 that the stock of stores of provisions and ready-made clothing should now be sufficient for the settlement for one year.

With the quantity of clothing shipped in mid-1794, there would be a sufficient supply for 2,500 men and 700 women, according to the last official report of numbers.' Mr. Henry Dundas (British MP) insisted that the convicts should be made to wear the clothing for a full year.'

The Colonial Office insisted that 'Each ship was to carry supplies for the trip and for maintenance upon arrival, for both convicts soldiers and sailers.' (15th February, 1794)

King, as Governor of Norfolk Island on the 20th July 1794, recorded that the island had produced a second crop in sufficient quantity for storage for the next year.—being 11500 bushels + 4000 reserved for seed, stock, and the producing families.'

'Stores were ordered from the Cape of Good Hope for the settlement and the hospital on 22nd June, 1788 to be selected by John Hunter, as captain of the Sirius.

Governor Hunter submitted a plan on 10th June, 1797 saying that "were Government to establish a public store for the retail sale of a variety of articles—such as clothing, or materials for clothing, hardware, tools, sugar, soap, tea, tobacco and every article that labouring people require—supported by a reputable shopkeeper who should produce regular accounts and charge a small premium to cover these other costs, then the people would get what they wanted with easer, and at far less expense than in any other way."

Governor Hunter repeated his request for a public store on 10th January, 1798 "If my suggestion is adopted, a branch of the store should be placed on Norfolk Island. Such a store should lessen the expense of maintaining the convicts and into the store, I would also suggest the retailing of liquor and spirits, for the purpose of putting a stop to the importation of that article."

Again on the 25th May, 1798 Hunter recommended "the public store as a means of controlling the high price of grain. Such a store would operate as an encouragement to industry. Without some form of price control on grain the settlers cannot live let alone provide for a family The speculators and the monopolists all contrive to keep the settlers in a continual state of beggary and retard the progressive improvements of the colony." The success of Simon Lord's colonial merchandising in 1801 evidences that Hunter was on the right track with his 'public' store.

The Colonial Secretary wrote to Hunter in 3rd December, 1798 about the meat supply "when the livestock belonging to the crown, added to that of individuals, is in so flourishing a state as to supply the needs at 6d a pound or less, it is evident the Government will gain by supplying the settlement with fresh meat instead of sending salted provisions from England. This request was later modified to limit the store purchases for meat to those from farm settlers.

On 2nd February, 1800, William Broughton, a Churchman and Magistrate was also appointed to be the storekeeper at Parramatta to replace a man sacked by Hunter for fraud.

Governor King recorded his success in conserving the stores by writing that "since I took office, I have reduced the full rationed people relying on the public stores by 450. This has saved annually the amount of 10488 pound using the rate of 23 pound per head. I have also reduced the price of wheat to 8d per bushel, pork to 6p per lb, maize to 4s instead of 5s per bushel."

When Hunter was recalled to England, the Commissary was left with many debts owing by settlers. Hunter was concerned that these would be denied and he be held responsible. He wrote to the new Governor, King, 'I trust it is clear that there has been no lavish waste, and no improvident use of the public stores during my authority. These debts are just, even though many of the individuals may doubt their being indebted to the Government for so much. "It appears there were doubtful debts of over 5,000 pound due to the store.

In response King made demand on the settlers and accepted grain at a higher price than usual in settlement of the debt. When the public demands became known it also produced an unusual response from John Macarthur, who suddenly recalled that much of what he had taken from the stores, and charged against the public account, over the previous twelve months was in fact his personal responsibility and he settled with the stores on this basis.

King appointed a new head of the store on 7th November, 1800-A Mr Palmer. Other appointments included Broughton to Norfolk Island and Deputy Chapman from Norfolk to Sydney and William Sutter as Storekeeper at Parramatta.

In order to conserve grain, King reduced the ration to 13.5 lb of wheat per week per person.

Palmer, at the time of his appointment had been handed a set of instructions, which included the instruction that:

a. all troops and convicts in the territory were to be properly supplied and a stock of 12 months supply to be kept at the store.

b. transmit annually a list of expected consumption.

c. purchases were to be made under the authority of the Governor and prices paid to be no greater than market prices

d. all bills of exchange must be accompanied with an affidavit of purchase countersigned by the Governor

e. you will make receipts for all payments in the presence of at least one witness—preferably a magistrate—and make three sets of all vouchers, one for the treasury, one with the accounts and one for the store use.

f. keep a separate account of all items transmitted from England.

g. make a survey of any stores lost or damaged—which goods are to be sold or destroyed at the Governors discretion.

h. Make up annually an account of all receipts and expenditures, accompanied by one set of vouchers.

i. You are responsible for the preservation of all stores and provisions and the employees who work for you, and to the public.

A set of notes on how the commissary should operate was prepared by the Duke of Portland and handed to Governor-in Chief Phillip Gidley King on 28th September 1800. These notes are attached for historical purposes.

OFFICIAL INSTRUCTIONS FOR THE COMMISSARY—28th September, 1800

Instructions to the Commissary by Captain Philip Gidley King, Governor-in-Chief, &c., in and over His Majesty's territory of New South Wales and its Dependencies, 28th September, 1800.

In consequence of my instructions, you are hereby required to conform to the following directions for your conduct:-

1st. You are to be present yourself as much as possible, and control the receipt and issue of all stores and provisions into and from His Majesty's stores; and as you are answerable for the conduct of those under you and about the different stores, if you should have any cause to be dissatisfied with their conduct in discharge of their duty you are to report the same to me, when a proper notice will be taken thereof.

2nd. You are not to receive or issue any articles whatever, either public or purchased, into or from the stores, but by a written order from me, delivering me an account thereof, on the receipt or issue having taken place, taking care to comply with all such general orders as I may judge necessary respecting your department.

3rd. When any grain or animal food raised by those at government work, or received from England or elsewhere, is delivered into your charge, you are to furnish me with a particular receipt for it, specifying the place and person you received it from, charging yourself with it as provisions received for the public use, and to observe the same with respect to all stores belonging to the Crown, and to deliver the quarterly accounts of the expenditure and the remains thereof, or oftener, if required.

4th. When there is not a sufficiency of grain and animal food raised by the convicts at public labour for the use of those necessarily maintained by the Crown, and that it becomes necessary to purchase the deficit required from the settlers, you are to give me an account of the quantity that may be absolutely necessary weekly, or at a stated period, but not to require more gain at a time than can be kept from the weevil. After my approval thereof, and the price at which such articles are to be purchased is fixed, you are to give public notice thereof, and open a list at the different settlements for the insertion of those persons' names who can spare any quantities of the articles required from the reserve necessary for seed and their own use; such persons being freemen, possessed of ground are known cultivators, are to be regularly entered on the list in preference to any other description of persons, as they offer themselves, and their required produce to be received in the stores without any preference or partiality. The grain thus purchased is to be measured at such times as I may direct in front of the storehouse, and from thence lodged in the store in the presence of a superintendent and another creditable person. When the receipt is ended for the day, a return thereof it to be made the next morning to me, specifying the person's name and quality from whom it is received, the superintendent and other witnesses attesting the same, one or both of whom are to sign their names to the witness column in the voucher when payment is made.

5th Being particularly directed to reform the irregularity that has existed in the mode hitherto followed in making payment for such articles as have been purchased from the inhabitants for the public use, the persons who take your printed receipts, audited by me, for their respective produce being lodged in the stores, may transfer them from one to another for their accommodation; all such receipts to be called in as often as I may judge proper, when payment will be made by me of all outstanding receipts by a bill on His Majesty's Treasury for the amount of such receipts as may be in the hands of individuals, such bills not to be drawn for less than (Pounds) 100, and the vouchers in support thereof to be verified by liquidating your receipts in rotation. And whenever such payments are made you are to take care that five complete sets of vouchers with their documents, agreeable to the annexed form, be prepared to be signed before me at the time of payment being made, which I am directed to control and superintend.

6th. When it is absolutely necessary for any stores, clothing or provisions being purchased from masters of ships, or other strangers, after the price is regulated by two proper persons on the part of Government, and the same on the part of the proprietors, the Commissary will be ordered to receive such articles into the stores in the presence of two respectable witnesses, who are to sign the vouchers, two of which are to be delivered to me, with the proprietor's receipt for the payment, witnessed by two other respectable persons.

7th. As I am directed to forward my account current, made up to the 10th of October annually, with the Right Honourable the Lords Commissioners of His Majesty's Treasury, to the Inspector General of Public Accounts, under cover to His Majesty's Principal Secretary of State for the Home Department, you are therefore not to fail in delivering to me, on or before the 10th day of October, for my inspection and auditing, the following books and papers in support of your account current with the Lords Commissioners of His Majesty's Treasury, together with the surgeon's account of the expenditure of stores and necessaries received from you, in order that those accounts may be sent with mine by the first opportunity after the above date, viz.:-

First—A census book, containing each man, woman, and child's name that has received any provisions from the stores during the year, distinguishing those in the different rations.

Second—A clothing and slop expense book, for those supported by the Crown, expressing as above.

Third—A book specifying the receipts of stores, provisions, and clothing from England or elsewhere, belonging to the Crown, also the quarterly expense thereof, and remains at the time of making up the public accounts, which is to be distinctly stated and carried over the next year's account, as a charge.

Fourth—A book of the particular expense, and the application of the above described provisions and clothing issued by you during the year, to those supported by the Corn, also another book stating the expense and application of the above described stores issued by you for the use of the public, and signed relatively by the superintendent, overseer, or other person to whom they have been delivered.

Fifth.—A store purchasing book, specifying the different quantities of grain and animal food bought from settlers, &c., noting the time of purchase, quantity and application thereof, with a reference to the proper vouchers in support of the receipt and payment, which documents are to be annexed to this book.

Sixth._ A similar book to the above, specifying the different quantities of stores, &c., purchased from masters of ships, or other strangers, verified by proper vouchers, &c., as last above, to which book you are to annex the general expenditure thereof and remains at the time of making up the public accounts, which is to be distinctly stated; and carried over to the next year's account as a charge. At the end of this book you are to insert whether such articles have been paid for in grain, meat, or money, and to debit yourself accordingly, either in your account current of cash, or store account, and to charge yourself in the same manner with any other payment made to you on behalf of the Crown.

Seventh.—A list of all births, deaths, and absentees during the year.

You are not to fail (on peril of being subject to an exchequer process) in delivering me for my examination all the above books and papers, with every other explanatory document, on the thirty-first day of October, annually, which accounts you are to attest before me previous to my transmitting them to England and you carefully to preserve correct copies thereof, in case of any accident happening to those sent to England. You are to keep an open list in your office, containing the names of each class of people in the colony, according to the form you are provided with, in which you are to make regular entries and discharges as they occur.

Eighth.—Exclusive of the above papers, when any ship is going from hence to England, you are to furnish me with a general return of the inhabitants, according to the annexed form, also a return of the expenditure and remains of Government stock.

Ninth.—The issue of provisions is to be attended by a superintendent, or principal overseer, and a non-commissioned officer, for the purpose of detecting and reporting any improper proceedings; but no report will be attended to that is not made on the day of the issue. A weekly victual and store-issue book are to be kept at each store by the person who has charge of it. No person whatever is to be put on or off the store but by a written note from me, or by a note from the person who has the superintendence of the district where the stores are. The master carpenter, and every other description of persons that has charge of the workmen supplied with materials from the different stores for the public use, as well as such individuals as are allowed to receive that indulgence, are to apply for the orders on Monday mornings, and to give receipts for the same to the Commissary, delivery an account of the expense thereof to me weekly. By this regulation, the necessity of persons frequenting the stores on the intermediate days between stores and victual issue will be prevented, and the stores properly appropriated. The different storekeepers are to deliver you a weekly return of their expenditure and remains, keeping the same ready for my inspection when required, and you are to furnish me with a quarterly return of Government stock, charging yourself with any that may be killed and issued as a ration, accounting for it under the head of provisions raised by those at public labour. And as it is necessary the Deputy-Commissaries and storekeepers at detached places should be supplied with regular directions how they are to conduct themselves, you

are to furnish them with such parts of these Regulations as relate to their duty, and you are to direct them to deliver their returns and receipts to me, if I should be on the spot, or to the officer who has the direction of the public concerns in the district where they are stationed.

Philip Gidley King

In addition to the above instructions, the Commissary will give directions to the Deputy-Commissary and storekeeper to obey all such directions as they may from time to time receive from the Reverend Mr Marsden, at Parramatta, and Charles Grimes, Esq., at Hawkesbury, reporting to him all such orders on the day they send their weekly returns.

THE WORKING OF THE FUNDS 1800-1810

There were numerous 'funds' probably supported by accounts with the Bank of New South Wales from 1818, when the surplus balance of the Orphan Fund was ordered to be placed on deposit with the Bank of New South Wales. This was followed by the Military Chest, the Land Fund, the Commissariat Fund and many others, all of which were probably raised to simplify accounting recording and reporting—a Bank account can be used to greatly simplify accounting records.

a. The Police Fund is intended to cover the expense of all items relating to the goal and police, and replace the gaol fund but is entirely distinct from the female orphan fund. (from a dispatch by Governor Macquarie 31.03.1810 and effective 1st April, 1810

b. ¾ ths of all the duties and customs collected in the port and Town of Sydney are to be paid into the Police Fund. The remaining 1/4th to be paid to the Orphan Fund, which will be necessary to defray the expenses of that institution.

c. Liquor Licenses to be paid to the Police Fund. D'Arcy Wentworth to be Treasurer of Police Fund. Quarterly accounts for both funds to be completed, inspected and published.

d. The naval officer, previously responsible for collecting customs and duties to settle his accounts by the 31st May, 1810

e. John Palmer to close up and settle all accounts for the commissary and pass over control to his deputy William Broughton until Palmer's return from England

f. Samuel Marsden to be treasurer of the orphan fund

On 30th April, 1810, Macquarie wrote to Castlereagh concerning the two funds.

Previously all duties and customs collections have been allocated to the Gaol and Orphan Funds. I have revised this practice in favour of sharing the collections between the Police—¾ ths.—and Female Orphan 1/4 th—Funds.

From the Police Fund is to be defrayed the expense of the jail and police establishments, the erection of wharves, quays, bridges and making/repairing of roads. The second fund is to cover establishment of the orphanage and other charity schools.

The Second Period 1810-20

Timothy Coghlan in 'Wealth & Progress 1900-01' (P837) writes about the Land Fund

"When in 1831 it was decided to abolish the system of free land grants, and to dispose of the public estate by auction in lieu of private tender, it was also decided that the proceeds of land sales should be paid into what was called the Land Fund, from which were to be paid the charges incidental to the introduction of immigrants; and it was from the inability of the Land Fund to meet these charges that the public debt of NSW first had its rise. From 1831 to 1834 the Land Fund was sufficient, but in 1841 the engagements for immigration purposes were so heavy that it became necessary to supplement the fund in some way and it was decided to borrow against the security of the Land Revenue. On 28th December 1841 a debenture loan of 49,000 pound was offered in the colony through the Sydney Gazette, the first loan raised in any colony.

Sundry Funds 1864

From "The Epitome of History of NSW" P409, the Government Printer reports that:

"The deficiency for 1864 was 407,626.7.11 of which, the sum of 357,408 had been already paid with funds borrowed from accounts as follows:

- Treasury Bills 30,948.1.11
- 1865 revenue 98,714.10.8
- Bank of NSW 83,333.14.8
- Oriental Bank, Ldn 20,818.14.9
- Lodgements 92,238.16.4
- Church & School Fund 19,658.09.7
- Civil Service Super Fund 1,429.7.10
- Scab in Sheep Fund 10,267.2.10

It can be concluded from the above statement by the NSW Treasurer of 1864, that these funds were established as 'collectives' or depositories of segregated receipts and a means of trying to simplify an accounting, recording and reporting system. It is probable that the Church & School Fund, was operated by The Church & School Lands Corporation (under the Act of 1834; 'to provide for the maintenance of the police and gaol establishments of the colony, the surplus of the land revenue (land fund) and of the other casual Crown revenues had been placed at the disposal of the Council.

ON THE TRACK OF THE MANY COLONIAL FUNDS

From 1802, the first date that the Colony of New South Wales attempted to manage some of its fiscal destiny by recording certain transactions in the Colony, in the Orphan Fund or the Gaol Fund.

The Crown did not put its hand out for a share of colonial revenues until 1822, but as early as 1802, the colony applied duties and customs to imported items, as a means of raising necessary revenue to provide a small amount of independence to the Governor's operations. The first year's revenue of 900 pound did not amount to much but it was the start of something big. That revenue grew quickly to reach over 100,000 by 1829 and over 1 million pound by 1854.

The Goal & orphan Funds were shortly replaced by the Female Orphan and Police Funds sponsored by Governor Macquarie in 1810.

Later, during the 'Blue Book' period, the number of funds grew. From 1802 and the Orphan & Gaols Funds, the colonial revenue was distributed eventually through the Female Orphan & Police Funds, the 'Military Chest' Fund, The Land Fund, the Colonial Fund, and the Commissary Fund. Each with a unique role and purpose.

From an accounting viewpoint, the matter of allocating certain revenues must have caused some confusion. Thus the 'parliamentary grant to reimburse the local expenditure on the convicts' was handled by placing the revenue in a new category—"Receipts in Aid of Revenue". This was soon changed to the heading of "Revenue of the Crown".

A BANK ACCOUNT BY ANY OTHER NAME ?

The Colony was initially operated through a series of 'funds' which were simply a bank account by another name. For the first 32 years of the colonial administration, there was no 'treasury'; and so that fact, along with the administration of watching over a mere penal colony, a treasury was neither demanded or necessary. But times changed. There became a demand for immigration of free people, of both families and single women; there were the demands of the traders for a means of purchasing their wares and paying for them via an acceptable means of exchange; and then the dereliction of duty by the Marine Corps led to officer's influencing, if not controlling much of the economy of the colony, especially the Commissariat. A Treasury became essential and the first token Treasury came with the local recording of colonial revenue from customs duties and tariffs, tolls and rents. There were a number of such funds going back to 1802. The Colonial Treasury commenced in 1822 under the auspices of the Colonial Secretary and until 1827 the Colonial Treasury was the sole source of deposits of revenue and the source of expenditures. In 1827 we find the first mention of the 'Military Chest'. It is safe to assume that the successor to the Military Chest was the Land Fund whose functions, not unlike the military chest was to pool the 'revenue of the crown' raised in the colony from the sale of its 'waste 'or crown lands. We will consider the role and function of the Military Chest momentarily, but first there were a number of funds between 1802 and 1855 including:

* The Goal Fund 1802-1809
* The British Treasury 1788-1835
* The Commissariat Fund 1822-1850
* The Orphan Fund 1802-1822
* The Police Fund 1810-1822
* The Blue Book Period 1822-1857
* The Military Chest
* The Land Fund
* The Colonial Fund
* Scab on Sheep Fund
* Church & School Fund
* Civil Service Super Fund

Because these funds have never been discussed or identified in any texts, this work has been designed to uncover and discuss two of the many funds mentioned above and trace their use and activity.

It would appear from the use of these minor funds that a new accounting procedure was under-way. A simple and inexpensive recording and reporting mechanism could be maintained with a fair degree of accuracy, if separate bank accounts were used for each collection point, or each source of revenue was identified by a separate account, into which these funds could be deposited.

UNDERSTANDING THE FUNDS

a. THE MILITARY CHEST

With a name as romantic as 'the military chest', this story may be expected to unfold as a historic novel, but the 'military chest' was the first fund identified following the initiation of the 'Blue Book' period being the first formal accounts transmitted to England from the birth of the colony in 1788.

THE REVENUE OF THE CROWN OR the first LAND FUND

b. We note that in the following year, 1829, that a notation on the 'Receipts in Aid of Revenue' is that these deposits have been paid into the Military Chest. These deposits include:

- Consignment of specie (transfer of coinage from Britain to the Colony)
- proceeds of bills drawn by the Deputy Commissary
- proceeds of sale of stores sent from England

Sale of :

- crown stock (livestock)
- coals ex Newcastle
- wheat from Bathurst
- sugar & molasses grown at Port Macquarie
- the Schooner 'Alligator'
- sundry stores & articles
- miscellaneous receipts

A special notation on the accounts is made for 'receipts in aid of revenue (ie revenue of the crown) which are exclusive of the value of colonial produce delivered to the commissariat from the convict agricultural establishments'

In subsequent years, this statement is modified because sale of produce from the Government farms is listed, but the notation is modified to say that the value of convict labour (other than labour for hire) is excluded

Military Fund—Items of Revenue & Outgoings

proceeds of bills	civil establishment
proceeds of sale of stores	convict establishment
Saleof crown livestock	military establishment
:coal	retired army pay
:wheat	retired military pensions
:sugar & molasses	
:sundry stores	

a. The Military Chest usually made payments in the following categories:

    • civil establishment
    • convict establishment
    • military establishment
    • retired army pay & pensions

b. The main revenue and expenditures were deposited into and paid out of the 'Colonial Treasury'. The first reference to the balance in the Military chest is found in 1828, but the first reference to a balance in the Colonial Treasury is not found until 1829. From those dates, the closing balance at the end of each year is identified until 1831 when there are headings such as "Paid into the Colonial Treasury" "Defrayed from the Colonial Treasury" ;"Paid into the Military Chest", "Defrayed from the Military Chest", providing the means of tracking balances in each account.

c. In 1829, the disbursements on account of miscellaneous civil services states

    "total disbursements out of the military chest, in aid of the civil establishment of the colony"

d. In 1834, the 'Receipts in aid of Revenue' used each year, was changed to 'Revenue of the Crown'.

    The items included remained the same, viz. proceeds of land sales, quit rents, fees on delivery of deeds and leased land revenue. These revenues were claimed by the British Treasury for dedication to their exclusive use to offset treasury expenditure on items such as the civil list, the military and interim commissary expenditure on public stores for improvements, until the Commissary Fund was properly established in 1833.

e. Back in 1826, for the first and only time, there was an entry for the British "parliamentary grant for the charges of defraying the civil establishment of the colony for the year 1826". The amount involved is 8,283.15.0; however the financial statements show the full civil establishment as costing 62,554.18.2 ½. The British Government must have decided that the cost of supporting the full civil establishment was too expensive and that it would only contribute to the salary of selected personnel. The details as listed in the 1826 statement do not allow us to decipher how the 8,283 pound is made up, We can only assume that the Governor, the chief justice, and possibly the chief medical officer are covered. The reason we cannot identify the amount is that individual salaries were no longer being shown in the records, but rather the Governor and his establishment received a grant of 4933.06.5 ¾, whilst the judicial establishment receive a grant of 13,462.02.8 1/4.

f. The reference above to the 'notes' incorporated into each statement to the effect that 'the total is exclusive of the value of articles of colonial produce delivered to the commissariat from the convict agricultural establishment' stood until 1825 when the military chest received and deposited receipts from "the sale of articles of colonial produce delivered to the commissariat from the several convict agricultural establishments and coal mines". The first ever recognition that the production of convict labour should be shown as a 'crown receipt'.

g. The 1826 Financial Statements from the 'Blue Book' of that year record the consignment of specie as being 50,000.09.0 pound. Butlin "Foundations of the Australian Monetary System" refers to the copper coins sent to the colony at the instigation of Governor King in 1805, together with a second consignment in 1806 to Governor Hunter. Hunter recommended that the coins be circulated at "a greater value . . . . than their intrinsic worth."

h. Butlin suggests that the progress of government finance in the colony goes along these lines:

   • the earliest coins arrive in the pockets of the first Fleeters
   • Phillip's Bills & Dollars—bills on the English Treasury & Spanish dollars

- The 'Rum' Currency and Barter
- Promissory Notes—personally pledged
- Commissary's Store receipts and Bills of Exchange
- Paymaster's Bills & Notes—Copper coins of 1805
- Legal Tender & Colonial Currency
- 'Holey' dollars
- Macquarie's Bank & exchange rates

Butlin concluded that, between 1788 and 1803, the 'Colony had no treasury', but this omission was not to last long. The earliest funds were controlled out of England with even the colonial commissary operating purely on a barter system for the first fifteen years. The first colonial accounting was commenced in 1802 (through the Goal & Orphan Funds) with revenue amounting to 900 pound. The Colonial Fund commenced with the 'Blue Books'. The Land Fund according to the 'Australians: Historical Statistics' opened in 1833, although the 1833 financial statements do show the balance at the end of the year, in the Military Chest was 22,719 pound. It is logical, subject to further verification, that the Land Fund was the successor to the Military Chest; the main evidence being that, in 1834, the 'Receipts in Aid of Revenue' was changed to 'Revenue of the Crown' and included the proceeds from the sale of crown (waste) land, and other crown assets of the colony.

The names of the various funds changed at different times between 1802 and 1834, including:

- Gaol Fund
- Orphan Fund
- Police Fund
- Orphan School Fund
- 'Blue Books' & The Colonial Fund
- Military Chest
- Commissary Fund
- The Colonial Fund
- Land Fund

This was the story of how the Military Chest which became, during the Blue Book era, the holder of large balances in the Colony; became the main lender to an malnourished colonial treasury; and the beneficiary of the 'profitable' commissariat trading and discounting of bills drawn on the English Treasury. Its successor was termed the Land Fund, but we have little official recognition of this fund, other than what we learn from some of the economic historians.

The second THE LAND FUND

The military chest, as an account style for the colonial treasury was identified in the financial statements contained in the 'Blue Books', and we can readily identify the revenues credited to that account as well as the expenditures charged against the military chest.

However the Land Fund is without mention in the 'Blue Books' at least through the end of 1838, and the origin of this nomenclature must be accepted as 'untraceable' without proper basic evidence. We know only of its existence in firstly, the Australians: Historical Statistics P112, and then its mention in the works of economic historian, S.J. Butlin:

We find the following table in Historical Statistics of NSW
New South Wales Public Finance
Land Fund 1833-1850

Revenue '000				Expenditure '000			
Year	Land	Other	Total	Immign		Other	Total
1833	**	26.1	0.1	26.2	9.0	17.2	26.2
1834	48.2	42.9	60.8	7.9	52.9	60.8	
1835	88.9	121.3	131.9	10.7	121.2	131.9	
1836	131.4	121.1	263.3	11.8	251.5	263.3	
1837	123.6	202.6	254.9	44.4	210.5	254.9	
1838	120.2	185.8	353.8	108.0	245.8	353.8	
1839	160.8	148.8	321.8	158.3	163.5	321.8	
1840	325.3	283.6	480.0	148.0	332.0	480.0	
1841	105.8	21.4	386.5	331.6	54.9	386.5	
1842	44.1	51.7	117.2	112.0	19.7	131.7	
1843	29.3	49.3	56.5	11.6	44.9	56.5	
1844	16.9	126.0	127.5	69.0	58.5	127.5	
1845	38.0	131.0	127.9	20.0	107.9	127.9	

1846	38.8	153.5	146.5	1.2	145.3	146.5
1847	51.7	109.7	212.3	1.0	232.6	233.6
1848	51.7	109.7	212.3	113.8	98.5	212.3
1849	109.0	237.4	296.0	138.5	157.5	296.0
1850	158.5	104.8	373.1	166.2	206.9	373.1

** Receipts in aid of Revenue (ie. paid into military chest—no record of land sales)

This table extracted from Historical Statistics can only be verified by reference back to the Blue Book Financial statements for those years, provided we make a generous assumption.

That assumption must be as follows:

a. If the 'military chest' is accepted as a predecessor to the 'Land Fund' then its purpose must have been essentially the same. The military chest took its revenue from the proceeds of sale of crown lands, sale of stores sent from England, sale of produce from the Convict Establishments and sale of crown livestock. In other words, only material items possessed by the crown; and that is most probably why the notations on the Blue Books changed from 'Receipts in Aid of Revenue' to 'Revenue of the Crown'. This important change occurred in the 1834 financial statements.

b. Obviously the Land Fund was so designated either officially or by Australian Economic Historians to be the account into which official 'crown' revenue is deposited and from which crown reserved expenditures are drawn. The crown reserved its use of portion of the funds for conveying selected immigrants into the country, and for (15%) aboriginal welfare. We will return to the official sanctioning of these funds later.

c. S.J. Butlin in his masterwork "Foundations of the Australian Monetary System 1788-1851" makes several passing references to the 'Land Fund' without fully identifying its source or use.

Butlin writes that "in February 1838, William Rucker, a Melbourne storekeeper, announced the opening of a Derwent Bank agency, to 'receive deposits and discount bills and orders for account and under the responsibility of the Derwent Bank Company in Hobart. He fixed the discount rate at 20%, letting it be known that Hobart rates would apply when a court was established in which debts might be recovered. Attempts were made, with what success it is not clear, to secure the accounts of the Customs Officer and of the Land Fund for the agency. But the agency met with considerable difficulty."

In 1846 there was a squabble between Stuart Donaldson, NSW Treasurer, Murray MHR and Dr. Bland MLC as to where certain colonial debentures were to be funded. Donaldson wanted the subscription to come from the public; Murray thought the Trust and Loan Bank should do the funding, but "Dr Bland wanted the loans to come from the Land Fund"

P 490 "Because of its late settlement and mining boom, land purchase in South Australia was heavy in the late 'forties and the local accumulations in the Land Fund were more than the local commissariat required. The practice developed, with English blessing, that any surplus in the Fund was paid to the commissariat which shipped the specie to other colonial commissariats in need, especially that in New Zealand, the amount being credited to the colony's account with the Land and Emigration Commissioners in London"

P539 Grey, in South Australia, decided to use, contrary to official directions from London, to use any bank he chose for Government business, and he used the Bank of South Australia. Being contrary to official direction, this action permitted a penalty. The Land Fund, which was a transient deposit remitted to England for immigration payments, was divided between the Bank of Australasia and the Bank of South Australia, but all other government business was given to the Australasia."

P540 n "In 1851, the SA Treasury decided to require banks to hold cash at least equal to the government deposit, and to insist on this for the Land Fund."

Some of these references through doubt on the strict governmental use of the Land Fund. Other quotes come from 'Historical Records of Victoria—Volume 7'

P35 "It was Lord John Russell's opinion in 1840 that the general revenue ought to provide for the general expenditure, leaving the Land Fund, apart from 15 percent to be used for expenditure on Aborigines, free for immigration purposes as originally intended"

A. Coghlan in his extensive work "Labour & Industry in Australia "helps place some of these matters in relation to sale of crown land & immigration into perspective.

It was upon emigration from England at the cost of the land revenue that the colonial authorities finally placed their confidence. They offered in 1822 to set aside 10,000 pound from the Land Fund for emigration purposes; of this sum they desired that about two-thirds should be devoted to promoting the emigration of unmarried women, as the proportion of men in the colony was excessive, and that about one-third should be used in loans for the emigration of mechanics. The colonial office objected vigorously but the British Treasury agreed to the proposal with the proviso that no further sum should be expended upon immigration until the money received from the sale of land had reached 10,000 pound.

"It had been Edward Gibbon Wakefield's philosophy that the idea of land disposition in the colonies was adopted . . . . If the land was sold, the proceeds of the sale might aptly be applied to transferring labour from Britain to the colony without which labour the land would be of very little value. In 1831 the English Government resolved to alter the land system of Australia with the view of throwing open the country more freely to settlement, and thereby increasing immigration. In the first four months of 1832, 103 mechanics reached the colony but were disappointed to find pay rates considerably less than those promised in England. The female emigrants all found ready employment, chiefly as domestic servants. Considering its resources, the colony went into the immigration business in a big way. The estimated expenditure of 1838 was 120,000 pound of which 80,000 was spent in chartering 26 ships, and 40,000 expended on bounty immigrants. With the overall success of the program it was decided that the whole of the rapidly increasing land revenue of New South Wales should be devoted to immigration and in 1837. 3093 immigrants arrived of whom 2688 were sponsored and 405 arrived under the bounty regulation of the colonial government.

CHAPTER 3

THE FIRST POST-SELF GOVERNMENT FINANCIAL STATEMENT—1855

The first financial statement of a Treasurer to the New South Wales Parliament following self-government was that made by the Honourable Stuart Alexander Donaldson on 6th November 1856 to the new Legislative Assembly.

(This extract is taken from the Sydney Morning Herald of 7th November, 1856.)

In the LEGISLATIVE ASSEMBLY of *Friday, 6 November 1856.*

FINANCIAL STATEMENT of the COLONY

Mr Donaldson said: Sir, I am sincerely glad that in taking the course which I am now permitted to pursue, I am not proceeding contrary to the ruling of, or in any disrespect to, the honourable the Speaker of this House. The honourable Member, who sits at the head of the benches opposite, has spoken of the way in which this important matter has been introduced by the present Government, but I can only tell him that so far as the substantial part of the matter is concerned, we have taken the constitutional course. The financial affairs of the country must, in any instance, be indicated by the Governor himself, by message to this House.

The difference between the course adopted by the late Ministry and the present is that the late Ministry sent down a message from the Governor, in which the whole matter of the Ways and Means and the Supplies were included; while the present Ministry have adopted that constitutional plan recommended by the Opposition, of separating these matters. I hope the House will bear with me while I now proceed to make that financial statement of the affairs of the country which has been so long promised; and I also hope hon. Members will bear with me if I am compelled to trespass on the patience at some length, which, from the severe cold I labour under, will render my full exposition of the subject matter of some difficulty to myself. In making this statement of the financial affairs of the country, it will be my desire, as far as possible to exhibit not only the debit but also the credit side of the account. To show distinctly our present financial condition, how that condition was brought about, its historical antecedents, the policy which has led to it, and the principles on which we propose to proceed—in short, to exhibit, as fully as I possibly can, the position of our financial affairs, and to bring before the House, as fully as possible, the steps the present Ministry are prepared to take in regard to them. It may not be uninteresting if I commence my observations with a short synopsis of the financial history of the colony for some years bygone. You must remember we are now entering on a new sphere—which our financial arrangements, both of expenditure and income, are in future to be regulated by ourselves alone. Hat for the first time we are to run on our own legs, and it may not therefore be unapt that in order to guide our policy for the future, we should proceed to some review of the past. I shall therefore turn to a period of 20 years ago, and in a cycle of 20 years, in a young country like this, all must be well aware of the great changes in the position of the community—social, moral, and political—which must infallibly take place. It will not be necessary to me to detain the House with all the figures in detail to afford the House the information, which I now wish to supply. Fortunately, we have an intelligent and well-regulated Press—the influence of which will, I doubt not, enable the statements I am about to make to be put fully before the public. Well, Sir, I find that in the year 1836 the revenue of the colony was £340,533 the expenditure £287,376; in 1837, revenue £353,785, expenditure £398,496; in 1838 revenue £334,079, expenditure £463,161; in 1839 revenue £427,368 expenditure £567,966, in 1840, revenue £682,473, expenditure £561,023; in 1841, revenue £497,302, expenditure £756,580; in 1842 revenue £428,

730, expenditure £503,913; in 1843, revenue £350,891, expenditure £369,489; in 1844, revenue £386,617, expenditure £345,583; in 1845, revenue £436,920, expenditure £314,368; in 1846, revenue £346,481, expenditure £305,730, in 1847, revenue £369,259, expenditure £413,073; in 1848, revenue £396,862, expenditure £460,430; in 1849, revenue £575,692, expenditure £516,633; in 1850, revenue £633,711, expenditure £567,165; in 1851, revenue £486, 698, expenditure £444,108; in 1852, revenue £682,137, expenditure £600,322; in 1853, revenue £987,476, expenditure £682,621; in 1854, revenue £1,239,147, expenditure £1,136,568; in 1855, revenue £1,660,710, expenditure £1,657,024-making a total of revenue through the twenty years, £11,616,879, and of expenditure £11,369,540. If the House will take the average of these returns, they will find that the expenditure and revenue of the country for the last twenty years has a little exceeded £500,000 per annum. It is impossible for any man to read these returns without being struck with the enormous increase of the revenue and expenditure, particularly when it is considered that since the separation of New South Wales from the powerful and productive province of Victoria, the then joint revenues of the colony have been nearly doubled. That must prove to any man, theorize as he may, a progression in the resources of the country most marvellous—a progress that would appear to be absolutely chimerical, but which nevertheless is an absolute fact. In further explaining the present financial position of the country, I shall allude to the exports and imports, and in doing this I shall not take so long a period, but commence from the year 1839.

In the year 1839 the imports of the whole colony, Port Phillip included, amounted to £2,236,371, and the exports to £948,776. A period of seventeen years passed away, and what do we find to have been the result of the enterprise of the community?—Its eager grasp at the advantages, which the productive resources of these colonies held out to them. Why, they found that the increase in commercial enterprise had changed them from a mere province to almost the financial position of an empire.

In 1855 the imports to New South Wales were £4,668,525, while the exports were £2,884,130. The imports to Victoria, which I cannot but regard as one with us, as a great constituent of this Australian colony, were £11,568,904 the exports £13,469,194,—making a total of imports of £16,237,429, and of exports of £16,353,324.

These figures, I think, are sufficient to show the rapidly increasing importance of our commerce and of our social and political growth, while under the political guardianship of the empire to which we are proud to belong. But we are now to start on a new career; for the first time we have to run on our own legs, to guide our own footsteps, through all the intricacies of finance. I fear not for any retrograde movement of this country, and have such faith in her resources that I believe that the rate of progression in wealth, power, and importance, under her own Government, for the next twenty years, will compare with the twenty years that are just gone by. I believe that the same almost miraculous amount of progression of the year 1876 over the year 1856 will equal that of the year 1856 over the year 1836.

With such hopes, with such prospects, with such aspirations as these, who, Sir, can refrain from pride, mingled with awe, in taking charge of this infant Hercules?—And in no respect can this progression be influenced more than by the successful regulation of the finances of the country. I have now gone over the details of the revenue and expenditure, and of the exports and imports of the country for some years past, and it may be interesting on many accounts that I should now afford the House some statement in detail of its present indebtedness, and the causes from which that indebtedness arose. It is necessary that the different purposes for which these loans were incurred should be separately stated. I will now read the return which I hold in my hand, showing the debt of the Colony of New South Wales, the year in which the different loans were contracted, and the purposes for which the money was raised:—

Services	Years	Amounts	Totals
	1851	69,600	
	1852	130,400	
Immigration	1853	100,000	
	1854	60,000	
	1855	53,000	413,000

Railways		1853	50,000	
		1854	150,000	
		1855	534,400	
		1856	<u>352,900</u>	**1,087,300**
Public Works	18 Vic., No. 35	1855	21,000	
	18 Vic., No. 35		269,700	
	19 Vic., Nos 38 and 40	1856	<u>290,000</u>	
Sydney Waterworks		1854	10,000	
		1855	18,000	
		1856	<u>87,400</u>	**115,400**
Sydney Sewerage		1854	10,000	
		1855	44,900	
		1856	<u>123,400</u>	**178,300**
	TOTAL			**£2,087,700**

I must state in passing that these services properly pay their share of the interest on the debt contracted. I have said that I think it will be the duty of every Finance Minister to treat this debt under different heads and view them from different points. The debt incurred, for immigration for instance, does not stand on the same footing as the debt incurred for the construction of railroads, and the debts for railways and public works stand in a very different position to those incurred for any other purpose whatsoever. As I shall, however, have to allude to this matter when a proposition which will probably be brought before the House by the Government shortly, for the raising of revenue, is under consideration, I do no more than allude to it to-day in a passing way, in order that honourable gentlemen may be somewhat prepared for its discussion.

In connection with the tabular statement just read, I will read another, also intensely interesting, now that we are likely on the threshold of making great outlays on public works—more especially those for internal communication. I find from a statement I have in my hand of expenditure for works and buildings (exclusive of those provided for by loan) from

1836 to 1855, that for the last twenty years a very large portion of the public works of this colony,—larger perhaps than honourable Members who have not paid much attention to the matter have been accustomed to think—has been paid for out of the revenues of the colony from year to year. I think this statement is valuable. Our prospects are now growing clearer and clearer, and it is evident that the cost of our public works of former years, though large in amount, have been trifling to what we must look for in future. In the year 1836 the whole amount, as will be seen from the tabular statement, was only £8,621. One could almost smile at the triviality of such a sum when we consider that it is not nearly so much as one month's interest of our present debt.

The following is the statement to which I refer:—

Statement of Expenditure for Works and Buildings (exclusive of those provided by loan), from 1836 to 1855 inclusive.

Year	Amount		
1836	£8,621	0	7
1837	22,851	12	3
1838	63,937	18	7
1839	58,877	15	9
1840	49,703	2	11
1841	37,527	6	2
1842	33,195	19	0
1843	25,494	8	3
1844	22,262	8	8
1845	15,943	4	8
1846	17,070	0	1
1847	41,595	6	10
1848	32,013	18	1
1849	25,992	0	11
1850	16,163	15	7
1851	14,117	8	10
1852	17,823	6	5
1853	44,596	1	0
1854	101,878	14	8
1855	82,314	14	1
Total	731,980	3	4

The progress of the colony did not appear to attract the attention of the Government until 1854, when it took a sudden jump from £44,596 1s 0d to £101,878 14s 8d; and in 1855 to £82,314 14s. 1d. The total expenditure according to this statement during the last twenty years has therefore been nearly £732,000 without one farthing for roads. This, I think, is an interesting paper, especially as it has a bearing on the prospects of the colony in reference to public works for the time to come. With these preliminary observations, I now feel called upon to state to the House what is the actual financial condition of this colony at the present moment. I am sorry it should fall to my lot—but at the same time, as a public man, I have no right to expect that my path will be strewn with roses, or that I am to enter upon my duties as Finance Minister of this colony with nothing but that calculated to felicitate me.

I am sorry to begin my career as a public man with a state of affairs certainly not agreeable either to myself or to the country. It is no use, however, to conceal from the House that fact that in bygone years—I will not lay the blame on any individual or on any body of individuals, owing to the mode of Government, the propositions made by the Executive Government, as it were, added to the proposals of honourable Members representing constituencies, and owing to the weakness of the then Government when they could not carry their financial schemes—although they were bound by the necessities of the day to give way to the pressure for money—the expenditure had exceeded the income until it had left the colony in a bad state.

I am sorry I differ totally with my honourable friend opposite—if he will allow me to use such an expression to one so hostile as the late Finance Minister. I do not know what attention he may have paid to the particular department of which he was the head, but he stated—and statement coming *ex cathedra* are considered to have some weight—that the debt was about £30,000 (Mr Campbell: £40,000 or £50,000.) The honourable gentleman says £40,000 or £50,000; he has jumped up some 50 per cent, but even now he falls far short. I am afraid he had a pair of diminishing spectacles on when he turned his attention to the matter, if he could not see that the debt was much larger in amount. I have taken great pains to go through this matter, assisted by a gentleman whose able head and ready hand were at my disposal, and I am astonished to hear the honourable gentleman opposite make such a statement, whether he really had charge of the department of which he was ostensibly the head or not. The deficit at the end of 1855, estimated in the most fair and reasonable way, cannot fall short of £120,000 exclusive of the Supplementary Estimates before the House. That would be about a true statement, and I neither wish to conceal that fact, nor the difficulty with which I am encompassed. That deficit I must explain has not accrued during the year 1855-6; it is an accumulated debt since 1854. I have drawn up an account which, availing myself of the Press; I shall possibly be able to give to honourable members before it is laid upon the table of the House formally. This account of the estimated revenue and expenditure shows how the deficit arose. The revenue is enormously deficient of what was anticipated. I do not blame the late Government for this. They propounded a financial scheme objectionable to me, as a Member and also, I believe, objectionable to a majority of the House. I speak of the Government, which existed previously to the inauguration of Responsible Government. Whether they based their conclusions on the financial scheme they withdrew, or upon the result of the ways and means I cannot say. I am sorry to say all the calculations made fall far short of the truth. Their estimates were larger than had been realised.

It is a principle now acknowledged that if you have a tariff calculated to raise a certain revenue, and were to put 10% more upon it, it by no means follows that there would be 10% more revenue.

The fiscal scheme of the late Council was bad and there were other circumstances, which pressed upon the country. A reaction took place after the over-stimulated trade of 1853 and 1854-a reaction which it did not require a prophet to foretell. The Customhouse revenue fell short at the beginning of 1856. The late Government was also exposed to another difficulty. Some hon. Gentlemen who represented constituencies pressed the Government for a large expenditure, which was granted, with the expectation of support. I was not in the ranks of those who pressed the Government for a large expenditure while I refused to supplement their revenue. I felt it my duty to withhold from the Executive Government any extravagant expenditure for fear of an improper expenditure being expected afterwards.

I can recollect that even up to the close of the last session as much as £8,000.00s 0d were forced from them by this pressure from the representatives. The balance sheet for 1856 has been drawn in a tabular form and is as follows:

On the expenditure side of the account there is, the deficit on the 1st January 1855, £65,225. 17s 5d, and the late Government told us fairly enough that there would be a large deficit for us to commence with, though they estimated it at only £40,000 or £50,000, not being very much less than the actual amount. Then the appropriations voted in 1855, for the year 1866, amounted to £1,174,029; but we have been able, owing to some of the votes not being required for the services—such as the votes for the Artillery, and the steamer "Torch" about which so much had been said, and for other matters not necessary to particularize, to save out of this £57,000; thus leaving on £1,117,029 of appropriations to be met. Then follow the Supplementary Estimate of 30,689 14s 2d every farthing of which will be wanted: sums chargeable on loan, £4,181; for sewerage £22,235; and for water works, £82,023 6s 8d; making a total of £1,321,383. On the other side, to meet this expenditure, we have made an estimate as nearly as we can of the revenue for the current year. This we are able to make as accurate as will be necessary for all purposes, seeing that we have the actual receipts for the last ten months past; and that we can make with something like a certainty an estimate for the other two months; this we have set down at £1,060,000; and I will here say, that for some of the figures I have used I am indebted to the late Ministry, and although I have not been able altogether to agree with them, yet I own they have helped me very materially in my task. Then followed amounts to be raised by loan, viz., for public works and buildings, £4,181; for sewerage £22,235; and for water works £82,023; being the exact amounts charged on the other side; thus showing an estimated deficiency at the end of 1856 of £152,942. This deficiency will include the £65,225 deficiency on the 1st January 1856, and the supplementary estimate for the year.

Having now brought you to the end of 1856, I propose to carry you to the end of 1857, in order that we may take a view of what our position will then be. Taking the deficit remaining as I have just shown on the 1ˢᵗ January 1857, we have £152,944 as the first item to be provided for. I then estimate the expenditure of the year at £1,060,914; and it is a curious coincidence that the expenditure estimated for 1857 should be precisely the sum at which the revenue of the preceding year had been estimated. My colleagues and I have gone very carefully over both our Estimates of Expenditure and Ways and Means.

I therefore trust that whatever opinion may be entertained of our scheme as a whole, honourable Members opposite will not have it in their power to accuse us of rashness, seeing that we have computed no more for the future than we have received in the past. Then comes the following items:—Interest and special appropriations, £127,500; chargeable on loans, £563,200; sewerage, £60,932; water works, £103,935. This, it will be seen, would leave a deficit of nearly £150,000; but we propose to wipe off this in a way that I shall explain more in detail to the House later in my speech, when I hope to be able to make honourable Members confess that we are justified in the proposal we make, which is that the money should be raised on loan, by terminable annuities, and in a manner that I shall, by-and-by, proceed to explain. Taking this sum then to the credit side of the account, there would be an apparent credit balance of £14,749. This, no doubt, is not a very large amount for them to trade upon, and might be thought to be drawing the revenue and expenditure rather finely together. But then honourable Members opposite must remember that we propose no new taxation, we do not suggest any additional burden on the people; and if we can manage what we propose, it will be something worth remembering that we, the first responsible Ministry of New South Wales, though starting with a heavy load of debt upon our shoulders, had manager after the first year of our office to make *la carte blanche*; and that in the next year we could start with a clear balance, and that tough in debt we had nothing to do but to go steadily ahead and work it off. There is every hope that we shall go on improving, as I have shown we have hitherto done; and in proof of this I need but point to the revenue for the last ten months. When I held office with my honourable friend the Member for Stanley Boroughts as Treasurer, the amount of Customs' revenue received during the first six months was most disheartening, but since the month of June the unfavourable anticipations that were then justified have become entirely out of place, for our Customs; revenue has increased from that time in a most remarkable degree, but latterly more particularly; and I have only to hope that it will go on so increasing. No doubt a great deal of the falling off at the beginning of the year owed its origin to the uncertainty that mercantile men felt, and the unsettlement, as I may say, of the commercial mind, at the expected ministerial changes, and when alterations to the tariff had been counted on.

We all know how much this is the case, and that until the financial statement is made in England, by the Chancellor of the Exchequer public interest is excited, and the mercantile world remains in a state of uncertainty until the changes proposed are ascertained. In the Customs department this sensitiveness is always more particularly felt than in any other.

There are two things that are most sensitive, particularly of the acts of a Government—the public credit and the Customs revenue; the latter is more especially so, and if at all tampered with will never be a good one.

Although I am aware that there are great temptations now to interfere with the Tariff, because we could readily tax articles of luxury which are yet also articles of ever day consumption, and must have been tempted to take advantage of it,

CHAPTER 4

CONCLUSIONS AND SUMMARY

CONCLUSIONS

As a general conclusion to this work, a number of observations should be made by way of summary, on matters such as:

- Management of The Police & Orphan Funds
- The Consequences of transportation
- The Gains & Benefits by the British from Transportation
- Fiscal Management during the 'Blue Book' Period
- Other Financial Observations
- Observations on Crown Land Transactions
- Making Improvements in the Public Accounts

A. Management of the Police & Orphan Funds 1810-1822

Marsden and Wentworth were the official recorders of transactions in these two accounts, and as Treasurers of the respective funds, their appointment created the potential for major conflict of interest situations.

It is interesting to muse how a Reverend gentleman (Samuel Marsden—was the appointed trustee of the Female Orphanage as well as a Magistrate in Parramatta) who was paid from the Civil List at the rate of 150.0.0 pound per annum, could afford to operate 4,500 acres of pasture land and build up a flock of 3,500 sheep in a time-frame of less than twenty years. Even allowing that the land came about from grants, the sheep had to be purchased from the market place or the Governor's flocks and although the convict labour assigned to him was unpaid, they had to be kept, with huts, food and clothing furnished.

We might also ask why the monthly meat bill for the orphanage ran to over 60 pound (whilst the Baker's account averaged over 76 pound per month). Even though the Orphanage owned and operated a farm, and the farm regularly sold livestock 'on the hoof', the Orphanage for Young Females then bought back dressed meat from the same butcher.

Marsden, was also entitled, on behalf of the orphanage to draw rations from the commissary, especially grain.

For its annual sale of livestock in 1811-1812, Marsden received, on behalf of the orphanage, only 127 pound, but from the same source purchased over 700 pound of dressed meat(which at the going rate of 6d per Lb comes to 25,000 lb of meat each year).

The means were easy to share the spoils between those that could help him gain wealth and reach his target of becoming a large landowner and successful grazier. Marsden housed only female orphans aged from under 5 to 14. On an average month, Marsden paid the butcher over 60 pound, being for an average of 2,500 lb of meat. By the 30th September 1818, Marsden held 3,033 (pound) in the Orphanage account, and on average disbursed 550 pound each month from that account. The only 'admonishment' that Macquarie made (if one can imply from a regulatory change, an act of admonition). Macquarie, at this time, chose to modify the basis of the Orphanage Fund revenue and deleted an item by redirecting that revenue to the Police Fund. He also reduced the percentage of customs duty received by the orphanage from ¼ to 1/8th. Even so, the orphanage Fund built up a substantial balance, which was deposited in 1818 into the newly formed Bank of New South Wales.

Macquarie made no objection to Marsden misdirecting funds from the orphan fund to repairing St. John's Church in July 1811 to the extent of 56 pound, nor to paying the Matron of the Orphanage a monthly stipend of 5 pound (he recorded the payments as 'donations') when the going rate would have been only 1 pound per month, nor of paying 4.5.0 for a bonnet for his wife from the fund. Marsden was married with 5 young children to raise, and because he was a magistrate, he was entitled to draw on the government stores, in spite of his obvious pastoral (agricultural) wealth

Wentworth too had his questionable methods. He built up large surpluses of cash and bills receivable rather than spend funds on road, bridge or wharf construction; he expended large amounts through the military for 'repairs' to the streets of Sydney and other questionable contracts, never commented on by Macquarie. Wentworth was also the town Magistrate, responsible for fines, which were an important source of revenue to the Police Fund. Two items of regular expenditure open to abuse, and which appear to be inordinately high were purchase of firewood and oil and payment for the capture of absconding convicts. The Military personnel were fleecing the Government stores, operating the barter system in the Colony and were obviously getting even more ample rewards in cash from Wentworth. What we can't find any certainty of is who gave directions to Darcy Wentworth to make all these payments. It can only have been the Colonial Secretary or the Governor himself.

This raises questions of the 'arms length' treatment of revenues and expenditures, generally, in the Colony.

Events that shaped the Colony

There were a number of events that influenced the course of the early economy and impacted on the extent and rate of economic growth have been selected and outlined. The list of events is not extensive but indicative of sometimes-obscure events, which have impacted on economic growth eg education.

Although it may be suggested that the Report by Commissioner Bigge did not largely influence the Colonial economy, it must be stated that his recommendations to continue with the new Bank of New South Wales, which had been chartered incorrectly by Governor Macquarie, moved the economy along, as did his support for the continuation of the transportation of convicts to the Colony. His lack of support for land grants and early release of convicts may have slowed the economic growth until the consequences of his recommendation that the sale of Crown land be made, is considered. The revenue from customs duties, licenses, tolls and fines was considerable and kept the economy afloat, even if it was being badly managed, until 1810 and the arrival of Macquarie.

Other events tended to feed on each other and gather momentum by cross-pollination. Exploration across the mountains and uncovering the mystery of the rivers opened up huge pastoral areas of first class grazing land, especially that of the Bathurst Plains and fostered the growth of the sheep and wool industries. The continued growth of the pastoral industries all through the 1800s was eclipsed as the prime-exporting commodity only upon the 'official' discovery of gold. The discovery of gold also filled the Colonial coffers and set into motion the most remarkable of events, that of expanding the rail system across the Colony and to the other Colonies—a line was developed all the way from Adelaide to Brisbane. Instead of relying on sea transport, (the very reason that the major cities were located on harbours and bays), the cities were now to be connected by rail. The senior colony of New South Wales could now diversify its population, move livestock and produce from Ballina to Albury, Broken Hill to Parramatta. The most powerful benefit of the advent of the rail system is the most simplistic one. The Colonial labour-force learned how to engineer bridges (the Hawkesbury); how to construct gradients (crossing the Blue Mountains); lay track at record rates and lowest costs in the world; and engineer the iron horses themselves for local conditions. This new knowledge led directly to the growth of the large engineering shops and the likes of business adventurers such as Thomas Mort, whose remarkable drive, ingenuity and entrepreneurial ability led to the Mort Dry Dock & Engineering complex in Balmain, NSW Fresh Food & Ice, in Sydney and Lithgow, the Bodalla Cheese & Milk factory, relying on refrigeration, together with abattoirs, for the first time, in remote locations rather than in Sydney town.

We cannot overlook the value of education to a largely illiterate economy. Literacy rose by 1835 from 55% to 97% of the adult (15 yrs +) population. The placement of schools and churches throughout the Colony was responsible for this remarkable achievement.

There may well be more 'special events ', other than those discussed but it seems that these interlinking events boosted the Colonial economy in a remarkable way:

- The crown land policy and reform
- The growth of education
- The Report by Commissioner Bigge
- Exploration
- Pastoral expansion
- The expansion of the rail system
- The Fiscal impact of Federation
- Commonwealth-State Financial Relations

B. The Consequences of Transportation: The next conclusion must be to record some of the Consequences of Transportation to the Colony of New South Wales. It was during the time that convicts provided the principal source of labour for government purposes and private enterprise, that the consequences of transportation appeared to be measurable. One of the indirect consequences was the 'opportunity' cost to both Britain and the Colony of the transportation program. The Molesworth Committee in 1838, believing that their definitive opinion on the value of transported labour could only justify its continuation stated that transportation was an obstacle to continued economic growth. Some twelve years later, an advocate of transportation, (Archibald Atchison—Crime and Transportation) produced figures to show that just the opposite was true.—Transportation had been of great value to the Colony.

A consequence first raised by Samuel Marsden was that adult convicts were beyond re-training but that the young people needed education. A further social consequence was that the transfer of so many male convicts led, by 1841, to 'a dearth of females', a situation named as alarming by Ralph Mansfield 'Analytical view of the census of 1841 in New South Wales'.

Governor Phillip was the first to publicly recognise that the nature of the penal settlement required a 'peculiar form of government', but one of the goals of Commissioner Bigge was to review the legal side of Colonial administration and report on changes needed for the administration of justice. Bigge did make such a report and the recommendations were immediately adopted by Macquarie.

The Molesworth Committee report into transportation concluded that "Some persons contend that the pecuniary interests of the penal Colony require the continuation of transportation; that as the extraordinary commercial prosperity of these colonies was occasioned by the constant supply of convict labour, if that supply be cur off the colonies would be ruined, from great wealth be reduced to great poverty; and that this change in the fortune of inhabitants, especially if it were sudden, would necessarily produce the worst moral effects upon their character, and still further demoralise the already demoralised.

"The extraordinary wealth of these colonies was occasioned by the regular and increasing supply of convict labourers. The convicts were assigned to settlers as slaves, they were forced to work in combination, and raised more produce than they could consume; for this surplus produce Government provided a market, by maintaining military and convict establishments, which have cost this country above 7,000,000 pound of the public money.

"Labour is in short supply whilst capital has amazingly increased. The flocks of sheep are double the size they ought to be; a vast number perish for want of care; labour must be furnished from sources, other than convicts, if the colonies are to continue to flourish"

C. Analysing the Benefits to the United Kingdom

Although the more significant consequences of transportation of British convicts to the Colony of New South Wales may have been both economic and social, the general benefits of transportation of British convicts out of the United Kingdom are economic.

The essential question becomes—Would the United Kingdom have pursued a Colonial expansion policy if there had not been a need to transfer convicts from the Americas elsewhere?

The answer is of course, a simple—'yes'. The trade, defence and colonisation policies, in place, and under discussion, made territorial acquisition essential. The British Navy needed supplies of masts and spars to maintain its fleet in sailing condition. The British Trade tsars wanted to see further expansion, after a successful entrance into the Caribbean area, and the eyes of the East India Company wanted to spread further across the Asian region. Terra Australis—the great southland—was an obvious desire.

Therefore, it is fair to say that the gains to Britain were enormous in economic terms, especially in terms of the opportunity cost in dealing with the housing, feeding and guarding of the great surge of prisoners between 1750 and 1850.

Some of the direct advantages to Britain include:

a. The build-up of trade by the East-India Company
b. The advantage of a secure, in-house, supply of raw wool, to keep the spinning mills occupied
c. The opportunity cost of housing, feeding and guarding prisoners
d. The use of convict labour in the new Colony
   - Land clearing, farming, food production
   - For road construction
   - Public wharves
   - Barracks
   - Public Buildings
   - For Materials supply eg brick & tile production.
   - As unpaid day labour for the pastoral & agricultural industry
e. We can assume that Land grants, in the Colony, to men on the military and civil list was a form of 'fringe benefits' and should be quantified as an alternative to paid remuneration for these people.
f. Even land grants to emancipists were used as an incentive to increase food production.
g. We can quantify items C, D, E and F into a 'value of direct gain to the British economy of nearly 140,000,000 pound (refer details in the attached), compared with the publicly recorded expenditure

on transportation, supplies, and military personnel of 5,600,000 pound, between 1788 and 1822.

The extent of the benefits depends on the pound value attached to the opportunity cost of a prisoner housed in Britain. James Matra wrote in 1784 that the contract cost of a prisoner maintained on the Thames River hulks was 26.75 pound, probably significantly less than cost of prisoners housed in the London prisons especially Ludgate, which was probably costing close to 40.0.0 pound per head per annum. So if we assume an opportunity cost of 20 pounds in lieu of the 10 pound, our benefit rises to 180 million pound from 130 million.

The purposes of trying to quantify these benefits are to challenge to traditional concept that 'the British invested millions of pounds in the Colony of New South Wales'.

It is obviously only the case, that the British Treasury invested millions when the outlay is shown and by not accounting for the on going benefits for over fifty years, and indeed for two hundred years. It is still arguable that the Continent of Australia is, in Captain Arthur Phillip's words 'the best investment Britain will ever make'.

What the accounts don't tell us but in hindsight we could see happening is that the shortsighted English arrogance and limited social understanding was heading in a definite direction. They had no alternative plans for the placement of convicts after the loss of the American Colonies, except the earlier consideration of Africa, which idea was scotched before Botany Bay became so attractive, but there was a move, not long after the penal colony had been commenced that the transportation program was not going to work. We noted previously the negative observations in the Molesworth Report of 1828, however, John Howard, in 1770 wrote a serious report on 'The State of the Prisons in England and Wales' and noted:

> "The general prevalence and spread of wickedness in prisons, and abroad by the discharged prisoners will now be as easily accounted for, as the propagation of disease. It is often said, 'A prisoner pays no debts;' I am sure, it may be added, that a prison mend no morals. Sir John Fielding observes, that . . . .

'a criminal discharged by the court will generally, by the next sessions, after the execution of his comrades, become the head of a gang of his own raising'. Improved, no doubt, in skill, by the company he kept in gaol: petty offenders who are committed to prison, not to hard labour, but in idleness and wicked company or are sent to county gaols, generally grow desperate, and come out fitted for any villainy."

We can conclude that this view held a lot of sway with Pitt, the Prime Minister of the day. So, this view along with the projected cost of transportation and establishing the Colony, suggested that strong opposition would be prevalent within the Commons to stop the transportation program very quickly.

That funds were short in the British Treasury is suggested by a number of events, especially the pressure on each Governor, to trim costs. It took the appointment of the Chief Justice of Jamaica, John Thomas Bigge, sent to Sydney to review progress in the Colony, to muzzle the extravagances of Macquarie, because he took little interest in the pleadings and persuasion of Colonial Secretary Bathurst, who was concerned about the expense of new exploration, the expense of the new settlements in Newcastle and elsewhere. The substantial 'investment' in new buildings as well as the new roads and bridges in this vast and empty land as well as the early emancipation, conditional discharges and early release that were being handed out to many of the convicts, along with land grants.

Further support for cutting the high cost of the transportation program was forthcoming from the Report by the Select Committee on Finance released to the Commons on 26th June 1798.

"For the first twelve years of the transportation program, 5,858 convicts were transported at a cost of 1,037,230.6.7 ¾. This worked out at the extraordinary cost of 177 pound per head for naval expenses, supplies, civil salaries, military costs and establishment costs.

That this figure was inflated or padded by the British Treasury officials is without doubt, as the naval cost portion of the total charge of 1,037,230 pound was 166,341 or 29 pound per head. The contracted cost for the second fleet onward was less than 12 pound per head for convicts loaded in England, rather than the number unloaded in Sydney or elsewhere. This cost cutting exercise was the biggest contributor to the high loss of convict lives on route from London to Australia in the second and third fleet and was substantially due to the treatment received by the convicts from their handlers, the contractors, (whose sole goal was to complete the run at a profit) whereas Phillip lost no convicts or passengers, or military personnel during his long trip.

The Select Committee on Finance thought obliquely about the problems of making the Colony too attractive. They concluded" The more thriving the setting, the less terrible the threat. It may lose its terrors altogether, especially if by money or other means, servitude be avoidable." The original estimate of total cost, including transportation was 30 pound per head. This estimate was accompanied by a Government projection that within the first four years, 10,000 convicts would be shipped for this 30 pound per head rather than the 5,800 convicts shipped over twelve years at 177 pound per head. The Peel Plan of 1828 which had compared the original estimates with the actual results also concluded that 'should the authorities succeed in sending home to Britain the expected surplus produce, for which at the moment the Government are indebted to Powers which it would be their policy to suppress, they would effect a national good which time could not erase from the annals of British History.'

Thus the real argument was not one of not punishing the prisoners sufficiently or of releasing them before full redemption could be guaranteed, but of the cost to the British Treasury. No official in that day considered or noted the opportunity costs or the other benefits accruing to the Government, as has been analysed above.

D. Fiscal Management during the 'Blue Book' period.

The 'Blue Book' was kept by the Colonial Secretary as a record of all financial transactions affecting the Colony, and was reported annually to the British Colonial Office and the House of Commons Committee on Colonies.

The' Blue Book' was written in meticulous copperplate writing (until 1828), and contains detailed records and notes relating to the items of revenue and expenditure of the Colony in the years from 1822 to 1857. The records for the Year 1824 are missing and could not therefore be examined. In 1827, the records were recorded in a printed form, and can be reviewed in the photocopies in the Appendix to this Report. The handwriting makes it virtually impossible to photocopy the handwritten text. However, a copy of selected pages from the printed text of 1827 is attached as Exhibit A. These printed notes also include guidelines for recording and reporting items of revenue and expenditure. The reports were obviously made to conform to standard British Treasury recording methods and to comply with the then known parliamentary reports by the British Treasurer.

From the Exhibit, certain conclusions can be drawn, and these can be set out as follows:

a. There was a wide range of duties and taxes imposed on the early settlers, especially on alcoholic beverages. The general rate of duty on spirits was 10 shillings per gallon, and on wine it was 9 pence per gallon. On tobacco the rate was 6 pence per pound, while timber attracted a rate of one shilling per solid foot. General Cargo attracted duty at a flat 5% ad valorem rate.

b. There were also licenses and tolls. A Hawkers Licenses sold for 20 pound, and it cost a settler 2 pence (tuppence) to go from Sydney town to Parramatta town. A country settler (in the Hawkesbury) paid One penny to cross the Nepean River Bridge at Windsor.

c. References to crown land sales were recorded in the 1825 'Blue Book', and as set out in the decree by George 3rd in a Proclamation on 25th March, 1825, that a new 'rent' was to be imposed on crown lands at the rate of One shilling for every 50 acres, to commence 5 years after the date of the original grant. To-date all crown lands had been disposed of by way of grants, and this rent was a form of back door and back-dated compensation to the crown. In the official grant documents, the receiver of the land grant was given notice that further costs may attach at some future time to the land, and it was this opportunity that provided the Crown to raise this 'rent' charge on the land in 1828.

d. There was to be a Land-holders fee of Fifteen shillings per 100 acres of crown land reserved for each three years for free settlers, followed by a two shilling fee per 100 hundred acres redeemable after twenty years from purchase.

e. On the 18th May 1825, the 'rent' was changed, by order of Governor Macquarie, to a flat rate of 5% of the estimated value of the grants, without purchase (as opposed to purchased land), to commence 7 years from the date of grant. 'Rents' on any 2nd and subsequent grants were payable immediately, without the benefit of the 7 years grace period.

f. The table of Land Grants (1789-1850) shows the number of acres granted to settlers and the conclusion can be drawn that this revenue source of 'rents' on Corn Land grants could build into as considerable sum for the Crown.

g. By Proclamation, also dated 18th May 1825, George III authorised the sale of crown lands at the rate of 10 shillings per acre, to a maximum of 4,000 acres per individual or a maximum of 5,000 acres per family. Payment was by way of a 10% deposit and six equal half-yearly instalments.

h. The title pages to the 1822 'Blue Book' are entitled 'Abstract of the Net Revenue and Expenditure of the Colony of New South Wales for the Year 1822', which indicates (and as the detailed records also reflect) that all Colonial revenue and expenses were being accounted for in the 'Blue Book'. It is immediately recognisable that the Table of British Financial Costs in the Colony is incomplete and misleading in that the outgoing expenditures do not reflect any offset revenues which would provide a true net expenditure. The official Table thus overstates the expenditure by the British Treasury on the Colony.

i. The table on Civil List Salaries for 1792-1793) sets out the Governor's Salary at One Thousand Pounds. But in the 1822 statement of expenditures on the Civil Salaries, the Governor's Salary had increased to Two Thousand Pounds. By 1856 the Governor's salary had increased to 15,000 pounds.

j. In fact, the total of Civil List salaries in 1792 was only 4,726.0.0 pounds, but by 1822 the total had increased to 9,828.15.0 pounds, due to both individual salary increases as well as more people being placed on the Civil List.

k. The official 'Observations upon revenue for the Colony in 1828' (written by the Colonial Treasurer of New South Wales) makes an interesting point. It observes that the 'net colonial income' of the year 1828, as actually collected, is exclusive of sums 'in aid of revenue', i.e. items which cannot be viewed in the character of income. This item is further defined as 'the proceeds of the labour of convicts, and establishments connected with them, being applied to the reduction of the amount of parliamentary grants for their maintenance'. Thus it took 30 years for the Colonial Government to officially recognise the contribution of convict labour in the Colony.

l. The total quantity of alcohol imported and thus consumed in the Colony, even in 1828, and with only a population in 1820 of only 26, 000 people, of which adult numbers would be less than 15,000, was 162,167 gallons of spirits plus 15,000 gallons of Colonial distilled spirits (distillation from sugar was prohibited in 1828, but the high price of grain and the higher taxing of local manufactured spirits became a natural deterrent). In 1829, the only duties imposed on spirits in that year were upon spirits imported directly from H. M. Plantations in the West Indies. So the British authorities received double benefit by both international trading and local duties.

m. The quantity of dutiable tobacco in 1828 was 136,748 pounds (compared to 91,893 pounds in 1825). The Government experimented with locally grown tobacco at establishments in Emu Plains and Port Macquarie with the result being 51,306 pounds produced in 1830.

n. By 1827 shipping companies were also paying lighthouse charges, along with wharfage.

o. In 1828, the postage of letters attracted fees, for the first time, and the official Postmaster collected 598 pounds for general revenue.

p. The commencement of sales of both crown lands and crown timbers

Increased general revenues to the extent that in 1828, the amounts realised were:

Sales of Crown Lands	5004.19.2
Sales of Cedar cut on crown lands	744.15.11
Sales of other Timber	9365.11.4

The Governor imposed a fee of one halfpenny per foot for all cedar cut on crown lands. The 'Blue Book' makes the further observation that this charge 'has checked bushrangers and other lawless depredators by depriving them of ready means of subsistence by the absence of all restraint from cutting Cedar upon unallocated lands'.

In 1810, Governor Macquarie changed the designation of these two funds to 'Police Fund' and Orphan School Fund. The designated revenues were split 3:1 into each fund. The Act 3 Geo IV c.96 of 1822 gave further powers of taxation to the Governor.

E. Other Financial Observations

The analysis of Accounts extracted from the 'Blue Books' of 1822 through 1828 allows a number of conclusions to be drawn.

a. The initial claim by the author that the cost to the British Treasury of establishing and operating the Colony was NOT the millions of pounds claimed by other historians is now born out by detailed examination. The accounting records as maintained by Governor Macquarie from 1810 leads to a statement of 'net revenue and expenses' which purports to offset all revenues against all expenses, and includes as revenue certain convict maintenance charges. Even in 1822 the Colony was showing a small operating surplus. This surplus grew through 1828 until, other than for transportation of convicts to the Colony, the charges on account of the British Treasury were less than One Hundred Thousand pounds for protecting, feeding and housing nearly 5,000 fully maintained convicts. Against this cost, the charge for housing, feeding and guarding this same number of prisoners in Britain would have been substantially higher, since in addition to the 5,000 gully maintained convicts there were a further 20,000 being paid for by free settlers and used as supervised labour. Britain surely had found a cheap source of penal servitude for at least 25,000 of its former prisoners, and found a very worthwhile alternative to the American Colonies as a destination for its prisoners.

b. Revenue from Crown Land sales and rents was used to offset Civil (Crown) salaries and expenses.

c. It is probably incorrect, at this stage, to say that it cost Britain nothing or at best, very little, to establish and maintain the Colony, but it can be said that from 1822 the costs were limited to maintaining fewer and fewer convicts. But from these convicts great value in terms of agricultural produce, coal and other minerals was derived. Just in terms of coal for lighting, heating and power, the cost to the government of purchasing these items would have been substantial. The 'Blue Book' reflects the use of the coal as a cost rather than a gain as would be the accounting standard today.

d. A final conclusion could be given that there are much more known records available for this period (1788-1899) than the author originally thought. The reproduction and regional distribution of the 'Blue Book' by the State Archives Office on microfiche is a major step forward in understanding the economic challenges faced by settlers and convicts in the early Colony. The sourcing of material from the Blue Book unveils the financial statements and conditions of these early years. It is still considered that finance records of the period 1788 to 1822 are not re-constructible, but the author feels that a deep search through the microfilms forming the Joint Copying Project will provide additional information on the two Colonial operating funds of the period—the 'Police Fund and the Orphan Fund'.

e. An interesting observation is found in 'The Constitutional History of Australia' by W. G. McMinn (1979).

P 33 records "Subject to the need for a vice-regal message, accepting that any locally (Australian Colony) initiated legislation of a money bill nature requires the

Sovereign's ratification, the New South Wales Legislative Council was to

Have a general right to appropriate revenue from taxation, except for an
Amount of 81,600 pounds, the expenditure of which was to be in
accordance with
'Three schedules' to the Act; being 33,000 pound for the salaries of those
on the
Civil list eg Governor et al, the superintendent of Port Phillip and its
judges
And for the expenses of administering justice 18,600 pound for the chief
Civil officers and their departments, for pensions and expenses of the
council; And 30,000 pound for the maintenance of public worship."
Land and casual revenues were also reserved.

The Sale of Waste Land Act of 1832 raised the minimum reserve price of
crown land to one pound per acre, except that large remote areas might
be sold at a lower price, and established a formula for the use of the land
revenue; fifty percent was to be spent on immigration, the rest was to
be expended by the Governor in accordance with British Government
directives from time to time. The Governor was to continue to have
power to issue depasturing licences and to make regulations for the use
and occupancy of unsold lands, but the existence of the Sale of Waste
Lands Act placed an important restriction on the colony by implying a
prohibition against the Legislative Council legislating on these matters.
The first directive on how the Governor was to spend a portion of
the fund, enjoined the Governor to spend a proportion on Aboriginal
protection and another on the roads; he was left free to hand any surplus
over to the Council for appropriation; but it was made clear that the
whole of the fifty percent was to be considered as 'an emergency reserve
if the Council proved difficult'. McMinn sheds some further light on the
Crown Lands mystery but there still remains the question of whether, year
after year, these funds were fully used or whether they were just included
as a contribution to general revenue. It would appear that somewhere
there is a firm directive from the British Treasury that the revenues from
Crown Lands sale was to be used to 'offset' British costs of maintaining
the Colony. The 'Blue Book' is evidence that as general revenues, these
funds were already being used to pay for the costs of feeding, clothing,
housing convicts, and we know they were specifically used to pay for
'sponsored immigrants', aboriginal 'protection', and now roads. The costs
of the military establishment were charged against general revenues so

in the quite large 'pot', nearly all Colonial expenditures were subsidised or offset by revenues from the Sale of Crown Land. Britain put its hand in the till only; it seems, to pay for the shipping and supplies costs of getting their prisoners to the Colony. After 1828, we know that convict production—both agricultural and mineral—went a long way to paying their expenses, so perhaps the British Treasury did in fact get off very lightly indeed, especially for the benefits it derived.

The vexing question of Crown Lands revenues still remains. It is apparent from the 'Blue Book' notations that this revenue was 'reserved' for specific allocation by the Crown and remained in the Colony as an offset against British Government fiscal obligations (eg Civil List salaries) until self-government in 1855. A relevant quotation from the 1887 Financial Statements of the Colonial Treasurer of New South Wales, assists in clarifying the use of the revenues:

> "Prior to the passing of the Constitution Act, the Territorial Revenues of the Colony belonged to the Crown, but upon that Act coming into operation in 1855, they were placed at the disposal of the local Parliament, and together with the taxes, imposts, rates and duties were formed into one fund, under the title of the Consolidated Revenue Fund. In lieu of the Crown Revenues thus given up to the Colony, an annual Civil List of 64,300 pound was made payable to Her Majesty out of the Consolidated Revenues of the Colony." What this means is that the British Treasury allowed the offset of all direct British payments made on account of the Colony against revenues raised by the sale, rent or lease of Crown lands.

G. Observations on Crown Land Transactions

There was a major improvement in record keeping and reporting after self-government in 1855. The "Financial Statements of the Colonial Treasurers of New South Wales from Responsible Government in 1855 to 1881" provide a detailed accounting mechanism for recording classifications, and compilation of budgets and reporting to the Authorities. They contain 'explanatory memoranda of the financial system of New South Wales, and of the rise, progress and present condition of the public revenue'.

The interest in this period (from 1822 to 1881) is that these records, firstly of the 'Blue Book' period and then of the printed Financial Statements to 1881, provide the first detailed identification of the items included in the revenue and expenditures for the Colony and the appropriation and approval process. This historical data is relevant to understanding the social conditions in the Colony, the application of duties, tariffs, tolls and fees which embraced the essential revenue of a Colony that was designed to be self-sufficient and which was being given minimal economic support by the British Government, even though the opportunity cost of housing 'prisoners' in the Colony was a fraction of the cost of housing them in England.

Governance of Public Finance

The appendix to the 'Financial Statements of 1887' (refer Appendix this work) records that:

> "The Financial System of the Colony of New South Wales is regulated chiefly by the Constitution Act of 1855 and the Audit Act of 1870, and in matters relating to Trust Funds and Loans by special Appropriation Acts of the local legislature.

The Imperial Act granting a constitution to the Colony of New South Wales was assented to on 16th July 1855, and became effective on the 24th November 1855. This Act provides for a Legislative Council (Upper House) and a Legislative Assembly. The Upper House members were to be nominated by the Governor, while the Lower House members were to be elected by inhabitants of the Colony.

We know that the first official empowerment of the Legislative Council to impose 'taxes' by way of customs duties was in 1823, but the payment (commenced in 1788) by the British Government of Civil salaried officials remained until 1853. So before the 1853 self-government, the British authorities maintained a civil list of officials who were paid for by the Crown.

The British Treasury directed revenues from crown land sales and rents from squatters' and pastoralists' leases (imposed from 1853) be used to meet local expenses and running costs, as well as Civil List Salaries.

The reserve sale price of crown land had been originally set at 50 pence per acre in 1833, but by 1839 it rose to 12 shillings an acre and shortly thereafter (1842) it rose to one pound per acre, and it is likely, based on the revenues from Crown Lands and the annual surplus recorded in the Colonial 'Blue Books', that the British Treasury made a surplus on its Colonial possession of Australia.

To draw this conclusion, a number of premises were made:

a. The British Government lists its Civil payments to the key officials of the Colony eg Governor, Attorney-, Surveyor-General, Chief Justice etc, but makes no mention of revenue collected from the Colony.

b. The three related Acts (59 Geo III c.114; 2 Geo IV. c.8 and 3 Geo IV. c.96) give the Colonial Governor the power to impose local taxes in the shape of Customs Duties on spirits, tobacco etc from about 1823,

c. The Legislative Council of 1851 adopted a Select Committee Report protesting that the more recent 'constitutional' Acts (13 & 14 Vic c.59) did not place the control of all revenue and taxation from the Colony in the hands of the legislature. The key omitted and thus missing elements—in the eyes of the Council—were the control of waste lands (i.e. Crown lands—specifically excluded by Act 9 Geo IV c.83) and revenue from mining operations.

d. The discovery of gold and the burgeoning wealth of the Colony prompted the Legislative Council in 1852 to seek the British Government's acceptance of an offset arrangement whereby the Colony of New South Wales would accept responsibility for all civil (i.e. official) salaries, provided the British Government surrendered all Colonial revenues to the discretion (under a proposed new constitution) of the Legislature.

e. The British authorities accepted Colonial funds, raised from the earliest sale and lease of Crown Land to be used for the funding of 'free immigration' to the Colony.

f. The concurrent Napoleonic wars being undertaken by the British, as well as the ongoing American War of Independence placed a substantial burden on the public purse, and the British Treasury was seeking every opportunity to limit, defray or offset expenses relating to the Colony in the Great South Land.

The conclusion should be (by implication), that the British Government had, (all during the period from 1788 to 1852) been in control of crown land (wasteland) revenues, as well as the revenue from mining. It was thus some portion of the crown land revenue that was used to pay the transportation charges for the first 'free' immigrants from Britain, until, some three years afterwards, numerous Colonial merchants supported and underwrote the transportation costs of 'free' settlers and guaranteed them jobs on arrival.

(a.) The Crown Land charges rose from 5 shillings in 1833 to 12 shillings in 1839 and then 1 pound in 1842. This revenue was used to defray Civil expenditures in the Colony, by being retained in the Colony and the Governor directed its use, on behalf of the Crown, for the payment of salaries to officials on the Civil list, to Military personnel, for government expenses in day to day running of the Colony, and it would take a mere accounting or book-keeping entry to offset such revenue and expenses.

We know from the public record (Wealth & Progress in NSW—1887) that revenue from Taxation in 1886 amounted to over two million pounds. This was largely customs duty on wines, spirits, coffee, tea and sundry other imported items such as rice and dried fruits. Stamps and license fee raised a further almost five hundred thousand pounds making the total Taxation revenue a sum of 2,611,835 pounds for 1886.

TABLE A   REVENUES FROM TAXATION 1886

Colony	Rail	Water etc	Immign	Other	Total '000
NSW	31380	4122	569	10573	46646
Vic	29282	5638	0	2706	37627
Qld	15374	221	2621	7623	25840
SA	11374	3321	0	5739	20435
WA	824	.05310	0	541	1371
Tas	.0173	0	.0235	4609	5019

TABLE B   REVENUE FROM SALE AND OCCUPATION OF CROWN LAND 1871-1886

1871	197978	1879	1632024
1872	840453	1882	2914394
1873	1137914	1884	1753345
1875	2020629	1885	1876452
1876	2773003	1886	1643955

The research undertaken in writing this paper has led the writer to certain conclusions, all of which reflect on the early economic progress of the Colony.

1. The British authorities were ignorant of the radically different nature of the climate, soils and natural environment of the new colony;

2. There was no sound planning to develop agriculture, and provide the basics of self-supported living for the early population;

3. Basic farming equipment and building tools were not supplied in sufficient quantities, nor training or guidance provided by experienced persons;

4. The members of the New South Wales Corps were more interested in pursuing their own interests than in supervising the convicts and promoting self sufficiency;

5. There was no system of proper supervision and training of convicts, leading to low levels of productivity; Governor Phillip had, on numerous occasions requested professional supervisors for the convicts but was repeatedly ignored.

6. The discovery of Gold was kept secret whilst convict transfers were still being undertaken, lest the 'dream' of great wealth became stronger than the requirement to work out a penal service.

7. Despite the lack of basic necessities and poor motivation of most of the population, the enterprise of a small number of individuals, both convict and 'free immigrant' provided a catalyst for the progress and prosperity of all.

8. Needless to say, in hindsight, progress to self sufficiency could have been hastened and much suffering avoided, if appropriate planning, and economic encouragement had been provided.

9. The discovery of large tracts of good grazing land and its associated export development of wool, and the discovery of large gold deposits rapidly boosted the fortunes of the Colony, but the driving force and critical factor was the motivation, energy and determination of the early entrepreneurs, acting initially and mainly in their own interest, but inevitably taking the bulk of the Colony with them in the progress towards prosperity.

After 1828, we know that convict production—both agricultural and mineral—went a long way to paying their expenses, so perhaps the British Treasury did in fact get off very lightly indeed, especially for the benefits it derived.

Another question arises after analysing the pre-Federation period. How did the Colony build up a debt to the Mother Country of 159 million pound—This figure was quoted in 1893 at the Corowa Federation Conference by A.J. Peacock MLA (Mildura). Peacock was later to become the Minister for Lands in the first Government of 1900, and was knighted for his contribution to the Federation Movement. The answer is that Peacock quoted this figure in error and in truth the sum of 159 million pound is the total indebtedness by the Colonies to bondholders in the City of London. This was a Colonial obligation at attractive interest rates and due over an extended period of time.

Interpreting the Public Accounts

The purpose of this work has been accomplished—the purpose being that of identifying and analysing public financial statements from 1800-1899. A niche was identified and one worthy of filling. That there could be an interest in relating and understanding the economic fundamentals of the Colony onto Federation is not surprising but a study of the early Government financial reporting can unleash an understanding of so much information relating to the social economic and political progress of the early settlers. What was the progress of the early social infrastructure? The hospital, the roads, the water supply, the sewerage disposal; the growth of industries—retail, pastoral, mineral, timber, whaling and sealing; citrus? What was the progress of education? The health and the nutritional state of the nation? Were the settlers housed properly? Did the settlers enjoy the benefits of travel, telegraph, refrigeration and other results of the ongoing industrial revolution? What did their entertainment consist of; what were the working conditions?

The government accounting and reporting system answered all these questions, and more. So, if the aim of the Government accounts was to analyse the condition of the Colony and inform its people, then the system worked well. We learnt where the revenue of the Colony was derived from, and the advent and then taxation in the Colony. We learnt where all that revenue was expended, and the resulting measurable standard of living achieved by the settlers. Government accounting was the official measure of the performance of the Colonial administrators for the British Colonial Office in London.

Interpreting the Direct and Measurable Gain to the British Authorities from the Colony of New South Wales.

The original estimate of direct gains by the British authorities from the original and continuing investment in the Colony of New South Wales was based on 5 (five) identifiable and quantifiable events

1. The opportunity cost of housing, feeding and guarding the convicts in the Colony compared with the cost of doing the same thing in Britain.

    The original estimates, in this category, were based on an estimated differential of ten pound per head—an arbitrary assessment of the differential cost.

    However recent and more reliable information has come to hand which gives further validity to a number of 20 pound per head per annum, compared with the original 10 pound per head per annum.

    A letter to Under Secretary Nepean, dated 23rd August 1783, from James Maria Matra of Shropshire and London assists us in this regard.

It was Matra who first analysed the opportunity of using the new Colony as a Penal Colony; only his estimates were incorrect and ill founded. He had advised the Government that it would cost less than 3,000 pound to establish the Colony initially, plus transportation cost at 15 pound per head and annual maintenance of 20 pound per head.

In fact the transportation was contracted for the second fleet at 13 pound 5 shillings per head and Colonial revenues from 1802 offset annual maintenance.

However, Matra made a significant statement in his letter to Nepean, when he pointed out that the prisoners housed, fed and guarded on the rotting hulks on the Thames River were being contracted for in the annual amount of 26.15.10 per head per annum. He also writes that 'the charge to the publick fore these convicts has been increasing for the last 7 or 8 years' (Historical Records of NSW—Vol 1 Part 2 Page 7)

Adopting this cost as a base for comparison purposes, it means that the benefit to Britain of the Colony increased from 140,000,000 pound to 180,000,000 pound. This benefit assesses the Ground 1 benefit at 84,000,000 pound.

2. Benefit to Britain on Ground Two (2) is put at 70, 000,000 pound which places the value of a convicts labour at 35 pound per annum. Matra had assessed the value of labour of the Hulk prisoners at 35. 85 pound.

2. The valuation of convict labour in the new Colony should reflect the convicts not only used on building sites, but also on road, bridge and wharf construction. This would add (based on 35 pound per annum) a further 21,000,000-pound.

3. The Molesworth Committee (A House of Commons Committee investigating transportation) concluded that the surplus food production by the convicts would feed the Military people and

this, over a period of 10 years, would save 7,000,000 pound for the British Treasury.

4. The benefits of fringe benefit grants of land to the Military etc can be estimated (based on One pound per acre) at over 5,000,000 before 1810.

5. We learn from Governor King's Report to Earl Camden (which due to a change of office holder, should have been addressed to Viscount Castlereagh as Colonial Secretary) dated 15th March 1806 that the Convicts engaged in widely diverse work. The Report itself (Enclosure #2) is entitled

"Public Labour of Convicts maintained by the Crown at Sydney, Parramatta, Hawkesbury, Toongabbie and Castle Hill, for the year 1805

Cultivation—Gathering, husking and shelling maize from 200 acres sowed last year—Breaking up ground and planting 1230 acres of wheat, 100 acre of Barley, 250 acres of Maize, 14 acres of Flax, and 3 acres of potatoes—Hoeing the above maize and threshing wheat.

Stock—Taking care of Government stock as herdsmen, watchmen etc

Buildings—
- At Sydney: Building and constructing of stone, a citadel, a stone house, a brick dwelling for the Judge Advocate, a commodious brick house for the main guard, a brick printing office
- At Parramatta: Alterations at the Brewery, a brick house as clergyman's residence
- At Hawkesbury: completing a public school
- A Gaol House with offices, at the expense of the Colony
- Boat and Ship Builders: refitting vessels and building row boats
- Wheel and Millwrights: making and repairing carts

Manufacturing: sawing, preparing and manufacturing hemp, flax and wool, bricks and tiles

Road Gangs: repairing roads, and building new roads

<u>Other Gangs</u>: loading and unloading boats"
(Historical Records of NSW—Vol 6 P43)

Thus the total benefits from these six (6) items of direct gain to the British comes to well over 174 million pound, and this is compared to Professor N. G. Butlin's proposal that the British 'invested' 5.6 million.

Historical Records of NSW Vol 1 Part 2

<u>The Opinions of Captain Arthur Phillip as Governor of the Colony of NSW</u>

<u>HRNSW Vols 1-7</u>

a. (P7)—Cost of Convicts (-J.M. Matra Letter)

- The estimate to create a settlement there (in Africa) amounted to 9865 pound, and the annual charge for each convict would be 15.14.0. The Government pays annually to the Contractor for each convict employed on the hulks 26.15.10
- the 1,000 felons is currently costing over 20,000 per annum

b. (P10)—The plan by Sir George Young as presented to Lord Sydney included a list of benefits for Britain. These included:

- The geographical position
- Trade with South America
- The commercial position
- Variety of climate and productions
- Facilities for trade
- Tropical products
- Flax
- Commercial centre
- Metals of every kind
- Settlers from China
- The American Loyalists
- Felons
- Expense

- Number of ships required
- Guard-ship
- Exploring ship
- Cheap transportation
- Back-loading

c. (P32) Estimates of Expense for equipment & supplies

b. (P67) Phillip's Commission

- "Our will and our pleasure is that all public monies which shall be raised be issued out by warrant from you and disposed of by you for the support of the Government or for such other purpose as shall be particularly directed and not otherwise"
- "We do likewise give and grant unto you full power and authority to agree for such lands, tenements as shall be in our power to dispose of and them to grant to any person upon such terms and under such moderate quit rents services to be thereupon reserved . . . ."

e. (P87) Economy

- "You shall use every proper degree of economy and be careful that the commissary so transmit an account of the issues to our Treasury, from time to time . . . ."

f. (P91) Emancipation and land grants

- "You have full power and authority to emancipate and discharge from servitude any of the convicts under your superintendence who shall be deserving of such favour"
- "You may issue your warrant to make full and careful surveys of land and may pass grants to any of the convicts emancipated eg to every male 30 acres, and if married, a further 20 acres more."

g. (P146) Bricklayers Wanted

- In at least two despatches—those of 9th July 1788 to Lord Sydney and that of 28th September 1788 to U/Secretary Nepean, Governor Phillip drew the British attention to the severe shortage of carpenters and bricklayers in the Colony.

BIBLIOGRAPHY

Shann, E. O. 'Economic History of Australia'

Yarwood, A. T.—Samuel Marsden (1977)

Collins, David 'An Account of the English colony in NSW' (1798)

Steven, Margaret 'Merchant Campbell 1769-1846)

Bigge, John Thomas 'Report of Commissioner of Inquiry, on the State of
    Agriculture and Trade in New South Wales' (1823)

Palmer, L.H. 'Our John's Adventures' (1988)

Carter, W. E. R. 'John Palmer: Father of the Colony' (1986)

Beckett, G. W. 'The Development of Public Finance in the Colony'

Crawley, Frank 'Colonial Australia 'Vol 1

The Sydney Gazette 1803-1809-1816-1821

The Australian Chronicle

H.R.A. series 1 vol 1-10 (10-p651)

HRNSW Vols 1-IV

Marjorie Barnard—"A History of Australia"

Foster, Josephine "John Palmer' Journal Royal Aust Hist, Soc Vol 11
    (1925)

Mackaness, G. 'The Life of William Bligh'

Coghlan, T. A. 'Labour & Industry in Australia Vol 1-IV (1918)'

Butlin, N. G. 'Forming a Colonial Economy'

Report of the Committee of Inquiry into Transportation—Evidence by
    John Palmer 1812

The Late John Palmer. An article in "New South Wales Magazine—vol
    1834"

Lea-Scarlett, Errol 'Queanbeyan—The District & Its People.

Evatt, H. V. 'The Rum Rebellion'(1938)

Illustrated History of Australia

Flannery, T (Ed)—'The Birth of Sydney'

The Oxford History of Australia

Hughes, R—'The Fatal Shore'

Macquarie Publishing 'A Colonial Time-Line'